OECD Investment Policy Reviews

OECD Investment Policy Review: Bulgaria

OECD
BETTER POLICIES FOR BETTER LIVES

Please cite this publication as:
OECD (2022), *OECD Investment Policy Review: Bulgaria*, OECD Investment Policy Reviews, OECD Publishing, Paris, https://doi.org/10.1787/6a0325b7-en.

ISBN 978-92-64-96195-1 (print)
ISBN 978-92-64-58132-6 (pdf)
ISBN 978-92-64-54573-1 (HTML)
ISBN 978-92-64-72284-2 (epub)

OECD Investment Policy Reviews
ISSN 1990-0929 (print)
ISSN 1990-0910 (online)

Photo credits: Cover © valio84sl / via Getty Images; © Denis Babenko/Shutterstock.com; © Xebeche/Shutterstock.com.

Corrigenda to publications may be found on line at: www.oecd.org/about/publishing/corrigenda.htm.

Foreword

The *OECD Investment Policy Review of Bulgaria* assesses the climate for domestic and foreign investment in Bulgaria and discusses the challenges and opportunities faced by the government of Bulgaria in its reform efforts. Capitalising on the *OECD Policy Framework for Investment*, the review includes chapters on trends in foreign investment and their socio-economic benefits, foreign investor entry and operations, the legal and institutional framework for investment protection, investment promotion and facilitation, public governance, and policies to promote and enable responsible business conduct. The review then highlights potential reform priorities to help Bulgaria fulfil development ambitions that align with its commitment to comply with the principles of openness, transparency and non-discrimination as a new Adherent to the *OECD Declaration on International Investment and Multinational Enterprises* (Declaration).

This review is the result of a two-year collaborative process to provide Bulgaria with a systematic approach to investment climate reform and to accompany Bulgaria's application for adherence to the *Declaration*. The OECD team worked with an inter-ministerial task force, led initially by the Ministry of Economy and then, from January 2022, by the Ministry for Innovation and Growth.

This review was drafted under the aegis of the OECD Investment Committee and forms part of the OECD's broader engagement with Bulgaria. It draws on a report prepared by the OECD Secretariat to support the OECD Investment Committee's assessment of Bulgaria's ability to comply with the principles of openness, transparency and non-discrimination and responsible business conduct practices, as well as its policy convergence with the *Declaration*. The report was adopted by the Investment Committee on 18 November 2021 and Bulgaria became the 51st adherent to the *Declaration* in June 2022.

The review was prepared, under the supervision of Frédéric Wehrlé, Head of Adherence to the OECD Declaration on International Investment, OECD Investment Division, by Boryana Kiskinova, Coralie Martin, Fernando Mistura, Andrea Marin Odio, Joachim Pohl, Baxter Roberts and Monika Szlajerowska, all from the OECD Directorate for Financial and Enterprises Affairs. Overall guidance was provided by Stephen Thomsen, Deputy Head of the Investment Division, and Ana Novik, Head of the Investment Division. The review has benefitted from inputs, comments and suggestions from other parts of the OECD Secretariat, including the Directorate for Public Governance; the Economics Department; the Centre for Entrepreneurship, SMEs, Regions and Cities; the Directorate for Science, Technology and Innovation; the Competition Division; the Corporate Governance and Corporate Finance Division; the Anti-Corruption Division; and the Centre for Responsible Business Conduct.

The information in this review is current as of June 2022.

Table of contents

FIGURES

TABLES

Acronyms and abbreviations

AFAA	Anti-Corruption and Forfeiture of Assets Act
AI	Artificial Intelligence
AIC	Actual Individual Consumption
AIP	Act on Investment Promotion
APIA	Access to Public Information Act
BCAP	Bulgaria's Code of Administrative Procedure
BDD	Bulgarian Development Bank
BCCI	Bulgarian Chamber of Commerce and Industry
BEEPS	EBRD-World Bank Business Environment and Enterprise Performance Survey
BGN	Bulgarian Lev
BIA	Bulgaria Industrial Association
BIT	Bilateral Investment Treaty
BNB	Bulgarian National Bank
BSMEPA	Bulgarian Small and Medium-sized Enterprises Promotion Agency
CA	Concessions Act
CAP	Common Agricultural Policy
CCUAAA	Counter-Corruption and Unlawfully Acquired Assets Forfeiture Act
CIT	Corporate income tax
CITA	Corporate Income Tax Act
CINDE	Costa Rican Investment Promotion Agency
CoM	Council of Ministers
CPC	Commission on Protection of competition
CPDP	Commission for Personal Data Protection
CPI	Corruption Perception Index
CRM	Customer Relationship Management
CVM	EU Commission Co-operation and Verification Mechanism
DDP	Detailed Development Plan
EBF	European Banking Federation
EBRD	European Bank for Reconstruction and Development
EC	European Commission
ECI	Economic Complexity Index
ECT	Energy Charter Treaty
ECtHR	European Court of Human Rights
EEA	European Economic Area
EIA	Environmental Impact Assessment
EIS 2021	European Innovation Scoreboard 2021
EITI	Extractive Industries Transparency Initiative
ERM II	Exchange Rate Mechanism II
ESI(F)	European Union Structural and Investment (Funds)
EU	European Union
EUR	Euro
FDI	Foreign direct investment

FET	Fair and equitable treatment
FSC	Financial Supervision Commission
FVA	Foreign value added content
GATS	General Agreement on Trade in Services
GCR	Global Competitiveness Report
GDP	Gross Domestic Product
GDPR	General Data Protection Regulation
GMOs	Genetically modified organisms
GPA	Agreement on Government Procurement
GVCs	Global value chains
IBA	InvestBulgaria Agency
ICAA	Bulgarian International Commercial Arbitration Act
ICSID	International Center for the Settlement of Investment Disputes between State and Nationals of Other States
ICT	Information, Communication and Technology
IDB	Inter-American Development Bank
ILO	International Labour Organization
IMF	International Monetary Fund
IPA	Investment Promotion Agency
IP	Intellectual Property
IPR	Investment Policy Review
iREG	OECD Indicators of Regulatory Policy and Governance
ISDS	Investor-state dispute settlement
IT	Information Technology
JEREMIE	Joint European Resources for Micro-to-Medium Enterprises
JVs	Joint ventures
LPE	Law on Public Enterprises
LPP	Law on Political Parties
MFA	Ministry of Foreign Affairs
MFN	Most-Favoured Nation
MoE	Ministry of Economy
M&A	Mergers and acquisitions
MoF	Ministry of Finance
MLDA	Fourth European Union Money Laundering Directive
MTITC	Ministry of Transport, Information Technology and Communications
NAPR	National Centre for Parliamentary Research
NCP	National Contact Point for the OECD Guidelines for Multinational Enterprises
NCIZ	National Company Industrial Zones
NDP	National Development Programme: Bulgaria 2020
NDP BULGARIA 2030	National Development Programme BULGARIA 2030
NEK	National electricity company
NGO	Non-Governmental Organisation
NRA	National Risk Assessment
NRRI	National Roadmaps of research infrastructure
NSI	National Statistical Institute
NT	National treatment
NTi	National treatment instrument
OECD	Organisation for Economic Co-operation and Development
OPT	Operational Programme on Transport
OSCE	Organisation for Security and Co-operation in Europe
OSS	One-stop solution
PCA	Protection on Competition Act
PECA	Public Enterprises and Control Agency
PDPA	Personal Data Protection Act

PFI	Policy Framework for Investment
PMR	Product market regulation
PPA	Public Procurement Act
PPCA	Privatisation and Post-Privatisation Control Agency
PPPs	Public Private Partnership
PTA	Preferential Trade Agreement
RBC	Responsible Business Conduct
R&D	Research and development
R&I	Research and Innovation
RIA	Regulatory impact assessment
RIEW	Regional inspectorates for the environment and water
SBA	Small Business Act for Europe
SEGA	State e-Government Agency
SEWRC	State Energy and Water Regulatory Commission
SJC	Supreme Judicial Council
SMEs	Small and Medium-Sized Enterprises
SOEs	State-Owned Enterprises
SPA	State Property Act
SPE	Special Purpose Entity
SRSS	Structural Reform Support Service
T+IN	Technology and Innovation Network
TiVA	Trade in value added
TFEU	Treaty on the Functioning of the European Union
TUAC	Trade Union Advisory Committee to the OECD
TRIPS	Agreement on Trade-Related Aspects of Intellectual Property Rights
UBOs	Ultimate beneficial owners
UCITS	Undertakings for collective investment in transferable securities
UN	United Nations
UNCITRAL	United Nations Commission on International Trade Law
UNCTAD	United Nations Conference on Trade and Development
UNCTADstat	United Nations Conference on Trade and Development statistics
USD	US dollar
VAT	Value-added tax
VET	Vocational Education and Training
WBG	World Bank Group
WEF	World Economic Forum
WPRBC	Working Party on Responsible Business Conduct
WIPO	World Intellectual Property Organisation
WTO	World Trade Organisation
YOY	Year-over-year

Executive summary

This investment policy review of Bulgaria looks at challenges and opportunities for attracting more and better investment and the resulting development impact of that investment.

Bulgaria has achieved a large degree of policy convergence with the *OECD Declaration on International Investment and Multinational Enterprises*, building on a number of reforms which have underpinned the country's economic and social progress. This is particularly true with respect to the country's ability to comply with the principles of openness, transparency, and non-discrimination and responsible business conduct that are an integral part of the OECD approach to investment.

Bulgaria has taken significant steps to provide adequate levels of investment protection in general. Bulgaria's investment legislation includes the principle of non-discrimination against foreign investment and general provisions on foreign investment protection. Efforts have been made to create an open and transparent environment for foreign investment by adopting new laws reinforcing and simplifying the protection of businesses. To encourage investment further, Bulgaria has also introduced significant reforms to improve the governance of state-owned enterprises (SOEs) and increase transparency in public procurement, while opening its market to private companies.

Despite these advances, Bulgaria's low score in several international rankings and businesses low levels of trust in the judiciary remain a cause of concern for both domestic and foreign investors. Although substantial structural reforms have been made to reduce corruption and mitigate its effects on the country's economy, corruption and favouritism remain widespread. According to the 2019 EU Flash Eurobarometer on business attitudes towards corruption in the European Union, 85% of respondents operating in Bulgaria described corruption as widespread; 50% of respondents felt that corruption had increased in recent years and more than 80% considered that bribery was still the easiest way to obtain public services. A strong judiciary is also lacking, which is essential for winning investor trust.

The review also analyses Bulgaria's track record in promoting responsible business conduct (RBC). Authorities have undertaken important policy reforms aimed at creating an enabling environment for businesses to act responsibly. The review proposes options that would help to promote RBC further, such as the active implementation of the OECD *Guidelines for Multinational Enterprises* and the establishment of an effective and impartial National Contact Point to promote the *Guidelines* and help to resolve RBC issues related to environment, labour, human rights and governance.

The Bulgarian authorities are well aware that private investment can play a role in enhancing the country's growth potential and in improving living standards. These goals can be advanced by creating a more modern investment promotion platform. The institutional set-up for investment promotion appears fragmented and a more explicit national strategy for investment attraction could help ensure better co-ordination among the different actors, without prejudicing specific efforts targeting activities and regions that require further assistance. Realising the full potential of investment requires a comprehensive and coherent policy package. Narrowing the gap in living standards will require an intensification of structural reforms as well as improvement in the overall business climate. Bulgaria still has some way to go towards a sustainable market economy status.

1 Assessment and recommendations

This chapter documents the overall development context in Bulgaria since the late 1990s, describing the current economic situation and the main investment policy reform efforts and identifies specific challenges that hinder investment, economic growth and well-being. It summarises the key findings in each policy areas covered by the Review and provides tailored recommendations.

Introduction

Bulgaria's reform trajectory has been nothing short of remarkable. In under three decades, successive structural, regulatory and economic reforms have propelled it from one of the poorest Eastern European countries to an upper-middle income economy. In the years leading to its European Union (EU) membership, the country made impressive progress based on continued reforms to attract investors and support private sector development. Since then, deepening integration with the EU has further allowed progress despite disruptions caused by, first, the financial global crisis in the late 2000s and then the COVID-19 crisis. Although the COVID-19 pandemic interrupted Bulgaria's impressive progress in terms of GDP growth, economic growth rebounded by 4.2 % in 2021 after real GDP contracted by 4.1% in 2020.

Foreign direct investment (FDI) has been pivotal in this success. In the late 1990s and during the 2000s, Bulgaria experienced rapid growth in FDI with a peak in 2007, the year that Bulgaria became an EU member, with FDI inflows amounting to EUR 10.1 billion. Bulgaria started with a small inward FDI stock in the 1990s (accounting for 3.5% of GDP in 1995), which increased at a spectacularly high rate over the following decade. For the 1995-2007 period, the share of inward FDI stock to GDP increased from 3.5% of Bulgaria's GDP in 1995 to 85% in 2007. FDI inflows in Bulgaria in the recent years were higher compared to all its EU regional peers. Until the outbreak of the COVID 19 crisis, FDI inflows averaged about 2.6% of GDP in the period 2014-19, albeit lower compared to the pre-financial crisis annual average of more than 10% of GDP.

Due to the global financial crisis, foreign direct investment in Bulgaria declined, dropping from 28% in 2008 to about 2% of GDP in 2018. The COVID-19 pandemic further affected FDI trends. In the first half of 2020, Bulgaria experienced a significant drop in FDI inflows, representing a 32.8% year-on-year decline. In 2021, foreign direct investment in Bulgaria stood at EUR 1.04 billion, the equivalent of 1.5% of GDP according to Bulgaria's National Bank data. According to statistics from the Bulgarian National Bank issued in June 2022, FDI in Bulgaria in the first four months of 2022 stood at EUR 653.2 million, the equivalent of 0.9 % of the GDP; in the same period of 2021, FDI was EUR 196.8 million.

Bulgaria continues to face challenges to meet its objectives of ensuring long-term sustainable growth and development that can deliver benefits for all and protect the planet as well as supporting local productive capacity, innovation and competitiveness to help the country prepare for the future. This *Investment Policy Review of Bulgaria* (hereafter: the *Review*) considers the extent to which FDI can contribute to achieving these objectives and how different aspects of investment policies in Bulgaria can help support their realisation. It assesses Bulgaria's policy convergence in the framework of the country's June 2022 adherence to the OECD *Declaration on International Investment and Multinational Enterprises* (hereafter: the OECD *Declaration*), including the country's ability to comply with the principles of openness, transparency and non-discrimination and responsible business conduct (RBC) practices (Box 1.1). Capitalising on the OECD *Policy Framework for Investment* (Box 1.2), the *Review* studies other policy areas that are of key relevance to investment and sustainable and inclusive development in Bulgaria such as investment protection, promotion and facilitation; innovation; the state of infrastructure; and public governance.

Box 1.1. The Declaration on International Investment and Multinational Enterprises

The Declaration is a policy commitment by Adherents to provide an open and transparent environment for international investment and to encourage the positive contribution multinational enterprises can make to economic and social progress.

The Declaration consists of four elements (each underpinned by a decision of the OECD Council on follow-up procedures):

The Guidelines for Multinational Enterprises: Recommendations on responsible business conduct (RBC) addressed by governments to multinational enterprises operating in or from Adherents. Adherents commit to promote the Guidelines and establish their built-in implementation mechanism – the National Contact Points (NCPs) to further their effectiveness.

National Treatment: A voluntary undertaking by Adherents to accord to foreign-controlled enterprises established on their territories treatment no less favourable than that accorded to domestic enterprises in the same situations.

International investment incentives and disincentives: Adherents recognise the need to give due weight to the interest of other Adherents affected by laws and practices in this field; they need to strengthen international co-operation in this area and endeavour to make measures as transparent as possible.

Conflicting requirements: Adherents agree to co-operate so as to avoid or minimise the imposition of conflicting requirements on multinational enterprises.

As of June 2022, all 38 OECD member countries had adhered to the Declaration, as had 13 non-member countries: Argentina (22 April 1997), Brazil (14 November 1997), Egypt (11 July 2007), Jordan (28 November 2013), Kazakhstan (22 June 2017), Morocco (23 November 2009), Peru (25 July 2008), Romania (20 April 2005), Tunisia (25 May 2012), Ukraine (10 March 2017), Croatia (17 October 2019) Uruguay (25 February 2021) and Bulgaria (9 June 2022).

Box 1.2. The Policy Framework for Investment

The Policy Framework for Investment (PFI) helps governments to mobilise private investment in support of sustainable development, thus contributing to the prosperity of countries and their citizens and to the fight against poverty. It offers a list of key questions to be examined by any government seeking to create a favourable investment climate. The PFI was first developed in 2006 by representatives of 60 OECD and non-OECD governments in association with business, labour, civil society and other international organisations and endorsed by OECD ministers. Designed by governments to support international investment policy dialogue, co-operation, and reform, it has been extensively used by over 35 countries as well as regional bodies to assess and reform the investment climate. The PFI was updated in 2015 to take this experience and changes in the global economic landscape into account.

The PFI is a flexible instrument that allows countries to evaluate their progress and to identify priorities for action in 12 policy areas: investment policy; investment promotion and facilitation; trade; competition; tax; corporate governance; promoting responsible business conduct; human resource development; infrastructure; financing investment; public governance; and investment in support of green growth. Three principles apply throughout the PFI: policy coherence, transparency in policy formulation and implementation, and regular evaluation of the impact of existing and proposed policies.

The value added of the PFI is in bringing together the different policy strands and stressing the overarching issue of governance. The aim is not necessarily to break new ground in individual policy areas but to tie them together to ensure policy coherence. It does not provide ready-made reform agendas but rather helps to improve the effectiveness of any reforms that are ultimately undertaken. By encouraging a structured process for formulating and implementing policies at all levels of government, the PFI can be used in various ways and for various purposes by different constituencies, including for self-evaluation and reform design by governments and for peer reviews in regional or multilateral discussions.

The PFI looks at the investment climate from a broad perspective. It is not just about increasing investment but about maximising the economic and social returns, which can differ substantially from region to region, even within a country. Quality matters as much as the quantity as far as investment is concerned. It also recognises that a good investment climate should be good for all firms – foreign and domestic, large and small. The objective of a good investment climate is also to improve the flexibility of the economy to respond to new opportunities as they arise – allowing productive firms to expand and uncompetitive ones (including state-owned enterprises) to close. The government needs to be nimble: responsive to the needs of firms and other stakeholders through systematic public consultation and able to change course quickly when a given policy fails to meet its objectives. It should also create a champion for reform within the government itself. Most importantly, it needs to ensure that the investment climate supports sustainable and inclusive development.

The PFI was created in response to this complexity, fostering a flexible, whole-of-government approach which recognises that investment climate improvements require not just policy reform but also changes in the way governments go about their business.

Bulgaria's FDI trends and macroeconomic performance

Bulgaria has been a member of the European Union (EU) since 2007. It is a relatively small, upper-middle-income economy, with a population of about 7 million (the 13th smallest in the EU in 2020). Around

1.3 million people lived in the capital city of Sofia in 2021.The transition from a centralised, planned economy to an open, market-based one begun in February 1991 and was initially hampered by slow institutional restructuring, opaque privatisation, high indebtedness, a deep economic and banking crisis, and a loss of savings. Gross domestic product (GDP) was correspondingly low and the promises of convergence failed to materialise. The situation started to improve in the late 1990s, thanks to the introduction of the currency board in 1997 as the key component of a broad macroeconomic stabilisation programme.

Since then, Bulgaria has established itself as a country with a strong macroeconomic performance and sound monetary and fiscal stability. In the late 1990s, a broad range of structural reforms ensured Bulgaria's transition from a command economy to an open market economy. The 2000s were a decade of economic growth and improved living standards. Although some of those gains were undone by the global economic crisis (GDP contracted in 2009), even in the most difficult moments inflation was kept low, in line with trade partners. The fiscal deficit was trimmed to less than 1% of GDP in 2012-13 from 4.2% in 2009. In 2011, Bulgaria exited the excessive fiscal deficit procedure. Government debt increased slightly to about 25% of the country's GDP in 2020, the third lowest in the EU. Throughout the years ahead of Bulgaria's accession to the EU, FDI trends followed an upward trajectory. Since then, deepening integration with the EU has further allowed progress despite the disruptions caused by the financial global crisis in the late 2000s and the COVID-19 crisis. Although Bulgaria's economy declined in 2020 as result of the COVID-19 pandemic, growth for 2021 as a whole totalled 4.2%, contrasting the 4.3% contraction recorded in 2020. GDP growth surpassed pre-crisis level by mid-2021, thanks to strong consumption supported by significant fiscal support and buoyant wage growth.

Many investors have continuously seen Bulgaria as an attractive investment destination. Prior to the COVID-19 crisis, the share of inward FDI stock stood at 78.5% of GDP, above the OECD and EU averages (of 46% and 59%, respectively), an illustration of Bulgaria's attractiveness to foreign investors. In 2020, Bulgaria's FDI flows were EUR 2.2 billion corresponding to about 3.5% of 2020 GDP, compared to 1.9% of GDP in 2019. Figures for January 2022 showed that FDI had more than doubled compared to January 2021. Among the world's leading manufacturers, the country ranks among the top locations for outsourcing production activities. With economic development, Bulgaria has also become an important investor abroad. According to preliminary figures issued by Bulgaria' Central Bank in June 2022, Bulgarian investment abroad increased by EUR 107.2 million in the first four months of 2022, compared to EUR 62.6 million in the same period of 2021.

Bulgaria's competitive stance

Tackling the challenge of sustaining efforts to promote innovation, digitalisation and better infrastructure

The COVID-19 crisis has brought up the importance of digitalisation and innovation, where Bulgaria is lagging. Further investment in Bulgaria's communication infrastructure networks and innovation across all regions is essential to support Bulgaria's economic recovery and attracting FDI. Yet low levels of public and private investment in R&I, fragmented public science base, lack of ICT skills as well as insufficient science-business linkages are still challenging Bulgaria's digital and innovation ecosystem. Progress in this direction would ensure greater social inclusion in the post-COVID-19 times.

With respect to infrastructure, Bulgaria started in the late 1990s to invest in the development of key physical infrastructure as a fundamental element of national integration. This effort was particularly important in road and rail transport. Nonetheless, despite significant progress achieved in improving both road and rail infrastructures, Bulgaria still suffers from a rather poor state and big disparities of infrastructure and big regional disparities as highlighted in international organisations' reports such as the World Bank *Doing*

Business 2020 report. Significant infrastructure disparities remain across regions, which is still a challenge for unlocking their potential for investment and growth. For Bulgaria to attract more private investment, several obstacles for investment would need to be addressed such as poor road quality, insufficient railroad connectivity as well as a slow-pace implementation of ongoing projects and reforms.

Labour market and skills

A set of factors such as Bulgaria's relatively high level of enrolment in education, low employment costs compared to other EU member states as well as Bulgaria's EU membership have made Bulgaria's labour market attractive for investors. The adult literacy rate in Bulgaria is 98.4% (15 years and older) according to the most recent data from the UN's Human Development Report, although illiteracy is higher among some minorities such as the Roma population. Against the background of a rapidly ageing population and negative net migration flows, Bulgaria will need to pursue its efforts to improve the labour and social context and to decrease the brain drain of Bulgaria's population.

SOEs reforms have advanced

Poor governance and economic performance of Bulgaria's State-Owned Enterprises (SOEs) has been seen for many years as an obstacle to private investment. Bulgarian SOEs still dominate large parts of the economy in key sectors such as energy, health, and transport. In order to diffuse these concerns, significant changes have been introduced by Bulgaria to improve the legal framework for SOEs through the adoption of a new Law and bylaws in line with the OECD *Guidelines on Corporate Governance of State-Owned Enterprises ("SOE Guidelines").* Strengthening the governance of SOEs, including local SOEs, has become one of the main priorities of Bulgaria's government.

For the past six years, reforms to improve governance and promote the integrity of SOEs have progressed. In December 2019, Bulgaria became adherent to the SOE *Guidelines* and as such has committed itself to further promote the implementation of the *Guidelines* and defining a framework for the corporate governance of SOEs. In October 2019, with the technical and legal support of the OECD Secretariat, Bulgaria adopted the Law on Public Enterprises (LPE). One of the main novelties introduced by the LPE is the establishment of an ownership co-ordination entity, the Public Enterprises and Control Agency (PECA) (a transformation of the former Agency for Privatisation and Post-privatisation Control). PECA's new role responds to the need to improve the decentralised SOEs model of the country. In April 2020, Bulgaria adopted the "PECA's rules of procedures" as well as the "Rule of Implementation of the Law on Public Enterprises". Despite these encouraging developments, these reforms are still recent and need to be practically implemented by relevant authorities in order to be effective.

Competition policy

For the past two decades, Bulgaria has taken steps to promote entrepreneurship and to guarantee a level playing field for both domestic and foreign investors. As part of EU membership requirements, Bulgaria has aligned its legal and institutional framework with EU standards. Bulgaria has a competition authority to promote competition and entrepreneurship and enable FDI. Still, Bulgaria's market functioning has been of concern for some investors. Bulgaria has an opportunity to leverage its standards and practice in the context of its work with the OECD Competition Committee.

Bulgaria's investment regime and policy framework for investment

Bulgaria is open to foreign investment

Since the early 2000s, attracting investment has been a top priority of the government, as evidenced by Bulgaria's national development strategy plans and other governmental strategic documents. With a view to enhancing FDI inflows, continuous efforts have been made to reform the regulatory framework under favourable terms in line with the European legislation and other international standards. Bulgaria is open to foreign investment, with few formal ownership restrictions, and the key standards of investor treatment and protection are guaranteed under the Constitution and other laws.

There are no generalised screening or approval mechanisms for new investments or established companies in Bulgaria. In addition, Bulgaria does not impose limits on access to local finance and incentives (e.g. tax concessions) or government purchasing markets for foreign-controlled enterprises incorporated in the country. National treatment of foreign investors in the post-establishment phase is guaranteed, which means that foreign investors, when incorporated and headquartered in Bulgaria, are considered domestic legal entities, with all the rights and obligations that are applied to domestic investors. The few existing exceptions to national treatment are limited to foreign ownership restrictions in a handful of sectors, namely in the acquisition of land (agricultural, for commercial purposes and real estate), forestry, air and maritime transport, as well as restrictions for the provision of rail transport, legal services and mining.

Other existing barriers to FDI mainly concern conditions imposed at establishment (e.g. establishment requirements for investment in energy, private security, legal services and selected financial services). These barriers are few, mostly sector-specific, and typically limited in their scope, applying almost exclusively to investors from outside the EU, the European Economic Area (EEA) or Switzerland, or to investors from countries that are not WTO members. As a result, using the methodology of the OECD FDI Regulatory Restrictiveness Index, which is based on statutory measures that are discriminatory in nature, Bulgaria's degree of restrictiveness is low in comparison to both the OECD average and the average of non-OECD economies that have adhered to the *Declaration*.

The key standards of investor treatment and protection, including with respect to intellectual property rights, are guaranteed under the Constitution and ordinary laws. The protection of investment, combined with effective enforcement mechanisms, is an important pillar of a sound investment climate. Protecting investors from improper treatment can lower their perception of risk for new investments, and investors who perceive lower risks will generally make capital and resources available at a lower cost and with longer amortisation process.

Protection of investment is strong

Bulgaria's domestic framework provides investor protection aligned with international standards. Bulgaria's Constitution includes protections for local and foreign investors against forcible expropriation of property, and property rights and regulations on acquisition, benefits and use of property are well defined.

Bulgaria also benefits from a modern intellectual property (IP) legislation that is aligned with the EU norms and standards, which is an important precondition for attracting and retaining investment. Bulgaria grants constitutional-level protection to IP rights, in particular to scientific and technological creativity, as well as inventors' rights, copyrights and related rights. Bulgaria is also a party to all international treaties and conventions on intellectual property administrated by the World Intellectual Property Organization (WIPO), with the exception of the Geneva Act of the Lisbon Agreement on Appellations of Origin and Geographical Indications. National laws are aligned with EU directives, even going beyond the minimum requirements of the WTO Agreement on Trade-Related Aspects of Intellectual Property Rights (TRIPS).

Bulgaria is also arbitration and mediation-friendly. It has also made tangible progress in reducing delays related to contract enforcement as illustrated in the 2020 World Bank Doing Business report, in which Bulgaria ranked 42nd in the ease of enforcing contracts among 190 economies, moving up 33 spots since its 2015 ranking. Progress in reforming the judicial system has been steady since Bulgaria's accession to EU membership, in particular towards strengthening the independence and professionalism of the judiciary. Challenges nevertheless remain to tackle judicial and administrative delays and costs to enforce contracts.

A significant network of investment treaties adds protection for foreign investors

Like many other countries, Bulgaria grants additional and preferential protections to some foreign investors through its network of investment treaties with broad range of countries. Most of these treaties, which nominally cover over 50 jurisdictions and a large share of Bulgaria's inward and outward FDI stock, were concluded in the 1990s and early 2000s. They bear the hallmarks of agreements concluded at a time when few treaty-based claims had been brought by investors, awareness of treaty implications was lower among governments and belief in the potential benefits of such treaties was greater than it is today.

Bulgaria has changed its approach to investment treaties in recent years. Some of this change corresponds to commitments that Bulgaria made as part of EU accession and a new role for the European Commission on investment policy in the EU since 2009. It also likely reflects Bulgaria's experiences facing claims by investors in arbitration cases under its older treaties – at least ten such cases at the time of writing of this report – and intensification of policy debates regarding effects, designs and outcomes of investment treaties.

Central in these debates is the desire to strike an appropriate balance in these treaties between investment protection and sovereign rights to regulate in the public interest. A new Bulgarian model BIT, which was approved by the Council of Ministers in November 2018, seeks to achieve a more balanced approach and serve as a basis for future treaty negotiations with non-EU countries. This represents an important achievement but seeking to update existing treaties remains a separate challenge. Bulgaria is keenly aware of these issues through its participation in several ongoing inter-governmental treaty reform processes.

Bulgaria has modern investment promotion mechanisms for FDI attraction

Bulgaria's policy framework for investment also contains modern and well-co-ordinated investment promotion mechanisms. Over the years, Bulgaria's governments have developed several framework documents that provide the overall vision for the country's medium and long-term socio-economic development and the role of investment promotion and facilitation within it. In particular, the Act on Investment Promotion (AIP) sets out the specific objectives of the national investment promotion policy, delineates responsibilities of different bodies, and outlines the criteria for state support.

The Ministry of Economy until recently has been in charge of the development of the national investment promotion policy, aided in its implementation by InvestBulgaria Agency (IBA), at the national level, and by regional governors and mayors at the sub-national level. In addition, several bodies have aimed to facilitate cross-institutional co-ordination, for example the high-level permanent taskforce of the Ministry of Economy, the National Economic Council and the National Council for Tripartite Co-operation. Given the commitment of the new government established in late 2021 to update the rules for doing business in Bulgaria, developing an action plan with specific planned government initiatives listed, responsible institutions and applicable timelines could help ensure that crosscutting reforms are implemented as envisioned.

Bulgaria relies on the provision of investment incentives to attract entrepreneurs

Bulgaria has a relatively low rate of corporate taxation and a well-developed framework for provision of investment incentives. Fiscal incentives are regulated by the underlying tax legislation and financial incentives by the AIP. As an EU Member State, Bulgaria is also subject to the EU State Aid rules. Overall, there are four types of certified investment projects in Bulgaria – Class A, Class B, Class C (which are provided by municipalities) and priority investment projects – that can benefit from government support. The certificates differ in the application process and the eligibility criteria, which relate to the character of the economic activity, size of investment and job creation effect, among others. About 300 investment projects were certified in Bulgaria in 2004-20 (most of which were Class A projects), which were associated with a creation of over 70 000 direct jobs.

Bulgaria also offers investors advantages associated with locating in one of the industrial zones. Importantly, industrial zone users in Bulgaria do not benefit from a reduced profit tax rate. Instead, such zones exist for custom purposes only, and they aim to provide investors with high-quality infrastructure. Technological parks are also available, which need to satisfy the conditions of an industrial zone and host predominantly scientific research and development activity, education, information technologies or advanced manufacturing. According to AIP, investment projects aiming to create an industrial zone or a technological park are eligible to become certified investment projects and the planned legislation on technological parks aims to regulate the parks' creation and management. In the future, improving monitoring and evaluation of such instruments can help ensure their optimal use.

The national investment promotion agency, IBA, plays an important role in facilitating the process of investors' applications to become a certified investment project and more generally help attract investment. IBA is an executive public agency. Beyond processing investment project applications, its task is to provide free-of-charge information, contacts and project management support to potential investors. Relative to OECD agencies, IBA is small and has relatively low levels of institutional independence. In order to maximise its positive impact, the agency could consider boosting its proactive prioritisation efforts, monitoring and evaluation and co-operation with regional bodies to fully embed its policies with regional development policies. It could also reflect on the feasibility of extending its aftercare services and offering information on local suppliers/buyers to embed them better to the region, personnel recruitment or training support to help bridge the skills gaps in the country.

EU funds also play an important role in mobilising investment

Another aspect influencing Bulgaria's investment attraction policy is the availability of EU funds. Bulgaria is one of the countries that has benefitted most from the EU support during the budget cycle between 2014 and 2020. These funds provide additional source of financing for firms and can mobilise additional private capital, improving the overall liquidity. In the medium and long run, they can also support building of necessary infrastructure and educating the labour force, helping to improve Bulgaria's attractiveness as an investment destination. For example, a large share of EU funding goes towards greening of the economy, educational and vocational training initiatives, research and innovation and high-quality employment programmes. Several EU programmes are also specifically geared towards supporting SMEs in Bulgaria, including in the aftermath of the COVID-19 pandemic. Yet, Bulgaria's system for managing EU funds in the 2014-20 programming period was centralised in the hands of national managing authorities, and lacked a place-based and integrated approach. In addition, the use of EU funds have been highly concentrated in large cities, where substantive infrastructure is located. This unbalanced use of EU support has further entrenched diverging development trends among regions and localities in Bulgaria.

Bulgaria has undertaken a number of actions to reduce administrative burden but additional efforts are required

Bulgaria has undertaken a number of initiatives to reduce administrative burdens. For example, several consecutive programmes involved reaching of quantitative targets. Legal changes in 2016 have also improved the legal requirements of creating new regulations; and an SME Test has been introduced to assess possible regulatory effects on smaller firms. Bulgaria has also made strides in digitising administrative procedures and offering e-services, including to business. Yet, international rankings and feedback from the private sector suggest that the ease of obtaining licenses and permits remains a challenge to doing business in Bulgaria. For example, there were 18 procedures for dealing with construction permits in Bulgaria at the time of writing of this *Review*. Overall, it took 97 days to deal with the 18 procedures according to the 2021 OECD *Review on Decentralisation and Regionalisation in Bulgaria*. In this context, the government could consider if establishing a single window for investment could be a useful and feasible step and continue the process of improving the overall quality of regulations in the country.

Strengthening public governance

The quality of public governance at the national, regional and local level has a significant influence on the climate for business and investment. Poorly designed or loosely applied regulations can slow business responsiveness, divert resources away from productive investments, hamper or delay entry into markets, reduce job creation and generally discourage entrepreneurship. Nothing contributes more to investor confidence about regulation than predictability and that rules achieve their state objectives. The quality of public services also significantly influences the investment climate, and this includes the quality of the justice system. Integrity is also a crucial determinant of a favourable investment climate.

Bulgaria has made progress in strengthening its anti-corruption and public integrity framework but challenges persist

Bulgaria has made progress in reducing opportunities for corruption and limiting discretion in public decision-making. The Criminal Code prohibits various corruption offences, including extortion, trading in influence, facilitation payments and, in line with the OECD *Convention on Combating Bribery of Foreign Public Officials in International Business Transactions*, bribery of foreign public officials. In late 2017, Bulgaria adopted a comprehensive anti-corruption law, setting up a single anti-corruption agency based on a merger of existing institutions, to tackle corruption among high-level officials and to deal with issues such as conflicts of interest and declaration of personal assets. The new legislation also introduced new principles such as legality, transparency and impartiality. New anti-money laundering legislation was adopted in 2018, following the Fourth European Union Anti-Money Laundering Directive (AMLD4) of 2015.

Nevertheless, the complex legal framework and weak enforcement have hampered Bulgaria's ability to effectively tackle all challenges related to corruption, as illustrated by the April, July and November 2021 legislative elections during which anger over corruption weighed on the campaign period. Despite the many encouraging steps taken, corruption continues to be perceived to be widespread. According to the 2019 EU *Flash Eurobarometer* on attitudes towards corruption, 85% of businesses operating in the country described corruption as widespread. In the *Transparency International Corruption Perception Index* for 2021 released in January 2022, Bulgaria remained below other EU member states, ranking 78th overall in the report, the worst ranking of an EU country among 180 countries surveyed. Bulgaria still lacks a solid criminal record of accomplishment of concrete results on high-level corruption cases as well on tackling corruption at the local level that would help to build public trust. In 2017, the *Local Integrity System Index* developed by Transparency International Bulgaria showed that the 27 municipalities-district centres had an average score of 3.29 (on a scale from one to five). The EU Co-operation and Verification Mechanism

(CVM) specifically included a recommendation concerning the need to fight against corruption at the local level.

Judicial reform has advanced although challenges remain

Bulgaria has undertaken noticeable reforms to tackle major issues of concern to businesses such as the perceived judiciary's lack of professionalism and impartiality. Policy steps have been taken to enhance the independence of magistrates. The Bulgarian authorities have also seen building the capacity of the judiciary as critical. Because of these efforts, the latest and last (2019) EU Co-operation and Verification Mechanism report assessed positively the progress of Bulgaria in the area of judicial reforms. Because of these policy developments, the Commission proposed that Bulgaria exit the mechanism, which was initially set up at the time of its EU accession in 2007.

Despite these encouraging developments, public perception of Bulgaria's judiciary has improved only marginally. According to the 2021 Index of Economic Freedom of the Heritage Foundation, court backlogs and delays have continued to be perceived as a significant issue and the judicial system has remained the least trusted Bulgaria's institution. Similarly, according to the 2020 EU Justice Scorecard, the perceived independence of Bulgaria's judiciary was among the lowest in the EU. This suggests that further progress towards improving judicial independence is required.

Reforms of Bulgaria's public procurement system is on-going under guidance of the European Commission

Unfair or opaque procurement processes may send negative signals to businesses and mislead them into considering that corruption is part of the normal course of doing business in a country. An average of around BGN 5 billion is spent annually through public procurement in Bulgaria. For years, public procurement in Bulgaria has been considered as vulnerable to corruption. For example, the amount of allegedly corrupt procurement represented 36% of the total public funds spent by municipalities in 2015 according to a 2021 OECD report on decentralisation and regionalisation in Bulgaria.

Administrative capacity has been another challenge for the procurement system, causing formal errors and delays. Persistent concerns have also related to the lack of consistency and 'formalistic' ex ante and ex post controls of procurement procedures. According to the EU Single Market Scorecard, Bulgaria's public procurement performance in 2019 was average, a performance comparable to the performance of other EU countries such as Belgium, France, Germany, Hungary, Italy, Ireland, and the Slovak Republic.

In response to these concerns, Bulgaria has continuously reformed its public procurement system in an effort to make it both compliant with the EU acquis and improve performance in terms of competition, openness and transparency – reforms that have affected all spheres of the procurement cycle, including oversight and law enforcement. For example, the Bulgarian National Strategy for the Development of Public Procurement Sector 2014-20, and its accompanying Action Plan, were elaborated to meet the requirements that stem from the new EU public procurement directives, the country specific recommendations proposed by the European Commission and adopted by the Council of the EU, the National Reform Programme 2014-20 and the EC Co-operation and Verification Mechanism. The strategy aimed at reducing the risk of irregularities in public procurement through measures in five areas: legislation, law enforcement, publicity and transparency, strengthening of administrative capacity and professionalism and control systems. It also contained actions, related to the adoption of e-procurement, which resulted in the operationalisation of e-procurement platform, together with amendments in the Law on Public Procurement.

Bulgaria has made strides in improving the quality of its overall regulatory system

In response to concerns by the business community about the regulatory environment in Bulgaria that has been characterised by complexity and lack of transparency, Bulgaria has made strides in improving the overall quality of its regulatory system. This is reflected in the country's scores on the World Bank's *World Governance Indicators* and the OECD *Indicators of Regulatory Policy and Governance* (iREG). For example, recent legislative changes improved the legal framework for publishing draft laws, conducting public consultations, preparing regulatory impact assessment and ensuring better regulatory oversight.

Still, in the area of conducting *ex post* evaluations of regulations, Bulgaria could achieve further progress to reach the levels found in other OECD countries. In particular, reducing administrative burdens and mixed feedback in reaching quantitative reduction targets point that this area is an ongoing challenge and will require further efforts to review and, wherever possible, streamline most burdensome regulations. Ensuring that the requirements of prior publication, public consultations and *ex ante* regulatory impact assessment are respected in practice when preparing draft regulations will also be important. Addressing recommendations stemming from the OECD *Regulatory Policy Scan of Bulgaria* released in 2022 could be helpful in this regard.

Promoting and enabling responsible business conduct

Promoting and enabling responsible business conduct (RBC) is vital to attract and retain quality investment and ensure that business activity contributes to broader value creation and sustainable development. Internationally recognised RBC principles and standards such as the OECD *Guidelines on Multinational Enterprises* set out an expectation that all business avoid and address negative impacts of their operations, while contributing to sustainable development where they operate.

Bulgaria has taken steps to promote RBC, including through the adoption of a National CSR Strategy and the mainstreaming of RBC principles and several policies and sectoral strategies. Various actors, notably business associations have been active in RBC promotion. These efforts have resulted in a growing awareness of RBC in the country. Understanding and implementation of RBC however vary significantly across businesses. Moreover, the concept of due diligence – a key process for the implementation of RBC principles – is not yet at the forefront of the public discourse and national efforts on RBC. Promoting a common understanding of RBC based on internationally recognised RBC standards, can help promote sound business practices, while supporting the government national priorities for Bulgaria's sustainable development.

Furthermore, deepening efforts to promote RBC due diligence could go a long way in addressing some of the main environmental and social risks that are associated with certain industries, for example the garment, mining and energy production sectors. The government could consider leveraging and actively disseminating international standards and tools to help businesses better manage such risks, improve industrial relations and maximise the contribution of the sectors to economic, but also environmental and social outcomes.

Beyond promoting standards, the government can play a role by facilitating the due diligence process, and creating an enabling environment for RBC. Ensuring that stakeholders, workers and journalists can play their role in consultative and accountability processes is key to ensure that businesses can meet international RBC standards. More broadly, a sound judicial system, as well as predictable and transparent processes are important elements to underpin RBC. As noted above, the government has made efforts in that regard. Bulgaria is encouraged to deepen reforms to support further uptake and implementation of RBC.

Countries that are Adherents to the OECD *Declaration* are required to set up a National Contact Point (NCP) for the *Guidelines*. NCPs are created to further the effectiveness of the *Guidelines*, and Adherents are required to make human and financial resources available to their NCPs so they can effectively fulfil their responsibilities, taking into account internal budget priorities and practices. In addition to promoting the *Guidelines*, NCPs contribute to the resolution of issues that arise relating to their implementation in specific instances. Throughout the year 2021, Bulgaria took important steps to establish its NCP as evidenced by the Council of Ministers Decision No. 682 adopted on 17 September 2021 establishing and organising the activities of Bulgaria's NCP for the implementation of the *Guidelines*. During the first half of 2022, in the context of its formal adherence to the *Investment Declaration*, Bulgaria made additional efforts to operationalise its NCP.

Challenges ahead

Political instability has been of concerns to investors. Although the political situation in Bulgaria stabilised in 2017 up to the end of 2020, for most part of 2021 Bulgaria did not have a functioning parliament. After this prolonged political crisis, a new coalition government was formed in December 2021. In summer 2022, Bulgaria was nevertheless facing new risk of political instability after a no confidence vote in parliament that led to the resignation of the government formed in December 2021.

The war in Ukraine has also clouded the economic outlook. While the economic recovery from the COVID-19 crisis was gaining momentum in 2021, the war has been dampening growth.

The many years of expansion until the COVID-19 crisis saw deep transformation in the economic structure, in particular of exports, which have proven to be particularly important given the small size of the Bulgarian economy and therefore the relevance of trade for overall economic performance. Exports of goods and services was equal to 65% of 2015-19 GDP (as against 29% in OECD, 41.5% in Romania and 33.6% in Greece during the same period). Until the COVID-19 crisis, private consumption expanded at a robust rate based on low inflation and favourable labour market conditions. Between 2015 and 2020, GDP growth was well in excess of 3%. Exports, supported by increasingly strong linkages with global value chains (GVCs), especially with EU countries, have been the key driver for growth. In late 2019, before the COVID-19 crisis, more than 50% of all Bulgarian exports were sourced and sold in GVC linkages. Bulgaria's GVC participation was above the EU-28 level, although lower than in countries such as the Slovak Republic and Hungary. Bulgaria is highly integrated in the regional value chain with the EU: in 2019, 48% of foreign value added content (FVA) in Bulgarian exports were sourced from EU (mainly Germany and Spain).

The global economic fallout resulting from the COVID-19 outbreak affected Bulgaria. Economic activity contracted sharply when confinement measures were first introduced to contain the pandemic. According to data issued by the National Statistical Institute (NSI) in March 2021, Bulgaria's economy dropped by 4.7% in the fourth quarter of 2020. In annual terms, the economic drop in the third quarter of 2020 was 4.2% compared to the same period of 2019.[1] Overall GDP fell by 4.1% in 2020. Employment fell, eroding recent gains. The reduced actual and expected business activity because of the COVID-19 crisis prompted domestic and foreign companies to postpone investment plans. Thanks to anti-crisis measures, including fiscal ones, adopted by the government in the aftermath of the COVID-19, economic growth rebounded by 4.2% in 2021, primarily driven by domestic demand and exports. According to the OECD June 2022 *Economic Forecast Summary*, growth was nevertheless expected to weaken to 2.5 % in 2022 and 2.25 % in 2023 because of the war in Ukraine.

In the context of this challenging time, business environment improvements could further support investment and growth. As recognised by Bulgaria's authorities, further efforts are required to attract high-value added investment to support the modernisation of the economy to achieve the country's goal of ensuring long-term sustainable growth and development that can deliver benefits for all as well as supporting local productive capacity and innovation and competitiveness to help the country prepare for the future. Further investments in infrastructure, more and better-targeted public policies in digitalisation and in R&D, completion of the major reform of the corporate governance framework of state-owned enterprises (SOEs), additional measures to strengthen the judiciary, and effective enforcement of the anti-corruption legislation, could help attracting more domestic and foreign direct investment and strengthen business competitiveness. Targeted investment promotion could also help to tackle regional disparities and unlock growth potentials in all regions, particularly in the North-West region (OECD, 2021).

It is important that policies and institutions take into account regional heterogeneity – as firms certainly do when making decisions on where and what to invest. An existing concept that already begins to do this is the EU Smart Specialisation Strategy. This strategy works on identifying local assets and then increasing the competitiveness of these assets, including through diversifying within this realm to higher value added operations. It also identifies a region's weaknesses and works to mitigate them for example through increasing service and infrastructure linkages to higher achieving regions. Thus, one of the best ways to ensure investment will lead to spill overs is to attract the foreign or domestic firms that match regional assets and ambitions.

Policy recommendations

National treatment of investment

- Evaluate the costs and benefits of continuing to open up the economy to international investment by further reducing the exceptions to the OECD National Treatment instrument. Discriminatory measures only serve the broader public interest to the extent that their potential costs in terms of forgone investment and efficiency gains are compensated by broader social and economic benefits. For this reason, they need to be constantly re-evaluated to determine whether such restrictions still fulfil their original roles in an efficient manner and no other non-discriminatory alternative measure is available for such purposes. This should include an assessment of the proportionality of the measure to ensure they are not greater than needed to address specific concerns and objectives.

Investment protection

- Consider recognising foreign-based conciliation commissions and foreign-based mediation procedures as an alternative method of resolution of legal and non-legal disputes, as done with mediation that takes place in Bulgaria. This would avoid the current burdensome requirement for out-of-court settlements to undergo the general procedures for enforcement of contracts.
- Take additional steps to reduce the length of judicial procedures. These measures should include specific rules of procedure to prevent or limit dilatory measures and fixed time limits for the performance of each judiciary step, eliminating the need of interested parties to resort to the superior court to avoid time-delaying tactics.
- Continue to reassess and update the government's priorities with respect to investment treaty policy. An important issue in this regard is an evaluation of the appropriate balance between investor protections and the government's right to regulate, and how to achieve that balance in practice. Clearer specification of key provisions in older BITs would likely help to reflect government intent and ensure policy space for government regulation. It has proven difficult for governments to update older treaties but some multilateral reform initiatives are underway. Depending on whether the parties wish to clarify original intent or revise a provision, it may be possible to clarify language through joint interpretations agreed with treaty partners or treaty amendments. Replacement of older investment treaties by consent may also be an appropriate option in some cases.
- Continue to participate actively in and follow closely government and other action on investment treaty reforms at the OECD, UNCITRAL and for the ECT. Consideration of reforms and policy discussions on frequently invoked provisions in ISDS cases and whether investment treaties are achieving their intended purposes are of particular importance in current investment treaty policy. Emerging issues such as the possible role for trade and investment treaties in fostering responsible business conduct as well as ongoing discussions about treaties and sustainable development also merit close attention and participation.
- Continue to develop ISDS dispute prevention and case management tools. The government advised during the course of this Review that there is currently no dedicated unit responsible for handling investor grievances before they become ISDS cases under investment treaties. The government may wish to consider drawing on examples of institutional frameworks in other countries for the prevention of investment disputes and policy-setting activities. It may also wish to consider ways to promote awareness-raising and inter-ministerial co-operation

regarding the government's investment treaty policy and the significance of investment treaty obligations for the day-to-day functions of line agencies.

Investment promotion and facilitation

- Establish a list of priority investment climate reforms and specific projects with clearly identified timelines and responsible institutions. The plan should build on the existing strategic planning documents and diagnostics. It could be made publically available and periodically updated. The National Economic Council (NEC) and the ministry in charge of investment policy could play a lead role in this regard, supported by high-level of government.
- Strengthen regional component in investment promotion and develop terms of reference for co-operation across agencies at the central and sub-national level. Differentiate investment promotion according to regional comparative advantages. Use the EU Smart Specialisation framework to aid in this exercise. Rules for engagement with sub-national investment promotion bodies appear limited to processing of certified investment projects. For example, InvestBulgaria Agency (IBA) does not have a regional development mandate and lacks terms of reference for engaging with sub-national bodies. The development and implementation of such rules could help ensure complementarity of efforts and attraction of FDI into different regions.
- Consider strengthening the aftercare services and technical capacity of InvestBulgaria Agency (IBA) and of local initiatives such as InvestinSofia agency. While IBA performs all standard investment facilitation functions in the pre-establishment stage, it does not offer many aftercare services to firms (outside of certified investors). In particular, considering skilled labour shortages in Bulgaria and potential spillovers from SME-MNE links, the agency could consider developing such programmes. Specific projects, supported by international donors, could also help strengthen IBA's monitoring and evaluation and prioritisation capacity.
- Continue reducing administrative burdens. Administrative burden may be necessary for fair taxation, health, safety, environmental stewardship and other governmental commitments in line with the OECD *Guidelines on Multinational Enterprises* to improve social progress and the overall quality of citizens' life. Still, from the perspective of business, administrative burdens can be a cost, delay and source of uncertainty with respect to operations and projects. Given the number of procedures that companies have to comply in order to establish a business in Bulgaria, including registration with the Commercial (Business) Register at the Registry Agency (which takes two days) and registration for VAT at the National Revenue Agency (which takes 12 days), and the overall time needed for establishing a business in Bulgaria (23 days in total according to the World Bank's 2020 *Doing Business* report), these could be natural areas of focus in the short run. In the medium term, the government could consider whether establishing a one-stop solution for investment would help businesses deal with government regulations. In the long run, progress in improving the quality of regulations would also help reduce the stock of burdensome requirements.

Public governance

- Build on the progress made in improving the overall quality of regulations across all levels of government by systematising and improving the oversight and transparency of regulatory processes. In particular, ensure that the requirements of prior publication, public consultations and ex ante regulatory impact assessment of draft regulations are respected in practice. Also, advance on conducting ex post evaluations to reduce administrative burdens and implement any specific recommendations identified as part of the 2022 OECD Regulatory Policy Scan of Bulgaria.

- Continue ongoing promising reforms to combat corruption, notably by perfecting Bulgaria's public integrity framework at national and local levels.
- Continue judicial reforms to strengthen judicial independence and increase public confidence; implement an effective and transparent accountability mechanism for the Prosecutor General in line with international standards.
- Develop an adequate framework for the protection of whistle-blowers in compliance with the 2019 EU Whistleblowing Directive, which requires the EU Member States to adopt national whistleblowing legislation no later than December 2021 and launch a campaign to enhance officials and public acceptance of whistleblowing.

Responsible Business Conduct

- Establish an effectively functioning NCP to further the effectiveness of the OECD Guidelines. All Adherents to the OECD Declaration have an obligation to establish an NCP, in accordance with the Decision of the Council on the OECD Guidelines for Multinational Enterprises. Bulgaria should ensure that structure of the NCP retains the trust of stakeholders and guarantees its impartiality. In this context, further clarify the relations between the NCP's Chair, Secretariat and Working Group as well as its relation with the National Economic Council with respect to NCP's impartiality as highlighted in the OECD Procedural Guidelines.
- Promote policy coherence and ensure co-ordination on RBC-related policies within the government. In particular, the government should ensure that the mandates of different bodies, including those created through the process of establishing the NCP, are clearly delineated and co-ordinate adequately. As Bulgaria plans to develop a NAP on RBC, ensuring consistency and complementary with the existing CSR Strategy will be of particular importance. The government should also make sure that the development of the NAP follows international best practice notably with regards to the consultation processes and involvement of stakeholders.
- Set clear expectations as to what RBC entails, including in relation to due diligence. The governments could leverage the presence of large business associations active in RBC promotion to translate and disseminate the OECD Guidelines as well as all OECD due diligence guidance, to establish a common understanding across businesses of what RBC means and what government expectations are in that respect.
- Actively promote the Guidelines and the NCP among businesses operating in Bulgaria and Bulgarian companies operating abroad, as well as workers and stakeholders. This entails organising awareness raising events, capacity building activities and consultations on RBC with all stakeholders to identify priorities and needs. Ensuring that RBC principles and standards, as well as the NCP mechanism, are known among all relevant stakeholders is an important aspect of ensuring that the NCP can effectively fulfil its mandate.
- Promote the use of the OECD sectoral due diligence guidance, in particular the OECD Due Diligence Guidance in the Garment and Footwear Sector, OECD Minerals Guidance and OECD Guidance in Extractive Industries, through active support to these enterprises in implementing the recommendations of the due diligence instruments. Countries that adhere to the OECD Declaration commit to also adhere to all of the related OECD legal instruments aimed at supporting the implementation of the OECD Guidelines, including the OECD due diligence guidance. Promoting and supporting implementation of these instruments will contribute to facilitate businesses in meeting RBC expectations in Bulgaria.
- Facilitate meaningful stakeholder engagement in the design and implementation of RBC policies and processes. This includes ensuring that all stakeholders are empowered to express their views and take part in the public debate and encouraging companies to consider

the views of stakeholders and affected communities. The OECD Due Diligence Guidance for Meaningful Stakeholder Engagement in the Extractive Sector can provide a useful framework that can be particularly relevant for the coal industry.

- Ensure full compliance with EU legislations related to RBC, including the EU Non-Financial Reporting Directive, and support businesses in observing RBC-related laws and expectations. The government could consider leveraging the NCP to identify challenges faced by businesses and provide relevant tools and guidance to facilitate businesses in meeting RBC expectations.
- Seize the momentum created by SOE reforms to promote and implement RBC standards within SOEs, including local SOEs. As an economic actor in its own right and owner of enterprises, the government could take steps to establish clear expectations and requirements for SOEs about RBC performance and due diligence, and reporting on RBC-related risks. The government could rely on OECD due diligence guidance to practically operationalise RBC in Bulgarian SOEs.

References

OECD (2021), *Decentralisation and Regionalisation in Bulgaria: Towards Balanced Regional Development*, OECD Multi-level Governance Studies, OECD Publishing, Paris, https://doi.org/10.1787/b5ab8109-en.

Notes

[1] See Gross Domestic Product for the Fourth Quarter of 2020 (Flash Estimates), published on 16 February 2021, www.nsi.bg/sites/default/files/files/pressreleases/FlashEstGDP2020q4_en_ZPA374U.pdf.

2 Economic trends and the role of investment

This chapter outlines investment trends in Bulgaria. It provides information on the evolution of inward and outward FDI flows and stocks and compares Bulgaria's performance to other similar countries. It also provides information on the relative importance of greenfield FDI and mergers and acquisitions. Bulgaria has performed relatively strongly in attracting foreign investment, but there is need to diversify FDI by destination sector, source country and mode of entry as well as support further internationalisation of domestic firms.

Introduction

Bulgaria has undergone a significant transformation over the past three decades. A broad range of reforms has been designed to accomplish macroeconomic stabilisation and the transition from a planned economy to an open, market-based, upper-middle-income economy anchored in the European Union (EU).[1] The increased co-operation with the World Trade Organisation (WTO) – that Bulgaria joined in 1996 – and the EU in the context of the accession process acted as an external anchor for reforms. Bulgaria applied to become an EU Member State in December 1995 and has been an EU member country since 1 January 2007.

Through the process, Bulgaria has engaged in many structural reforms including privatisation of State-Owned Enterprises (SOEs), adoption of a favourable investment regime, and liberalisation of trade, and the strengthening of the tax system. As a result, the 2000s were a decade of economic growth and improvements in living standards except the year 2009 when the global financial and economic crisis affected Bulgaria's economy. Since it joined the EU in 2007, Bulgaria has made additional progress, with living standards raising from 41% of the EU average in 2007 to 53% in 2019, measured in terms of purchasing power parity according to figures released by EU statistics agency Eurostat. These achievements have also been reflected in the pre-crisis sustained increase of foreign direct investment (FDI) inflows, which in turn played an important role in Bulgaria's development. As the global financial crisis started to spill over Bulgaria, investment activity contracted substantially and, despite the recently witnessed recovery of business investment, remained below pre-crisis levels in 2019.

The COVID-19 pandemic sent shockwaves through the Bulgarian economy, resulting in a revision of the 2020 GDP from expected growth of about 3% to a 4.2% contraction.[2] Notwithstanding the decline of FDI in the first half of 2020 due to the COVID-19 crisis, by the end of 2020 Bulgaria recorded more FDI inflows than in 2019. According to estimates from the Bulgarian National Bank at the time of this *Review*, FDI inflows reached approximately EUR 2.1 billion in 2020, an increase of about EUR 590 million compared to 2019 when FDI inflows amounted to approximately EUR 1.5 billion. Given the role that investment has played in Bulgaria's development during the past two decades, attracting more and better investment, including FDI, has taken central stage in the National Development Programme: Bulgaria 2020 (NDP BG 2020) and the National Development Programme BULGARIA 2030 (NDP BULGARIA 2030). FDI has been seen as potentially mitigating the impact of the COVID-19 crisis and reinforcing the economic recovery of countries by financing the public debt, creating more and better-paid jobs, decreasing poverty, and boosting productivity, among others (WB, 2020a).

This chapter presents Bulgaria's situation in terms of its overall economic performance and FDI trends over the past three decades to provide key insights into the role and evolution of foreign investment in the Bulgarian economy.

Bulgaria's economic performance

Bulgaria has experienced a significant transformation over the past decades. The transition from a planned economy to an open, market-based economy begun in 1991. It was initially hampered by slow institutional restructuring, opaque privatisation, high indebtedness, a deep economic and banking crisis, and a loss of savings. GDP growth was correspondingly low and the promises of convergence failed to materialise. This period was characterised by a low level of foreign investments due to macroeconomic and political instability in the country.

In 1996, Bulgaria faced a severe economic and banking crisis, which culminated in February 1997 with a short period of very high inflation and important shortages of basic items. The situation started to improve in the late 1990s thanks to the introduction of the currency board in 1997 as the key component of a broad macroeconomic stabilisation programme, the deepening of structural reforms, and the legislative and institutional harmonisation with the EU ahead of the 2007 accession. With the rule of law more firmly established, the 2000s were a decade of economic growth and improvements in living standards (e.g. lower incidence of unemployment and poverty and longer life expectancy at birth). Substantial improvements in several dimensions of material and human well-being marked this period. Bulgaria's GDP annual growth marked its highest peak in 2005 with the rate of 7.2% and then decreased to 0.6% in 2010 because of the global financial crisis.

For the 2010-19 period, Bulgaria's GDP growth fluctuated between 0.5% and 4% per year (Figure 2.1). In PPP terms (current international USD), GDP per capita considerably increased from USD 17.5 000 (approximately EUR 14 700) in 2010 to USD 23 300 (approximately EUR 19 600) in 2019. Poverty declined from 8.5% in 2015 to 7.1% in 2018 (at the USD 5.5 per day line, approximately EUR 5.0).

Figure 2.1. GDP growth and GDP per capita in Bulgaria, 1990-2019

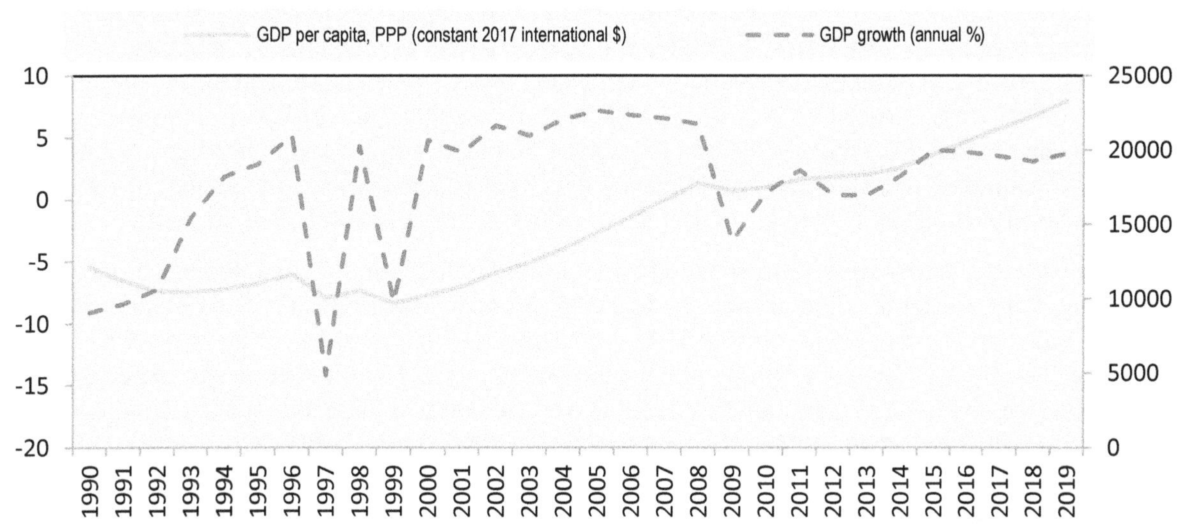

Note: Annual percentage growth rate of GDP at market prices based on constant local currency. Aggregates are based on constant 2010 USD. GDP is the sum of gross value added by all resident producers in the economy plus any product taxes and minus any subsidies not included in the value of the products. It is calculated without making deductions for depreciation of fabricated assets or for depletion and degradation of natural resources.
Source: World Bank (2021), World Bank national accounts (database), https://data.worldbank.org/country/bulgaria.

The most recent period, prior to the pandemic, witnessed growing optimism, with annual GDP growth averaging 3.6% in the years 2015-19. For example, real GDP expanded by 3.7% in 2019. Exports, underpinned by growing links with EU value chains (notably with Germany and Italy), as well as strong household consumption have been the main driver of economic growth. Private consumption expanded robustly thanks to low inflation and favourable labour market conditions. The employment rate for the 20-64 age group[3] reached 72.4% in 2018, while the unemployment rate[4] decreased to 5.2% in 2018 (EC, 2020). In 2019, Bulgaria recorded even better results, with a 4.2% unemployment rate.[5]

While some of the progress before the pandemic has been wiped out by the global economic crisis, even in the most difficult time inflation was kept low. The fiscal deficit was brought down to less than 1% of GDP in 2012-13 from 4.2% in 2009; and in 2011 Bulgaria exited the excessive fiscal deficit procedure. Bulgaria's general government debt decreased to 20.2% of GDP at the end of the fourth quarter of 2019, remaining the second lowest in the EU at that time.[6]

The past years also led to profound changes in the economic structure, especially in exports, which have proved particularly important given the small size of the economy and thus the importance of trade for

Bulgaria's overall economic performance. Export of goods and services was equivalent to 65% of GDP in 2015-17 (compared to 42% in Romania and 30% in Greece), while trade per capita – at around EUR 5 400 in 2018 – was significantly higher than in Romania (EUR 4 612) and Republic of Türkiye (hereafter 'Türkiye') (EUR 3 011) (WTO, 2018). Foreign trade has followed broad trends consistent with Bulgaria's accession to the WTO in 1996 and then with improving trade and tax-related legislation to make it consistent with EU trade policy and internal market rules in the scope of Bulgaria's accession to the EU in 2007. Bulgaria's economic performance largely reflects the growing integration into the world economy that the country has gone through (Figure 2.2).

Once a country that was in many ways closed off to the global economy, Bulgaria's involvement in global value chains (GVCs) grew robustly. As a small open economy, prior to the COVD-19 pandemic, Bulgaria sourced more foreign inputs than large economies such as the EU countries and hence had predominantly backward GVC participation (Ivanova and Ivanov, 2017). Bulgaria's relatively high openness level was reflected in its TiVA (trade in value added) and GVC (global value chain) statistics. For example, foreign value-added share in Bulgaria's gross exports amounted to 36% in 2015, the latest available year (while the OECD average was 9%). Meanwhile, Bulgaria has lower levels of forward GVC participation[7] as the share of domestic value added embodied in foreign exports was 16% in 2015 (compared to 18% at the OECD). In other words, the comparison with OECD GVC reveals that the foreign value added share of exports is higher in Bulgaria, whereas the domestic value added sent to consumer economy is lower than in OECD economies. In addition, between 2012 and the COVID-19 pandemic, the number of automotive parts manufacturers doubled to almost 100 with a workforce of more than 33 000 in the sector.[8]

In the past decades, there has also been strong trade growth in Bulgaria. Bulgaria has had traditionally a trade deficit, but the balances are broadly comparable to other peer countries. For instance, in 2018, Bulgaria's merchandise trade ratio amounted to 109% and was higher than in Greece (48%) Croatia (74.5%) but lower than in Slovenia (160%), and the Slovak Republic (178%).[9] FDI has played a significant role in supporting these economic transformations. Over the last two decades, actual FDI inflows as a percentage of GDP have grown, notably during the years 2004-07, reaching 28% of Bulgaria's GDP. They then sharply declined in 2008-10 (3.1% of GDP in 2010) and then again in 2014 (0.8% as a percentage of GDP) and 2016 (1.9%), primarily as the result of the global financial crisis and the steady decline of FDI flows globally. From 2016 to 2019, FDI stocks in Bulgaria followed an upward trend, which continued during the first quarter of 2020 before the COVID-19 crisis spread across Europe.

Figure 2.2.GDP, trade and FDI in the Bulgarian economy, 1990-2019

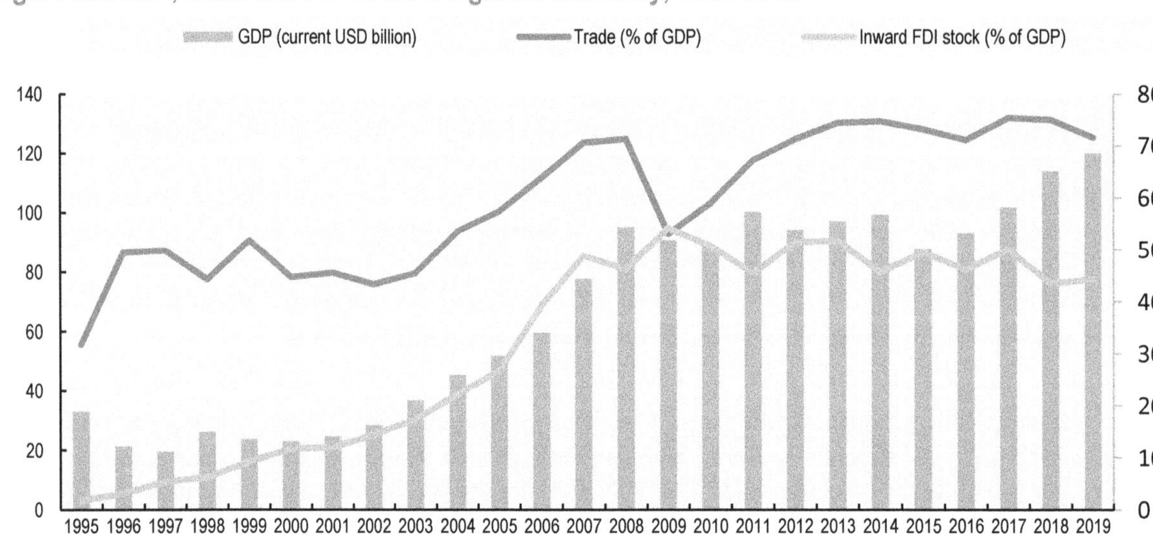

Source: World Bank (2021), World Bank national accounts (database), https://data.worldbank.org/country/bulgaria.

Yet, the COVID-19 pandemic has affected Bulgaria's economy. In the course of 2020, the export and import sectors decreased by 11.3% and 6.6%, respectively.[10] Employment fell, eroding recent gains. Bulgaria's unemployment rate of 5.9% recorded in December 2019 increased to 8.9% in April 2020[11]. A recovery was nevertheless underway in 2021 : according to the statistics of the Ministry of Labour and Social Policy, the unemployment rate was approximately 6.7% in December 2020[12] and further decreased to 4.60 % in April 2022. Economic growth rebounded by 4.2% in 2021 after real GDP contracted by 4.1% in 2020 as a result of the coronavirus pandemic, thus bringing the economy to pre-pandemic levels of output. According to the OECD *Economic Survey of Bulgaria*, a growth of 3.7% was expected in 2022 (OECD, 2021), whereas the European Commission expected a 4.7% GDP growth in 2022 (Table 2.1).

Since then, the outlook for 2022 and 2023 has nevertheless worsened owing to the war in Ukraine, the OECD expecting growth to weaken to 2.5 % in 2022 and 2.25 % in 2023 and be accompanied by a surge in inflation (OECD, 2022). Investment will be essential to overcome the impacts of the COVID-19 crisis and the war in Ukraine. Boosting the economy will require ambitious reforms. The economy is still in the process of convergence. Bulgaria's GDP per capita, in purchasing power standards, was the lowest in the EU in 2019, at half of the EU average. Bulgaria ranked last in the EU in terms of actual individual consumption (AIC) – 57% of the EU average.[13] According to the National Statistical Institute of Bulgaria, in 2018, four of the seven European regions with the lowest standard of living were in Bulgaria. North-West Bulgaria was the region with the lowest standard of living, at 34% of the EU average, followed by North-Central Bulgaria (35%) (NSI, 2019a).

Since 2012, income inequality in Bulgaria has been increasing and is the highest in the EU, with the Gini coefficient reaching 39.6 in 2018 (World Bank 2019).[14] Along these lines, Bulgaria still faces an important income gap vis-à-vis the EU average, and additionally faces unfavourable demographic prospects. In 2018, more than a quarter of Bulgaria's population (32.8%) was at risk of poverty or social exclusion followed by Romania (32.5%), Greece (31.8%), Latvia (28.4%), Lithuania (28.3%), Italy (27.3%) and Spain (26.1%) (Eurostat, 2019).[15]

Table 2.1. Economic forecast for Bulgaria, 2020-22

Indicators	2020	2021	2022
GDP growth (%, yoy)	-4.2	3.5	4.7
Inflation (%, yoy)	1.2	1.6	2
Unemployment (%)	5.1	4.8	3.9
General governement balance (% of GDP)	-3.4	-3.2	-1.9
Gross public debt (% of GDP)	25	24.5	24
Current account balance (% of GDP)	4.1	6	7.5

Source: The European commission, Directorate-General for Economic and Financial Affairs (DG ECFIN), May 2021, https://ec.europa.eu/info/business-economy-euro/economic-performance-and-forecasts/economic-performance-country/bulgaria/economic-forecast-bulgaria_en, https://ec.europa.eu/economy_finance/forecasts/2021/spring/ecfin_forecast_spring_2021_bg_en.pdf.

Importance of FDI in Bulgarian economy

Foreign direct investment has established itself as an important driver of economic development in Bulgaria since the very start of the market transition, which determined the establishment of a liberal foreign investment regime. In December 2020, FDI accounted for 10% of all financial assets and 66% of all financial liabilities in Bulgaria, respectively (Figure 2.3).

Figure 2.3. Bulgaria's International investment position by functional type of investment, 2010-20

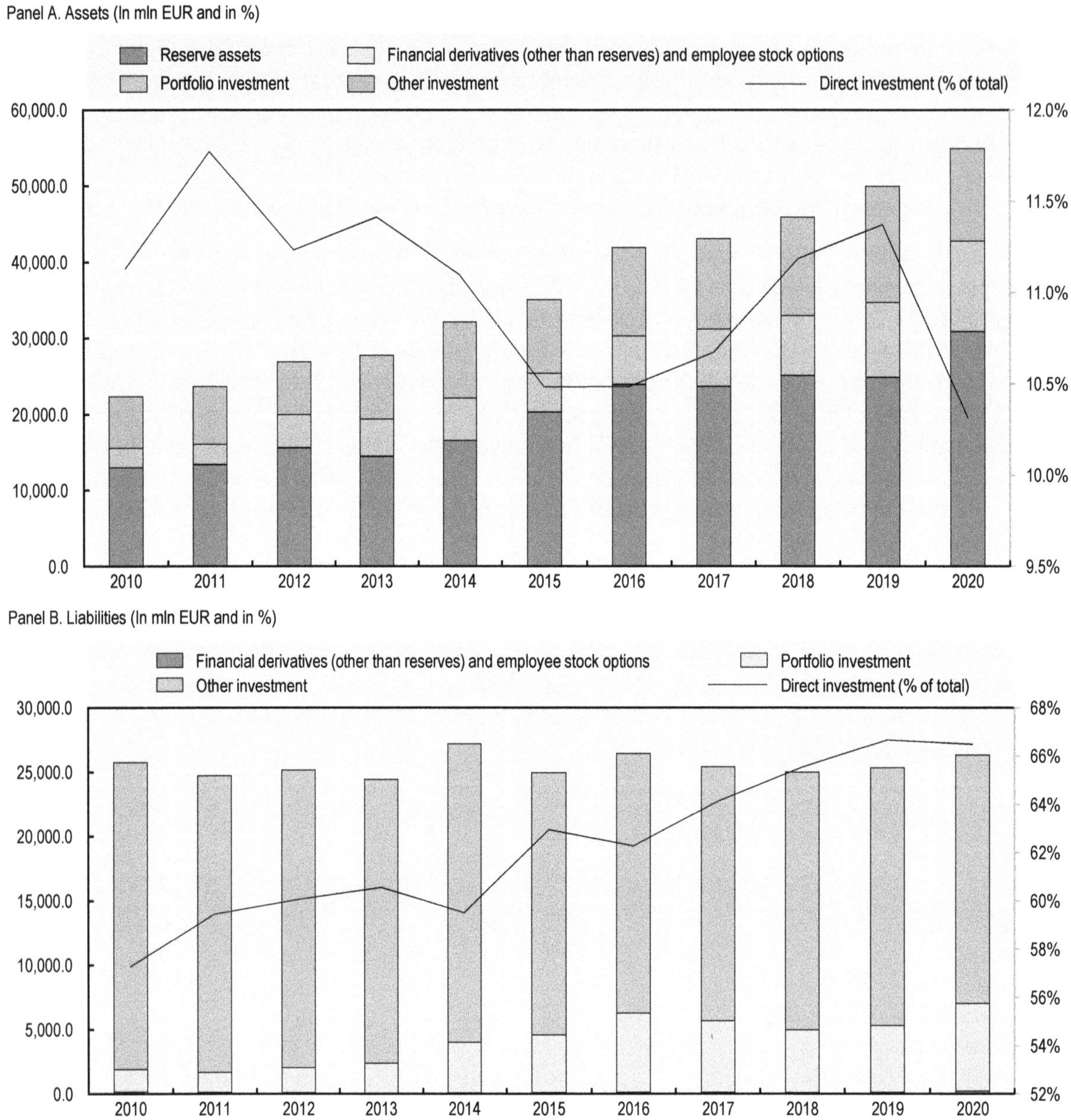

Source: Bulgarian National Bank (March 2021), International Investment Position.

Over the last two decades, inward foreign investment increased, reflecting the country's openness towards foreign investors, the absence of screening from the government, and of limits on foreign ownership or control of firms as well as other reforms undertaken by the authorities as described throughout this Review. Following the global financial and economic crisis, FDI activity contracted: the share of inward FDI stock to GDP fell to 85.1% in 2008 (corresponding to an amount of approximately EUR 37 billion) but then quickly recovered. In particular, the share of inward FDI stock in GDP increased dramatically at the beginning of the past decade, representing 87.6% of Bulgaria's GDP (approximately EUR 36.8 billion) in 2012. After a recovery in the period 2013 – 2015 (reaching 87.4% of Bulgaria's GDP, approximately EUR 40 billion, in 2015), it followed a downward trend, reaching approximately 77% of GDP (EUR 46.9 billion) in 2019 (Figure 2.4). As of the end of 2020, the inward FDI stock in GDP stood at EUR 48.7 billion (80.3% of

GDP). Like in many countries of the world, for the past decade direct investments by foreign-owned firms in Bulgaria have remained more important than investments by Bulgarian firms abroad as illustrated in Figure 2.4.

Figure 2.4. Inward and outward stock as a share of GDP, 2010-20

In percentage and mln EUR

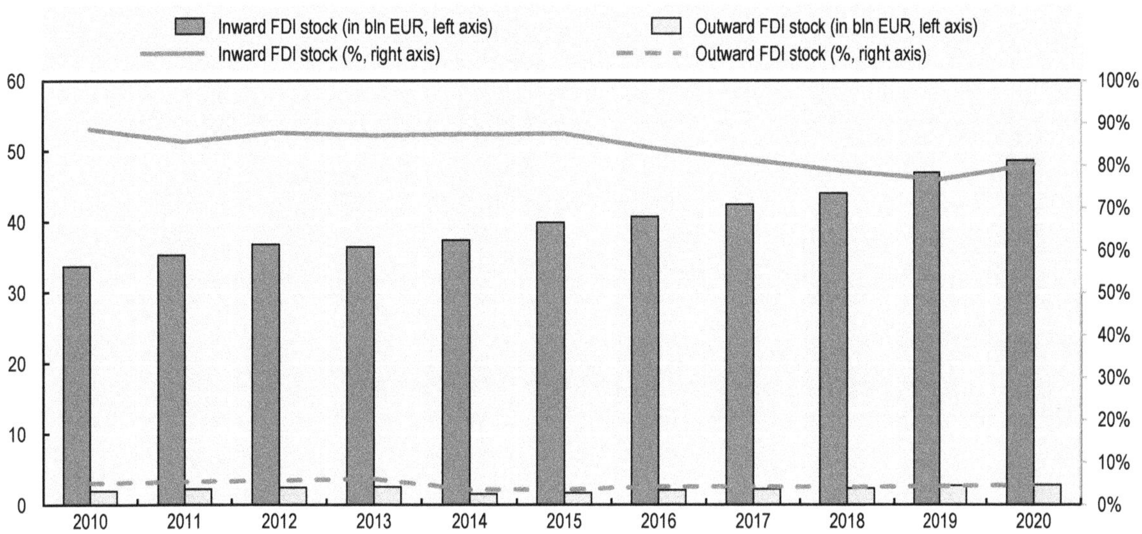

Source: Bulgarian National Bank and Eurostat (2021).

Considering data on the activities of affiliates by type of control and location, in 2018, foreign-controlled firms located in Bulgaria accounted for 5.3% of all foreign-controlled firms in the EU while the share of foreign affiliates of Bulgaria firms in the EU-28 equalled to 0.3% (Figure 2.5).

Figure 2.5. Number of enterprises by type of control and location, 2018

Panel A. Foreign-controlled EU enterprises

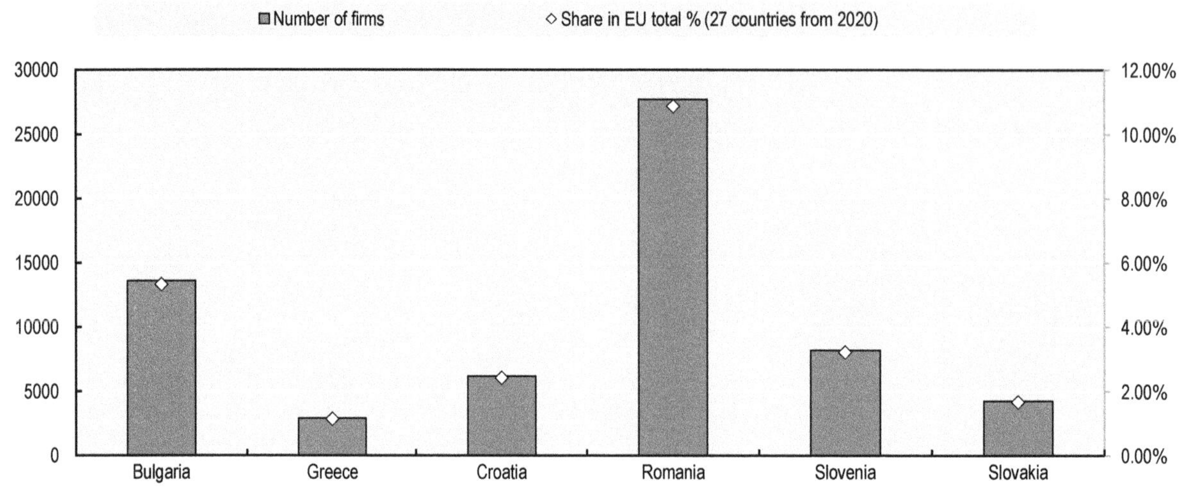

Panel B. Foreign affiliates of EU enterprises

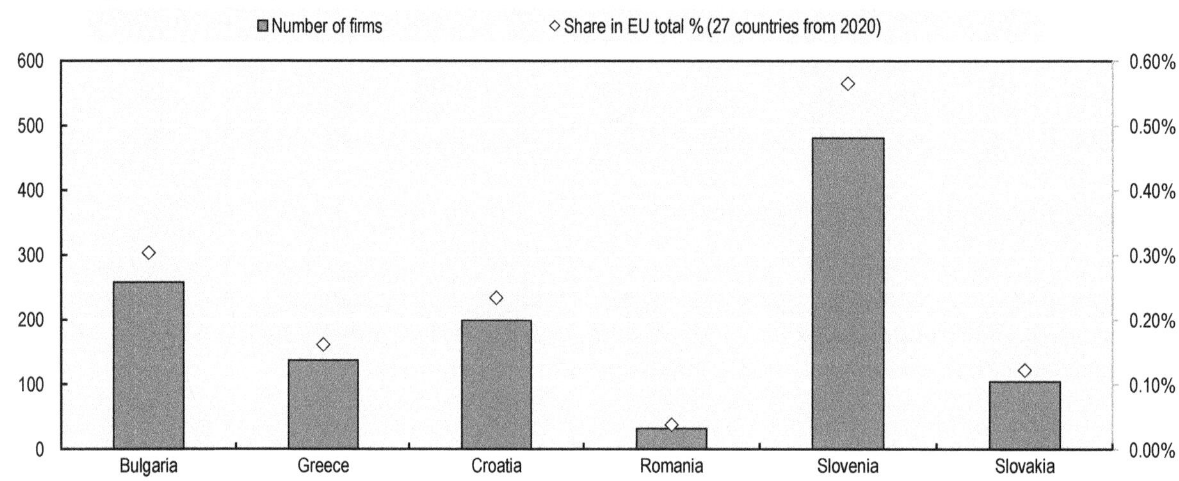

Note: Foreign affiliates in the framework of inward FATS (Foreign Affiliates Statistics) mean an enterprise resident in the compiling country over which an institutional unit not resident in the compiling country has control. Number of enterprises refers to the number of 1) foreign controlled enterprises resident in the compiling economy for inward FATS (Panel A); and 2) foreign affiliates abroad that are controlled by an institutional unit resident in the compiling country for outward FATS (Panel B).
Source: Eurostat (2021).

Evolution of FDI over time

As noted in the introduction to this chapter, the importance of FDI inflows in the Bulgarian economy has been growing over time. The ratio of outward FDI stock to GDP has also generally increased, with a pace higher than in other economies in the region (Figure 2.6). In absolute terms, inward FDI has increased significantly since 2010 Bulgaria's inward FDI increased from about EUR 33.7 billion in 2010 to EUR 48.7 billion in 2020. Meanwhile, during the same period (2010-20), the amount of direct investment abroad increased significantly from approximately EUR 1.9 billion to EUR 2.8 billion.

Figure 2.6. Share of inward and outward FDI stock as a share of GDP in Bulgaria and selected EU countries, 1995-2019

Panel A. Inward FDI stock

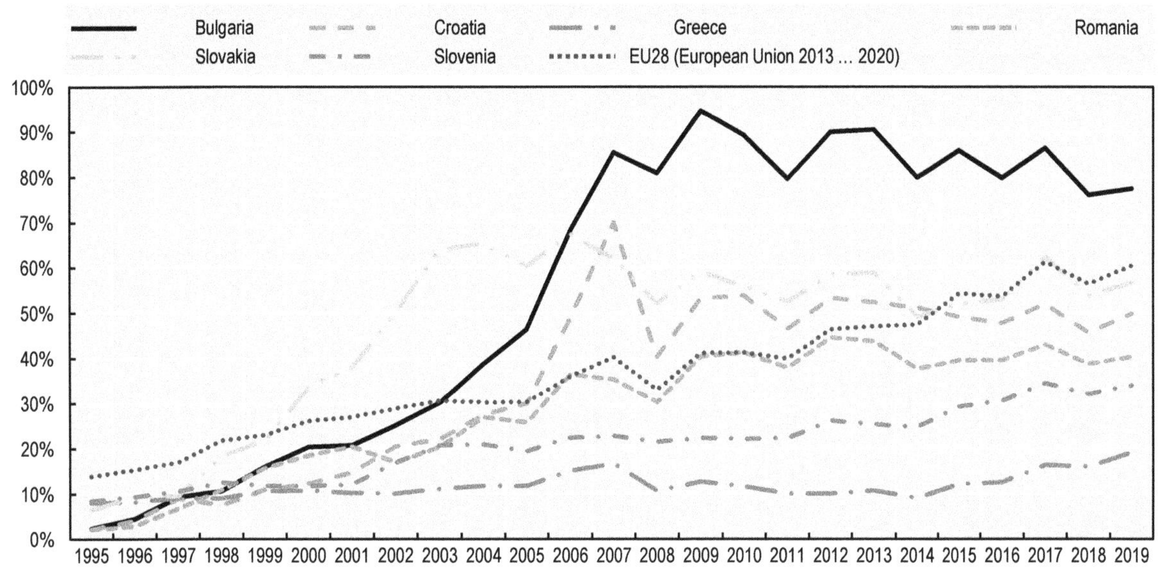

Panel B. Outward FDI Stock

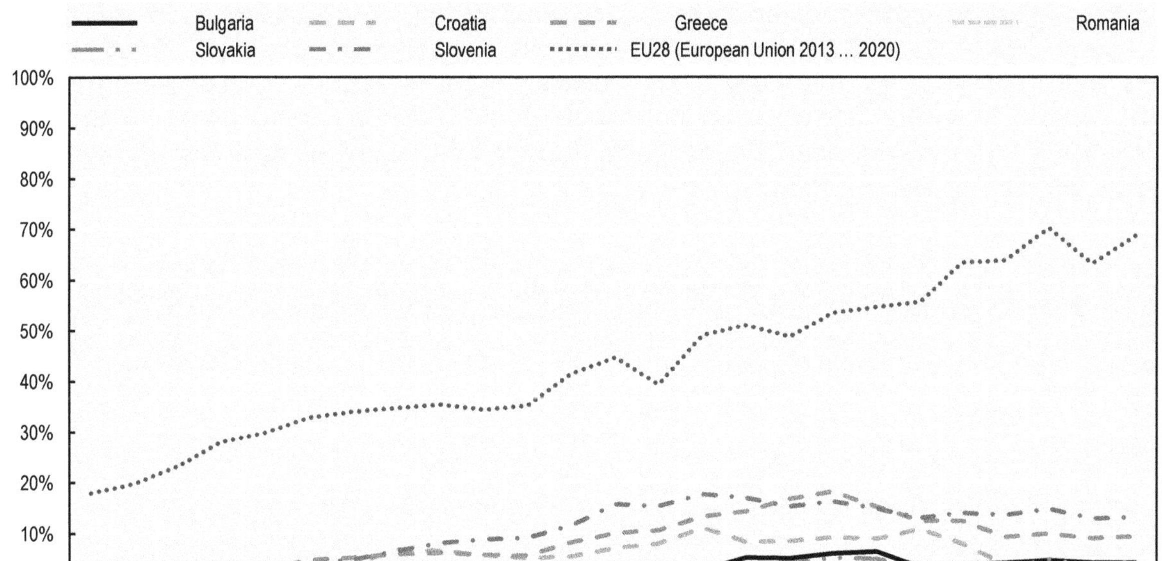

Note: EU membership and region are the criteria used in the selection of countries.
Source: UNCTADSTAT (2020), Data centre, https://unctadstat.unctad.org/wds/TableViewer/tableView.aspx?ReportId=96740.

Concerning FDI flows, they declined for the first time in 2008 after six years of sustained growth, dropping to approximately EUR 6.7 billion. In 2009, FDI inflows dropped to approximately EUR 2.4 billion, about one-third of the 2008 level. The same trend continued in 2010, with FDI inflows amounting to just over EUR 1.2 billion, the lowest figure since 2003. Thus, just between 2007 and 2010, FDI flows to Bulgaria dropped by almost 87% (Figure 2.7).

Figure 2.7. Bulgaria's inward and outward FDI flows as a share of GDP, 2010-20

In % and in EUR mln

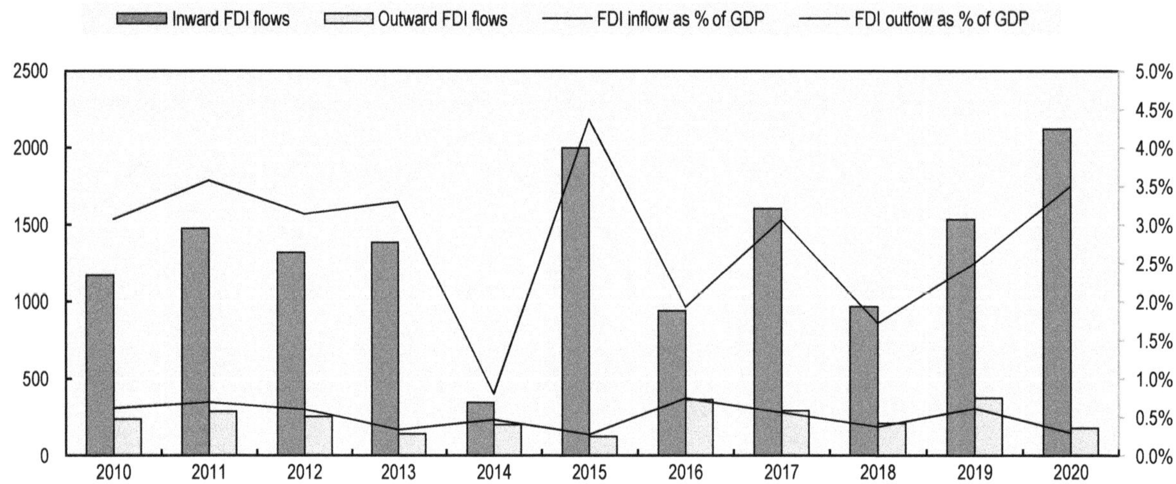

Source: Bulgarian National Bank (2021).

The importance of FDI for Bulgaria's economy is similar to other peer economies. Figure 2.8 compares Bulgarian FDI inflows and outflows relative to other economies in the region in absolute and relative terms (as a share of GDP). Generally, the share of FDI flows to GDP in Bulgaria has been comparable to those found in other, similar countries in the region. For example, in the years 2015-18, FDI inflows in Bulgaria accounted for 2.7% of GDP (slightly above the EU average of 2.3%). FDI outflows meanwhile accounted on average for 0.5% of Bulgaria's GDP, below the EU average of 2.4% and more than the average of Bulgaria and the selected countries (0.3%).

Figure 2.8. Inward and outward FDI flows as a share of GDP in Bulgaria and selected EU countries, 1995-2019

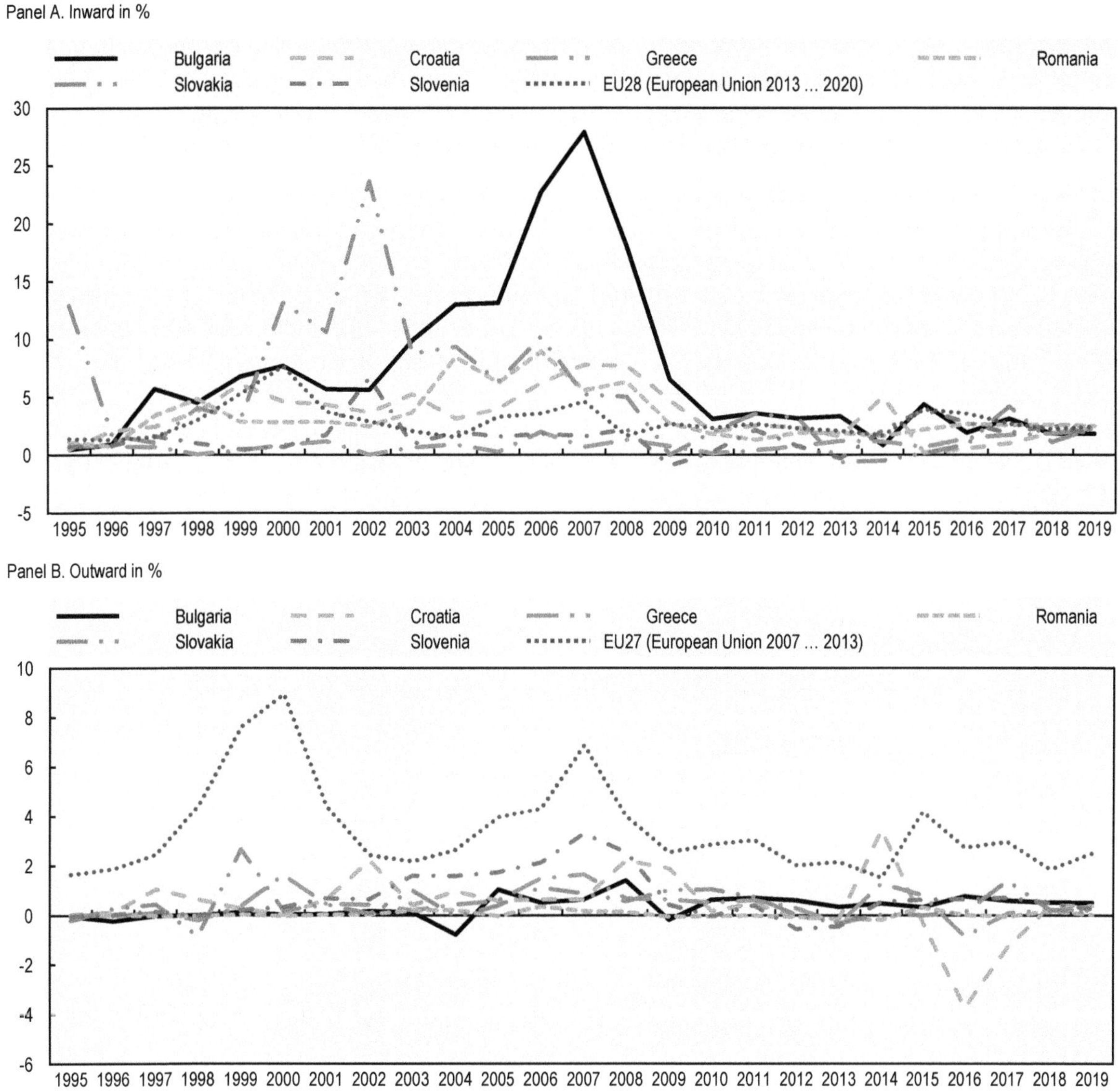

Note: EU membership and region are the criteria used in the selection of countries.
Source: UNCTADSTAT (2020), Data centre, https://unctadstat.unctad.org/wds/TableViewer/tableView.aspx?ReportId=96740.

Greenfield FDI has picked up

Transition reforms such as the privatisation of SOEs have offered scope for the emergence of FDI projects, first through the creation of joint ventures (JVs) and subsequently, and increasingly, through cross-border mergers and acquisitions (M&A) of existing companies or the creation of new so-called greenfield investments (Sakali, 2013).

Similarly to other economies in the region that experienced big waves of privatisation in the 1990s, most of FDI in Bulgaria has taken place through so-called brownfield investments (i.e. via privatisations and mergers and acquisitions) rather than greenfield investments (i.e. foreign direct investment in which a parent company creates a subsidiary in Bulgaria, building its operations from the ground up). According to the FDI Greenfield Performance Index (which captures the country's share in the world's total of announced greenfield FDI projects to the country's share in world GDP), Bulgaria attracted more greenfield FDI than suggested by the size of its economy between 2006 and 2018. It also performed better than countries such as Croatia, Greece and Slovenia for the same time period (Figure 2.9). Software & IT (Information and technology) services, automotive components, industrial equipment, transport and warehousing, business services have been among the top sectors for greenfield investment in Bulgaria. In 2019, greenfield investment into the Bulgarian technology sector recorded seven new projects amounting to USD 76.3 million (approximately EUR 69.4 million) of which more than 83.4% were from US companies.

Greenfield FDI has played an important role in job creation. Between 2015 and 2018 alone, the number of job-creating greenfield FDI projects into the technology sector in Bulgaria increased by 300% (fDi Markets, 2019). In 2019, leading international companies such as Facebook opened offices in the city of Sofia to provide ICT (Information, communication and technology) services (Financial times, 2019). For the past five or six years, the development of new sectors related to innovation and technology such as Machinery (SKF, Lufthansa, Technik, Montupet), IT & Telecoms (ICB, Cisco, Microsoft, HP, VMWare), shared services centres (Coca-Cola, HP, AIG), Electrical engineering (Siemens, ABB, Honeywell, Liebherr), Automotive (Witte Automotive, Sumitomo Electric, Yazaki Corporation), Lifesciences (Pharmaceutical Product Development, TEVA Pharmaceuticals) has increasingly attracted greenfield investment projects (CMS, 2018).

Figure 2.9. Greenfield FDI index, 2003-18

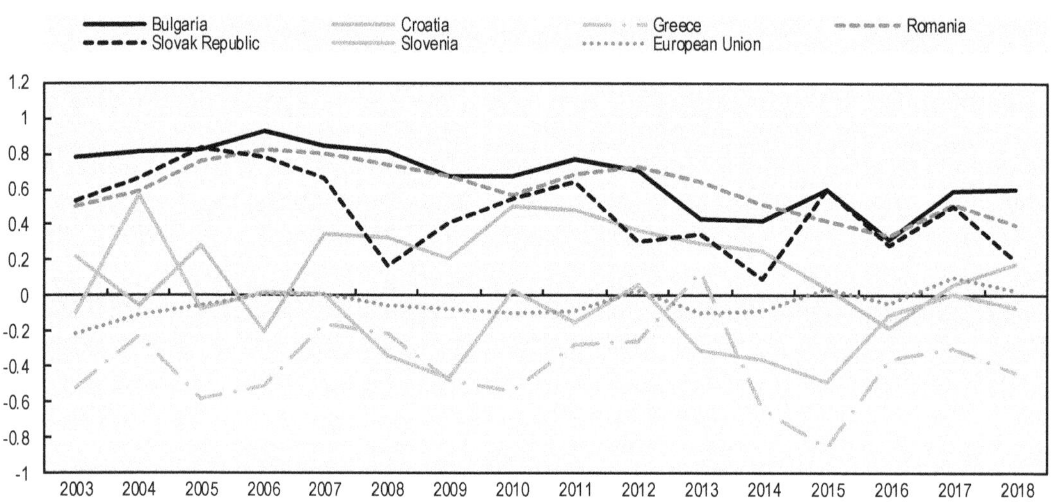

Note: The Index is calculated as a share of the value of greenfield FDI projects announced in the country to the world's total value of greenfield FDI projects divided by the share of country's GDP in the world's GDP (normalised around 0). A value > 0 means that a country attracts more FDI than suggested by the size of its GDP.
Source: Authors calculations based on UNCTAD, using on information from the Financial Times Ltd, fDi Markets (www.fDimarkets.com).

Table 2.2. Greenfield investment projects to Bulgaria, 2010-19 Q3

In USD mln

Year	Projects	Capex (USD m)
2010	63	2.186
2011	73	4.706
2012	49	2.296
2013	47	1.074

Year	Projects	Capex (USD m)
2014	41	1.040
2015	38	1.873
2016	46	1.033
2017	51	1.614
2018	54	2.285
2019 (Q1-Q3)	39	1.368

Note: Authors elaboration.
Source: The Financial Times (2019), www.fDimarkets.com.

FDI patterns in Bulgaria

The relative concentration of FDI in trading and retail activities and real estate as well as in specific regions suggests that there could be scope for diversifying the portfolio of FDI projects in Bulgaria through improvements of the business climate and targeted investment promotion policies.

FDI remains regionally concentrated

A large amount of FDI has been located in Bulgaria's relatively prosperous areas such as South Bulgaria and the large economic zones near Sofia, Plovdiv, and Haskovo. In 2018, the capital of Sofia benefited from half of the total FDI stock in non-financial enterprises; less than 2% of inward FDI was distributed to the North-West region.

Table 2.3. FDI regional distribution of non-financial sector in Bulgaria, 2018

Region	Districts	Total (EUR thousand)
North West (Severozapaden)	Vidin, Vratsa, Lovech, Montana, Pleven	469 721.3
North Central (Severen Tsentralen)	Veliko Tarnovo, Gabrovo, Razgrad, Ruse, Silistra	1 111 657.2
North East (Severoiztochen)	Varna, Dobrich, Targovishte, Shumen.	2 579 480.7
South East (Yugoiztochen)	Burgas, Sliven, Stara Zagora, Yambol	3 203 109.3
South West (Yugozapaden)	Blagoevrgrad, Kiustendil, Pernik, Sofia, Sofia capital,	14 562 477.3
South Central (Yuzhen tsentralen)	Kardzhali, Pazardshik. Plovdiv, Smolyan, Haskovo	2 993 143.5

Note: FDI in non-financial enterprises as of 31.12 2018 by statistical regions and districts. NSI statistics on the non-financial sector FDI represents stock at the end of the statistic period (2018) and not the annual FDI inflow for 2018. The data is from the annual statistical survey conducted by the NSI on foreign direct investment in enterprises in the non-financial sector.
Source: National Statistical Institute (2018).

European countries dominate the FDI landscape

European countries dominate the FDI landscape in Bulgaria, topping the list of major destination and source countries (Figure 2.10). Among the largest investors, some countries have been traditionally associated with the presence of special-purpose entities (SPEs), which can serve as a conduit for pass-through capital motivated by tax purposes, e.g. Hungary, Luxembourg, and the Netherlands (see Box 2.1); other European countries, such as Austria, Italy, Germany, the United Kingdom as well as the Russian Federation have been the main sources of FDI inflows.

Meanwhile, in 2020, outward FDI flows of Bulgaria were targeted primarily at EU and neighbouring countries – in particular, Austria, the Czech Republic, Germany, Greece, Luxembourg, Malta, the Republic of North Macedonia, Moldova. This is congruent with Bulgaria's geographic location, history, EU membership, and the country's trade structure.

Figure 2.10. Top ten destination and source countries, 2020

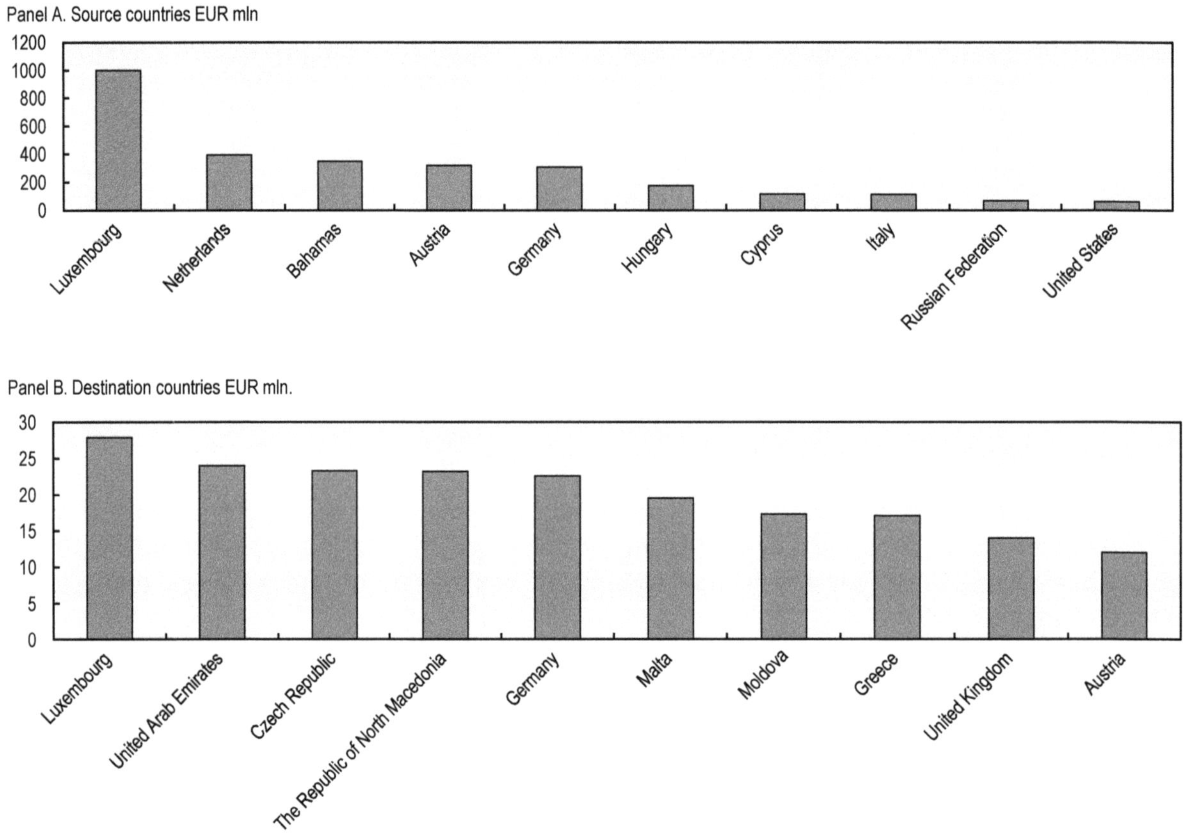

Source: Bulgarian National Bank (March 2021), www.bnb.bg/Statistics/index.htm.

Box 2.1. Special purpose entities: Why do they matter for FDI statistics?

Special purpose entities (SPEs), such as shell or shelf companies, are companies that do not have substantial economic activity in the country but that are used by companies to raise capital or to hold assets and liabilities. With the proliferation of international activities and increase in intra-firm trade, including in intangibles, it has become increasingly easy for companies to shift profits across jurisdictions according to the most favourable tax environment through corporate structures built for that purpose. Just as gross trade flows may obscure the destination and origin of value-added produced in a given economy due to multiple shipments of goods across borders during the production process that spans several countries, so the passing of funds through SPEs can lead to the inflation of FDI statistics and the obscuring of the ultimate source and destination of FDI.

The OECD Revised Benchmark Definition of Foreign Direct Investment (BMD4) recommends that countries compile their FDI statistics excluding resident SPEs, and, then, separately for resident SPEs to provide a more meaningful measure of direct investment into and out of an economy (see OECD, 2008). For the country hosting the SPEs, this recommendation improves the measurement of FDI by excluding inward FDI that has little or no real impact on their economies and by excluding outward FDI that did not originate from their economies. Four countries-Austria, Hungary, Luxembourg, and the Netherlands-have reported FDI flows and positions excluding resident SPEs to the OECD for several years. With the implementation of the latest standards, 30 OECD countries currently report FDI data excluding resident SPEs. In some countries, such as Luxembourg, the Netherlands or Hungary, SPEs account for a sizable share of inward FDI stock (and, if not accounted for, could distort FDI statistics. Even in countries where SPEs do not play a significant role currently, it is useful to be able to identify resident SPEs in the FDI statistics so that their role can be monitored, especially as, by their nature, SPEs are easily established and can grow rapidly and can distort investment flows in particular years.

Source: OECD (2019)

Services account for the majority of FDI stock in Bulgaria

In 2020, services accounted for the majority of FDI stock in Bulgaria. More than half of the inward stock was composed of private services, in particular real estate activities (22%), manufacturing (18%), financial and insurance activities (18%), wholesale and retail trade (15%); electricity, gas steam and air conditioning supply (6%); and professional, scientific and technical activities (5%). Information and communication accounted for 3% and construction accounted for 3%. (Figure 2.11, Panel A). While there is a high variation across countries, generally real estate, accommodation and construction services tend to play a less prominent role in OECD economies, suggesting that there could be scope for diversifying the portfolio of FDI projects in Bulgaria.

Figure 2.11. FDI stock by sector, 2020

Panel A. Inward FDI stock by sector

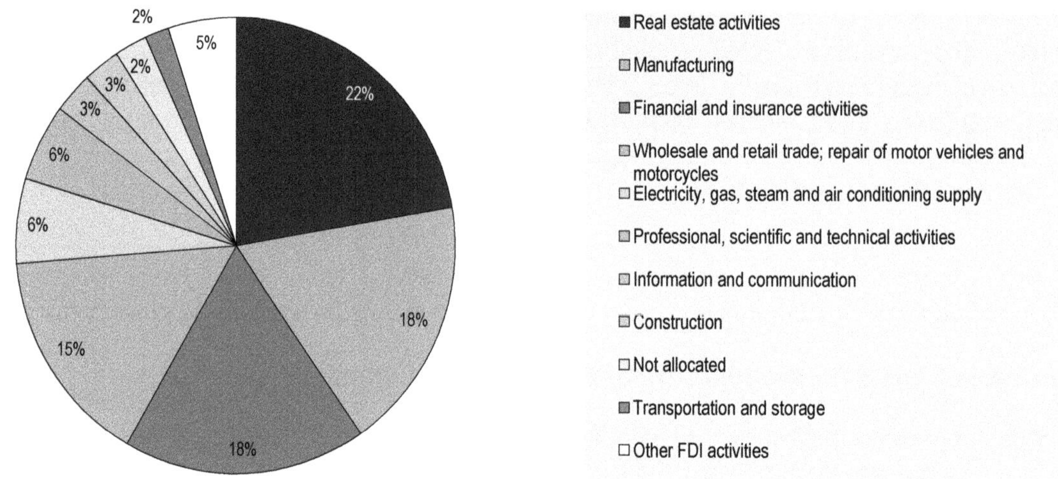

Panel B. Outward FDI stock by sector

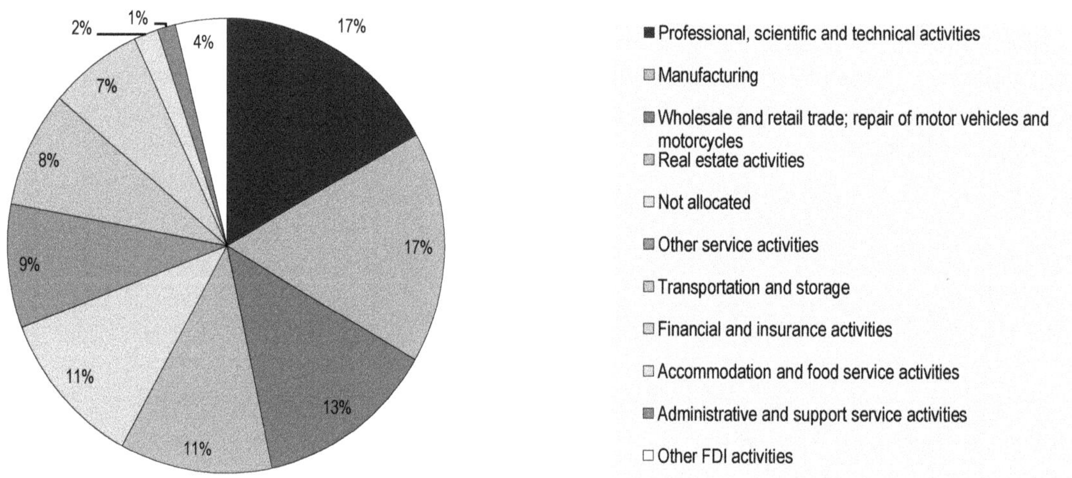

Source: Bulgarian National Bank (March 2021).

Activities of Bulgarian companies abroad

As reflected in total outward and inward foreign affiliate statistics, the activities of Bulgarian companies abroad have remained significantly less important than activities of foreign-owned enterprises in Bulgaria. Statistics on outwards activities of foreign-controlled affiliates provide further insights into internationalisation of domestic firms. According to Eurostat, in 2018, 258 Bulgarian companies were operating outside of the EU that jointly employed over 9 717 people and had a total turnover of approximately EUR 1 billion, which represents 0.3% of European firms operating outside of the EU in 2018 (Figure 2.12). These levels are comparable to those encountered in EU economies with similar market sizes and per capita income levels, although they are among the lowest in the EU. Considering the central and strategic location of Bulgaria as well as some robust sectors, such as IT, machinery, and software, there could be scope for further growth in future years. Figure 2.11 (Panel B) above shows that outward FDI stock has been primarily composed of professional, scientific, and technical activities (17%), manufacturing (17%), wholesale, and retail (13%).

Figure 2.12. Data on EU-controlled foreign affiliates in selected EU 28 countries, 2018

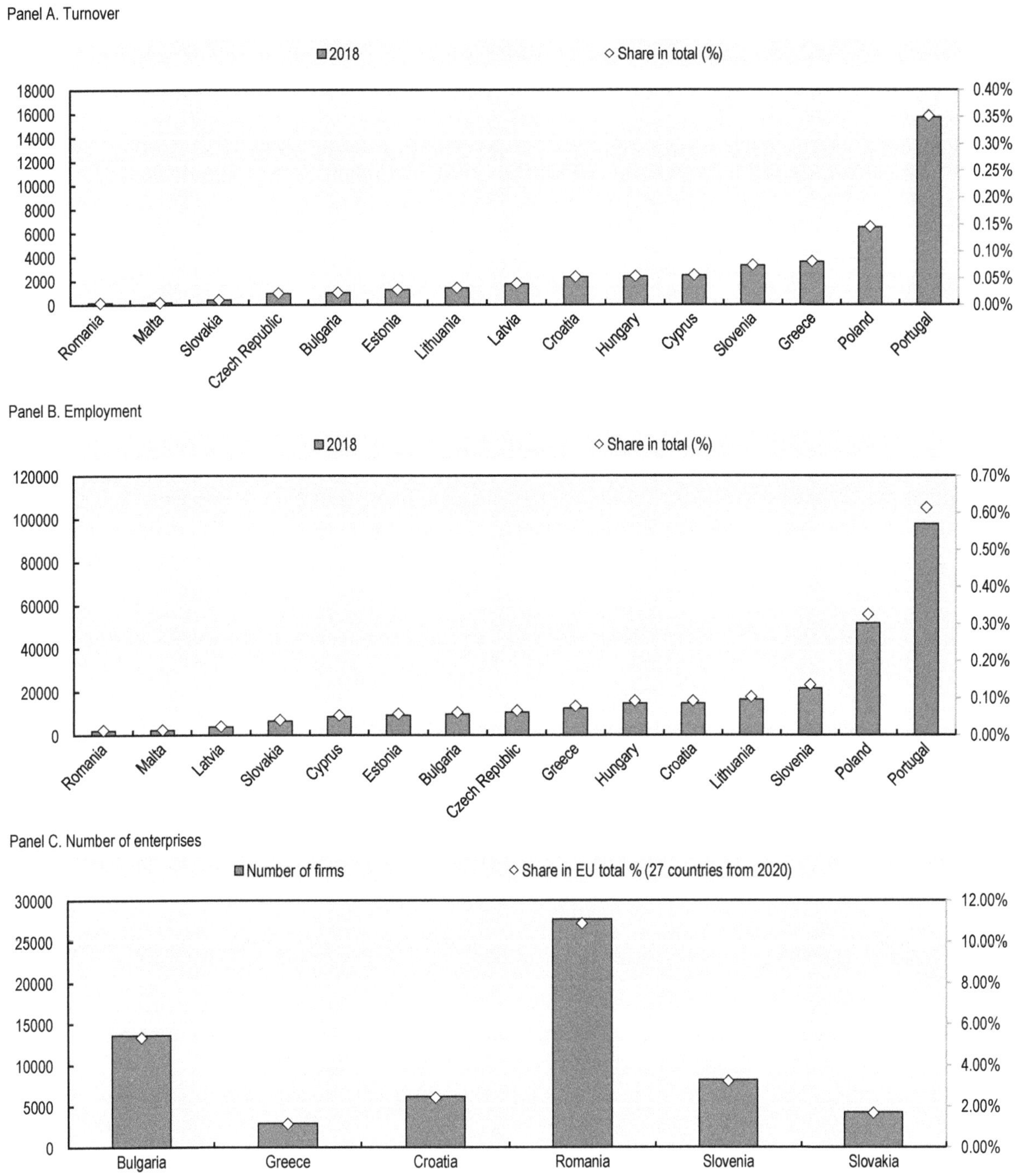

Source: Eurostat (2021).

In 2018, 20 Bulgarian companies were among the top 500 largest firms in Central and Eastern Europe, according to the ranking compiled by COFACE (COFACE, 2019). Utilities and public services as well as oil, minerals, wholesale and retail trade dominated the list of companies. Still, outward FDI is an incipient phenomenon in Bulgaria. Active export promotion and investment promotion policies (see Chapter 6), including for outward FDI and the overall improvements in the country's investment climate, could have a role to play in promoting Bulgarian investments abroad.

Outlook

FDI has played an important role in Bulgaria's development over the past two decades. While Bulgaria experienced a relatively slow start due to political instability in the early 1990s, it experienced rapid growth in FDI in the late 1990s and the 2000s – with a peak in 2007, the year that it became an EU member, with FDI inflows amounting to EUR 10.1 billion. Recent years have nevertheless been challenging for Bulgaria, with foreign direct inflows going up and down. Bulgaria received approximately EUR 1.6 billion in 2017 and EUR 2.1 billion in 2020, more than in 2019 when it attracted EUR 1.5 billion. FDI in the first three months of 2022 stood at EUR 1.06 billion, more than during the same period of 2021 when FDI was EUR 244.1 million.

Improving further the framework conditions for foreign investment has become among the authorities' foremost priorities for boosting economic growth and improving citizens' well-being. The relative concentration of FDI in trading and retail activities and real estate, which account for most of the foreign investment in Bulgaria, suggests that there could be scope for diversifying the portfolio of FDI projects in Bulgaria through improvements of the business climate and targeted investment promotion policies, discussed in the following chapters.

While the prominence of European countries in terms of FDI inflows is understandable, extra efforts may be needed to attract investments from other regions, including large emerging economies. There is also considerable potential to increase outward investment and the internationalisation of Bulgarian companies, especially as immediate non-EU neighbouring countries accelerate their journey towards European integration.

References

Bulgaria (2021), *National Development Programme BULGARIA 2030*, www.minfin.bg/upload/43546/Bulgaria+2030_EN.pdf

CMS Law & Tax (2018), *Greenfield investments in CEE*, https://cms.law/en/media/local/cms-china/files/publications/greenfield-investments-in-cee-2018-english.

Council of Ministers of Bulgaria (2020), *National Development Programme: Bulgaria 2020* (NDP BG 2020), www.strategy.bg/StrategicDocuments/View.aspx?lang=bg-BG&Id=766

COFACE (2019), CEE Top 500 Companies, www.cofacecentraleurope.com/News-Publications/Coface-CEE-Top-500.

European Commission (2021), "European Economic Forecast Spring 2021", *European Economy Institutional Papers,* Luxembourg: Publications Office of the European Union 2021, https://ec.europa.eu/info/sites/default/files/economy-finance/ip149_en.pdf.

EUROSTAT (2021*),* Statistics on the structure and activity of foreign affiliates (FATS*)*, https://ec.europa.eu/eurostat/web/structural-business-statistics/global-value-chains/foreign-affiliates

IMF (2019), Bulgaria: 2019 Article IV Consultation-Press Release; Staff Report; Staff Supplement; and Statement by the Executive Director for Bulgaria, IMF Country Report No. 19/83, www.imf.org/en/Publications/CR/Issues/2019/03/22/Bulgaria-2019-Article-IV-Consultation-Press-Release-Staff-Report-Staff-Supplement-and-46702.

Ivanova, N. and E. Ivanov (2017), "The Role of Bulgaria in Global Value Chains", *Discussion Papers*, No. 105/2017, Bulgarian National Bank, www.bnb.bg/bnbweb/groups/public/documents/bnb_publication/discussion_2017_105_en.pdf.

NSI (2019a), Foreign direct investments in non-financial enterprises as of 31.12.2019 by statistical regions and districts, www.nsi.bg/en/content/6196/foreign-direct-investments-non-financial-enterprises-3112-statistical-regions-and.

NSI (2019b), *Population and demographic process in 2019*, www.nsi.bg/sites/default/files/files/pressreleases/Population2019_en_XE8MEZL.pdf.

OECD(2022), *Bulgaria Economic Snapshot: Economic Forecast Summary (June 2022)*, https://www.oecd.org/economy/bulgaria-economic-snapshot/

OECD (2021), *OECD Economic Surveys: Bulgaria 2021: Economic Assessment*, OECD Publishing, Paris, https://doi.org/10.1787/1fe2940d-en.

OECD (2020), *OECD Foreign direct investment flows in the time of COVID-19*, https://read.oecd-ilibrary.org/view/?ref=132_132646-g8as4msdp9&title=Foreign-direct-investment-flows-in-the-time-of-COVID-19.

OECD (2019), OECD Investment Policy Reviews: Croatia 2019, *OECD Investment Policy Reviews*, OECD Publishing, Paris, https://doi.org/10.1787/2bf079ba-en.

World Bank (2020a), "Spring 2020: Fighting COVID-19", *Europe and Central Asia Economic Update*, World Bank, Washington, DC, https://openknowledge.worldbank.org/handle/10986/33476.

World Bank (2020b), *World Development Indicators database*, https://databank.worldbank.org/data/source/world-development-indicators.

World Bank (2020c), *Global Investment Competitiveness Report 2019/2020: Rebuilding Investor Confidence in Times of Uncertainty*, World Bank, Washington, DC, https://openknowledge.worldbank.org/bitstream/handle/10986/33808/9781464815362.pdf?sequence=2&isAllowed=y.

WTO (2020), *Member Information: Bulgaria and the WTO*, www.wto.org/english/thewto_e/countries_e/Bulgaria_e.htm.

WTO (2003), *Trade Policy Review: Secretariat Report*, www.wto.org/english/tratop_e/tpr_e/tp220_e.htm

Notes

[1] See *World Bank country classification*, https://datahelpdesk.worldbank.org/knowledgebase/articles/906519-world-bank-country-and-lending-groups.

[2] Bulgarian National Bank, Metronomic Indicators as of 26 March 2021, www.bnb.bg/Statistics/StMacroeconomicIndicators/index.htm.

[3] The employment rate refers to the 20-64 age group of Bulgaria's population.

[4] The unemployment rate is determined as the share of the registered unemployed in the economically active population aged 15-64, established in the 2011 Census.

[5] See www.nsi.bg/en/content/6503/unemployed-and-unemployment-rates-national-level-statistical-regions-districts.

[6] See https://ec.europa.eu/eurostat/databrowser/view/sdg_17_40/default/table?lang=en.

[7] The percentile rank of a score is the percentage of scores in its frequency distribution that are equal to or lower than it. For example, a test score that is greater than 75% of the scores of people taking the test is said to be at the 75th percentile, where 75 is the percentile rank.

[8] "Bulgaria's auto parts industry powers up", *Financial Times*, 29 November 2016.

[9] World Bank (2020), *World Bank national accounts (database),* https://data.worldbank.org/country/bulgaria.

[10] National Statistical Institute, Gross Domestic Product annual data, published on 9 March 2021, www.nsi.bg/en/content/5490/gdp-final-expenditure-percentageE2%80%93-total-economy

[11] Ministry of Labour and Social Policy Employment Agency, information about the unemployment, the active employment policy and the implementation of the operational programme "*human resources development*" in April 2020, www.az.government.bg/bg/stats/view/2/312/.

[12] Ministry of Labour and Social Policy Employment Agency, Information about the unemployment, the active employment policy and the implementation of the operational programme "human resources development" in December 2020, www.az.government.bg/bg/stats/view/2/331/.

[13] Actual individual consumption, abbreviated as AIC, refers to all goods and services actually consumed by households. It encompasses consumer goods and services purchased directly by households, as well as services provided by non-profit institutions and the government for individual consumption (e.g. health and education services). In international comparisons, the term is usually preferred over the narrower concept of household consumption, because the latter is influenced by the extent to which non-profit institutions and general government act as service providers. See Eurostat Glossary: Actual individual consumption (AIC), https://ec.europa.eu/eurostat/statistics-explained/index.php/Glossary:Actual_individual_consumption_(AIC).

[14] Gini index measures the extent to which the distribution of income (or, in some cases, consumption expenditure) among individuals or households within an economy deviates from a perfectly equal distribution. A Gini index of 0 represents perfect equality, while an index of 100 implies perfect inequality, https://datacatalog.worldbank.org/gini-index-world-bank-estimate-1.

[15] See Eurostat, "Downward trend in the share of persons at the risk of poverty or social exclusion in the EU", *News release*, 158/2019, 16 October 2019, https://ec.europa.eu/eurostat/documents/2995521/10163468/3-16102019-CP-EN.pdf/edc3178f-ae3e-9973-f147-b839ee522578.

3 Bulgaria in transition: Challenges and opportunities

This chapter examines Bulgaria's current challenges and ongoing reforms. It looks at various indicators which, taken together, determine the country's ability to attract investment. It also summarises various measures that can be taken to improve the investment climate in the country, notably by investing in innovation and infrastructure projects, addressing skills shortages, implementing SOEs reforms and enhancing competition policy.

Introduction

Achieving the ambitious long-term strategic vision of more inclusive and sustainable goals for all citizens is one of the top priorities of Bulgaria's 2030 National Strategy. In this respect, foreign investment can generate positive socio-economic and other benefits in Bulgaria that help make progress towards sustainable development. Under the right conditions, foreign direct investment (FDI) can enhance growth and innovation, create quality jobs, develop human capital, raise living standards and strengthen regional development. Realising these gains is not a given, however. While, in principle, foreign investment has the potential to advance sustainable and inclusive development, the policy context plays a critical role.

This chapter looks at actions taken by Bulgaria to improve the investment climate and make the country more attractive to foreign investment. It focuses on ongoing reforms, challenges and opportunities in sectors such as innovation, physical and digital infrastructure, skills and competition, which good functioning is a prerequisite for attracting long-lasting investment. Other chapters in this *Review* will examine how reforms in various policy areas can further promote investment.

The innovation system

Foreign investment can benefit a host economy. The policy context nevertheless plays a critical role in realising this potential. In this line, the host country's innovation policy can drive foreign investment, offering business opportunities for international and domestic investors.

Attracting more and better investment, including FDI, was a focus of the National Development Programme (NDP) Bulgaria 2020. For instance, under priority 5 (Support of innovation and investment activities to increase the competitiveness of economy), sub-priority 5.1 focused on the creation of conditions for developing an institutional environment in favour of innovations, and investments in products and services with high added value and high technologies, as well as the development of the small and medium-sized Enterprises (SMEs) sector. Priority 6 aimed at strengthening the institutional environment for higher efficiency of public services for citizens and businesses. Such policies have been seen as contributing to enhancing economic growth, reaching higher R&D expenditure share in GDP, increasing investments in tangible fixed assets, attracting FDI, and accelerating productivity growth.

Bulgaria has since adopted the NDP BULGARIA 2030, the main strategic document in the hierarchy of the national programming documents, which determines the vision and overall goals of development policies in all sectors of government, including their territorial dimensions (EC/OECD 2021, STIP Compass Bulgaria Overview). The document sets out three strategic goals, five development areas (axes) and 13 national priorities in which attracting more and better investment and consolidating efforts on innovation policy remain Bulgaria's priority. According to the Programme, "efforts to build capacity and develop human resources in the R&D system will continue, with interventions focusing on enhancing the attractiveness of scientific careers and attracting and retaining scientists and researchers". In addition, "co-operation between higher education institutions, research institutes and businesses will be stimulated to effectively gear R&D towards the needs of the market and society, as well as to increase their value added by harnessing the synergies arising from such cross-sectoral links".

Bulgaria also adopted a National Research Strategy "Better Science for Better Bulgaria 2017-30" and an Innovation Strategy for Smart Specialisation aimed at fostering innovation (Bulgaria, 2017a). The National Roadmaps of research infrastructure (NRRI) development have also been important for implementing national research and innovation strategies. Bulgaria's NRRI, adopted in 2010 (Council of Minister, Decision No.692), defined the national needs in relation to research infrastructure (RI). In 2014, the NRRI was updated (Council of Minister, decision No.569 of 31 July 2014) to support the National Research Strategy "Better Science for Better Bulgaria 2017-30" and address the priorities under the Innovation Strategy for Smart Specialisation.

Yet, Bulgaria's research and innovation (R&I) system suggests that Bulgaria continues to face challenges such as insufficient modern infrastructures, lack of skilled human resources and weak science-business linkages, irregular territorial and thematic distribution of the RI, financial instability of companies as well as inadequate engagement of the private sector (Bulgaria, 2017b, NRRI). These shortcomings have been assessed by the EC as hampering the potential development of Bulgaria and contribution of R&I to economic growth and investment attraction (EC, 2020a).

Box 3.1. Main innovation national strategies and policy initiatives

National strategy

- Bulgaria's National Strategy for Development of Scientific Research 2017-30 sets up the new R&I targets for Bulgaria in line with the Europe 2020 strategy and defines priority areas for the development of scientific research in the country.

Policy initiatives

- National Roadmap for Research and Infrastructure: the roadmap is one of Bulgaria's key instruments for implementing the national research strategies for development aligned with the EU priorities. The roadmap supports the policies defined in the National Research Strategy "Better Science for Better Bulgaria 2017-30"; addresses the priorities under the Innovation Strategy for Smart Specialisation.
- Institutional funding for a public research initiative to Support the Bulgarian Academy of science with an estimated budget expenditure range per year between EUR 50-100 million.
- Sofia Tech Park is a state-owned company creating the first science and Technology Park in Bulgaria with the mission of realising projects fostering the development of the research, innovation, and technological capacity of the country.

Source: EC/OECD (2021), STIP Compass Bulgaria Overview, generated from https://stip.oecd.org/stip/countries/Bulgaria on 25 June 2021.

Despite an increase of 7.2% between 2014 and 2021 in the 2021 European Innovation index, Bulgaria was rated as among the worst performers (emerging innovators)[1] according to the European Innovation Scoreboard 2021 (EIS, 2021), with an overall level below 70% of the EU average. According to the Scoreboard, with a score of 50.1, Bulgaria ranked second from the bottom to the top among the EU-28 countries. As far as Gross Domestic expenditure on R&D (GERD) as a percentage of GDP is concerned, in 2019, Gross domestic expenditure on R&D (GERD) in Bulgaria amounted to only 0.75% of GDP compared to average spending of about 2.5% of GDP found in the OECD countries and 2.1% in the European Union (Figure 3.1).

Figure 3.1. Gross domestic expenditure on R&D (GERD) – Bulgaria in comparative perspective

In percentage of GDP

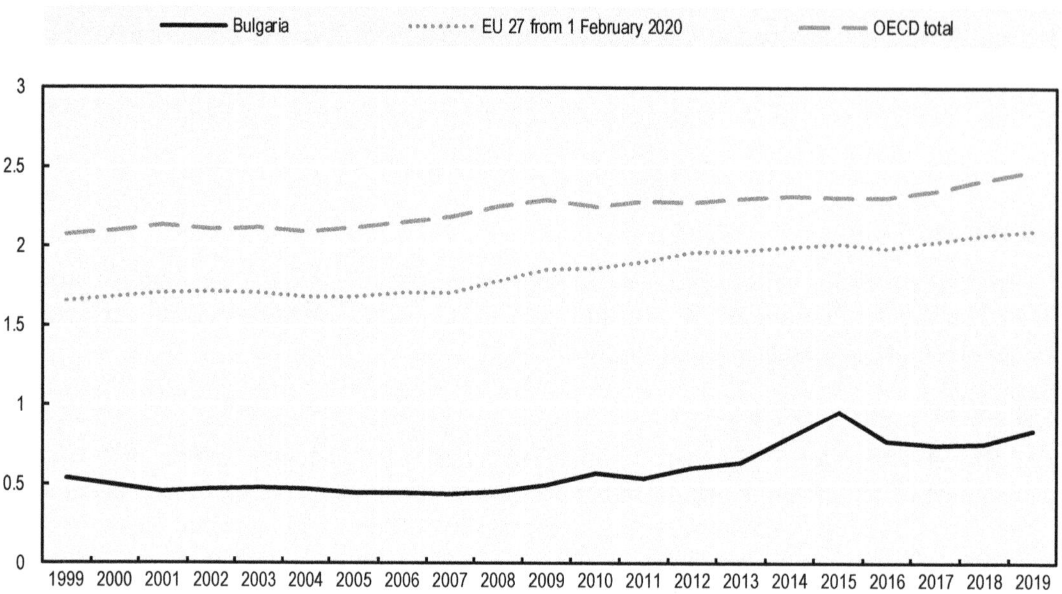

Note: Gross domestic expenditure on R&D (GERD), totals all expenditure on inputs used in performing R&D, in a given territory. For OECD member countries, zone totals (OECD and EU), Argentina, the People's Republic of China, Romania, the Russian Federation, Singapore, South Africa and Chinese Taipei: OECD, Main Science and Technology Indicators Database, http://oe.cd/msti. For Bulgaria, Cyprus, Croatia and Malta data (if available): OECD calculations based on Eurostat, Statistics on Research and Development. For other countries: OECD calculations based on UNESCO Institute for Statistics (UIS) data.
Source: MSTI database (March 2021), www.oecd.org/sti/scoreboard.htm.

Bulgaria's innovation performance differs from region to region. According to the Regional Innovation Scoreboard 2021 (a regional extension of the European Innovation Scoreboard), Bulgaria's performance has increased across all regions compared to 2014. Still, in 2021 all six regions in Bulgaria were emerging innovators, of which Yugozapaden – the capital region (South West) is the best performing one, whereas Severozapaden (North West) continues to be the worst-performing region in the country (Table 3.1).

Table 3.1. Regional innovation Scoreboard 2021 – regional performance in Bulgaria

Region	"2 021" – score relative to EU 2014	"2 021" – score relative to EU 2021	Change over time	Performance group
North West (Severozapaden)	29.9	26	4.7	Emerging innovator-
North Centrat (Severen tsentralen)	40.1	34.9	2.1	Emerging innovator
North East (Severoiztochen)	40.8	35.5	8.4	Emerging innovator
South East (Yugoiztochen)	31.2	27.2	0.7	Emerging innovator
South West (Yugozapaden)	63.8	55.6	11.4	Emerging innovator+
South Central (Yuzhen tsentralen)	41	35.7	6.2	Emerging innovator

Note: Regional Innovation Scoreboard 2021 – Relative performance to EU in "2 014".
Source: Regional Innovation Scoreboard (2021) database.

In 2021, Bulgaria's performance related to innovation improved by 7.2% compared to 2014. According to the 2021 edition of the EIS, intellectual assets, employment impacts, and environmental sustainability were the strongest innovation dimensions. Environment-related technologies, design applications, and trademark applications scored relatively high, above the EU average. The country was nevertheless still underperforming in areas such as finance and support and the attractive research system with the lowest score in the EU. Bulgaria's lowest performance has been in R&D expenditure in the public sector, enterprises providing ICT training, public-private co-publications, lifelong learning, and most-cited publications. Bulgaria directs half of the entire business sector's R&D investment to large multinational companies (EIS, 2021). The low levels of public and private investment in R&I, fragmented public science base, lack and ageing of skilled human resources, weak science-business linkages, and ineffective governance have been identified as remaining challenges for the potential role of R&I in boosting the productivity of the Bulgarian market and attract foreign investors. Putting in place competitive salaries for researchers would help attract well-qualified Bulgarian and foreign talent and address the problem of the ageing research community and shortages (OECD, 2021a).

All possible efforts should be undertaken by the national authorities to significantly increase Bulgaria's public funding of R&D in order to reach a level that should be well above that of the past decade. To be successful, these R&I investments should be accompanied by structural reforms with regard to the research and innovation system to boost efficiency and quality. In this respect, stronger participation of businesses to encourage investments in the innovation sector would be welcomed. The OECD *Guidelines for Multinational Enterprises*, in Chapter 10 on Science and technology, include recommendations that aim to promote the diffusion by businesses of the fruits of research and development activities among the countries in which they operate. Businesses are notably encouraged to perform science and technology development work, develop ties with local universities, public research institutions, and participate in co-operative projects with local industry or industry associations. Bulgaria has an opportunity to leverage the *Guidelines* to involve businesses in the development of innovative capacities, including through the implementation of RBC principles and standards.

The state of infrastructure

The Infrastructure sector is of paramount importance to Bulgaria as it is vital to the country's economic growth, inward investment and international competitiveness. Quality infrastructure helps businesses compete and grow, attract and keep foreign investors, and maintain a high quality of life for the population. Failure to invest in infrastructure means a failure to sustain economic and social development.

Bulgaria has made substantial efforts to modernise and build sustainable infrastructure as a strategic factor for the success of the economy. In particular, the long-awaited EU membership has allowed the country to benefit from EU funding for infrastructure projects. As a result, in the past decade, infrastructure including communication infrastructure, has improved. Nonetheless, Bulgaria still suffers from a poor perception of the state of public infrastructure, as revealed by its 101 position out of 141 countries in the 2019 *Global Competitiveness Report*, with a score of 3.4 out of 7 (WEF, 2019).

Bulgaria's road infrastructure has improved but still has a way to go

For the past decades, the government has taken important steps to improve Bulgaria's physical infrastructure and connectivity by investing in motorways and road projects. According to data of Bulgaria's National statistical institute (NSI, 2019), Bulgaria's national road network length reached 19 879 kms of which the motorways accounted for 790 kms. In October 2015, Bulgaria completed the Maritsa Motorway project. Trakia, Maritsa, and Lyulin motorways were entirely completed with total lengths of 360 kms, 117 kms, and 19 kms respectively (KPMG, 2017). An important part of Bulgaria's motorway projects, such as Struma[2] motorway and sections of Hemus[3] motorway, are under construction.

Despite this progress, the country still suffers from an inadequate road infrastructure as revealed by its 26th position out of 28 countries in the 2020 EU *Transport Scoreboard* focusing on the Trans-European Transport Network (TEN-T). According to it, Bulgaria was one of the worst EU performers along with Croatia and Romania (EC, 2020b). Of particular note have been the unequal distribution and the insufficient connectivity of Bulgaria's roads at regional level (Table 3.2). For instance, only 18 kms of motorways pass through the North-West region whereas 454 kms of motorways pass through South-West and South-Central Bulgaria. It should be recalled that South-West Bulgaria is among the poorest regions among EU countries and hence, the least attractive for foreign investors. Lack of road maintenance and poor pavement quality are particularly pronounced in some northern regions, which increases travel time (OECD, 2021a). In addition, the road infrastructure is struggling to keep up with the demand, which is due to a steady rise in traffic and in car ownership, which has increased with 60% for the 2017 and 2019 period (EBRD, 2019).

Another weak spot has been investors' low trust in the public procurement process for infrastructure projects. According to investors that the OECD Secretariat met during its fact-finding mission in the framework of this Review, contracts would sometimes be given to companies amidst procedural irregularities and tailor-made award criteria.[4] For example, in 2016, a publication on a leading investigative journalism website reported a number of irregularities with respect to the mountain section infrastructure project between Separeva Banya and Panichishte (5 kms), in particular as regards its alleged disproportionate funding, the participation of questionable companies, the use of cheap construction materials despite the high financing of the project and a number of invoiced activities that had not been fulfilled.[5]

Table 3.2. Regional distribution by road category 2019

Regional distribution by road category (2019)	Total (in km)	Motorway (in km)	Category I Roads[1] (in km)	Category II Roads[2] (in km)	Category III roads and road connections such as crossroads and junctions[3] (in km)
North and South-East Bulgaria	12 382	336	1 948	2 612	7 486
North-West region	3 435	18	399	763	2 255
North Central Region	2 962	-	462	636	1 864
North-East region	2 682	95	487	467	1633
South-East rehion	3 303	223	600	746	1 734
South-West and South Central Bulgaria	7 497	454	952	1407	4684
South-West region	3 422	262	536	623	2 001
South Central	4 075	192	416	784	2683

Notes:
1. Designed for long-distance transit (mainly from border to border).
2. Designed for transit movement over medium distances.
3. All other republican roads that do not enter in Category I and II.
Source: National Statistical Institute (2019), www.nsi.bg/en/content/7203/national-road-network-road-category.

Bulgaria's railway network needs further improvement

Efficient rail transport services and infrastructure is necessary not only to support investment in all Bulgaria's regions but also to allow social and territorial inclusion. As most physical infrastructure investment has gone into roads, there is still an important gap in railways quality in Bulgaria despite recent efforts made by Bulgaria to modernise its railway network, notably as part of the investment plan and priorities set out in the "Programme for the development and operation of the railway infrastructure 2019 –

2023".[6] According to the 2019 *Global Competitiveness Report*, Bulgaria's quality of railroad infrastructure decreased from 3.3 (one worst and seven best) in 2018 to 3.1 in 2019.

Although the bulk of the rail network is composed of double-track and electrified ways with a total length of 4 030 kms,[7] the operational and technical condition of the railway infrastructure is poor. Considerable parts of the railway lines have been constructed more than 50 or 60 years ago, for speeds up to 100 km/h. As a result, it takes approximately eight hours to go by train from Sofia to Burgas (an approximate distance of 400 kms), almost twice long as by car. In terms of extension, the insufficient rail network connections with neighbouring countries, such Greece, Romania, Serbia and Türkiye, has been assessed as creating obstacles for trading with them (EC, 2019). There is also currently no railway link with the Republic of North Macedonia (the rail link between Sofia and Skopje should be completed in 2025-27).

Ramping up investment in Bulgaria's railway network is therefore crucial, not only to sustain robust rates of economic growth and integrate more fully the country into regional and global value chains but also to ensure greater social inclusiveness. In this respect, foreign investment and financial assistance from international organisations can help. For example, with respect to the latter, the EU, in November 2018, allocated EUR 293 million to fund the modernisation of the railway connection between two of Bulgaria's biggest cities, Plovdiv and Burgas.[8] For the period 2015-19, the annual funding from the EU dedicated to railway infrastructure was estimated at approximately EUR 140 million according to the 2014-20 Operational Programme on Transport (OPT). To ensure inclusiveness of all regions, Bulgaria will need to further provide support to investments in lagging behind regions. For instance, for the use of the EU funds, in the next programming period (2021-27), Bulgaria is already reinforcing the regional approach promoting integrated investment. It provides opportunities to pool resources of the OPT with other Operational Programmes (OPs) to support regional programmess, which can direct funds in a more place-based approach (OECD 2021, Decentralisation and Regionalisation in Bulgaria). As Bulgaria's economy will likely continue to grow in the post COVID-19 phase, donor financing will likely decline, underlying the need for Bulgaria to mobilise additional resources, notably from the private sector.

The investment required to improve Bulgaria's rail network is also an opportunity for the government to promote infrastructure investment projects, which can have positive impacts on Bulgaria's society, including lower environmental impacts and better well-being of Bulgarian's inhabitants. Indeed, certain infrastructure projects may have negative impacts on sustainable development, which can range from conflicts with communities over land, water, and resettlement, to unsafe working conditions during construction or significant environmental (including climate change). In line with the OECD *Guidelines for Multinational Enterprises*, Bulgaria should encourage enterprises to conduct due diligence with a view to identify, prevent, mitigate, and account for how they address their actual and potential adverse impacts, including in the course of investment in infrastructure. The OECD *Due Diligence Guidance for Responsible Business Conduct* provides practical support to enterprises on the implementation of the *Guidelines*. In addition, the OECD *Policy Framework for Investment* and the OECD *Principles for Private Sector Participation in Infrastructure* (OECD, 2007) encourage governments to clearly communicate RBC expectations to their private partners.

Bulgaria's digitalisation is lagging behind OECD standards

The deployment of digital economy has reshaped the traditional global business and investment landscape. As illustrated by the COVID-19 crisis, the digitalisation of business operations is an opportunity for investors to protect themselves from supply-chain disruptions. The deployment of new digital tools, such as blockchain technology for supply change management and machine learning for tracking risks, can not only boost country's economic growth but also enable businesses to further comply with the RBC standards.[9] Nevertheless, with these opportunities come new challenges that governments need to address carefully. The digital transformation is changing the nature and structure of investment and raising concerns about social equity and inclusion, as well as privacy and data protection. Against this background, Bulgaria could establish itself as one of the leading European countries in terms of digitalisation and attract a new generation of intangible FDI.

Bulgaria has a modern legal framework on data protection and privacy, aligned with EU law. The right to privacy is a constitutional right recognised and protected by the Constitution of the Republic of Bulgaria (Article 32 para.1, Constitution of the Republic of Bulgaria). The main legislative act that governs data protection and privacy in Bulgaria is the General Data Protection Regulation (Regulation (EU) 2016/679) (GDPR). Bulgaria implemented the EU Data Protection Directive 95/46/EC by updating the 2002 Personal Data Protection Act (PDPA) in February 2019. The PDPA as amended in 2019, implements the GDPR into Bulgarian legislation and also transposes Directive (EU) 2016/680 of the European Parliament and of the Council of 27 April 2016, on the protection of natural persons concerning the processing of personal data by competent authorities for the prevention, investigation, detection or prosecution of criminal offences or the execution of criminal penalties, and the free movement of such data, and repealing Council Framework Decision 2008/977/JHA. The supervisory authority in charge of performing tasks and exercising powers under the GDPR and the PDPA is the Commission for Personal Data Protection (CPDP). The Inspectorate to the Supreme Judicial Council supervises the processing of personal data by the courts, prosecutors, and investigative bodies in their capacity as judicial authorities.

For the past ten years, the Bulgarian authorities have made important efforts in the direction of the country's digital transformation. For example, in November 2019, Bulgaria adopted a National Programme "Digital Bulgaria 2025" as well as a roadmap for its implementation, both setting out the conditions for building an innovative digital infrastructure. In July 2020, the Council of Ministers of the Republic of Bulgaria approved the National Strategic Document "Digital Transformation 2020-30 Programme" focusing on digital transformation for growth. In December 2020 Bulgaria's Ministry of Transport, Information Technology, and Communications (MTITC) adopted the "Concept of the development of Artificial Intelligence in Bulgaria until 2030" which is the country's national Artificial Intelligence (AI) strategic document. The connectivity of Bulgaria's population has also improved considerably over the past ten years. For instance, mobile broadband subscriptions increased in Bulgaria from 13 in 2009 to almost 29 in 2019.[10] Yet, these figures are still lower compared to the OECD countries, where the number of subscriptions grew from 32 subscriptions per 100 inhabitants in 2009 to almost 113 subscriptions per 100 inhabitants by June 2019 (OECD, 2020a).

Despite Bulgaria's ambitious programmes aimed at establishing the country as one of the EU leaders in terms of speed of mobile and internet networks, there are still some obstacles that need to be addressed. In 2020, Bulgaria was ranked last (out of 28 countries) in the Digital Economy and Society Index (DESI) with an overall score of 36.4 (out of 100) compared to the EU average of 52.6 (out of 100). Bulgaria performs relatively well in connectivity, specifically as regards the wide availability of ultrafast (i.e. 100 Mbps or higher and mobile broadband networks)[11] (EC, 2020c). Approximately 67% of Bulgarians use the Internet (compared to 85% EU average) while 24% have never used it which is the highest percentage among all EU member states. According to the 2021 OECD economic survey of Bulgaria, household usage rates in the country are still relatively low, and in some regions, only about 60% of households have internet access (OECD, 2021a).

The COVID-19 crisis has further underlined the importance of digitalisation and innovation not only for the functioning of the economy but also for the protection of people's health and welfare. Digital technologies, such as mobile and biometric applications and online learning platforms, are being adopted in innovative ways to improve the effectiveness of government front-line responses to COVID-19 and to ensure continuous education for children and students. While disclosures of personal information can help the public to identify potential COVID-19 infections and track the spread over time, current digital solutions for monitoring and containment have varying implications for privacy and data protection (OECD, 2020b).

The enforcement of social distancing, lockdowns, and other measures in response to the COVID-19 pandemic have disrupted Bulgaria's market and economy. In this regard, Bulgaria has made additional efforts for enhancing digitalisation and improving the information exchange between the institutions and citizens (Box 3.2).

Regarding data relevant to the economic recovery during the ongoing COVID-19 crisis, Bulgaria is lagging compared to its EU peers in the introduction of 5G network,[12] the digital skills, and the digitisation of business indicators. In the deployment of the high capacity networks (VHCNs),[13] Bulgaria ranked 20th out of 28 countries in 2020, and its performance in digital public services was still relatively weak (EC, 2020d). Building up investment in Bulgaria's digital infrastructure networks is therefore crucial, to not only sustain robust rates of economic growth and integrate more fully the country into regional and global value chains but also to ensure greater social inclusion in Bulgaria's post-COVID-19 context.

In order to overcome the challenges created by the development of the digital economy and, at the same time, to attract FDI projects, Bulgaria should consider taking additional steps to address the digital skills shortcomings in the country for both individuals and businesses by providing trainings and increasing financial resources for the less advantaged socio-economic groups in the country. In addition, Bulgaria could also take further actions to ensure the implementation of its digital programme and ensure more supportive mechanisms for digitisation projects.

Box 3.2. The COVID-19 crisis and the importance of digitalisation in Bulgaria

In response to the COVID-19 crisis, Bulgaria launched two projects underlying the importance of digitalisation and access to the Internet to preserve the functioning of the health and education sector. Still, Bulgaria needs to address two major concerns – i) how to ensure broad access to digital technologies so that all children can exercise their rights, and ii) how to mitigate against increased risks for data privacy violations that may arise out of the increased use of COVID-19 applications, and e-learning platforms.

- In April 2020, Bulgaria approved the ViruSafe mobile application developed by Bulgarian IT specialists. The application was created to assist society and governmental institutions in the fight against COVID-19. ViruSafe allows users to track their symptoms and health status. If necessary, users can share their health status with practitioners or with the national health authority. The Bulgarian Ministry of Health is now working on the introduction of a National Health Information System to enhance the effectiveness of the institutions. Yet, concerns have been raised concerning the lack of information on whether the COVID-19 application had undergone independent audit in terms of data security and data protection.
- Shortly after the declaration of the state of emergency in Bulgaria in March 2020, amendments to the Electronic Communications Act (ECA), introduced the possibility for the Ministry of the Interior to monitor the telephone numbers of those who do not observe quarantine without restrictions and only subsequently to notify the court of this. In April 2020, a group of Members of Parliament challenged before Bulgaria's Constitutional Court (CC) the amendments to the ECA allowing the Ministry of Interior to obtain access to traffic data. The applicants claimed that the provisions represented disproportionate interference with the right to privacy and the confidentiality of correspondence and communications as defined in the Constitution, the European Convention of Human Rights, and the EU Directive on privacy and electronic communications. In November 2020, Bulgaria's Constitutional Court (CC) ruled that the preventive collection of traffic data on location for six months constitutes a serious, disproportionate intrusion into the right to privacy and protection of personal data.[14]

- In March 2020, 89% of Bulgaria's students were enrolled in the e-learning platform launched just a few days after Bulgaria's state of emergency was announced. School education content has been also broadcasted through the national television channels BNT 2 and BNT 4. To support distance learning, the Ministry of Education and Science (MES) has developed a National Electronic Library of Teachers (e-Content Repository), which provides materials for pedagogical specialists for working in e-learning environments. A 2020 study of the Institute for Research in Education (IRE) on the impact of distance learning on the quality of education showed Roma children were less prepared for the transition of schools to distance learning. According to the research, about 64% of schoolchildren speaking the Romani language at home had a smartphone, only 21% had a computer, and just 50% had internet access. These figures are significantly lower than the share of those speaking the Turkish language (79%, 46%, and 72% respectively) or the Bulgarian language at home (95%, 70%, and 84% respectively).

Source: World Bank (2020), www.worldbank.org/en/topic/edutech/brief/how-countries-are-using-edtech-to-support-remote-learning-during-the-COVID-19-pandemic, European Union Agency for Fundamental Rights (2020) https://fra.europa.eu/sites/default/files/fra_uploads/bg_report_on_coronavirus_pandemic_-_may_2020.pdf.

State-Owned Enterprises reform

State-owned enterprises (SOEs) still represent a large part of the economy in Bulgaria and many of them are at local level: by 2016, according to OECD data, there were 581 fully or majority-owned municipal enterprises, compared to 350 SOEs at the central level. The latter provide utility services (electricity, gas), transport and other community services, e.g. waste management, water supply, cultural centres, etc. In spite of the rapid privatisation of businesses in the 1990s and 2000s (Table 3.3), Overall, Bulgaria retains control over some of the most important economic sectors of the country such as energy, water, health care and transport services.

The privatisation process in Bulgaria started in 1992 with the adoption of the Law on Transformation and Privatisation of State and Municipal Enterprises and the establishment of the Privatisation Agency (PA). The Law divided SOEs into three categories depending on their value, and the Privatisation Agency was responsible for the privatisation of the largest enterprises while line ministries were in charge of the privatisation of the smallest enterprises.

In 2019, according to Bulgaria's National Statistical Institute (NSI), more than 300 SOEs were under the central government and 580 were under the sub-national government units, including municipalities.[15] More than 200 central SOEs were under line ministries control. Bulgaria was also a minority shareholder (10-50% stake) in 41 enterprises through different ministries such as the Ministry of Agriculture, Food and Forestry, the Ministry of Energy, the Ministers of Economy, and the Ministry of Health. Hospitals and medical centres account for around half of SOEs in Bulgaria (OECD, 2019a).

Table 3.3.Waves of privatisation

	Main features
1992	Adoption of the Transformation and Privatisation of State-Owned and Municipal Enterprises Act and creation of the Privatisation Agency.
1995 -97	Establishment of a Mass Privatisation Centre privatised SOEs through investment vouchers. According to the government Program for Mass Privatisation, stakes varying between 10 and 90% of shares in 1 050 SOEs were included in a list of companies to be privatised through the voucher system. 10% of every stake offered was to be transferred free to the company's workers and managers; the remaining 90% was to be offered to the public through centralised public auctions.

	Main features
1999	A second wave of mass privatisation started in 1999, offering 12.5 million shares from 547 enterprises for sale and approximately 17% of state-owned assets were privatised. (IMF, 2001).
2002	Privatisation and Post-Privatisation Control Act (PPCA) was adopted under which the whole activity as regards the sale of state interest in the enterprises was centralised in the Privatisation Agency, while the municipal councils or bodies specified by them did the privatisation of municipal property. The line ministries preserved their role of principals and representatives of the state, as owner of the state interest in the company capital.
2010	The Privatisation and Post-Privatisation Control Agency (PPCA) was established by the Government of of Bulgaria in 2010 with the unification of the former Privatisation Agency and Post-Privatisation Control Agency responsible for the accomplishment of the privatisation process in the country and the supervision of the concluded privatisation contracts.
2019	The Agency for Privatisation and Post-privatisation Control was transformed into the Public Enterprises and Control Agency (PECA) and endorsed an additional function.

Note: Authors' elaboration.
Source: Multiple data sources and context analysis.

Table 3.4. The presence of the State in Bulgaria's economy and its peers

Sector	Situation in		
	Bulgaria	Croatia	Romania
	Ownership	Ownership	Ownership
Electricity	37.5%	71.43%	19.91%
Natural gas	46.15%	42.70%	43.01%
Fixed e-communications	0%	2.51%	100%
Mobile e-communications	0%	100%	100%
Air transport	53.85%	82.34%	65.89%
Railways	71.43%	55.56%	51.72%

Note: Authors' elaboration based on the OECD Product Market Regulations Indicators database (2018). The OECD has developed a range of indicators of product market regulation at both the economy-wide and sectoral levels. All of these indicators measure the extent to which policy settings promote or inhibit competition in areas of the product market where competition is viable.
Source: Product Market Regulations (2018).

Table 3.5. List of largest SOEs in Bulgaria in 2019

SOE	Legal form	Responsible ministry
Bulgarian Energy Holding (BEH EAD)	Single shareholder joint-stock company	Ministry of Energy
NPP Kolzoduy	Single shareholder joint-stock company	100% owned by BEH EAD; Ministry of Energy
Electricity System Operator	Single shareholder joint-stock company	100% owned by BEH EAD; Ministry of Energy
Bulgartransgaz	Single shareholder joint-stock company	100% owned by BEH EAD; Ministry of Energy
National Electricity Company EAD (NEK)	Single shareholder joint-stock company	100% owned by BEH EAD; Ministry of Energy
MaritsaEast Mining	Single shareholder joint-stock company	100% owned by BEH EAD; Ministry of Energy
TPP Maritsa East 2	Single shareholder joint-stock company	100% owned by BEH EAD; Ministry of Energy
National Railway Infrastructure Company	State enterprise	Ministry of Transport, Information Technology and Communications
BDZ Holding	Single shareholder joint-stock company	Ministry of Transport, Information Technology and Communications

SOE	Legal form	Responsible ministry
Bulgarian Ports Infrastructure Company	State enterprise	Ministry of Transport, Information Technology and Communications
Bulgarian Development Bank	Joint-stock company	Ministry of Economy
Vazovski Mashinostroitelni Zavodi EAD (VMZ	Single shareholder joint-stock company	100% owned by State Consolidation Company (DKK EAD), Ministry of Economy

Source: OECD (2019).

Given the importance of SOEs in Bulgaria, SOE's performance has been an area of concern. Weaknesses in SOEs' governance has been pointed out by multilateral governmental organisations as implying risks for economic and financial stability (IMF Article IV Report 2016). Economic losses, poor governance, insufficient transparency, monitoring and control, the non-competitive selection process for the board of directors, and frequent board management changes have been seen as among the main issues of the SOEs sector in Bulgaria (OECD, 2019a). In addition, exposure to the risk of political patronage, conflict of interest, and corruption including bribery of SOEs employees by other parties or the risk of employees and board members using their positions for gaining a personal advantage for themselves have been viewed for a long time as a challenge (OECD, 2019a).

In order to defuse concerns about weak governance and potential risks of corruption, significant legislative and regulatory changes have been introduced to enhance the performance, transparency and integrity of SOEs. For example, in 2017 Bulgaria introduced new provisions in the Accountancy Act, according to which enterprises, including all SOEs, are required to draw up non-financial declarations describing environmental, social, employees, human rights and anti-corruption-corruption policies (Article 48, Accountancy Act). The Law on Public Enterprises adopted in 2019 further specifies that SOE board members cannot hold a "senior public office" or be a member of a political cabinet or a municipality's secretary. The state ownership regulations for fully corporatised SOEs and the Counter-Corruption and Unlawfully Acquired Assets Forfeiture Act (CCUAAA) also contain disposition on anti-corruption and integrity in SOEs boards and provide a definition of conflict of interest (CCUAAA, Chapter 8) as well as a requirement that board members sign a "Declaration of Assets and Interest", which is to be regularly updated (Article 22 of the state ownership regulations). Certain SOEs are also obliged to develop internal regulations for potential conflicts of interest within their boards (OECD, 2019a).

Overall, strengthening SOEs governance has become one of the top priorities for Bulgaria. Reforms aimed at improving the governance and fostering the integrity of SOEs have advanced rapidly in Bulgaria for the past few years. As part of its ERM II and Banking Union accession commitments, Bulgaria started a legislative reform process to improve the governance of SOEs by revising and aligning its legislation with the OECD *Guidelines on Corporate Governance of State-Owned Enterprises*.

In support of Bulgaria's reform process, in 2018 the European Commission and the OECD began to implement an *improving the governance of state-owned enterprises in Bulgaria* project. With such support, Bulgaria adopted in late 2019 an entirely new law, the Law on Public Enterprises (LPE), which addresses the main issues of SOEs practices in the country as identified in the 2019 OECD *Review* of the Bulgaria. The LPE has been assessed as being in line with the OECD *Guidelines on corporate governance for SOEs*, incorporating international standards for corporate governance including stronger ownership, co-ordination, accountability, qualification for the managing bodies, independence, and transparency in their nomination, disclosure and publicity obligations, to address the main weaknesses of the SOEs governance in Bulgaria (OECD, 2019a).

At the central level, the new legislation applies to fully and majority-owned SOEs and their subsidiaries, except for the Bulgarian Development Bank. Stricter requirements may be required for large SOE as defined in Chapter 2, Section I and II of the Accountancy Act. Chapters 2, 5, 6, and 7 of the LPE apply to municipal level SOEs. The LPE has also transformed the Agency for Privatisation and Post-privatisation

Control into the Public Enterprises and Control Agency (PECA), giving the PECA an additional role of monitoring and policy co-ordination body (Box 3.3).

Box 3.3. Public Enterprises and Control Agency's new role under the Law on Public Enterprises

Art. 11. (1) The Agency for Public Enterprises and Control shall act as a unit responsible for the co-ordination of state policy with regard to public enterprises and shall monitor and report its implementation to the Council of Ministers. (2) The Executive Director of the Agency for Public Enterprises and Control shall be accountable to the Council of Ministers and shall work under the supervision of the Prime Minister or a Deputy Prime Minister appointed by the latter. (3) Persons with higher education – a master with at least 10 years of professional experience in the field of finance, state governance and/or the sector of real economy, of which at least three years at a managerial position, shall be appointed members of the Executive Board of the Agency for Public Enterprises and Control.

Art. 12. The Public Enterprises and Control Agency shall carry out the functions under Article 11(1) by:

1. developing the policy in the field of state shareholding in the capital of public enterprises
2. monitoring the implementation of the policy in the field of state shareholding in the capital of public enterprises and preparing its updating
3. assisting the authorities exercising the powers of the State in formulating the general strategic objectives of the enterprises and the key financial and non-financial performance indicators in the business programmes of the enterprises
4. monitoring the activities of public enterprises and preparing an aggregate report for the previous year in the format and scope defined by law
5. co-operating with other state administrations, non-governmental and international institutions on issues related to the management of public enterprises
6. publishing updated information and reports on the activities of public enterprises, incl. financial and non-financial information on the enterprises
7. monitoring the competitive selection procedures and the procedures for the appointment of the members of the management and control bodies
8. evaluating the implementation of the approved business programmes of public enterprises and making proposals for improving their management
9. exercising the powers of the State in public enterprises when delegated by the Council of Ministers
10. on request, assisting the municipalities with regard to the management of municipal public enterprises
11. preparing an assessment and analysis of the approved business programmes of public enterprises and their implementation as well as recommendations regarding the risks and effects on public finances, including the potential effects and risks for the consolidated debt and deficit/surplus indicators of the State Governance Sector
12. giving instructions on the application of this Law.

Source: Law on Public Enterprises (2019),

The establishment of a co-ordination unit in the face of the PECA has been assessed by the OECD as being in line with the OECD *SOEs Guidelines* and as responding to the need to improve the decentralised SOE model in Bulgaria in which 17 ministries oversee a portfolio of 221 SOEs (OECD, 2019a). In addition, the LPE introduces new requirements with regards to selection criteria for board members such as reputation and integrity, suitable education, and solid professional experience amongst other aspects (Art. 20(1), LPE). The LPE also contains minimum requirements for independent members on SOE boards, which must constitute at least 1/3, but not more than half of board composition and introduces independence requirements (Art. 23(1), LPE).

The Bulgarian Development Bank (BDB), which is a state-owned financial institution in charge of financing companies and projects in support of national economic development, is the only SOE exempted from the LPE's scope because it is subject to regulations and supervisory rules governing financial institutions. The proposal for its exclusion came from deputies between the first and second reading of the LPE draft. In July 2019, the Minister of Finance submitted an opinion, according to which such an exclusive approach towards the BDB contradicts the main purpose of the LPE.[16]

For a long time, Bulgaria's Development Bank, a financial institution 99.9% owned by the Bulgarian state, has been pointed as a vulnerable SOE because of its management (IMF, 2017). After adopting the LPE, the Bulgarian authorities kept working with the OECD on the adoption of a secondary legislation. In these lines, Bulgaria promulgated PECA's rules of procedures.[17] In parallel, the OECD also supported Bulgaria's legislative and institutional reform efforts by providing administrative and technical support in developing the new "Rule of Implementation of the Law on Public Enterprises" which was adopted on 30 April 2020[18] and came into force in May 2020.

Both the implementing Rules for the LPE and PECA's rules of procedures have been assessed by the OECD as being in line with the OECD *SOE Guidelines'* principles and as further enhancing the legislative foundation for more effective ownership co-ordination and monitoring of the SOEs in Bulgaria (OECD 2019). It can reasonably be argued that the steps taken by Bulgaria are moving in the right direction. Bulgaria's governance system for SOEs is nevertheless work in progress. Reforms are expected to take time to permeate through the system. For example, the OECD, in its report on corporate governance of SOEs in Bulgaria (OECD, 2019), noted that not all SOEs in Bulgaria were consistently establishing internal controls, ethics and compliance measures including those dedicated to preventing corruption as recommended in the OECD *Guidelines for Multinational Enterprises,* the OECD *SOE Guidelines* and the OECD *Anti-Corruption and Integrity Guidelines for State-Owned Enterprises*. The report further noted that the government had not yet established or communicated specific expectations concerning SOEs' compliance with RBC standards. The OECD is currently providing additional technical and legal assistance to PECA on the implementation of the Law and related regulations.

Labour market and skills

Bulgaria's low employment costs as well as its EU membership have played an important role in attracting investors. Because of Bulgaria's steady economic growth since 2015, the country recorded historically high employment rate of 72.4% (for the group of people between 20 and 64 years old) in 2018, with an unemployment rate of 5.2% (EC, 2020d). A mismatch between the labour market needs and workforce skills and availability has nevertheless been identified as a challenge by foreign and domestic investors met in the course of this *Review* (Box 3.4).

Box 3.4. Mismatch priority occupations in Bulgaria

Shortage occupation in Bulgaria

- ICT Professionals
- Teachers
- Health Professionals
- Engineering professionals
- Financial and mathematical professionals
- Sales and purchasing agents and brokers
- Administration and business services professionals

Surplus occupation in Bulgaria

- Street Workers
- Workers in mining, construction, transport and manufacturing
- Cleaners and helpers
- Agriculture, forestry, fishery

Source: Cedefop (2016), https://skillspanorama.cedefop.europa.eu/en/analytical_highlights/bulgaria-mismatch-priority-occupations.

Regional disparities also remain high. Some regions in the country are less attractive for investors for numerous factors, not only because of poor infrastructure as discussed above but also with respect to inadequate educational characteristics of the workforce. Such characteristics vary across regions and are more pronounced in the least advanced ones such as the North-West. In 2020, the North West region recorded a 13.3% unemployment rate compared to a 5.2% national average unemployment rate for the Bulgarian population in the 15-64 age group.[19] Policies should push for relevant vocational courses, digital and administrative skills training to meet the market needs not only on central but also on a regional level.

Bulgaria, like many countries in Central and Eastern Europe, has experienced higher educational attainment (such as years of education and level of education completed) following an upward trend since the start of country's economic transition. The level of educational attainment, however, is not necessarily a proxy for measuring actual skills, as proven by performance in international student assessments that measure cognitive skills such as PISA. Scores reveal that Bulgarian youth accumulates poor cognitive foundation skills, which leaves them ill prepared for the demands of a competitive, innovation-driven economy. The gap is the widest in reading literacy, the main topic of PISA 2018, where 15-year-olds in Bulgaria score 420 points compared to an average of 487 points in OECD countries. Girls perform better than boys in Bulgaria do, with a statistically significant difference of 40 points. Social-economically advantaged students outperformed disadvantaged students in reading by 106 score points in PISA 2018. This is larger than the average difference between the two groups (89 score points) across OECD countries (OECD, 2018).

Another weak area in terms of labour and skills in Bulgaria has been the insufficient integration of the Roma minority, which makes up one-tenth of Bulgarians and which lives in socially excluded neighbourhoods (EC, 2020c). Facilitating access to the labour market of the Roma population, in particular young Roma women, whose labour inactivity is to some extent due to the cultural peculiarities of this ethnic group, could contribute to greater labour market participation. Implementation of responsible business conduct (RBC) principles and standards by businesses could help in that regard.

Notwithstanding the recent decline in the share of young people who are neither employed nor enrolled in training or education programmes, the early school leavers' proportion remains high. Bulgaria also records a low level of individuals with above basic overran digital skills. According to the 2021 European Innovation Scoreboard, Bulgaria ranked second from the bottom to the top among the EU-28 countries, scoring below neighbouring non-EU countries such as the Republic of North Macedonia and Serbia. The tertiary higher education level alignment with labour-market demand remains limited. Although Bulgaria has made progress with respect to vocational education and training (VET) reform, yet the employment rate in VET remains low (European Commission, 2020c).

The brain drain, i.e. the departure of skilled nationals, is another problem plaguing Bulgaria, affecting all sectors its national economy and labour force. Since the 1990s, Bulgaria has experienced a huge dip in its population, falling from nearly 9 million in 1989 to less than 7 million in 2019.[20] Current forecasts predict that by 2050 the population will have shrunk by another quarter – a projection so high that the country is neck-and-neck with countries such as Lithuania for the fastest shrinking population in the world.

There is scope for improving the quality and the inclusiveness of education and aligning it to the needs of the labour market. Bulgaria's labour and skills shortages constitute a significant obstacle to the creation of a favourable investment climate. Government spending on education for increasing teacher's salaries, to make the best professionals stay in the country, as well as modernisation of the education system, would help address current shortcomings.

In terms of policy responses to alleviate brain drain, there is some promising evidence that suggests governments can successfully encourage the return of their high-skilled diaspora by putting in place "returning scientists programmes" to attract scientists back to their home country for temporary stays (brain circulation) or permanent returns. Another way to attract Bulgarian experts is to make use of scientific diaspora networks by connecting scientists abroad to the scientific community at home countries. The return of high-skilled professionals could also be supported by granting tax incentives to returning emigrants.[21]

The entry of young and highly qualified people into the education system would improve the knowledge and skills that students acquire. In addition, of particular concern are the extremely high rates of unemployed (formal) or untrained (NEET) youth among the Turkish and Roma populations, while the share of NEET among ethnic Bulgarians is close to the EU average (OECD, 2021a). Establishing a better dialogue between business and education institutions is a key step for making their curricula adequate concerning labour market needs.

Market functioning: Enhancing competition policy

Over the past decades, Bulgaria has undertaken a series of steps in the field of market functioning, establishing a strong legal and institutional framework for competition policy. Bulgaria has a modern legal and institutional framework aligned with the EU norms and standards.

Bulgaria's main legal instruments on competition include the Protection of the Competition Act (PCA), adopted in 2008 and which has been designed to protect and foster competition and free enterprise in economic activity. The law protects against agreements, decisions and concerted practices and regulates abuse of stronger bargaining power on the market, and any other actions and operations which may result in prevention, restriction or distortion of competition in Bulgaria and/or affect trade between EU Member States, as well as against unfair competition or against abuse of dominant position when contracting (Article1, PCA). The scope of the Act is large and comprises every kind of undertakings, which carry out their activities within or outside Bulgaria if they explicitly or tacitly prevent, restrict, distort or may prevent, restrict or distort competition in the country (Article 2, PCA). The PCA also regulates merger control aligned with the EU merger control regime and applies equally to foreign and domestic mergers. The central body responsible for ensuring the protection and creating conditions for the development of competition and free enterprise is the Commission on Protection of Competition (CPC, the Commission), an independent state agency.

Although steps undertaken by Bulgaria in the area of competition policy have been welcomed by the OECD (OECD 2019b), the enforcement of the Competition Law has been perceived by some international investors met by the OECD Secretariat in the framework of this *Review* as being sometimes inconsistent or, as suggested by some authors across the Bulgarian media, prone to political influence. One of the controversial cases concerning the consistency of Bulgaria's competition watchdog practice has been the PPF/Nova case in the context of which the CPC prohibited the acquisition of the largest media conglomerate in Bulgaria, Nova Broadcasting Group AD, by PPF, owned by a the Czech businessperson. The CPC decision came under criticism for its alleged lack of valid economic arguments, despite the use by the Commission of the SIEC ("significant impediment of effective competition") test that the European Commission also uses when applying the EC Merger Regulation.[22] For some observers,[23] it was not clear how the CPC concluded that the acquisition of Nova would lead to a strengthening of PPF's dominant position on the relevant markets. The CPC claimed that the transaction would impede effective competition, but the acquiring entity, reportedly, had only a negligible presence on the market where their activities overlapped (0-5%). In addition, in its prohibition decision, the CPC underlined the significant power of Nova, but allegedly failed to explain how this position would change if the acquisition by an insignificant market player was cleared.

Alleged or actual inconsistent decisions may have a chilling effect on investment decisions and economic activity. From an investor's perspective, a level playing field is crucial for Bulgaria's investment climate attractiveness. In this regard, despite limited financial resources, Bulgaria should maintain its efforts aimed at strengthening the institutional capacity of the Commission as a regulator, notably by providing additional training to its officials and case handlers in the framework of competition law proceedings (infringements of competition law and merger cases). At the time of writing this *Review*, Bulgaria was in process of changing its Protection of the Competition Act to transpose into Bulgarian legislation the provisions of Directive (EU) 2019/1 of the European Parliament and of the Council of 11 December 2018 aimed at empowering the competition authorities of Member States to be more effective enforcers. With the transposition of the Directive provisions on the financial independence of EU competition authorities in to the PCA, the Competition Commission expected that it would found itself in a better position to obtain additional financial resources for professional training of the CPC expert staff.

Outlook

Fifteen years after becoming an EU member state, Bulgaria continues to face challenges despite significant efforts to improve the country's overall investment climate. As part of EU membership requirements, Bulgaria's legal and institutional framework for investment has gradually become aligned with EU norms and standards. For example, substantial progress has been achieved with respect to the SOEs sector through the adoption of an entirely new Law aligned with the OECD standards.

Issues such as ageing population, brain drain and weak integration of national minorities have nevertheless been perceived as areas of concern by investors. Bulgaria's insufficient state of infrastructure (both road and railroad) has been another issue for businesses. The COVID-19 context has also highlighted the importance of digitalisation and innovation where Bulgaria's performance is still lagging compared to many of its EU peers and OECD countries.

In order to overcome the above-mentioned challenges, Bulgaria should consider pursuing specific policies. For example, it seems necessary to improve investment in infrastructures. There is also the need for Bulgaria to keep working on securing the inclusiveness of its education system both at the central and regional level. There is also scope, as recognised by Bulgaria's Commission for Protection on Competition, for enhancing its institutional capacity as a regulator, notably by strengthening the skills and competencies of its officials and case handlers on competition law enforcement. Despite progress in reforms aimed at strengthening the governance of SOEs, given that they are still present in some key sectors of the economy such as railways and the postal service as well as in the energy, health care and infrastructure sectors, additional steps in line with the OECD *Guidelines on Corporate Governance of State-Owned Enterprises* should be taken to ensure a stronger level playing field. Bulgaria has an opportunity to leverage its standards and practice in the context of its work with the OECD Competition Committee.

References

Bulgaria (2021), *National Development Programme Bulgaria 2030*, www.minfin.bg/upload/43546/Bulgaria+2030_EN.pdf

Bulgaria (2020), *National Development Programme: Bulgaria 2020* http://www.strategy.bg/StrategicDocuments/View.aspx?lang=bg-BG&Id=766.

Bulgaria (2017a), *National strategy for development of scientific research in the Republic of Bulgaria 2017 – 2030 – Better science for better Bulgaria*

Bulgaria (2017b), *National Roadmap for Research Infrastructure 2017-23*, ec.europa.eu/research/infrastructures/pdf/roadmaps/bulgaria_national_roadmap_2 017_en.pdf

Bulgaria (2014), *Innovation Strategy for Smart Specialisation 2014-20*, www.mi.government.bg/en/themes/innovation-strategy-for-smart-specialisation-of-the-republic-of-bulgaria-2014-20-is3-1470-287.html.

EC/OECD (2021), *STIP Compass Bulgaria Overview*, generated from https://stip.oecd.org/stip/countries/Bulgaria on 25 June2021.

European Commission (2021), European Innovation Scoreboard 2021, https://ec.europa.eu/docsroom/documents/46013; https://ec.europa.eu/docsroom/documents/46032.

European Commission (2020a), *Research and Innovation analysis in the European Semester 2020 Country Reports,* https://rio.jrc.ec.europa.eu/sites/default/files/report/2020_Compilation%20R%20and%20I%20sections%20CRs.pdf.

European Commission (2020b), *EU Transport Scoreboard, Investments and infrastructure*, https://ec.europa.eu/transport/facts-fundings/scoreboard/countries/bulgaria/investments-infrastructure_en

European Commission (2020c), *The Digital Economy and Society Index (DESI*), https://ec.europa.eu/digital-single-market/en/desi.

European Commission (2020d), 20*20 European Semester: Assessment of progress on structural reforms, prevention and correction of macroeconomic imbalances, and results of in-depth reviews under Regulation (EU) No 1176/2011*, https://eur-lex.europa.eu/legal-content/EN/TXT/?qid=1584543810241&uri=CELEX%3A52020SC0500.

European Commission (2019), *Country Report Bulgaria 2019, Including an In-Depth Review on the prevention and correction of macroeconomic imbalances*, https://ec.europa.eu/info/sites/info/files/file_import/2019-european-semester-country-report-bulgaria_en.pdf.

Eurostat (2019), *Regional Innovation Scoreboard 2019*, https://ec.europa.eu/growth/sites/growth/files/ris2019.pdf.

IMF (2019), *Bulgaria article IV consultation*, IMF Country Report No. 19/83, www.imf.org/en/Publications/CR/Issues/2019/03/22/Bulgaria-2019-Article-IV-Consultation-Press-

Release-Staff-Report-Staff-Supplement-and-46702.

IMF (2016), *Bulgaria selected issues paper*, IMF Country Report *No. 16/345*, www.imf.org/external/pubs/ft/scr/2016/cr16345.pdf.http://www.imf.org/external/pubs/ft/scr/2016/cr16345.pdf/

Ivanova K. and G. Spasov (2019), “Dominance and Monopoly”, *The Law Reviews 2019*, https://thelawreviews.co.uk/edition/the-dominance-and-monopolies-review-edition-8/1228440/bulgaria.

KPMG (2017), “Investment in Bulgaria”, https://assets.kpmg/content/dam/kpmg/bg/pdf/Investment-in-Bulgaria-2017-WEB.pdf.

Milatovic, J., M. Szczurek (2019), *Bulgaria Diagnostic*, EBRD, www.ebrd.com/publications/country-diagnostics

OECD (2021a), *OECD Economic Surveys: Bulgaria 2021: Economic Assessment*, OECD Publishing, Paris, https://doi.org/10.1787/1fe2940d-en.

OECD (2021b), *Decentralisation and Regionalisation in Bulgaria: Towards Balanced Regional Development*, OECD Multi-level Governance Studies, OECD Publishing, Paris, https://doi.org/10.1787/b5ab8109-en.

OECD (2020a), *OECD Digital Economy Outlook 2020,* OECD Publishing, Paris, https://doi.org/10.1787/bb167041-en.

OECD (2020b*), Tracking and tracing COVID-19: Protecting privacy and data while using apps and biometric*s, OECD Publishing, Paris, https://doi.org/10.1787/8f394636-en.

OECD (2019), “The road to 5G networks: Experience to date and future developments”, *OECD Digital Economy Papers*, No. 284, OECD Publishing, Paris, https://doi.org/10.1787/2f880843-en

OECD (2019a), *Review of the Corporate Governance of State-Owned Enterprises: Bulgaria*, www.oecd.org/corporate/ca/Corporate-Governance-of-SOEs-in-Bulgaria.pdf

OECD (2019b), *Annual Report on Competition Policy Developments in Bulgaria 2018*, https://one.oecd.org/document/DAF/COMP/AR(2018)50/en/pdf.

OECD (2018), *Bulgaria: Student performance,* PISA 2018 Results, https://gpseducation.oecd.org/CountryProfile?primaryCountry=BGR&treshold=10&topic=PI

OECD (2011), *OECD Guidelines for Multinational Enterprises,* 2011 Edition, OECD Publishing, Paris, https://doi.org/10.1787/9789264115415-en

OECD (2007), *OECD Principles for Private Sector Participation in Infrastructure*, OECD Publishing, Paris, www.oecd.org/daf/inv/investment-policy/38309896.pdf

WEF (2019), *The Global Competitiveness Report 2019*, www3.weforum.org/docs/WEF_TheGlobalCompetitivenessReport2019.pdf

Yotov, P., A. Kinaneva (2018), “PPF Mergers in Bulgaria – a Tale of Double Standard”, *Kluwer competition blog*, 20 September 2018, http://competitionlawblog.kluwercompetitionlaw.com/2018/09/20/ppf-mergers-bulgaria-tale-double-standard/?doing_wp_cron=1592256034.6131310462951660156250.

Notes

[1] According to the 2021 European Innovation Scoreboard, the group of emerging innovators includes seven Member States that show a performance level below 70% of the EU average. This group includes Bulgaria, Croatia, Hungary, Latvia, Poland, Romania, and the Slovak Republic.

[2] Struma motorway is a part of Pan-European Corridor IV, the EC Priority Project No. 7 as well as the TENT network on the Bulgarian territory. The motorway begins from the end of Liulyn Motorway (approximately 20 kms south-west of Sofia at Daskalovo Junction) and ends at the border crossing with Greece at Kulata. See https://keep.eu/projects/17403/.

[3] Hemus motorway starts from the Sofia Ring Road and ends in Varna. It is a part of extended TEN-T. The sections Yana – Yablanica, and Belokopitovo – Varna are already completed. At the time of writing of this *Review*, two sections were under construction – from Sofia Ring Road to Yana (8.5 kms) and from Kaspichan to Belokopitovo (8 kms). In 2020, the section from Sofia Ring Road to Yana (8.5 kms) and from Kaspichan to Belokopitovo (8 kms) was still under construction. See https://keep.eu/projects/17405/.

[4] See www.fnf-southeasteurope.org/our-work/black-book/black-book-of-government-waste-in-bulgaria-eu-edition/the-myth-of-cheap-bulgarian-roads/.

[5] See https://bivol.bg/sapareva-bania-road-prsr.html.

[6] Available at: www.mtitc.government.bg/sites/default/files/pril_1_pet_god_programa_2019_2023_s_prilojeniya_of.pdf.

[7] See www.nsi.bg/en/content/7191/length-railway-network.

[8] See www.mtitc.government.bg/en/category/1/ec-allocates-293-million-euro-plovdiv-bourgas-railway-line-modernization.

[9] See www.oecd.org/investment/investment-policy/The-digital-economy-multinational-enterprises-and-international-investment-policy.pdf.

[10] International Telecommunication Union (ITU) World Telecommunication/ICT Indicators Database https://data.worldbank.org/indicator/IT.NET.BBND.P2?locations=BG.

[11] See https://ec.europa.eu/commission/presscorner/detail/en/MEMO_19_2933.

[12] 5G will support simultaneous connections, increase masse capacity, and deliver multi-Gbps peak rates and ultra-low latency. 5G is the fifth generation mobile network succeeding 4G, which was still being deployed in Bulgaria in 2021. The fifth generation of wireless networks, or 5G, is intended to meet the IMT-2020 specifications. That is, 5G is being developed with three main generic use case scenarios: enhanced mobile broadband (eMBB); massive machine type communications (mMTC); and critical communications/applications (Ultra-reliable and low latency communications, URLLC) (OECD, 2019). It is intended to support simultaneous connections, increase masse capacity, and deliver multi-Gbps peak rates and ultra-low latency.

[13] Article 2(2) of the European Electronics Communications Code EECC defines the term ‘very high capacity network’ as follows: “’Very high capacity network’ means either an electronic communications network which consists wholly of optical fibre elements at least up to the distribution point at the serving location, or an electronic communications network which is capable of delivering, under usual peak-time conditions, similar network performance in terms of available downlink and uplink bandwidth, resilience, error-related parameters, and latency and its variation.”, available at: https://eur-lex.europa.eu/legal-content/EN/TXT/PDF/?uri=CELEX:32018L1972.

[14] Constitutional Court of the Republic of Bulgaria, Resolution No 15 17 November 2020 (Promulgated SG, issue 101 of 27.11.2020), http://www.constcourt.bg/bg/Acts/GetHtmlContent/871b6834-64cd-47b3-9fbd-5a9fc570a96d.

[15] Note that in 2019 the NSI reports different numbers than the 2019 OECD Review of Bulgaria as they count also other entities, which would not typically, fit within the category of SOE.

[16] See "MEPs removed BDB from stricter rules for public companies", *Kapital*, 26 September 2019, www.capital.bg/politika_i_ikonomika/bulgaria/2019/09/26/3968585_deputatite_izvadiha_bbr_ot_po-striktnite_pravila_za/.

[17] CoM Decree No 68 of 13 April 2020, https://lex.bg/bg/laws/ldoc/2137202005.

[18] CoM Decree No 85 of 30 April 2020, https://dv.parliament.bg/DVWeb/showMaterialDV.jsp?idMat=147723.

[19] National Statistical Institute, Unemployed and unemployment rates – national level; statistical regions; districts, https://www.nsi.bg/en/content/6503/unemployed-and-unemployment-rates-national-level-statistical-regions-districts.

[20] See https://data.worldbank.org/indicator/SP.POP.TOTL?locations=BG.

[21] See https://blogs.worldbank.org/europeandcentralasia/there-policy-remedy-brain-drain-europe.

[22] Council Regulation 139/2004 of 20 January 2004 on the on the control of concentrations between undertakings.

[23] See "Bulgaria: New purchaser new rules. CPC clears the acquisition of Nova TV by Domuschievi brothers in "fast-track" proceeding", *Schonner*, 22 May 2019, www.mondaq.com/broadcasting-film-tv-radio/805348/new-purchaser-new-rules-cpc-clears-the-acquisition-of-nova-tv-by-domuschievi-brothers-in-fast-track-proceeding. See also Plamen Yotov (Kambourov & Partners) and Aleksandra Kinaneva, "PPF Mergers in Bulgaria – a Tale of Double Standard", Kluwer Competition Law Blog, September 2018, http://competitionlawblog.kluwercompetitionlaw.com/2018/09/20/ppf-mergers-bulgaria-tale-double-standard/

4 The framework for investment in Bulgaria

This chapter provides an overview of the legal framework for starting and expanding a business in Bulgaria. Particular attention is given to the conditions Bulgaria imposes on the entry of foreign investors and the extent it provides them national treatment once they are established. The chapter also benchmarks Bulgaria's overall openness to investment, an area where the country performs well.

Introduction

As noted in the previous chapters, since the beginning of Bulgaria's transition towards a market economy, the government has considered FDI as an important driver of economic development. This is reflected by the quick move to enact several laws promoting openness towards FDI during the 1990s, even in the midst of macroeconomic and political instability. The legal certainty provided by the 1990s legal framework and the prospect of EU membership, which materialised in 2007, have been considered by international organisations as the main drivers of the increase of FDI inflows in Bulgaria in the 2000s.

Investment in general is central to growth and sustainable development. According to OECD research, investment has the capacity of expanding an economy's productive capacity, driving job creation and fostering income growth (OECD, 2015). While both domestic and international firms carry out investments, foreign investment has proven to grant additional advantages to host countries through enhanced productivity, diffusion of technology and expertise, as well as acting as a vehicle for transformation of domestic production through better integration with global value chains (Echandi, Krajcovicova and Qiang, 2015).

In order to attract and retain FDI, economies have put in place measures to ensure that their legal regime is conducive to the establishment and cross-border provision of services, eliminate discriminatory barriers to invest and defend transparent capital flows. The OECD regulates these issues through two of its investment instruments: the Codes of Liberalisation (comprised of the Code of Liberalisation of Capital Movements and Code of Liberalisation of Current Invisible Operations),[1] and the National Treatment instrument (Box 4.1), which is part of the OECD *Declaration on International Investment and Multinational Enterprises*. Adherents to these instruments are encouraged to uphold the principle of non-discrimination at entry (between residents and non-residents, and across the latter) and thereafter (between nationals and foreigners) as a way of creating an enabling environment for foreign investment, and to be transparent about any departures from such principle.

On 18 January 2018, the OECD Council invited Bulgaria to adhere to the Codes of Liberalisation, subject to the outcome of a full examination by the Investment Committee. A first review by the Investment Committee took place in May 2020, supported by a note by the Secretariat (OECD, 2020c). In addition, in January 2022, the OECD Council invited Bulgaria to adhere to the OECD *Declaration on International Investment and Multinational Enterprises*; Bulgaria became Adherent to the Declaration in June 2022. As an Adherent to the *Declaration*, Bulgaria is committed to providing national treatment to foreign investors, this is, to treat enterprises operating on its territory, but controlled by the nationals of other adhering countries, no less favourably than domestic enterprises in like situations. National treatment is an integral part of the non-discrimination principle, one of the fundamental aspects of any international investment regime, since it ensures that once the investment has been accepted into the territory, it will operate under the same conditions as those controlled by nationals.

Bulgaria's commitment to national treatment is reflected under the National Treatment instrument (NTi) (Annex A). In addition, to further strengthen transparency on policies regarding national treatment, Bulgaria has reported, for transparency purpose, measures that do not constitute exceptions to national treatment, but are important determinants of policies in the context of national treatment (for example measures related to national security, corporate organisation or public and activities covered by monopolies and concessions) (Annex B). The present chapter elaborates on Bulgaria's FDI regime and measures departing from national treatment or that may have an adverse impact on the attraction of FDI and the investment climate in general.

Box 4.1. The OECD National Treatment instrument for foreign-controlled enterprises

National treatment is the commitment by an Adherent to the *Declaration on International Investment and Multinational Enterprises* to treat enterprises operating on its territory, but controlled by the nationals of another country, directly or indirectly, no less favourably than domestic enterprises in like circumstances.

The term "operating in its territory" in the instrument conveys the idea of doing business from a place of business in the host country, as distinct from conducting business in the country from abroad. This recognises that adhering countries' practices differ regarding recognised forms of business but that the main forms of doing business are through locally incorporated subsidiaries and branches. The principle of national treatment applies regardless of the home country's treatment of enterprises from the host country (OECD, 2005).

The National Treatment instrument consists of two elements: a declaration of principle, which forms part of the *Declaration*, and a procedural OECD Council Decision, which obliges Adherents to notify their exceptions to national treatment and establishes follow-up procedures to deal with such exceptions. The Decision comprises an Annex that lists exceptions to national treatment, as notified by each Adherent and accepted by the OECD Council. The Investment Committee periodically examines the exceptions.

Only measures concerning legal entities are reported for the purpose of the National Treatment instrument, and thus any measure that may apply to natural persons is not reflected in the list contained in the Annex to the Council's decision.

To ensure transparency, Adherents to the *Declaration* also commit to report any measures that, while not representing exceptions to national treatment, have an impact on it. The lists of these exceptions and measures are published and regularly updated. There are featured in Annexes A and B to the present *Review*.

Bulgaria has a legal regime conducive to the attraction and retention of investment

Attracting investment and further improving the country's institutional framework are key government priorities, as evidenced by Bulgaria's strategic documents such as "Vision, Goals and Priorities of the National Development Programme BULGARIA 2030 (Decision 33 of the Council of Ministers, 20 January 2020),[2] which is the basis for the approved NDP BULGARIA 2030 (Protocol 67 of the Council of Ministers, 2 December 2020).

According to the Bulgarian authorities, efforts to improve the quality, efficiency and fairness of the legal and regulatory framework aim to improve the business climate and the investment environment, without any difference, in principle, between foreign-owned and local-owned foreign companies. The key standards of investor treatment and protection are guaranteed under the Constitution – the highest legal authority- and dedicated laws. Bulgaria's FDI legal regime includes enforceable principles for protection of foreign investors, investment promotion and transparency requirements.

Protection of foreign investors

Bulgaria's Constitution provides that foreign and local persons, whatever form they take, enjoy equal rights when conducting economic activities, except where otherwise provided by the law.[3] Foreign investors may establish or participate in establishing a company in Bulgaria and may acquire rights and obligations as national investors. In addition, Bulgaria guarantees the principle of equal treatment between national and foreign citizens or entities through the 2004 Investment Promotion Act (IPA). Both the Constitution and the IPA guarantee the national treatment of foreign economic operators.

According to the IPA, the Minister of Economy is in charge of the implementation of the law and investment policy in general, in collaboration with central and local authorities (i.e. the regional Governors and the Mayors of the municipalities). In addition, the InvestBulgaria Agency (IBA) assists potential local and foreign investors by providing information, contacts and project management support at all stages of the investment (see Chapter 7 of this *Review*).

Local and foreign investors are also protected against unlawful expropriation, in a non-discriminatory manner. According to the Bulgarian Constitution,[4] expropriation of immovable property may be carried out only in accordance with the procedures laid down in the State Property Act and in the Municipal Property Act, provided that they fulfil state or municipal needs that cannot be otherwise satisfied.

The conditions under which expropriation is allowed are expressly detailed in Bulgarian law (Spatial Development Act, Article 205) and include the construction and redevelopment of physical infrastructure for transport and other networks and facilities (roads, railways, water supply, sanitary sewerage, electricity supply, physical infrastructure for the deployment of electronic communications networks); implementation of environmental and natural resources protection activities, actions to remove and eliminate geologic hazards; construction of public health care facilities, social assistance facilities, educational establishments; construction of special-purpose installations related to national defence and security; and construction of industrial zones or technological parks with the technical infrastructure necessary to attract investments. Expropriation may be undertaken only after providing previous monetary compensation (State Property Act, Article 32, para. 1).

Investment promotion

As further detailed in Chapter 6 of this *Review*, Bulgaria's investment framework contains several investment promotion mechanisms, applicable to both national and foreign investors and in line with the requirements of the National Treatment instrument. Investment projects in industry and services that meet certain criteria may apply for a "Certificate for investment project" from the Ministry of Economy. This certificate entitles the investor to a number of administrative and financial incentives, such as: partial reimbursement of the obligatory social and health insurance contributions; shortened terms for administrative service; and financial support for technical and professional development.[5] Both the IPA and its implementation rules clarify the steps that investors must follow to obtain the required certification and indicate a number of priority sectors for the country.[6] The assignment of these certificates is based on objective criteria, depending on the type of investment envisaged and the priority Bulgaria has given to each sector. It does not take into account the nationality of the investor, allowing for non-discriminatory allocation of investment preferences. This is reflected in the great number of Certified Investment Projects in Bulgaria granted to companies with some form of foreign participation over the years.[7]

Investments can also benefit from incentives through the Corporate Income Tax Act, which provides for tax relief constituting *de minimis* aids and regional aids (Articles 184, 188-189) for investments in underemployed regions. These tax reliefs are in line with EU state aid legislation and do not discriminate against third country investors.

Transparency requirements

As for transparency, all investors (Bulgarians and foreigners) have the right to participate in public consultations and access public information, in line with the Access to Public Information Act (APIA). Public consultations are set as an obligatory stage before adopting primary and secondary legislation, both at national and sub-national (local) level[8] and before the adoption of administrative decisions by the council of ministers.[9] Although the authorities may make specific requests to local authorities and organisations, any person, regardless of their nationality, may participate in these consultation processes. In addition, Bulgaria introduced in 2016 a regulatory impact assessment (RIA) requirement system, whereby regulatory proposals are subject to either a partial or full assessment. The RIA examines the ratio of defined goals to expected results and can also be performed after the adoption of the law. All approved laws are available online in English, as well as all acts (decisions and determinations) of the Bulgarian Commission on Protection of Competition.

As discussed later in this *Review*, selected investment proposals are subject to an Environmental Impact Assessment (EIA), mandatory for any investment in infrastructure, energy, minerals, chemicals, pharmaceutical products, transport, water resources and tourism (Annex I of the Environmental Protection Act). The final decision on the EIA is taken by the Ministry of Environment and Water or the regional inspectorates for the environment and water (RIEW), including vast participation with local authorities, non-Governmental Organisations (NGO's) and stakeholder consultations, with no discrimination of treatment based on nationality. All EIA decisions are made public through the national mass communication media and the Internet site of the Ministry or RIEW. Intra-EU public participation is also mandatory for decisions concerning the deliberate release of genetically modified organisms (GMOs).

General applications for access to information can be submitted electronically by email, and a register of written and oral applications for access to public information can be found directly on the IBA English website.[10] Transparency requirements from the part of the investor are also taken into account by Bulgarian authorities when granting the benefits deriving from the "Certificate for investment project", in accordance with the requirements of EU State Aid Regulation and Bulgarian law.[11]

Bulgaria is open to foreign direct investment

Bulgaria is largely open to FDI. National treatment of foreign investors in the post-establishment phase is guaranteed, which means that foreign investors, when incorporated and headquartered in Bulgaria, are considered domestic legal entities, with all the rights and obligations that are applied to domestic investors. The existing exceptions to national treatment are limited to foreign ownership restrictions in a handful of sectors, namely in the acquisition of non-agricultural and agricultural land, forestry, air and maritime transport and legal services as well as restrictions for the provision of rail transport and mining.

Other barriers to foreign direct investment mainly concern conditions imposed at establishment (e.g. establishment requirements for investment in energy, private security, legal services and selected financial services), fall outside the remit of the Investment *Declaration*. These barriers are few, mostly sector-specific, and typically limited in their scope, applying almost exclusively to investors from outside the EU, the European Economic Area (EEA) or Switzerland, or to investors from countries that are not WTO members.

There are no generalised screening or approval mechanisms for new investments or established companies in Bulgaria and the only horizontal exception to national treatment is related to the foreign acquisition of land (for commercial purposes and real estate) in Bulgaria for investors from outside the European Union and the European Economic Area (EU/EEA). Bulgaria does not impose limits on access to local finance and incentives (e.g. tax concessions) or government purchasing markets for foreign-controlled enterprises incorporated in the territory.

As a result, Bulgaria's degree of restrictiveness is low in comparison to both the OECD average and the average of non-OECD economies that have adhered to the *Declaration*, according to the OECD *FDI Regulatory Restrictiveness Index* (FDI Index) (Figure 4.1). The FDI Index measures statutory restrictions on foreign direct investment in 22 economic sectors across 69 countries, including all OECD and

G20 countries. In comparison with other 25 EU member states covered by the FDI Index, Bulgaria is in the third quartile of most restrictive EU economies to FDI.

Figure 4.1. OECD FDI Regulatory Restrictiveness Index, 2019

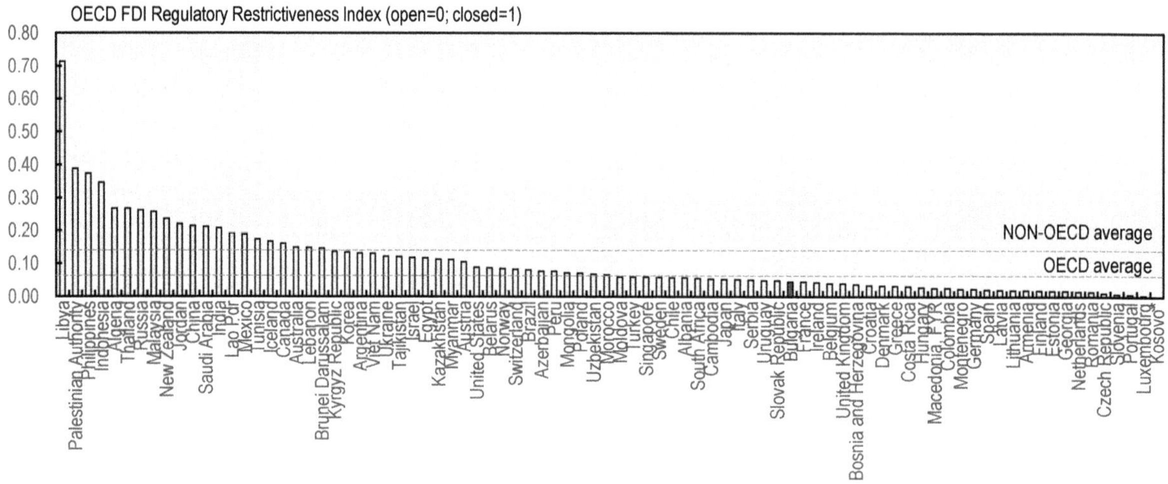

Note: The OECD *FDI Regulatory Restrictiveness Index* covers only statutory measures discriminating against foreign investors (e.g. foreign equity limits, screening and approval procedures, restriction on key foreign personnel, and other operational measures). Other important aspects of an investment climate (e.g. the implementation of regulations and state monopolies, preferential treatment for export-oriented investors and SEZ regimes among other) are not considered. Data reflect regulatory restrictions as of end-December 2019. For Bulgaria, information reflects the regulatory environment as of June 2020. Please refer to Kalinova et al. (2010) for further information on the methodology.
Source: OECD FDI Regulatory Restrictiveness Index, www.oecd.org/investment/fdiindex.htm.

Bulgaria also compares generally well on a sectoral basis against the OECD average, except in agriculture and legal services where foreign ownership limitations apply (Figure 4.2). The horizontal restrictions on the acquisition of land by foreign investors, even if for business purposes, explains the slightly more restrictive environment for FDI in a few other sectors. As such, any particular difficulty in attracting FDI into Bulgaria is unlikely related to the regulatory environment for foreign investors.

All the measures constituting statutory barriers to FDI are further discussed below. Bulgaria's list of measures constituting an exception to national treatment at national and territorial level is reported in Annex A of this *Review*. Annex B contains the list of measures reported for transparency reasons (e.g. measures based on national security considerations, as well as non-discriminatory corporate organisation requirements, and public and private monopolies and concessions). For clarity, measures restricting investments by natural persons are not reported because the OECD NTi does not cover these.

Figure 4.2. OECD FDI Regulatory Restrictiveness Index, 2019: Sector breakdown

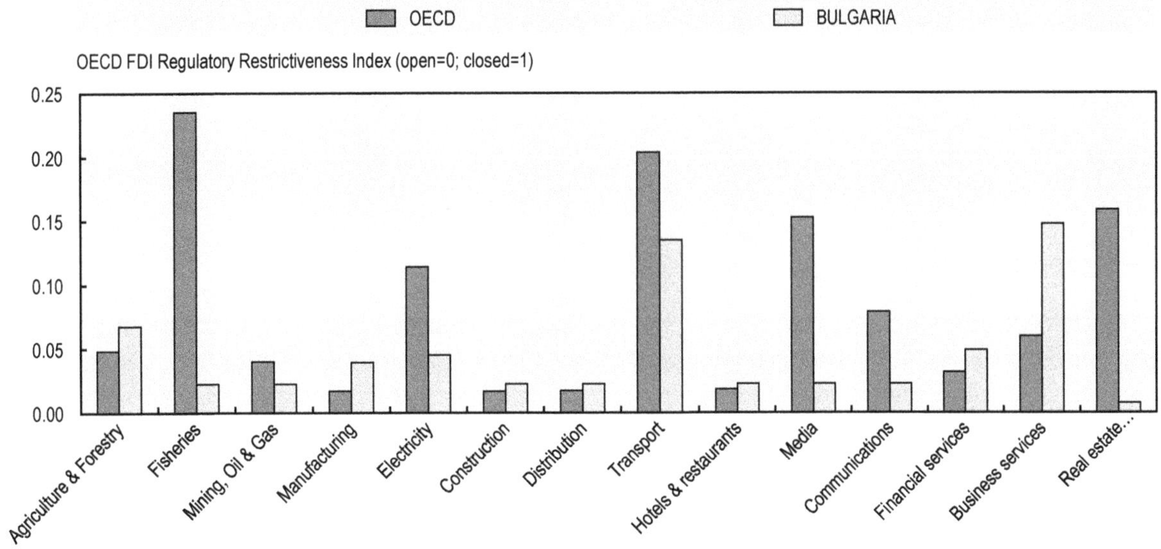

Note: See Figure 4.1.
Source: OECD FDI Regulatory Restrictiveness Index, www.oecd.org/investment/fdiindex.htm

Cross-sectoral measures affecting foreign investment

Bulgaria has no cross-sectoral exception to national treatment. Existing trans-sectoral measure is limited to entry conditions for non-EU/EEA investors for land acquisition and ownership.

Foreign acquisition of land is restricted in Bulgaria

The issue of acquisition and use of land has been of primordial importance for Bulgaria ever since its independence from the Ottoman Empire in the late 19th century. Between 1 878 and 1946 almost 80% of the Bulgarian population consisted of small, predominantly subsistence farmers, with 1 million production units owning on average 4.3 hectares of land each (Csaki et al., 2000). Following the end of World War II, the government abolished the previous concept of property of land. Small farms were grouped into large state-controlled units ran by co-operatives, known as "agro-industrial complexes" and other types of land such as real estate was labelled as "personal property", allowing Bulgarian citizens to own residential property in their city or town of residence (Parusheva and Marcheva, 2010). It was not until the end of the socialist regime that property rights to land in Bulgaria were protected by the Constitution (Articles 21 and 22 of the 1991 Constitution). Collective farms were officially disbanded in 1991 and property rights for land returned to the families that held them prior to collectivisation (Meurs and Bogushev, 2008).

On 1 January 2012, companies established in EU/EEA Member States were allowed to acquire real estate land (for commercial purposes or housing) in Bulgaria. For third country foreigners, acquisition of real estate and land remains restricted. Companies established outside the EU/EEA can only acquire land (for real estate and business purposes) by virtue of an international treaty or by inheritance. To date, Bulgaria has not concluded any international treaty with third countries providing for the acquisition of land. However, foreigners may bypass these restrictions by incorporating a company in Bulgaria, in which case the company will be treated as a Bulgarian national. Bulgaria imposes additional restrictions for the acquisition of agricultural land by foreign investors, which are detailed below.

Sector-specific measures affecting foreign investment

The sector-specific exceptions to the NTi notified by Bulgaria apply to non-EU/EEA investors in the areas of acquisition and ownership of agricultural land, forestry, air transport, maritime and inland waterway transport, rail transport, legal services and mining (see Annex A to this *Review*). Other sector-specific measures discussed below refer to measures imposing conditions on the establishment of foreign investors in Bulgaria. While not covered by the NTi, they constitute statutory barriers to entry and are covered in the OECD *FDI Regulatory Restrictiveness Index.*

Acquisition and ownership of agricultural land

The Treaty of Accession to the European Union required Bulgaria to lift restrictions on the acquisition of agricultural land by nationals and legal entities of other Member States after a period of seven years from 01 January 2007. Accordingly, in 2014, Bulgaria substantially amended the Bulgarian Ownership and Use of Agricultural Land Act 1991,[12] to allow for the following legal entities to acquire and own agricultural land in Bulgaria:

- Commercial companies in which shareholders are:
  - Nationals from EU/EEA countries;
  - Foreign legal entities established in the EU/EEA; and
  - Natural and legal persons from third countries with whom Bulgaria has concluded an international treaty containing provisions on the acquisition of agricultural land.[13]

Companies in which shareholders fail to meet such qualifications, as well as companies with bearer shares and companies in which shareholders are, directly or indirectly, legal entities registered in jurisdictions with preferential tax regimes are not allowed to acquire or own agricultural land in Bulgaria.

In addition, acquisition of agricultural land by foreign companies requires a mandatory five-year establishment in Bulgaria (Article 3c of the Bulgarian Ownership and Use of Agricultural Land Act). This provision has been the subject of an infringement procedure by the European Commission since March 2015.[14]

Pursuant to a Decision of the National Assembly of 19 September 2017 (SG, issue 77 of 2017), amended by a Decision of 12 October 2018 (SG, issue 85 of 2018) and a Decision of 27 February 2019 (SG, issue 19 of 2019), a draft Law on Agricultural Lands has been prepared. At the beginning of November 2019, the bill was published for public discussion on the website of the Ministry of Agriculture, Food and Forestry and on the Public Consultation Portal and was submitted for interdepartmental co-ordination. Given the need to comply with the legislative framework in the field of agriculture with the requirements of the new Common Agricultural Policy, with a Decision of the National Assembly of 18 December 2019, the deadline for drafting the bill has been extended.

Forestry

The Bulgarian state enjoys exclusive ownership rights over the vast majority of forests located in the country (Bulgarian Constitution, Article 18). Nonetheless, certain wooded areas are open to acquisition and exploitation by EU and EEA companies, as established in the Forestry Act.

Non-EU/EEA foreign legal persons may acquire wooded areas pursuant to the provisions of an international treaty in accordance with Article 22 of the Constitution, as well as by way of legal inheritance (Article 23.5 of the Forestry Act). To date there are no such international treaties concluded with third countries. In the absence of such treaty, foreigners that have acquired ownership right of wooded areas by way of legal inheritance must, within three years from discovery of such inheritance, transfer ownership thereof to Bulgarian or EU/EEA persons or companies entitled to acquire such properties (Article 24 of the

Forestry Act). Third-country foreigners may nevertheless bypass these restrictions by incorporating a company in Bulgaria, in which case the company will be treated as a Bulgarian national.

As for the activity of wood processing in Bulgaria, it is usually reserved to incumbent wood processors, since wood in State-owned forest areas (the vast majority of forests) can only be obtained through auctions. According to the Ordinance on the control and protection of forest areas (Number 1 of 30 January 2012, Article 13) only registered wood processors can participate in auctions for the purchase, processing and use of wood from state-owned forests. In order to determine if a company qualifies as a "wood processor", it must submit a proof of the volume of processed wood during the previous calendar year, in a registered establishment inside Bulgaria. Although this requirement grants an advantage to locally established firms, foreign investors face no restrictions for the acquisition of a Bulgarian wood-processing firm.

Air transport

Bulgaria maintains restrictions for enterprises that are majority-owned by foreign investors, other than EU/EEA investors, to obtain an air transport license and to manage and operate civilian airports.

Restrictions to obtain an air transport license derive from EU Regulation 1008/2008, which states that airlines licensed to operate in an EU country must be majority owned and effectively controlled by EU Member States or nationals of an EU member country, unless otherwise provided for through an international agreement to which the EU is a signatory (Articles 3 and 4).

Bulgaria has transposed EU Regulation 1008/2008 into the Civil Aviation Act of 1972, under which licenses for the provision of air transport can only be granted to companies where at least half plus one of the shareholders are EU/EEA Member States or EU/EEA nationals (Article 64). In addition, air transport companies and companies dedicated to the management and operation of civilian airports in Bulgaria must be controlled, directly or indirectly by EU/EEA Member States or EU/EEA nationals (further detailed in the section on Corporate organisation and key personnel).

The air transport sector showed substantive growth after Bulgaria's accession to the EU, due to the development of business and tourism industries and targeted investment policy. Bulgaria's aircraft fleet was updated and the international airports in Sofia, Varna and Burgas underwent modernisation programs to improve their competitiveness through the EU funded 2014-20 Operational Programme on Transport (OPT).[15]

Maritime and inland waterways transport

There are two main international ports on the Bulgarian coast: the port of Varna and the port of Burgas. These ports and their adjacent terminals are open to international freight traffic, without any differentiation as to who owns the freight. As for internal water transport, the four major river ports on the Danube have open access for foreign vessels and foreign shipping companies, with restrictions for the provision of inland water services (cabotage). Since Bulgaria's accession to the EU, extensive investment has been dedicated to modernise logistic, navigational and information systems for the Black Sea and the Danube River, improving navigation conditions and reducing the risk of incidents.[16]

Transportation within the territory of Bulgaria (cabotage) can be provided only by vessels using the Bulgarian flag or that of an EU country (Shipping Merchant Code, Article 6). Third-countries may only provide these services by entering into an international treaty with Bulgaria or, in the absence of such treaty, via a decision of the Council of Ministers. At present Bulgaria is not a party to any international treaty permitting vessels from third countries to provide transportation within the territory of Bulgaria (cabotage). In addition, such a permission has not been granted by the Council of Ministers to any third country.

The Shipping Merchant Code provides that the Bulgarian flag is to be granted only to vessels that are: i) property of the Bulgarian State; ii) property of Bulgarian or EU natural or legal persons; iii) more than 50% owned by a Bulgarian natural or legal person (Article 27).

Third-country foreigners may own a vessel flying the Bulgarian flag by incorporating a company in Bulgaria, in which case the company will be treated as a Bulgarian national. This is also the case for enterprises providing maritime services, which must be incorporated in Bulgaria, however with no limitations for foreign investors to own or manage the enterprise established in Bulgaria.

Since the registration and incorporation requirements for non-EU investors are considered pre-establishment requirements, this is, they do not entail a differentiated treatment to foreigners once established in the country through a Bulgarian legal person, measures are covered in the OECD *FDI Regulatory Restrictiveness Index*.

Rail transport

Railway infrastructure in Bulgaria is managed by the National Railway Infrastructure Company, which is a state-owned enterprise. Foreign railway operators licensed and certified in an EU Member State have the right to carry out passenger and/or freight transportation by rail, and to access the relevant infrastructure of Bulgaria. Railway operators licensed by a third country railway administration may use the Bulgarian railway infrastructure to conduct its transportation services if so provided in an international agreement ratified by Bulgaria (Article 43, Paragraph 2 of Railway Transport Act). No such agreement has been concluded or ratified by Bulgaria, thus no non-EU/EEA railway operators is allowed to conduct railway transportation services in the country.

Although Bulgaria's railway density is relatively high – with 500 km of railway network per million inhabitants and 1 189 km2 of lines per 10 000 km2, above the EU average of 437 km per million inhabitants and over 500 km^2 of lines per 10 000 km^2 (Global Mass Transit, 2017),[17] as noted in Chapter 3 of this *Review*, considerable parts of the railway lines have been constructed more than 60 years ago and are suitable for speeds of only up to 100 km/h. In recent years, financial assistance from the EU has helped improve the technical conditions of Bulgaria's railway infrastructure. In addition, network connections with neighbouring countries are being improved, as for example the creation of a railway link with the Republic of North Macedonia expected to be concluded before 2027. For the period 2015-19, the annual funding from the EU dedicated to railway infrastructure was estimated at approximately EUR 140 million according to the 2014-20 Operational Programme on Transport (OPT).[18]

Energy – electricity market

Since 1999, with the establishment of the State Energy and Water Regulatory Commission (SEWRC), Bulgaria has been engaged in energy sector reforms to improve its energy efficiency and related infrastructure. The state-owned national electricity company (NEK) was divided into six independent generators, a national transmission system operator and seven regional distribution system operators. Between 2002 and 2012, most of the government-owned electricity generation and distribution businesses were privatised (CMS Sofia, 2015).

In 2007, Bulgaria liberalised the access to its energy and electricity market for foreign investors, requiring only an operating licence by SWERC, in accordance with the Energy Act (Articles 39 and 40). Among the requirements for the license, companies must be registered or have an incorporated subsidiary either in Bulgaria or in another EU Member State. Incorporated foreign-controlled enterprises are treated equally with domestically owned firms in this matter. At the time of writing this *Review*, there were 239 licensed electricity companies incorporated in Bulgaria or other EU member countries, many of them fully controlled by third-country foreign interests. Since there is no restriction for foreign investors to incorporate a Bulgarian company, there is no exception to national treatment as reported in Annex A.

Mining

Bulgaria allows for foreign investment in mining, with certain restrictions. A permit or concession is necessary for the prospecting, exploration or extraction of natural resources, including thorium ores.

Companies registered in preferential tax treatment jurisdictions and those related, directly or indirectly, to such companies are not allowed to participate in open procedures for mining permits or concessions, and to operate an existing permit or concession. This restriction extends to the registration of geological or commercial discoveries of a deposit, as a result of exploration.[19]

Bulgaria forbids hydraulic fracturing technology or fracking for activities of prospecting, exploration or extraction of oil and gas, both for nationals and for foreigners (Decision of the National Assembly of the Republic of Bulgaria of 18 January 2012). Other mining-related activities not allowed in Bulgaria include the exploration and extraction of shale gas (ISIC Rev. 3.1 10, 3.1 11, 3.112, 3.1 13, 3.1 14) and the extraction and processing of uranium ores (Council of Ministers Decree 163 of 20 August 1992). Since these restrictions are non-discriminatory, they do not entail a departure from national treatment and therefore are not listed as exceptions to the National Treatment instrument in Annex A.

Professional services (legal services)

Investment in companies providing legal services is not authorised, neither to Bulgarians nor to foreigners.[20] This is a non-discriminatory restriction and as such, it does not entail an exception under the NTi. Enterprises providing legal consultancy services (law firms) and partnerships can only be created by groups of lawyers authorised to practice in Bulgaria, the EU/EEA or Switzerland. In addition, law firms must be locally incorporated and registered in the Bar Council (Bar Act, Articles 57 and 61).

Private security services

According to the Law on Private Security Activities, in order to provide such services, companies must be incorporated, headquartered and licensed in Bulgaria for such purposes (Article 2.2.1); companies incorporated, headquartered and licensed in another EU/EEA Member State or Switzerland may carry out private security activities after obtaining a certification by the competent Bulgarian authorities that they comply with the requirements of the Law (Article 2.2.2). The requirements for obtaining this certificate are similar to those for obtaining a licence (Section III of the Ordinance 8121з-610 of 11 June 2018) and must include an address in Bulgaria. (Article 2.2.2). Third-country foreigners may establish a company in Bulgaria, which, when incorporated and headquartered in Bulgaria, is considered a domestic legal entity, with all the rights and obligations that are applied to domestic investors. This company can apply to obtain a license as per Article 2.2.1 of the Law.

Financial services (banking, insurance, private pension and other financial services)

Financial services in Bulgaria are generally open to foreign investment. Restrictions refer to conditions on the establishment of non-EU/EEA foreign investors in Bulgaria. While not covered by the NTi, they constitute statutory barriers to entry and are covered in the OECD *FDI Regulatory Restrictiveness Index*.

For banking, the Law on Credit Institutions governs the terms and procedures for granting licenses, conducting activities and supervising the compliance with the prudential requirements and termination of credit institutions (banks).[21] Foreign legal persons are allowed to acquire or incorporate a credit institution in Bulgaria without any market entry restriction, as well as to establish branches subject to authorisation by the Bulgarian National Bank (BNB), after meeting the corresponding prudential and financial requirements. EU/EEA credit institutions are not subject to authorisation by the BNB, in line with the single passport rules.

Before the transition to a market economy, the BNB performed almost all of the functions in the banking market, acting as a commercial bank and a central bank simultaneously. In the 1990s, a number of commercial banks were created, albeit all state-owned. It was only until 2003 that Bulgaria privatised the banking sector, attracting a large number of foreign investors and large international banks. According to BNB official data, by December 2020, there were 25 banks operating in Bulgaria, seven of them foreign bank branches. The market share of domestic banks was 22.4% by December 2020 while the share of EU subsidiaries was of 74.5% (BNB, 2020).

For insurance, according to the Insurance Code, foreign legal persons are allowed to register a branch or to acquire or incorporate an insurance company in Bulgaria through a joint stock company registered under the Law on Commerce, a co-operative registered under the Law on Co-operatives or an EU/EEA insurer under the terms and conditions of the freedom of establishment or freedom of services. Insurance companies established in another EU/EEA country benefit from the single passport system and do not need to apply for an additional authorisation to offer their services in Bulgaria. As of the date of the *Review*, there are no branches of non-EU/EEA insurance undertakings in Bulgaria.

Non EU-EEA insurance undertakings require a license by the Financial Supervision Commission (FSC) under the terms and conditions of the Insurance Code (Article 12). The FSC may refuse the authorisation based on reciprocity, if the competent authority in the country where the headquarters of the insurer is based does not give access to Bulgarian insurers to the respective foreign insurance market (Article 58). This reciprocity requirement is not binding and has never been applied in practice. More importantly, the requirement is inoperable, as it is not compatible with Bulgaria's MFN obligations under the GATS, which take precedence over Bulgarian law under the Constitution as well as under the Insurance Code itself (Article 9 of the Insurance Code) (OECD, 2020c).

For private pensions, the provision of services is limited to companies established in Bulgaria, the EU and EEA, and with previous authorisation by the FSC (Art. 121 of the Social Insurance Code). Legal entities registered in a country outside the EU/EEA may incorporate a subsidiary in Bulgaria if: a) they are established as a joint stock company with a minimum capital of BGN 7.5 million, fully paid-up (Article 121, Article 121c (2) and (3)); b) its shareholders are Bulgarian or EU/EEA natural persons and legal entities, or third-country legal entities registered in their country of origin as a social insurance, insurance or other financial institution, subject to specialised financial supervision (Art. 121b). Branching is not allowed.

For other financial services, foreign investment is authorised, provided they obtain the relevant licence by the FSC. Cross-border services are not allowed by companies established outside the EU/EEA. Restrictions exist for foreign-owned companies providing financial services as a management company[22] or as an investment firm,[23] which must be registered as branches, and for depositories of undertakings for collective investment in transferable securities (UCITS) which must be incorporated in Bulgaria or another EU/EEA country, as required by EU law.[24]

Other policies affecting foreign-established companies that may have an impact on the investment climate

Other policies applied by Bulgaria, while not discriminating between foreign-controlled enterprises and domestic enterprises, may have an impact on the investment climate by potentially imposing a greater burden on established foreign controlled-enterprises. Policies on corporate organisation and key personnel may be more burdensome to comply for foreign-owned companies, which count with fewer local contacts. Likewise, policies based on public order and essential security considerations or the existence of public, private, or mixed monopolies may restrain access to certain sectors of national interest. As such, they are important determinants in the context of national treatment. Such measures are notified for transparency purposes by a country adhering to the OECD Declaration.

Bulgaria has reported only a few measures for transparency purposes under the NTi (see Annex B). These are related to conditions imposed for the safekeeping of essential security concerns; restrictions on the management and organisation of companies dedicated to air transport and civil airports, maritime and inland waterways transport, private security services, banking and private pensions; as well as a few sectors which are kept under public monopoly. These measures are further detailed below.

Essential security concerns

International instruments such as the OECD *Declaration* and the OECD *Guidelines for Recipient Country Investment Policies relating to National Security* recognise countries' rights to regulate and manage potential risks for the host country's national security or public order.

Although Bulgaria does not have a horizontal national security review mechanism, the existing legal framework provides for monitoring investment in critical infrastructure, which might pose a threat to its national security. Following the enactment of EU Regulation 2019/452, which establishes a framework for the screening of FDI into the EU, Bulgaria made a review of existing legislation and control mechanisms in force, which secure the protection of national interests of Bulgaria. After consultations with the relevant ministries and agencies, Bulgaria confirmed in June 2020 that the existing legal framework provides enough opportunities for monitoring of the investment in critical infrastructure, in accordance to Article 4 of Regulation 2019/452. No further changes to Bulgaria's legislation are envisaged to occur in the near future.

Bulgarian national security interests and priorities are detailed in the Updated National Security Strategy of the Republic of Bulgaria, adopted by the National Assembly in March 2018. For reasons of public order, safety and essential security, Bulgaria maintains a number of authorisation requirements to conduct the following activities, which can be performed exclusively by Bulgarians and traders incorporated in the EU/EEA and Switzerland:

- Fire safety of facilities and/or maintenance and servicing of devices, systems and installations related to fire safety, such as firefighting, firefighting maintenance[25] (Article 129 of the Ministry of Interior Act).
- Activities covered under the Weapons, Ammunition, Explosives and Pyrotechnical Products Act. This Act provides for authorisation regimes in connection with the manufacturing, trading, acquisition, safekeeping, carrying and use, transportation, import, export and transit, repair, discarding, destruction and utilisation of explosives, weapons, ammunition and pyrotechnical products.
- Activities covered under the Defence-Related Products and Dual – Use Items and Technologies Export Control Act of 2011. This act regulates the terms and procedures for export, import, transfer, transport, passage, carriage and transit of defence-related products and dual-use items import, brokering services with defence-related products and dual-use items and the control over such activities.
- Private security activities in accordance with the Law on Private Security Activities.

Corporate organisation and key personnel

Bulgaria imposes conditions on the corporate organisation and key personnel of companies operating in air transport, management and operation of civil airports, maritime and inland waterways transport, as well as private security services.

For air transport, companies must be effectively controlled, directly or indirectly by EU/EEA Member States or EU/EEA nationals; this is, they must exercise a decisive influence on the process of making decisions relevant to the operation and business of the company. These measures are also applicable to the management and operation of civilian airports in Bulgaria (Article 48c of the Civil Aviation Act).

Maritime and inland waterways transport companies must employ ship crew consisting of qualified seafarers, of which Bulgarian citizens must account for minimum 25% of the management and operational functions and 25% of the support level functions. In addition, the master and the chief engineer of a vessel must be Bulgarian citizens or citizens of the EU/EEA or Switzerland (Bulgarian Merchant Shipping Code, Article 88).

As for private security services, persons working as security guards or security guard manager must be citizens of Bulgaria, EU/EEA or Switzerland (Article 50 of the Law on Private Security Activities).

In addition, in the area of financial services, although Bulgaria does not impose any restrictions in terms of employment of key foreign personnel, at least one of the two required managers of a bank providing services in Bulgaria must be fluent in Bulgarian language (Article 10(1) of the Law on Credit Institutions). This same requirement applies for private pensions companies (Article 121f. of the SIC). This is considered a prudential requirement imposed on both foreign-owned and Bulgarian-owned companies.

Activities covered by public, private, mixed monopolies or concessions

Public monopolies

A number of activities are reserved to the Republic of Bulgaria as reported by the Bulgarian authorities in the framework of this *Review* (Table 4.1):

Table 4.1. List of public monopolies (2020)

Bulgargaz EAD*
Bulgartransgaz EAD**
Electricity System Operator EAD
National Railway Infrastructure Company (NRIC)
Independent Bulgarian Energy Exchange EAD
National Electricity Company EAD
State Enterprise radioactive waste (SERAW)
National Health Insurance Fund

Notes: *Bulgargaz EAD is the biggest natural gas wholesale company in Bulgaria.
**Natural gas transmission and storage operator and a subsidiary of Bulgarian Energy Holding EAD.
Source: OECD Secretariat, (2020) based on Bulgaria's replies to the adherence review questionnaires.

In addition, Bulgaria maintains ownership in several companies in areas related to infrastructure and distribution in electricity and gas markets as well as in railways and postal services.[26] These companies are detailed in Annex 1 to the Privatization and Post-privatisation Control Act (adopted on 19 March 2002 and as amended on 18 February 2020), which includes 179 SOEs and nine facilities in which the Bulgarian State holds more than a 50% interest. The protection of strategic companies owned by the Bulgarian state is ensured through their inclusion in the list, approved by the National Assembly, of companies not subject to privatisation. This list includes key companies from different economic sectors, including the national defence, technological and industrial. The Privatisation and Post-privatisation Control Law contains a restricting list of state companies not subject to privatisation.

Monopoly positions in Bulgaria may be granted only by law in the sectors listed in the Constitution, any other kind of granting of monopoly position is null and void (Art.19 (2) and (3) of the Law on Protection of Competition).

Concessions

Concessions play a central role in the provision of public services in Bulgaria. Concessions are time-bound and regulated through the 2018 Concession Act, which transposed Directive 2014/23/EU on the award of concession contracts. There are no restrictions to foreign-owned companies to participate in a concession process and be awarded a concession.

The Concession Act provides for non-discriminatory regulations for the participation in tender procedures and awarding of contracts. Currently, most concessions have been granted in the area of infrastructure and services in the field of transport and mineral water extraction. Public information is available directly at the National Concessions Register[27] of the Ministry of Transport and the Council of Ministers[28] (OECD, 2020c).

At the time of writing this *Review*, Bulgaria had awarded concessions to established foreign-owned companies for projects in the protected area of the Pirin National Park, which is subject to exclusive state property, as well as for the administration of Rosenets Port Terminal (part of the Burgas public transport port of national importance), and the Burgas and Varna civil airports. There were also concession contracts with foreign investors' participation in the field of extraction of mineral resources.

Procurement process below the EU thresholds are regulated by the Public Procurement Act (PPA) of 2016. Public contracts are awarded in accordance with the principles of the Treaty on the Functioning of the European Union (TFEU), more precisely with those regarding the free movement of goods, the freedom of establishment, the freedom to provide services, mutual recognition, as well as the principles deriving therefrom, such as equal treatment and non-discrimination, free competition, proportionality, publicity and transparency (Article 2, para. 1 of the PPA). Public procurement rules cover the acquisition of works, supplies or services by means of a public contract (whether they are implemented through purchase, leasing or other contractual forms).

According to Article 10 of the PPA, tenderers and candidates in procurement procedures may be Bulgarian and foreign natural and legal persons, groups (including temporary associations) of such persons, as well as other entities that have the right to supply goods, services and works under the legislation of the state where they are established. Branches of foreign companies may also be independent candidates or tenderers in a procurement procedure, provided that they are authorised to submit requests for participation or tenders and to sign contracts under the legislation of the state where they are established (Article 36, para 1 of the Rules for Implementation of the Public Procurement Act).

Starting and operating a company nevertheless remain cumbersome according to business surveys

While an open environment for foreign investment is important, this is not the only incentive to which investors respond to. Foreign investors are equally affected by deficiencies in the overall business environment impinging on domestic investors as well. Although Bulgaria has a fairly open regime for international investment according to the OECD *FDI Regulatory Restrictiveness Index*, and exceptions under the OECD NTi are limited, Bulgaria suffers from onerous business regulations that create regulatory barriers to firm entry and competition higher than most OECD countries based on the product market regulation (PMR) indicators (OECD, 2020b).[29]

This is in line with the findings of similar exercises, such as the World Bank's *Doing Business* indicators, where Bulgaria ranked 61st out of 190 countries in the 2020 edition, dropping two places from the previous report and being among the lower third in comparison with other EU countries, only above Greece, Luxembourg and Malta. When compared with non-OECD countries that are Adherents to the OECD *Declaration*, Bulgaria was in 2020 behind countries such as Croatia at 51, Morocco at 53 and Romania at

55, while being above Brazil at 124, Egypt at 114, Peru at 76, and Ukraine at 64. Bulgaria performs particularly poorly in the areas of starting a business and getting electricity, where it ranks, respectively, 113 and 151 out of 190 economies.[30] In some other areas, Bulgaria has achieved moderate improvements, but these have not been sufficient to improve its ranking as other countries have also progressed.

While *Doing Business* – which addresses ten business regulatory areas such as starting a business, dealing with construction permits and enforcing contracts – should not be construed as an overall measure of the investment climate, Bulgaria's relative poor performance, in particular in comparison with other EU countries, suggests that, despite reforms and on-going improvements, there is room for rendering administrative procedures speedier, more transparent and effective, and for improving the overall quality and transparency of public governance. This is attested by interviews with foreign and domestic investors conducted by the OECD as part of this *Review* where concerns were raised about administrative burdens in terms of time and costs and state-intervention in the economy. Businesses have been especially critical concerning the time spent on informing different parts of the government administration on various commercial operations and exiting a business, which they have seen as making day-to-day business activities cumbersome.

Table 4.2. Bulgaria in current international rankings (2019-20)

Indicator	Rank	Past Ranking
OECD Product market regulation (PMR) Index	1.93 (index scale 0 to 6)	1.57 in 2013
Doing Business 2020 edition (World Bank)	61/190	59/190 in 2019
Starting a business	113	99
Dealing with construction permits	43	37
Getting electricity	151	147
Registering property	66	67
Getting credit	67	60
Protecting minority investors	25	33
Paying taxes	97	92
Trading across borders	21	21
Enforcing contracts	42	42
Resolving insolvency	61	56
Global Competiveness Index Report 2019 (WEF)	49/141	51/140 in 2018
First pillar: institutions	57	70
Second pillar: infrastructure	56	58
Third pillar: ICT adoption	30	30
Fourth pillar: macroeconomic stability	43	52
2021 Corruption Perceptions Index (Transparency International)	78/180 in 2021	76/180 in 2020

Note: The OECD Product Market Regulation Index is updated every five years. OECD average for the year 2019 is of 1.38 (with the five most competition-friendly countries scoring 1.00 and the five least competition-friendly countries 1.82).
Source: Compiled by OECD Secretariat (2021-2022).

Bulgaria also suffers from relatively high levels of corruption, particularly with respect to concession and public procurement processes. While important steps have been taken to fight corruption in Bulgaria as further discussed in Chapter 7 of this *Review*, perceived corruption remains relatively high: According to one of the latest EBRD/World Bank Business Environment and Enterprise Performance (BEEPS) surveys, corruption was identified by Bulgarian firms as one of the top five business environment obstacles. In the latest (December 2021) Transparency International's Corruption Perception Index, Bulgaria was ranked 78th among 180 countries. For sure, when compared with other non-OECD countries that are Adherents to the *Declaration on International Investment,* Bulgaria is above countries such as Egypt (116th),

Kazakhstan (102nd) and Ukraine (122nd). It is nevertheless below other Adherents to the *Declaration* such as Argentina (96th), Croatia (63rd), and Romania (66th). As further discussed in Chapters 7 and 8 of this *Review*, continued progress in the fight against corruption remains essential for Bulgaria's citizens and businesses.

Outlook and policy recommendations

Bulgaria has an open regime for international investment according to the *OECD FDI Regulatory Restrictiveness Index*, both in comparison to the OECD average and the average of non-OECD economies that have adhered to the *Declaration*. On a sectoral basis, Bulgaria compares generally well against the OECD average, except in agriculture and legal services where foreign ownership restrictions apply, and horizontal restrictions are limited to the acquisition of land by foreign investors. In addition, Bulgaria's exceptions under the OECD *National Treatment instrument* are limited to restrictions in a few activities, mostly for non-EU/EEA investors (e.g. acquisition of commercial, real estate and agricultural land, forestry air transport, maritime and inland waterway transport, rail transport, mining, legal services). Likewise, regulatory barriers to entry are confined to a few sectors, and notably restricted to non-EU/EEA investors.

While an open and transparent environment for foreign investment is important since it expands market opportunities and enhances predictability for investors, this is not the only incentive to which FDI responds to. Foreign investors are equally affected by deficiencies in the overall business environment impinging on domestic investors too. Behind-the-borders regulatory challenges and perceived corruption and favouritism, which affect foreign and domestic investments altogether, should be seen in complement to market access and treatment of foreign investors. These other policies affecting the overall business environment are addressed in the next chapters.

Policy recommendations

- *Continue the reforms and on-going improvements to tackle current difficulties to start and operating a company.* Any particular difficulty in attracting FDI into Bulgaria is unlikely related to the regulatory environment for foreign investors and could point to difficulties in creating and operating a Bulgarian company, which still remain cumbersome according to business surveys, in particular since third-country investors need to incorporate a company in Bulgaria to conduct most business.
- *Evaluate the costs and benefits of continuing to open up the economy to international investment by further reducing the exceptions to the OECD National Treatment instrument.* Discriminatory measures only serve the broader public interest to the extent that their potential costs in terms of forgone investment and efficiency gains are compensated by broader social and economic benefits. For this reason, they need to be constantly re-evaluated to determine whether such restrictions still fulfil their original roles in an efficient manner and no other non-discriminatory alternative measure is available for such purposes. This should include an assessment of the proportionality of the measure to ensure they are not greater than needed to address specific concerns and objectives.

References

Bulgarian National Bank (2020), "Annual Report 2020", Sofia, www.bnb.bg/BankSupervision/BSCreditInstitution/BSCIRegisters/BS_CI_REG_BANKSLIST_EN

CMS Law firm (2015), "CMS Expert Guide to Electricity Bulgaria", Sofia, https://cms.law/en/int/expert-guides/cms-expert-guide-to-electricity/bulgaria

Csaki, Cs., J. Nash, A. Fock, and H. Kray (2000), "Food and Agriculture in Bulgaria: The Challenge of Preparing for EU Accession", *World Bank Technical Paper*, No.481, World Bank, Washington, DC, http://documents1.worldbank.org/curated/en/939501468769886584/pdf/multi-page.pdf

Echandi, R., J. Krajcovicova, C.Z. Qiang (2015), "The impact of investment policy in a changing global economy: a review of the literature", *Policy Research working paper; no. WPS 7437,* World Bank, Washington DC, http://documents.worldbank.org/curated/en/664491467994693599/pdf/WPS7437.pdf

ECORYS, the Netherlands (2006), "Study on Strategic Evaluation on Transport Investment Priorities under Structural and Cohesion funds for the Programming Period 2007-13", in *Country report Bulgaria*, No. 2005.CE.16.0.AT.014, Rotterdam https://ec.europa.eu/regional_policy/sources/docgener/evaluation/pdf/evasltrat_tran/bulgaria.pdf.

European Banking Federation (2019), *Bulgaria's banking sector: Facts & Figures*, Sofia, www.ebf.eu/bulgaria/

Global Mass Transit (2017), "Europe: Rail network density and utilisation rates", in *Global Mass Transit Report,* www.globalmasstransit.net/archive.php?id=24558

Meurs, M. and Bogushev, A. (2008), "Forward to the Past? Agricultural Restructuring in Bulgaria », *Revue géographique des pays méditerranéens*, 110 : 2008, p. 93-104

OECD (2020a), "Acquisition- and ownership-related policies to safeguard essential security interests: current and emerging trends, observed designs, and policy practice in 62 economies", *Research note by the OECD Secretariat*, www.oecd.org/Investment/OECD-Acquisition-ownership-policies-security-May2020.pdf

OECD (2020b), "OECD Product Market Regulation Indicators: How does Bulgaria compare?", *Product Market Regulation Country Note 2018*, https://issuu.com/oecd.publishing/docs/bgr_country_note_-_tot_final

OECD (2020c),"Bulgaria: Position under the OECD Codes of Liberalisation of Capital Movements and of Current Invisible Operations, Note by the Secretariat", unpublished

OECD (2005), *National Treatment for Foreign-Controlled Enterprises: 2005 Edition,* OECD Publishing, Paris, https://doi.org/10.1787/9789264012912-en

Parusheva, D. and L. Marcheva (2010), "Housing in Socialist Bulgaria: Appropriating Tradition", *Home Cultures,* Volume 7, Issue 2, 197-215, www.academia.edu/2387479/Housing_in_Socialist_Bulgaria_Appropriating_Tradition

World Bank (2020), *Doing Business 2020*, Washington, DC, www.doingbusiness.org/en/reports/global-reports/doing-business-2020.

Notes

[1] The Codes of Liberalisation are legally binding instruments regulating inward and outward cross-border capital flows (including investment), as well as the cross-border provision and establishment of financial services. As of November 2021, all 38 OECD members were Adherents to the Codes. Since 2011, non-OECD economies may apply for adherence. As of June 2021, six non-OECD countries were undergoing the process of adherence to the Codes (Argentina, Brazil, Bulgaria, Peru, Romania and South Africa).

[2] English version available at: www.minfin.bg/en/1394.

[3] Article 26, paragraph 2, of the Constitution of Republic of Bulgaria, according to which: "(2) Foreigners residing in the Republic of Bulgaria shall have all the rights and obligations provided for in this Constitution, with the exception of those rights and obligations for which the Constitution and laws require Bulgarian citizenship".

[4] Art.17, para.5 of the Constitution regulates the right of property, with the possibility of lawful expropriation for public purposes, after preliminary and equivalent compensation.

[5] Ministry of Economy of Bulgaria, *Application of the Investment Promotion Act* (more information at: https://mi.government.bg/en/themes/application-of-the-investment-promotion-act-95-284.html).

[6] The investor can receive a certificate for class of investment ("Class A" or "Class B") or a certificate for Priority Project based on the size of the investment, the economic sector and the region in which the investment is implemented.

[7] See the full list of Certified Investment Projects in Bulgaria from 2014-20: www.investbg.government.bg/en/pages/certified-investment-projects-in-bulgaria-217.html.

[8] Through the Bulgarian Portal for Public Consultation (http://strategy.bg/).

[9] Portal for Public Consultations under the CoM (www.strategy.bg/).

[10] InvestBulgaria Agency, www.investbg.government.bg/en.

[11] Regulation (EU) No 651/2014 Article 5; Regulation for the application of the IPA, section V Transparency and observation.

[12] Via Decree 114, adopted by the XLII National Assembly on 4 April 2014, and re-adopted on 29 April 2014. Released in Sofia on 30 April 2014.

[13] The Bulgarian authorities have confirmed that to date there are no such international treaties concluded with third countries.

[14] Due to a potential violation of Articles 49 (freedom of residence) and 63 (movement of capital) of the Treaty on the Functioning of the European Union (TFEU).

[15] EU Commission Implementing Decision C(2014) 10232. Operational programme under the 'Investment for growth and jobs' goal, Transport and Transport Infrastructure, CCI 2014BG16M1OP001.

[16] Op.cit.

[17] Global Mass Transit (2017), "Europe: Rail network density and utilisation rates", http://www.globalmasstransit.net/archive.php?id=24558

[18] EU Commission Implementing Decision C(2014) 10232. Operational programme under the 'Investment for growth and jobs' goal, Transport and Transport Infrastructure, CCI 2014BG16M1OP001 in relation to the 5-year Programme for development and operation of the railway infrastructure.

[19] According to Art. 3, point 7 from the Law on the Economic and Financial Relations with Companies Registered in Preferential Tax Treatment Jurisdictions, with the Persons Controlled by Them and with Their Beneficial Owners, companies registered in preferential tax treatment jurisdictions and persons controlled by them shall not, directly or indirectly, participate in procedures for granting a concession, as well for granting a subsurface resources extraction concession or a permit for prospecting and exploration or for exploration of subsurface resources under the Subsurface Resources Act.

[20] The practice of regulated professions is conditioned on obtaining a license. Measures that discriminate on grounds of nationality the granting of such licenses to foreign natural persons are not taken into account here, unless they also prevent foreign persons from taking a direct investment in the related business. For instance, this may occur when citizenship is required for membership in a professional association with regulatory powers, and such membership is required for practicing such profession and establishing a business for such purposes.

[21] Regulations of the typical banking transactions in Bulgaria are to be found mainly in the Bulgarian Commercial Act, while additional rules concerning credits, financial aids and loan securities are stipulated in the Bulgarian Obligations and Contracts Act.

[22] Article 88 of the Bulgarian Collective Investment Schemes and Other Undertakings for Collective Investments Act.

[23] Article 49, paragraph 1of the Markets in Financial Instruments Act (MFIA)

[24] EU Directive 65/2009/EEC.

[25] As well as anti-fire securing and conducting preventive and organisational events for provision of fire safety in sites; fire-extinguishing activities; rescuing activity; servicing of anti-fire equipment; maintenance and servicing anti-fire systems and facilities.

[26] A list of entities over which Bulgaria exerts control is available from the website of the Bulgarian Ministry of Finance, www.minfin.bg/upload/39707/Juridicheski%20lica%20sektor%20DU.pdf

[27] National Concessions Register

[28] Council of Ministers official webpage:
http://nkrold.government.bg/app?service=external/Browse&sp=206&sp=2832

[29] OECD's PMR Indicators assess the alignment of a country's regulatory framework with internationally accepted best practices. The Economy-wide Indicator measures the distortions to competition that can be induced through the involvement of the State in the economy, as well as the barriers to entry and expansion faced by domestic and foreign firms in different sectors of the economy.

[30] There have been some recent improvements, however, to the process of starting a business. According to the authorities, since 2019 it has been possible for a company to submit electronically a request for VAT registration at the National Revenue Agency together with its application for registration with the Commercial Register. The request is made by simply checking the related field in the application form for registration with the Commercial Register. The Registry Agency transfers the request to the National Revenue Agency automatically, by electronic way, at the moment the company is registered with the Commercial Register. Further improvements are, however, still much needed for streamlining the process of 'starting a business' according to the World Bank's Doing Business 2020 indicator.

5 Investment protection and dispute settlement in Bulgaria

This chapter provides an overview of provisions in both domestic legislation and Bulgaria's international investment agreements offering protections for investors. It looks into the rules of expropriation, contract enforcement and dispute settlement as well as the regimes for intellectual property rights and for access to land. It also reviews Bulgaria's international investment treaty practice and its legal framework for investor-state dispute settlement.

Introduction

The conditions faced by investors both when they establish and in their on-going business operations are only part of the overall investment environment. The previous chapter expanded on Bulgaria's measures in order to attract and retain FDI, as well as measures that might have an adverse effect in fulfilling this purpose (such as foregoing national treatment to foreign investors, this is, granting nationals better conditions to invest and conduct business than foreigners in like circumstances). However, for host economies to reap the benefits of foreign investment, additional policies should be in place to protect investments once established in the host country, allowing for a dual effect of attracting foreign investment and maximising the local benefits of FDI (Alfaro, 2016).

The protection of investment, combined with effective enforcement mechanisms, is an important pillar of a sound investment climate. Protecting investors from improper treatment can lower their perception of risks for new investments, and investors who perceive lower risks will generally make capital and resources available at a lower cost and with longer amortisation periods. Measures to ensure the protection of investments are taken at both domestic and international level. They include improving legal certainty and predictability, guarantees against expropriation, intellectual property rights protection, as well effective access to justice and effective dispute resolution mechanisms. This chapter addresses Bulgaria's measures for the protection of investment, at both the domestic and international level.

Bulgaria's domestic legal framework provides protection for investors in line with other EU policy regimes, reflecting the gradual adoption of the EU *acquis* and the country's transition towards a market economy. As an effective system of protection of intellectual property rights is an important precondition for attracting and retaining investment, Bulgaria has a modern legislation that is aligned with the EU norms and standards. The country is also arbitration-friendly. It has also made tangible progress in reducing delays related to contract enforcement as illustrated in the 2020 World Bank *Doing Business* report, in which Bulgaria ranked 42nd in the ease of enforcing contracts among 190 economies, moving up 33 spots since its 2015 ranking. This being said, challenges remain. Corruption in public administration, a weak judiciary, administrative delays and costs to enforce contracts and obtain reparations continue to hamper the country's investment climate and economic prospects, as discussed in Chapters 6 and 7 of this *Review*.

Protections afforded under Bulgaria's investment treaties are another important part of the legal framework for investment. Bulgaria has 62 investment treaties in force today. These treaties grant protections to certain foreign investors in addition to and independently from protections available under domestic law to all investors. Like treaties signed by many other countries, Bulgaria's investment treaties typically protect investments made by treaty-covered investors against expropriation and discrimination. They also give covered investors access to investor-state dispute settlement (ISDS) procedures, including international arbitration, in cases where they claim that the government has infringed these protections.

Bulgaria, like many other countries, has changed its approach to investment treaties in recent years. Some of this change corresponds to commitments that Bulgaria made as part of EU accession and a new role for the European Commission on investment policy in the EU since 2009. It also reflects Bulgaria's experiences facing claims by investors in arbitration cases under its older treaties – at least ten such cases to date – and intensification of policy debates regarding effects, designs and outcomes of investment treaties. Central in these debates is the desire of many governments to strike an appropriate balance in these treaties between investment protection and sovereign rights to regulate in the public interest. A new Bulgarian model BIT, which was approved by the Council of Ministers in November 2018, seeks to achieve a more balanced approach and serve as a basis for future treaty negotiations with non-EU countries. Bulgaria also participates in inter-governmental discussions regarding possible reforms of investment treaties, including UNCITRAL's Working Group III on ISDS Reform and the modernisation process for the Energy Charter Treaty, a prominent multilateral treaty to which Bulgaria is a party.

Like many other countries, Bulgaria still has a significant number of investment treaties with vague investment protections and ISDS provisions that may create unintended consequences in ISDS cases and ultimately undermine reform efforts. Updating existing treaties remains a separate challenge to negotiating new treaties with time, cost and resource allocation constraints. Recommendations to reconsider several aspects of the government's approach to investment treaties in this context are set out below. Whatever approach the government takes towards investment treaty making, these treaties should not be seen as a substitute for long-term improvements in the domestic business environment including through measures to improve the capacity, efficiency and independence of the domestic court system, the quality of the legal framework, and the strength of national institutions responsible for enforcing such legislation.

Domestic framework: Investor protection under Bulgarian law

Bulgaria offers a safe legal environment

Investor protection, together with effective and responsible public institutions that are sensitive to the needs of businesses and citizens, has been one of Bulgaria's key government priorities, as evidenced by strategic documents such as the "Vision, Goals and Priorities of the National Development Programme BULGARIA 2030" (Decision 33 of the Council of Ministers, 20 January 2020)[1] and NDP BULGARIA 2030 (Protocol 67 of the Council of Ministers, 2 December 2020).

Investor protection is guaranteed under Bulgaria's highest legal authority, the 1991 Constitution of Republic of Bulgaria (Articles 17, 19, 54, 117), as well as dedicated laws. The country's legal framework includes enforceable principles for the protection of private property, limits to the powers of administrative authorities and rules to ensure the predictability for the issuance and implementation of legislative acts/statutory instruments.

To ensure the policy stability and predictability of Bulgaria's legal framework, Article 4 of the Constitution asserts that the country shall be "governed by the rule of law". The practice of the Constitutional Court has repeatedly clarified this principle as comprising the application and consideration of both the principles of legal certainty (protecting investors against the arbitrary exercise of public power) and of substantive legality (requiring that laws must be laid down in advance[2]).[3] The implementation of these constitutional principles is found in Bulgaria's Code of Administrative Procedure (BCAP) (Article 4), which defines the limits of the powers of administrative authorities as well as the Bulgarian Statutory Instruments Act (Article 26), which provides for the preparation, issuance and implementation of the legislative acts/statutory instruments.

Moreover, according to Bulgaria's principle of proportionality, an administrative or legislative act, and the enforcement thereof, may not affect any rights and legitimate interests to a greater extent than the minimum necessary for the purpose for which the act is issued. In case an administrative act affects any rights or creates any obligations for individuals or companies, the more favourable measures shall be applied if the purpose of the law can likewise be achieved in this manner (BCAP, Article 6). Finally, Bulgaria protects foreign investors against changes in the national legislation. Any foreign investment made prior to the adoption of legislative changes imposing legal restrictions solely on foreign investments is to be governed by the legal provisions that were effective at the moment of implementation of the investment (IPA, Article 23).

As it will be developed below, Bulgaria is a party to various multilateral and bilateral agreements for the protection of investors, as well as to more than 130 agreements on mutual encouragement and protection of investments or avoidance of double taxation (Kolev and Targot, 2019).

Guarantees against expropriation

The right to expropriate is an undisputed prerogative of sovereign states, safeguarding their ability to pursue legitimate interests. Bulgaria's Constitution includes protections for local and foreign investors against forcible expropriation of property (Article 17.5). Property can only be expropriated by virtue of a law,[4] pursuant to State or municipal needs that cannot otherwise be met, and after fair compensation has been paid in advance.

Expropriation processes begin by a decision of public need by the Council of Ministers or a regional governor, and are regulated under the State Property Act (SPA) (Articles 32-40). Before commencing an expropriation process, a Detailed Development Plan (DDP) is published and discussed with the interested parties in order to determine the exact area(s) to be expropriated, the property appraisal and monetary compensation. According to the SPA, compensation will be calculated based on the market prices of properties with similar characteristics located near the expropriated property and determined before the DDP enters into force.

All decisions to expropriate are subject to appeal within 14 days of their notification. Expropriation actions by the Council of Ministers can be appealed directly to the Supreme Administrative Court, while a regional governor's expropriation can be appealed in the local administrative court at the location of the property. A property will only be seized after the monetary compensation has been transferred to the account of the owner and, in case the expropriated property is the sole home of the owner, three months after the payment of the compensation. The State Property Act includes additional protections in case of agricultural land and private forest territories, which must respect a certain size in order to avoid fragmentation of land and preserve their effective management and cultivation (Article 42.a).

Alternative dispute resolution mechanisms: Arbitration and mediation

Bulgaria's legal framework for arbitration is largely defined by the Act for International Commercial Arbitration (ICAA) – which regulates both international and domestic arbitration. In addition to the ICAA, provisions of the Civil Procedure Code are also applicable to arbitration proceedings. According to the latter, arbitration proceedings can be conducted on any property dispute, except for certain disputes such as real estate disputes, employment disputes, administrative and other public law disputes, and consumer related disputes (Article 19 and Supplementary Provisions of the 2006 Consumer Protection Act, Article 13, Item 1). Arbitration is also limited in cases of insolvency: once the proceedings have been initiated, all claims against the debtor must be filed before the insolvency court (Commerce Act, Article 637(6)).

The ICAA defines the rules applicable to international and national[5] commercial arbitration, based on a written arbitration agreement[6] when the place of arbitration is on the territory of the Republic of Bulgaria (Article 1(1)). Commercial arbitration under ICAA is open not only to private parties, but also to state or public entities having concluded arbitration agreements (ICAA, Article 3). Disputes include civil property proceedings resulting from foreign commercial relationships as well as disputes for filling in the gaps of a contract or its adaptation to changed circumstances (ICAA, Article 1(2)). Bulgaria is also party to the European Convention on International Commercial Arbitration since 1964.

Adopted in 1988, the ICAA is largely based on the UNCITRAL Model Law on International Commercial Arbitration (1985), thus transposing relevant regulations such as the right for the tribunal to resolve the dispute under the law chosen by the parties, the obligation for arbitrators to ensure equal treatment of the parties and equal opportunities to present their cases and the principle of competence-competence (ICAA, Articles 19, 22 and 38). In January 2017, responding to concerns regarding the proliferation of new arbitral institutions and the need to maintain the quality of their services (Draguiev and Georgiev, 2015), the ICAA was amended to explicitly provide eligibility criteria for arbitrators sitting in Bulgaria, who must, among other considerations, hold an university degree, have at least eight years' professional experience and high moral qualities (Article 11). Foreign citizens may act as arbitrators only if the arbitration is international. Certain arbitral institutions impose further restrictions – for example, some institutions restrict the choice of arbitrators to their lists and permit the choice of unlisted arbitrators to international cases only (Emanuilov, 2019).

National courts cannot interfere with pending arbitration proceedings (e.g. accepting to hear a dispute or an appeal to an award that the parties had agreed to submit to international arbitration); however, they could refuse to enforce a unilateral arbitration clause that grants only one of the parties a choice between arbitration and state courts.[7]

Although about 40 arbitral institutions are active in Bulgaria, there is one major national arbitration institution, which is the Arbitration Court (AC) at the Bulgarian Chamber of Commerce and Industry (BCCI). The AC-BCCI has been by far the busiest arbitral institution in Bulgaria; for example, in 2018 it registered some 200 domestic and 30 international new arbitration cases.[8] Other important Bulgarian arbitral institutions are the Arbitration Court at the Bulgarian Industrial Association and the Arbitration Court at the Confederation of Employers and Industrialists in Bulgaria (KRIB Court of Arbitration).

Recognition of foreign arbitral awards are regulated by the Bulgarian International Commercial Arbitration Act of 1988 (Article 51) and the Convention on the Recognition and Enforcement of Foreign Arbitral Awards (the New York Convention), which is part of Bulgaria's national law and with precedence over any conflicting provisions of domestic legislation since 1965 (1991 Constitution of the Republic of Bulgaria, Article 5(4)).

Mediation is also available as an alternative method of resolution of legal and non-legal disputes. According to the 2004 Mediation Act, mediation is possible in case of civil, commercial, labour, family and administrative disputes related to consumer rights, and other disputes between natural and/or legal persons, including for international disputes (Article 3(1)). The Mediation Act includes a non-exhaustive list of disputes subject to mediation, allowing for a broad approach to mediation in both national and international disputes. Agreements reached in a mediation process have the effect of an in-court settlement, subject to approval by regional courts in Bulgaria, who will verify it does not contradict the law or the principles of morality (Mediation Act, Article 18(1)). Bulgarian national law does not recognise foreign-based conciliation commissions and foreign-based mediation procedures. In case of out-of-court settlements, the general procedures for enforcement of contracts shall apply.

At the international level, Bulgaria is a party to the two founding instruments of the Permanent Court of Arbitration – the 1899 Convention for the Pacific Settlement of International Disputes and the 1907 Convention for the Pacific Settlement of International Disputes- since September 1900 and June 2000 respectively. Bulgaria is also a party to the Charter of the United Nations and thus the International Court of Justice since 1955, to the Convention on the Recognition and Enforcement of Foreign Arbitral Awards since 1965 and to the 1965 Convention on the Settlement of Investment Disputes between State and Nationals of Other States (ICSID Convention) since 2001.

Bulgaria actively participates in the initiative of the Secretary of the ICSID for the amendment of the ICSID Convention and ICSID Additional Facility Rules and is an active participant in the UNCITRAL Working group III Investor-State Dispute Settlement Reform, focused on reforms of investor-state dispute settlements in relation to the establishment of a multilateral investment court.

Protection of intellectual property rights

The protection of intellectual property (IP) rights is another important component of any policy aiming at attracting investment. Protection of IP rights fosters development and innovation since it safeguards associated research and development and give investors the confidence to share new technologies without fears of losing their ownership. It is widely acknowledged that a well-functioning and balanced IP system is key to promoting innovation and creativity, which are the main drivers of development of knowledge-based economies (OECD, 2015).

Main traits of Bulgaria's IP rights system

Bulgaria grants constitutional-level protection to IP rights, in particular to artistic, scientific and technological creativity, as well as inventors' rights, copyrights and related rights (Articles 17 and 54 of the 1991 Constitution). Bulgaria is also a party to all international treaties and conventions on intellectual property administrated by the World Intellectual Property Organization (WIPO), with the exception of the Geneva Act of the Lisbon Agreement on Appellations of Origin and Geographical Indications (adopted on 20 May 2015). National laws are aligned with EU directives, even going beyond the minimum requirements of the WTO Agreement on Trade-Related Aspects of Intellectual Property Rights (TRIPS).

Table 5.1. Bulgaria's regulations in force in 2020 on the protection of IP rights

Law on Patents and Utility models registration
Ordinance on drafting, filling and examination of patent
Ordinance on filling applications and supplementary protection certificates granting
Disputes Resolution Ordinance on Act on patents and registration of utility models
Instructions on the Patent and Utility model applications content
Instruction on the consideration of requests of provisional protection for the applications for the European patent and requests for effect on the territory of the Republic of Bulgaria of the granted European patent
Law on Trademarks and Geographical indications
Ordinance on drafting, filling and examination of Trademarks and Geographical indications applications
Ordinance on the procedure for drafting, submitting and examining oppositions on the Law on Trademarks and Geographical Indications
Disputes Resolution Ordinance on the Law on Trademarks and Geographical Indications
General Recommendation on the provisions considering the protection of the known trademarks, adopted by the Assembly of the Paris Union for the protection of Industrial Property and the WIPO General Assembly on its 34th series of the meetings of the Member States` Assemblies
Guidelines for the Application of Art. 11 and 12 of the Trademarks and Geographical Indications act
Law on Industrial designs
Ordinance on drafting, submitting and examination of the applications for registration of the Industrial designs
Law on topographies of integrated circuit
Instruction on drafting, submitting and formal examination of the applications for the topographies of integrated circuits
Law on the protection of new plant varieties and animal breeds
Instruction on the examination of the applications for the certificates for new plant varieties and animal breeds
Regulation on the border legal measures for the protection of the intellectual property rights
Ordinance for Representatives regarding Industrial Property
Ordinance on the Secret Patents
Organisational Structure Regulations of the Patent Office of Republic of Bulgaria
Tariff of Fees Collected by the Patent Office of Republic of Bulgaria
Regulation (EU) No 386/2012 of the European Parliament and of the Council of 19 April 2012 on entrusting the Office for Harmonization in the Internal Market (Trade Marks and Designs) with tasks related to the enforcement of intellectual property rights, including the assembling of public and private-sector representatives as a European Observatory on Infringements of Intellectual Property Rights
Directive 2004/48/EC of the European Parliament and of the Council of 29 April 2004 on the enforcement of intellectual property rights)
Directive 98/44/EC of the European Parliament and of the Council of 6 July 1998 on the legal protection of biotechnological inventions
Regulation (EC) No 1610/96 of the European Parliament and of the Council of 23 July 1996 concerning the creation of a supplementary protection certificate for plant protection products
Council Regulation (EC) No 2100/94 of 27 July 1994 on Community plant variety rights
Regulation (EC) No 469/2009 of the European Parliament and of the Council of 6 May 2009 concerning the supplementary protection certificate for medicinal products (Codified version)
Council Regulation (EC) No 491/2009 of 25 May 2009 amending Regulation (EC) No 1234/2007 establishing a common organisation of agricultural markets and on specific provisions for certain agricultural products (Single CMO Regulation)

Regulation (EC) No 110/2008 of the European Parliament and of the Council of 15 January 2008 on the definition, description, presentation, labelling and the protection of geographical indications of spirit drinks and repealing Council Regulation (EEC) No 1576/89
Regulation (EU) No 1308/2013 of the European Parliament and of the Council of 17 December 2013 establishing a common organisation of the markets in agricultural products and repealing Council Regulations (EEC) No 922/72, (EEC) No 234/79, (EC) No 1037/2001 and (EC) No 1234/2007
Regulation (EU) No 251/2014 of the European Parliament and of the Council of 26 February 2014 on the definition, description, presentation, labelling and the protection of geographical indications of aromatised wine products and repealing Council Regulation (EEC) No 1601/91
Regulation (EU) No 1151/2012 of the European Parliament and of the Council of 21 November 2012 on quality schemes for agricultural products and foodstuffs
Regulation (EU) 2017/1001 of the European Parliament and of the Council of 14 June 2017 on the European Union trademark (Text with EEA relevance)
Directive (EU) 2015/2436 of the European Parliament and of the Council of 16 December 2015 to approximate the laws of the Member States relating to trade marks (Text with EEA relevance)
Commission Regulation (EC) No 2245/2002 of 21 October 2002 implementing Council Regulation (EC) No 6/2002 on Community designs
Council Regulation (EC) No 6/2002 of 12 December 2001 on Community designs
Directive 98/71/EC of the European Parliament and of the Council of 13 October 1998 on the legal protection of designs
Council Regulation (EC) No 1650/2003 of 18 June 2003 amending Regulation (EC) No 2100/94 on Community plant variety rights
Paris Convention for the Protection of Industrial Property
Patent Co-operation Treaty (PCT)
Hague Agreement Concerning the International Registration of Industrial Designs
Madrid Agreement Concerning the International Registration of Marks and Protocol Relating to the Madrid Agreement Concerning the International Registration of Marks
Lisbon Agreement for the Protection of Appellations of Origin and their International Registration
International Convention for the Protection of New Varieties of Plants (UPOV)
Vienna Agreement Establishing an International Classification of the Figurative Elements of Marks
Nice Agreement Concerning the International Classification of Goods and Services for the Purposes of the Registration of Marks (as amended on 28 September 1979)
Locarno Agreement Establishing an International Classification for Industrial Designs
European Patent Convention (EPC), also known as the Convention on the Grant of European Patents
Strasbourg Agreement establishes the International Patent Classification (IPC) not available on the BPO`s site

Source: OECD Secretariat (2021) based on Bulgaria's replies to the OECD questionnaires.

Early during the market transition, through the 1993 Patent Law, the Bulgarian Patent Office was established as the authority overseeing the registration of intellectual property in Bulgaria. In parallel, a Copyright and Related Rights Directorate was created at the Ministry of Culture. In 2012, the Council for the Protection of Intellectual Property was created, headed by the Minister of Culture, as an advisory body for co-ordination and co-operation between state institutions, local governments and NGOs working in the field of IP protection (Decree 267 of 26 October 2012).

The average costs for registration of a trademark for three classes in Bulgaria is around EUR 300 and the process is completed in around six months. In 2019, out of 4 110 applications for trademarks, 3 467 of them were registered. As for inventions, utility models, designs, plant varieties and animal breeds, the average filling price is EUR150 and in 2019 Bulgaria registered up to 500 utility model registrations, while filings for patents where the substantive examination is required were about 200. For Geographic Indications (GI), the average cost is EUR 600, with 12 GIs for spirit drinks currently protected at EU level. To foster innovation and the protection of patents, in 2021 Bulgaria provided a 50% reduction in fees for micro, small and medium-sized enterprises, universities, schools, academic research organisations or registered inventors, as well as government-funded scientific organisations. In 2019, according to Bulgaria's replies to the OECD questionnaire, there were 52 filings for patents from universities and public research institutes.

Enforcement of intellectual property rights

Enforcement rules are the procedural complement of substantive protection. In Bulgaria, enforcement of IP rights is provided through civil, administrative, and criminal proceedings. In addition, investors can resort directly to the Bulgarian Patent Office, which is empowered to impose administrative penalties – fines or monetary sanctions – on infringers of rights of the owners of trademarks, GIs, patents, utility models and industrial designs. Administrative procedures at the Bulgarian Patent Office include cancellation and revocation of trademarks, cancellation of designs, invalidation of patents and cancellation of utility models.

Although there are no specialised courts that exclusively hear IP-related cases in Bulgaria, the decisions of the President of the Bulgarian Patent Office can be appealed before the Administrative court of Sofia City and the Supreme Administrative Court of Bulgaria. Civil cases concerning infringements of IP rights are also heard before the Sofia City Court.

Foreign authors enjoy the same rights as Bulgarian authors, unless otherwise provided by international treaties and agreements. Foreign legal entities and all persons with a domicile or seat outside Bulgaria may apply for the registration of a patent, trademark, GI and industrial design through their local IP representatives listed with Bulgaria's Patent Office.

The international registrations of patents under the Patent Co-operation Treaty, of trademarks in conformity with the Madrid Agreement, of geographical indications under the Lisbon Agreement, and of industrial designs under the Hague Convention have the same effect as if the applications were directly lodged and the registrations were made in Bulgaria in accordance to the relevant Bulgarian law. In addition, Bulgarian law will apply to foreign individuals and legal entities whose country of origin is a party to international agreements to which Bulgaria is a party as well. In case of no agreement, Bulgaria will apply the principle of reciprocity, that is, granting the same treatment as Bulgarian nationals and legal entities receive in the respective foreign country. This reciprocity treatment will be established by the Patent Office on a case-by-case basis.

Contract enforcement and dispute settlement

Appropriate contract enforcement is important for investment since it assures investors that their contractual rights will be respected and upheld. FDI recipient countries are encouraged to put in place non-bureaucratic, timely and straightforward settlement of contract disputes through an efficient and effective court system, both for private and state-related issues. In addition, alternative dispute resolution mechanisms such as arbitration, mediation and conciliation are vital to decongest the judicial system and grant alternatives to investors for resolving commercial disputes.

The Bulgarian legislation clearly defines the competent courts, judicial procedures for solving contractual disputes, requirements toward parties and rules for serving papers in the Civil Proceedings Code (State Gazette, Issue 59 of 20 July 2007, in force since 1 March 2008). Special provisions regarding the jurisdiction of the Bulgarian courts on international contractual disputes can also be found in the Private International Law Code (State Gazette, issue 42 of 17 May 2005, effective since 21st of May 2005).

Although court jurisdiction based on subject-matter cannot be contested, the parties may mutually decide to bring their dispute to a court located in another territorial jurisdiction within Bulgaria, with the exception of real estate-related disputes. In addition, Bulgaria has special rules to ensure fast settlement of contractual disputes, for example by reducing to two-weeks the terms for responding claims (instead of the one-month general term); allowing filing additional claims under the same dossier; the possibility for the court -upon parties' request- to examine and solve the dispute in a closed hearing;[9] and simplified claim enforcement when that claim is unlikely to be contested by the debtor (Civil Proceedings Code, Articles 109, 117 and Chapters XXXII and XXXVII). In addition to the ordinary civil courts, contractual disputes may be referred to alternative dispute settlement mechanism, such as domestic and international commercial arbitration, which are further explained below.

The cost and procedure of enforcing contracts

Contract enforcement in Bulgaria requires an effective court decision before the claim can be honoured. This entails costs for the investor in the form of state fees for the initiation of the process (equal to 4% of the material interest), additional costs for the collection of evidences, preparation of expert reports by specialists or for obtaining official documents from other public authorities. Such costs may vary, for example, the remuneration of the experts will depend on the complexity and the exhaustiveness of the report and can be estimated around BGN 100-600 (or EUR 50-300 on average) (Civil Proceedings Code, Chapter 8).

After a court decision is issued, the claimant will need to request the issuance of a writ of execution by the competent court. By law, this state fee is not costly, since it amounts to less than EUR 3. In case of requesting the recognition and enforcement of a non-EU foreign decision, the payable state fee ascends to BGN 50 or EUR 25. Nonetheless, parties face additional costs related with the execution of the court sentence, depending on whether it is enforced by a state or a private enforcement agent. Judgments rendered in another EU Member State, are enforceable in Bulgaria without the need to issue a writ of execution (Civil Proceedings Code, Article 622a). The rules for recognition and enforcement of foreign judgements are set forth in the Civil Proceedings Code (Part VII, Chapter LVII) and the Private International Law Code (Part IV, Chapter XII).

Contract enforcement simplification efforts

Efficient contract enforcement is essential to attracting investment, economic development and sustained growth. For many years, long and complex contract enforcement procedures in Bulgaria had been highlighted as one important barrier to doing business in the country. The judiciary – in principle the institution of choice for enforcing contracts- has not been trusted by companies as noted in previous chapters of this *Review*. Cross-country rankings, such as the World Bank's *Doing Business*, have regularly identified the number of procedures and time involved as an obstacle to doing business in Bulgaria. For example the 2015 *Doing Business* report noted that on average entrepreneurs in Bulgaria paid 23.8% of the claim value in attorneys, court and enforcement fees and needed 564 days to resolve a commercial dispute through the courts, while in countries such as Austria and Hungary entrepreneurs paid 18% and 15% of the claim value in attorneys and needed only 397 and 395 days respectively to resolve the same dispute. The whole procedure according to *Doing Business* 2015 took 38 separate steps. As a result, in *Doing Business 2015*, Bulgaria scored rather poorly, ranking 75th in the ease of enforcing contracts among 189 economies, and 18th out of 26 in the Europe and Central Asia region. According to the 2015 World Bank *Doing Business* database, under the indicator "Enforcing contracts", Bulgaria's distance to frontier was 61.27 compared to the OECD average of 69.82.

Since then, Bulgaria has made tangible progress in reforming its judiciary, as it will be further addressed in Chapter 7 of this *Review*. As a result, in the *Doing Business 2020* report, Bulgaria ranked 42nd in the ease of enforcing contracts among 190 economies, moving up 33 spots since its 2015 ranking. Still, there is room for improvement in terms of the number of procedures and time involved. According to some local observers, the average length of time required to obtain a final court resolution for enforcement of a contract in Bulgaria (including appealing procedures on second-instance and the Supreme Cassation Court) would be of four to five years (Mikov Attorneys, 2017). Afterwards, investors must conduct an enforcement procedure by a State or a private agent, which may take another two to three years.

Through the Inspectorate to the SJC, the Bulgarian Ministry of Justice has been working on a reform of its judicial system in order to address investors' concerns about the length of judicial procedures. For example, in February 2021, the Judges' College of the SJC adopted a roadmap to reorganise courts at district and appellate levels, which seeks to increase the number of judges significantly, allow for specialisation of judges, provide for mandatory court-ordered mediation in certain cases and improve overall efficiency in court procedures by optimising judicial workload across courts and judges. If implemented effectively, these proposals could go a significant way towards addressing concerns with court efficiency in Bulgaria.

Investment treaties

Bulgaria was party to 52 investment treaties in force as of June 2021. This included 51 bilateral investment treaties (BITs) and one multilateral trade and investment treaty – the Energy Charter Treaty (ECT) (see summary table in Annex 5.A). It is also a member country of two important multilateral treaties related to enforcement of arbitral awards issued in investor-state arbitration cases under investment treaties – the New York Convention (in force for Bulgaria since January 1962) and the Washington Convention (in force for Bulgaria since May 2001).

These numbers are likely to change in the near future. Almost a third of Bulgaria's BITs (19 in total) have recently been or will soon be terminated under an agreement between EU member states to terminate all BITs currently in force between them (the Intra-EU BIT Termination Agreement).[10] The Agreement was signed on 5 May 2020 and entered into force on 29 August 2020. It entered into force for Bulgaria on 13 December 2020 following the completion of Bulgaria's domestic ratification procedures. As of June 2021, 10 of 19 Bulgarian intra-EU BITs have been terminated under the Agreement.[11] The Ministry of Finance also advised during the process of preparing this *Review* that bilateral negotiations were underway to terminate existing Bulgarian BITs with Austria, Finland, Sweden and the United Kingdom, including sunset provisions that would extend treaty effects beyond termination.

Several other treaties signed by Bulgaria may also soon come into force. A trade and investment agreement concluded by the EU and its member states – the EU-Canada CETA (2016) – was not in force at the time of writing this *Review* but the parties apply provisionally some of the provisions in its investment chapter (notably on market access and non-discrimination). Bulgaria has signed two further investment agreements concluded by the EU and its member states with Singapore (2018) and Viet Nam (2019).[12] As of June 2021, the Bulgarian Parliament had not yet ratified these EU-led agreements.[13] None of them were in force pending the completion of ratification procedures in all 27 EU member states.[14] Bulgaria has also concluded six BITs that so far, according to Bulgaria's authorities, have not been not in force – with Austria (1981), Azerbaijan (2004), Ghana (1989), Democratic People's Republic of Korea (1999), Nigeria (1998) and Sudan (2002).

Bulgaria signed most of its investment treaties in the 1990s and early 2000s. A timeline appears in Figure 5.1. The government has not concluded a BIT since 2009. A significant development during this period was the transfer of exclusive competence over FDI, including negotiations for investment treaties, from EU member states to the EU in 2009 as a result of the Lisbon Treaty. EU member states are still able to negotiate and conclude investment treaties with non-EU partners provided they first seek approvals from the European Commission in line with EU Regulation No. 1219/2012. At the time of writing this *Review*, Bulgaria was negotiating possible BITs with Saudi Arabia, Türkiye and the United Arab Emirates under Commission-approved negotiating mandates.

Figure 5.1. Evolution of Bulgaria's investment treaty relationships

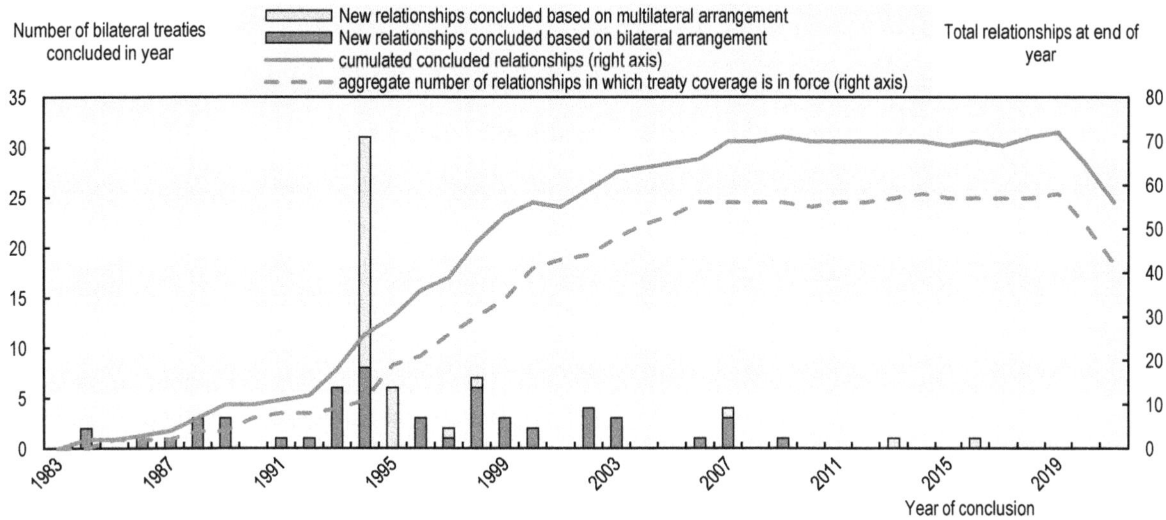

Source: OECD calculations based on OECD treaty database; Bulgarian Government.

Figure 5.2. Approximate evolution of Bulgaria's inward and outward FDI stock coverage from investment treaties in force

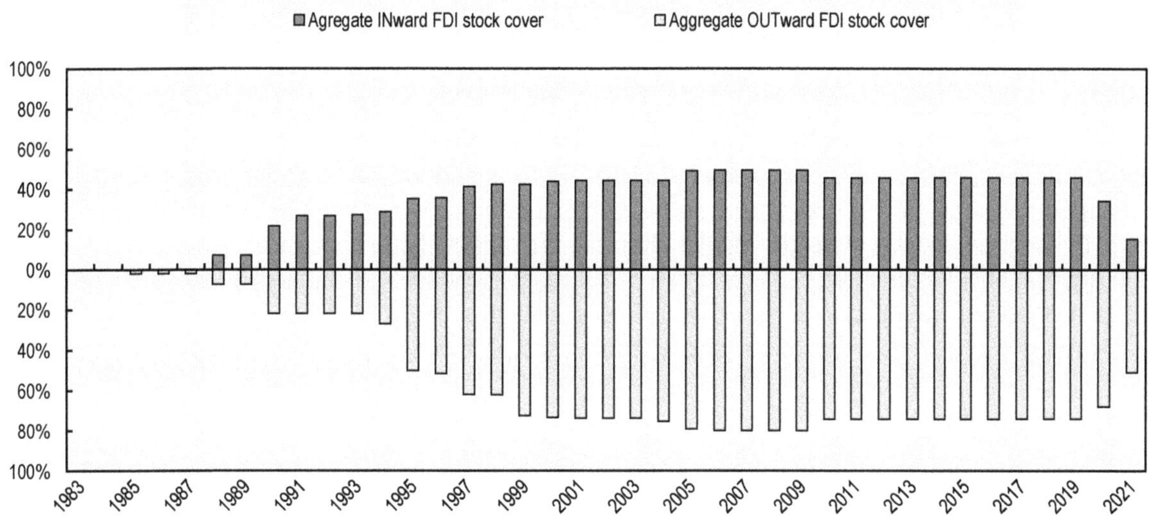

Note: This graph shows the approximate share of overall inward and outward FDI stock by matching investment treaty relationships in force as of October 2020 with aggregate immediate bilateral FDI data. FDI data shown here does not cover relationships or stock in country pairs where only the ECT is in force due to the lack of bilateral sector-specific FDI stock data.
Source: OECD calculations based on OECD investment treaty database. FDI data was taken from OECD FDI database and IMF Direct Investment Positions and reflects FDI stock as of 2018 rather than historical values.

Bulgaria's treaty making activity and choice of treaty partners has led to a significant coverage of its inward (approximately 46%) and outward (approximately 74%) FDI stock (see Figure 5.2). FDI trends are discussed in further detail in Chapter 2 but for current purposes it is notable that treaty relationships with the Netherlands cover significant portions of Bulgaria's inward (9%) and outward (9%) FDI stock. Treaty relationships with four other countries (Austria, Belgium, Luxembourg and Russia) also cover a significant portion of inward FDI stock (approximately 15% in total) and relationships with another three countries

(Republic of North Macedonia, Romania and Serbia) cover significant portions of outward FDI stock (approx. 39% in total). Many Bulgarian investment treaties in force today cover none of Bulgaria's FDI stock (inward or outward) or only negligible portions of it. This is a common phenomenon in many countries' treaty samples (Pohl, 2018).

Treaty use: ISDS claims under Bulgaria's investment treaties

Bulgaria has had several first-hand experiences defending formal legal claims brought by investors under investor-state dispute settlement (ISDS) provisions in its investment treaties. Based on publicly available information,[15] foreign investors have filed at least ten treaty-based claims against Bulgaria: nine under the auspices of the ICSID Convention[16] and one with an arbitral tribunal constituted under the UNCITRAL Arbitration Rules.[17]

Bulgaria's ISDS disputes have primarily concerned investments in power generation, waste management industrial processing and real estate projects. As of May 2021, four cases were still pending. At least one treaty-based ISDS claim has also been filed against one of Bulgaria's treaty partners by a Bulgarian investor operating abroad.[18]

Reconsidering Bulgaria's investment treaty policy

Bulgaria's investment treaty policy deserves continued attention. Many of Bulgaria's BITs in force today contain features often associated with older investment treaties concluded in great numbers in the 1990s and early 2000s. Such treaties are generally characterised by a lack of specificity of the meaning of key provisions and extensive protections for covered investors. Some of Bulgaria's most recent investment treaties – notably those concluded by the EU with Canada, Singapore and Viet Nam – contain more precise approaches in some areas. Bulgaria's older BITs nonetheless remain in force alongside these newer agreements and form an integral part of the country's legal framework for investment.

This scenario may expose Bulgaria to a range of unintended consequences, especially given the potential scope for ISDS claims under these treaties. While many countries have revised their approaches to negotiating new investment treaties in response to these and other concerns, retrospectively addressing older BITs has proven to be more challenging. Some governments have negotiated treaty amendments or joint interpretations with existing treaty partners to address individual treaties but these efforts can require significant time and resources. Ongoing multilateral initiatives at UNCITRAL and ICSID to consider possible reforms are primarily technical and narrow in scope (focussing on ISDS and ICSID's arbitration rules, respectively) while the ECT reform negotiations are focused on a particular sector and concern only ECT member countries.

Governments continue to weigh the growing consensus on the need to update older investment treaties with the potential benefits of these treaties. Some consider that investment protection provided under investment treaties can play an important role in fostering predictable rules for investment and providing more reliable, fair and enforceable remedies than domestic courts in some countries. Many also recognise that foreign investors are exposed to specific risks, at least under certain circumstances, and that such risks need to be mitigated to enable international investment. Government acceptance of legitimate constraints on policies can provide investors with greater certainty and predictability, lowering unwarranted risk and the cost of capital.

Investment treaties are also frequently promoted as a method of attracting FDI and this is a goal for many governments. Bulgaria's National Reform Programme (update 2022, April 2022) and the European Commission's 2020 Country Report on Bulgaria attest to the government's priority for attracting foreign investment to contribute to R&D as well as infrastructure upgrades, among other things. The fundamental assumption that international investment can contribute to prosperity, help overcome challenges such as the climate crisis and the need to transform economies, create employment, and address crises remains valid. Most immediately, international investment has a central role to play in a sustainable recovery from the COVID-19 pandemic and in coping with negative economic impacts of the war in Ukraine. Despite many studies, however, it remains difficult to establish strong evidence that protection components of treaties help to attract investment (Pohl, 2018). Some studies suggest that treaties or instruments that reduce barriers and restrictions to foreign investments have more impact on FDI flows than BITs focused only on post-establishment protection (Mistura et al., 2019). These assumptions continue to be investigated by a growing strand of empirical literature on the purposes of investment treaties and how well they are being achieved.

The government is well aware of these and other debates through its participation in several inter-governmental discussions regarding possible reforms of investment treaties, including UNCITRAL's Working Group III on ISDS Reform and multilateral negotiations for possible updates to "modernise" the ECT. The ECT modernisation process may have particularly important implications for Bulgaria. The ECT is the most frequently invoked investment treaty in ISDS cases: investors have filed more than 130 known ISDS cases under the ECT since the first claim was filed under this treaty in 2001 (Energy Charter Secretariat, 2020). Five of Bulgaria's ten publicly known ISDS cases were filed under the ECT. Importantly, the Intra-EU BIT Termination Agreement expressly does not apply to the ECT, which means that the ECT will remain in force between Bulgaria and other EU members. Formal negotiations regarding possible reforms to the ECT began in November 2019. An approved list of topics for discussion includes all core investment protections and ISDS provisions. The Energy Charter Secretariat published a set of policy options identified by the ECT Members on the various topics in October 2019 (Energy Charter Secretariat, 2019). Most ECT governments do not appear to have released public negotiating mandates but the European Council approved negotiating directives in July 2019 and the EU publicly released its text proposals in May 2020 (European Commission, 2020). The EU has promoted reform of the ECT and in particular its investment protection components, which share many characteristics with other older investment treaties. Some of these proposals are addressed below. EU parliamentarians have also urged that the ECT revisions should align with the EU's climate change agenda (Urtasun, 2020).

The balance of this section examines four key aspects of possible reform – the scope of three frequently invoked protections (FET, MFN and indirect expropriation) as well as dispute settlement mechanisms and ISDS. It then briefly outlines some other possible aspects of investment treaty reform.

Vague provisions referring generally to "fair and equitable treatment" generate risks and costs, and should be addressed where possible

Most of Bulgaria's investment treaties in force today contain provisions that require Bulgaria to provide covered investors and/or their investments with FET.[19] Since the early 2000s, the FET standard has become the most frequent basis for claims in ISDS. Most FET provisions were agreed before the rise of ISDS claims related to this treatment standard. Starting around 2000, broad theories for the interpretation of FET provisions by arbitral tribunals emerged as the number of ISDS cases increased markedly. Based on public information, investors in at least two of the ten known ISDS cases brought against Bulgaria have relied on FET provisions in investment treaties.[20]

Most FET provisions in investment treaties do not provide specific guidance on what treatment should be considered fair and equitable. Arbitral tribunals in ISDS cases under investment treaties have taken different approaches to interpreting such "bare" FET provisions. This creates considerable uncertainty and high litigation costs for governments and investors alike. It has also resulted in some broad interpretations of bare FET provisions that go beyond the standards of investor protection in the domestic legal systems of some advanced economies. Governments have reacted to these developments in various ways, including by adopting more precise or restrictive approaches to FET or excluding FET in recent treaties (Box 5.1). These recent approaches in broader treaty practice can serve as a useful point of comparison for varying approaches to FET in Bulgaria's investment treaties.

Box 5.1. Recent approaches to the FET provision and ISDS for FET claims

States are becoming more active in the ways in which they specify, address or exclude FET-type obligations in their treaties and submissions in ISDS. Dissatisfaction with and uncertainties about FET and its scope have also led some governments to exclude it from their treaties or from the scope of ISDS. Some important recent approaches are outlined below.

The MST-FET approach: Express limitation of FET to the minimum standard of treatment under customary international law (MST). This approach has been used in a growing number of recent treaties, especially in treaties involving states from the Americas and Asia (Gaukrodger, 2017). In addition to using MST-FET, the CPTPP clarifies that the claimant must establish any asserted rule of MST-FET by demonstrating widespread state practice and *opinio juris* (Article 9.6 (3)-(5), Annex 9A). Evidence of these two components has rarely been provided by claimants or arbitrators in ISDS cases. This approach has since been replicated by other states (e.g. Australia-Indonesia CEPA (2019), Article 14.7). The NAFTA governments have further reformed their approach to MST-FET claims in the USMCA (see below).

Exclusion of FET from ISDS, investment arbitration or from treaties. The recently concluded USMCA (which replaced the North American Free Trade Agreement (1992) on 1 July 2020) includes MST-FET but generally excludes it from the scope of ISDS (except for a narrow class of cases involving certain government contracts) (Article 14.D.3). ISDS under the USMCA generally applies only to claims of direct expropriation and post-establishment discrimination (and only to Mexico-United States relations); only state-to-state dispute settlement (SSDS) is available for MST-FET claims. India's Model BIT does not refer to FET and instead identifies specific elements; Brazil's model treaty and recent treaties also exclude FET.

The definition approach: Stating what FET means or listing its elements. Recent treaties negotiated by the European Union, China, France and the Slovak Republic contain defined lists for the elements of FET. This approach can vary greatly depending on the nature of the list. Some lists include elements such as a denial of justice, manifest arbitrariness, fundamental breach of due process, targeted discrimination on manifestly wrongful grounds, and/or abusive treatment of investors. This approach likely results in a broader concept of FET than MST-FET, especially if state practice and *opinio juris* must be demonstrated to establish rules under MST-FET.

Clarifications of treatment excluded from FET. Some recent treaties have also clarified that FET does not protect investors from certain types of treatment. Starting with the Australia-Singapore FTA as revised in 2016, and followed by the CPTPP signed in March 2018 and the Korea-United States FTA as revised in 2018, several treaties now exclude government measures that may be inconsistent with an investor's expectations concerning its investment from giving rise to a breach of the FET provision.[21] Several recent treaties concluded by Australia clarify that the modification of government subsidies or grants is not protected under the FET provision.[22]

Some Bulgarian BITs adopt some of these more precise or restrictive approaches to FET. The EU trade and investment agreements with Canada, Singapore and Viet Nam contain defined lists for the elements for FET.[23] At least seven Bulgarian BITs exclude FET from the scope of ISDS.[24]

Other formulations of FET in Bulgaria's investment treaties may leave scope for broad interpretations by arbitral tribunals. Most of Bulgaria's treaties contain an unqualified or "bare" reference to FET without any further specific guidance on its meaning. Some contain several different references to "bare" FET in the same treaty, which may generate additional uncertainty as to how these provisions should be interpreted.[25] The prevalence of "bare" FET provisions and of varying approaches more generally creates uncertainty as to the scope of these FET obligations and exposure to unpredictable interpretations by arbitral tribunals in

ISDS cases. More specific approaches to FET provisions could improve predictability for the government, investors and arbitrators alike. They could also potentially contribute to preserving the government's right to regulate in the context of investment treaties (Gaukrodger, 2017a, 2017b). In some cases, governments may be able to achieve greater clarity on the scope of FET by agreeing on joint government interpretations of provisions in existing investment treaties with treaty partners.[26] In other cases, agreement on new treaty language may be required to reflect government intent and preclude undesirable interpretations.

Members of the ECT, including Bulgaria, are considering the scope of FET as part of the ECT modernisation process. Most ECT Members agree on the need to update the existing provision on FET in the ECT to clarify further its scope (Energy Charter Secretariat, 2019). Issues for discussion include whether FET should be linked to the MST under customary international law, whether FET should be linked to other substantive protections or a stand-alone provision, and whether FET should refer to the concept of legitimate expectations. Some ECT Members, such as Switzerland, Türkiye and the EU, propose a list-based definition of FET. Other Members propose MST-FET but are open to considering list-based formulations that are consistent with prevailing understandings of the content of MST-FET.

Most-favoured nation (MFN) treatment provisions in Bulgaria's investment treaties may have a range of unintended consequences

Almost all of Bulgaria's investment treaties provide for MFN treatment.[27] Like national treatment (NT) provisions, MFN clauses establish a relative standard: they require Bulgaria to treat covered investments at least as favourably as it treats comparable investments by investors from third countries. As with FET provisions, most of the MFN treatment provisions in Bulgaria's investment treaties and the global sample of investment treaties are vague with little guidance on how to interpret or apply them. More specific approaches to MFN treatment provisions could improve predictability for the government, investors and arbitrators alike (Box 5.2).

Bulgaria has had first-hand experience of these interpretations in at least two ISDS cases (*Plama Consortium Limited v. Republic of Bulgaria* (ICSID Case No. ARB/03/24) and *ST-AD GmbH v. Republic of Bulgaria*, UNCITRAL, PCA Case No. 2011-06) where the claimants sought to rely on an MFN provision to benefit from more favourable dispute resolution provisions in other Bulgarian investment treaties.

Some of Bulgaria's investment treaties include specifications or restrictions on MFN provisions that reflect these recent treaty practices and debates. Almost all Bulgarian BITs that contain such provisions exclude benefits granted under existing customs, economic or monetary unions, double taxation agreements and/or multilateral investment agreements from MFN treatment.[28] At least four of these treaties also require an assessment of MFN treatment with respect to comparable investments.[29] The EU's recent trade and investment agreements adopt a range of approaches to MFN treatment – three of them clarify that MFN treatment does not extend to ISDS or substantive provisions in other treaties[30] while one omits MFN treatment provisions altogether.[31] None of Bulgaria's BITs contains similar exclusions that apply to MFN provisions for either ISDS provisions or substantive protections in other investment treaties. While the current text of the ECT does not contain any such specifications, the EU and several other ECT Members propose to update it to include them (European Commission, 2020).

Box 5.2. Recent approaches to MFN treatment provisions and ISDS for MFN treatment claims

Recent investment treaty policies and debates over MFN have centred on three key issues outlined below.

MFN clauses and treaty shopping. ISDS arbitral tribunals have frequently interpreted MFN provisions to allow claimants in ISDS cases to engage in "treaty shopping".[32] These interpretations allow claimants to use MFN provisions to "import" provisions from other investment treaties that they consider more favourable than the provision in the treaty under which their case is filed.[33] This can create uncertainty and also dilute the effect of investment treaty reforms. While MFN claims in trade law have centred on domestic law treatment of traders from different countries, most claimant attempts to use MFN in ISDS have sought to use the clause to access other treaty provisions.

Some governments have clarified in recent treaties that MFN provisions cannot be used to engage in treaty shopping at all. Others have limited treaty shopping to the importation of substantive provisions or limited the application of MFN clauses to cases where government measures have been adopted or maintained under the third country treaty. Article 8.7(4) of the CETA between Canada, the EU and EU Member States, for example, clarifies that "substantive obligations in other international investment treaties do not in themselves constitute 'treatment', and thus cannot give rise to a breach of [the MFN provision], absent measures adopted or maintained by a Party pursuant to those obligations". The CETA also prohibits "treaty shopping" for procedural provisions. The USMCA similarly clarifies that treaty shopping is excluded under its MFN clause for both substantive and procedural matters (Article 14.D.3(1)(a)(i)(A), footnote 22): "For the purposes of this paragraph [...] the "treatment" referred to in Article 14.5 (Most Favoured Nation Treatment) excludes provisions in other international trade or investment agreements that establish international dispute resolution procedures or impose substantive obligations".

Comparison criteria in MFN treatment provisions. A second area of interest and government action with regard to MFN treatment provisions involves the determination of what investments or investors are comparable. Many older-style treaties do not provide any specificity on this issue, leaving it to arbitral interpretations in ISDS. Some recent treaties provide that comparability requires "like circumstances". Further clarifications have also been added. For example, some recent clarifications have stated that deciding on whether there are "like circumstances" requires, among other things, consideration of whether the relevant treatment distinguishes between investors or investments on the basis of legitimate public welfare objectives.[34]

Negative lists, carve-outs or conditions. A third area of interest and government action with regard to MFN treatment provisions involves exclusions or limitations. Some recent treaties include negative lists of exclusions from MFN clauses in their investment chapters. Thus, a schedule may specify exceptions to MFN treatment for existing benefits granted under customs unions, other international treaties or specific domestic law schemes.

Vague provisions referring to protection for indirect expropriation should be clarified where possible

All of Bulgaria's investment treaties contain provisions that protect covered investments from expropriation without compensation. Many of these provisions refer to direct takings of investor property by the government (direct expropriation) as well as other government measures that have effects equivalent to a direct taking without a formal transfer or outright seizure (commonly referred to as indirect expropriation). Provisions on indirect expropriation have become the second most frequently invoked basis for claims in ISDS cases after provisions on FET. As with FET and MFN treatment provisions, most of these provisions in Bulgaria's treaties and the global sample of investment treaties are vague with little guidance on how to interpret or apply them.

Since 2003, some countries have included a range of clarifications on the scope of indirect expropriation in newly concluded investment treaties. Clarifications fall into four broad categories: (i) positive definitions of the concept of "indirect expropriation"; (ii) guidance on how to determine whether an indirect expropriation has occurred; (iii) clarifications that certain regulatory measures do not constitute indirect expropriation; and (iv) restrictions on the types of assets covered by this protection. None of Bulgaria's BITs contains any of these features. The EU's trade and investment agreements with Canada, Singapore and Viet Nam contain clarifications in categories (i), (ii) and (iii) above, albeit with some differences in treaty language used to express them.[35] The EU and other ECT Members have made proposals to update the existing ECT provisions on expropriation with these and other elements (Energy Charter Secretariat, 2019; European Commission, 2020).

Clarifications such as these are likely to improve predictability as to the scope of indirect expropriation and reduce the possibility for unintended interpretations in ISDS cases. They are also likely to continue to feature in debates regarding the balance between investment protections and governments' rights to regulate in investment treaties, including as part of ongoing discussions at the OECD. The impact of these clarifications may depend, however, on the scope of other provisions in the same treaty such as FET that have often been invoked in ISDS cases as a substitute basis for indirect expropriation claims. It also remains to be seen how arbitrators interpret such provisions as very few investor-state arbitrations have been brought under treaties that contain these features. At least one government (Brazil) has responded to this residual uncertainty by excluding indirect expropriation altogether from its investment treaties concluded since 2015 through clear language to that effect.

Bulgaria's investment treaties contain relatively few specifications or clarifications in dispute settlement provisions

Many investment treaties allow covered foreign investors to bring claims against host states in investor-state arbitration, in addition or as an alternative to domestic remedies. Investor-state arbitration generally involves *ad hoc* arbitration tribunals that adjudicate disputes in an approach derived from international commercial arbitration. Investor-state dispute settlement (ISDS) provisions appear in all of Bulgaria's investment treaties in force today. State-state dispute settlement (SSDS) is also an option under these treaties.

Recent treaty practice has seen both greater specification of ISDS and, in some cases, replacement of investor-state arbitration with more court-like systems. Treaties like the CPTPP and the EU-Canada CETA are among some recent treaties that have included investor-state arbitration reforms to reduce possible exposure to unintended consequences of ISDS. Common features in these treaties include time limits for claims, possibilities for summary dismissal of unmeritorious claims, mandatory transparency requirements, provisions for non-disputing party participation and possibilities for joint interpretations of the treaty by the state parties that are binding on the arbitral tribunal. The United States – Mexico – Canada Agreement (USMCA) contains many similar investor-state arbitration reforms but has reduced the scope for ISDS claims to direct expropriation and post-establishment discrimination (and only to Mexico-United States relations); only state-to-state dispute settlement (SSDS) is available for claims under other provisions, such as MST-FET claims. The EU, which supports the concept of a multilateral investment court, has included court-like dispute settlement in all its recent investment protection treaties. Brazil's treaties omit ISDS and designate domestic entities ("National Focal Points") to act as an ombudsperson by evaluating investor grievances and proposing solutions to a Joint Committee comprised of government representatives from both states. Under this model, state-state dispute settlement is also available if necessary. South Africa has terminated its BITs with European countries. South African domestic legislation governs the claims of foreign investors against the government in domestic courts and provides for the possibility of case-by-case agreement to arbitration.

ISDS provisions in some Bulgarian investment treaties contain reform elements that reflect recent treaty practice. Some of Bulgaria's BITs restrict the scope of ISDS to certain treatment provisions, such as expropriation and non-discrimination guarantees,[36] while others clarify that certain types of government conduct cannot be litigated under the treaty.[37] At least 16 Bulgarian BITs specify the governing law for ISDS cases, albeit using different formulations.[38] The EU's trade and investment agreements with Canada, Singapore and Viet Nam all contain detailed ISDS provisions with various reform elements. Once in force, investor claims under these treaties will be resolved through a court-like system including a first instance tribunal and an appellate tribunal, the members of which will be drawn from a standing body of 15 individuals appointed for fixed terms by the treaty parties. These treaties also envisage the creation of a multilateral investment court in the future.

The MoE has advised that Bulgaria's model BIT, approved by the Council of Ministers in November 2018, contains provisions addressing many of these issues on ISDS reform but no new treaties have yet been concluded under this model as of February 2021.The majority of Bulgaria's investment treaties, however, contain no such specifications regarding investor-state arbitration procedures. They thus leave substantial decision-making power to arbitrators or investors and their legal counsel. For example, in ISDS, the appointing authority in a case plays a key role notably because it chooses or influences the choice of the important chair of the typical three-person tribunal (Gaukrodger, 2018). Some Bulgarian treaties – including BITs with the Russian Federation (1993), Mongolia (2000), Albania (1994), and Denmark (1994) – remove this choice by providing for a single forum for investor-state arbitration. Other Bulgarian BITs include other types of limitations[39] but most Bulgarian treaties give claimants and their counsel a choice between at least two and as many as three different arbitration institutions at the time they file a claim.[40] This allows investors to choose or influence the choice of appointing authority and exacerbates the competition for cases between arbitration institutions (Gaukrodger, 2018).

Multilateral reform efforts for ISDS are underway in several fora, including at UNCITRAL and ICSID. The Bulgarian government participates actively as an observer in these discussions. Possible ISDS reforms under consideration at UNCITRAL and in the ECT modernisation process (no decisions have yet been reached) include both structural-type reforms (a permanent multilateral investment court with government-selected judges or a permanent appellate tribunal) as well as more incremental reforms such as a code of conduct for arbitrators or adjudicators.

Clearer specification of investment protection provisions would help to reflect government intent and ensure policy space for government regulation

Specifications on key provisions in investment treaties play an important role calibrating the balance between investor protection and governments' right to regulate. The MoE has advised that Bulgaria's model BIT, approved by the Council of Ministers in November 2018, was designed with this balance in mind. It is also an important part of the EU's policy on investment treaties and its proposals for a reformed approach to investment dispute settlement based on a court-like model for ISDS. Specifications seeking to achieve this balance should reflect policy choices informed by Bulgaria's priorities. Policy-makers need to consider the costs and benefits of these choices and their potential impact on foreign and domestic investors, together with the government's legitimate regulatory interests and potential exposure to ISDS claims and damages.

There are a range of techniques that governments can use to affect the balance between the right to regulate and investor protections under investment treaties (Gaukrodger, 2017a). The most obvious technique involves decisions about whether to include or exclude particular provisions, whether to draft them narrowly or broadly, precisely or in broader terms. The most important provisions in this regard are likely to be those most often the focus of alleged breach in investor claims such as the FET provision.

Depending on whether the parties wish to clarify original intent or revise a provision, it may be possible to clarify language through joint interpretations agreed with treaty partners or treaty amendments. These types of government action have been relatively rare in recent years, however, and can require significant time and resources to engage with individual treaty partners. Replacement of older investment treaties by consent in the context of new treaty negotiations may also be appropriate in some cases.

The government's experience with the COVID-19 pandemic and the impact of the war in Ukraine on Bulgaria's national economy may cause it to recalibrate the appropriate balance between investor protections and the right to regulate. Measures taken by governments to protect their societies and economies during the pandemic and the war in Ukraine have affected companies and investors. Investment treaties should be drafted with sufficient precision to provide flexibility for governments to respond effectively to the crisis and to take vital measures such as securing quick access to essential goods and services. While it may be too early to assess the consequences of the pandemic and the war in Ukraine for this area of investment policy, it is likely that experiences with the two events may refocus government attention on the balance between investor protection and governments' right to regulate, especially in times of crisis (OECD, 2020). Governments have been addressing the balance between investment protection and the right to regulate in investment treaties through analysis and discussion at the OECD (Gaukrodger, 2017a, 2017b).

Opportunities for investment treaties to address investor responsibilities

The OECD is currently considering how trade and investment treaties can affect business responsibilities including through their impact on policy space for governments, their provisions that buttress domestic law or its enforcement, or their provisions that directly address business by, for example, encouraging observance of RBC standards (Gaukrodger, 2020).

Some Bulgarian investment treaties contain provisions on RBC-related objectives and investor responsibilities. These provisions vary in terms of scope and level of generality; some are binding on arbitral tribunals in ISDS or SSDS but others may not be. Most notably, the EU's trade and investment agreements with Canada, Singapore and Viet Nam contain provisions aimed at preserving space for government policy making in RBC-related areas,[41] clarify that the expropriation provisions shall not restrict the parties' ability to regulate to achieve specified public interest objectives such as public health, safety and environmental protection[42] and exclude investments procured by corruption from the scope of ISDS.[43] These agreements also contain dedicated chapters on trade and sustainable development, labour and the environment that reaffirm government duties to regulate in key RBC-related areas.[44] Treaty provisions that buttress domestic law or its enforcement in key areas in host states remain rare but they are increasing in importance. Some EU trade treaties further buttress domestic law by clarifying the parties' understanding that it is inappropriate to encourage investment by relaxing environmental or health measures.[45]

Almost all of Bulgaria's BITs contain provisions that address investors directly on RBC-related issues. Most Bulgarian BITs contain legality requirements that restrict the scope of treaty protections to investments made in accordance with Bulgarian law. These requirements appear most frequently in provisions defining covered investments but also appear in provisions on the scope of application of the treaty. Some Bulgarian treaties also contain hortatory language in the preamble or substantive provisions reaffirming the importance of encouraging companies to respect corporate social responsibility norms.

Investment treaties concluded by some other governments address investor responsibilities in various other ways. For example, some treaties impose obligations on investors to uphold human rights and maintain an environmental management system; exclude the possibility for ISDS in relation to government measures relating to the treaty's environmental and labour provisions; refer to the parties' commitments to implement international standards related to RBC; and recognise that investments should contribute to the economic development of the host state (Gordon et. al., 2014; Gaukrodger, 2020).

The MoE has advised that Bulgaria's model BIT, approved by the Council of Ministers in November 2018, contains provisions on sustainable development and public welfare considerations but no new treaties have yet been concluded under this model. The government may wish to engage with ongoing intergovernmental discussions on this topic, including as part of the ECT modernisation process and at the OECD. Some ECT Members including the EU propose to update the ECT by including new provisions addressing sustainable development and RBC-related objectives (European Commission, 2020c).

Addressing the unique approach to claims for reflective loss in ISDS

Bulgaria should continue to engage in multilateral fora such as at the OECD and UNCITRAL to develop proposals to address the unique approach to claims for shareholders' reflective loss in ISDS. Shareholders incur reflective loss if a company in which they hold shares suffers a loss that results, in turn, in the shareholders suffering a commensurate loss, typically a loss in value of the shares. In contrast to the approach of domestic laws in many countries, many investment treaties have been interpreted to allow ISDS claims by covered shareholders for losses incurred by companies in which they own shares.

Governments have been considering these issues at the OECD since 2013 (OECD, 2016; Gaukrodger, 2014a, 2014b, 2013; Summary of 19th FOI Roundtable, October 2013, pp. 12-19; Summary of 18th FOI Roundtable, March 2013, pp. 4-9). Ongoing discussions at UNCITRAL's Working Group III on ISDS Reform are considering possible reforms to address these issues, which were underlined in a recent UNCITRAL Secretariat note (UNCITRAL, 2019d). At the request of the Working Group, these discussions are being conducted jointly with the OECD. Given that the current approach towards reflective loss in ISDS provides claimants with exceptional benefits and greatly expands the number of actual and potential ISDS cases, however, only government-led reform is likely to address the issues.

Evaluating overlaps between investment treaties

Bulgaria has two investment treaties – namely a BIT and the ECT – in force with 29 countries as of December 2021 (Figure 5.3).

Overlapping investment treaties that apply to investments by investors from the same country may raise some policy concerns. As a general matter, Bulgaria should strive to minimise inconsistencies between international obligations entered into with different countries. In the case of the ECT, any potential overlap with protections offered under BITs with the same partners applies to investments in energy or energy-related sectors – while the ECT applies only to these sectors, Bulgaria's BITs apply to investments in all sectors. In practice, this means that covered foreign investors in Bulgaria's energy or energy-related sectors may be able to rely on more favourably worded provisions in Bulgaria's older BITs in their dealings with the government or in ISDS disputes. This approach could potentially undermine the impact of the ongoing ECT modernisation process if investors in the energy sector can circumvent reforms to ECT provisions by relying on older BITs that are still in force.

Bulgaria may wish to evaluate the likely impact of these overlaps in treaty protection for investments in energy or energy-related sectors. It may also wish to consider engaging with relevant treaty partners to consider these overlaps and how they could be addressed as part of the ongoing ECT modernisation process.

Despite the concerns that may arise with overlapping treaties, some governments may consider that they need to provide certain extra incentives or guarantees to some treaty partners over others in order to attract FDI. This may be because they expect that investors from those countries are less likely to invest their capital in the absence of such treatment or assess that the broader benefits associated with attracting FDI from those countries are particularly lucrative. Some governments may also consider that similar provisions in different treaties, while framed differently, are likely to be interpreted in a consistent way. The balance between these interests and assessments is a delicate one and may evolve over time.

Figure 5.3. Overview of Bulgaria's overlapping investment treaty relationships in force as of December 2021

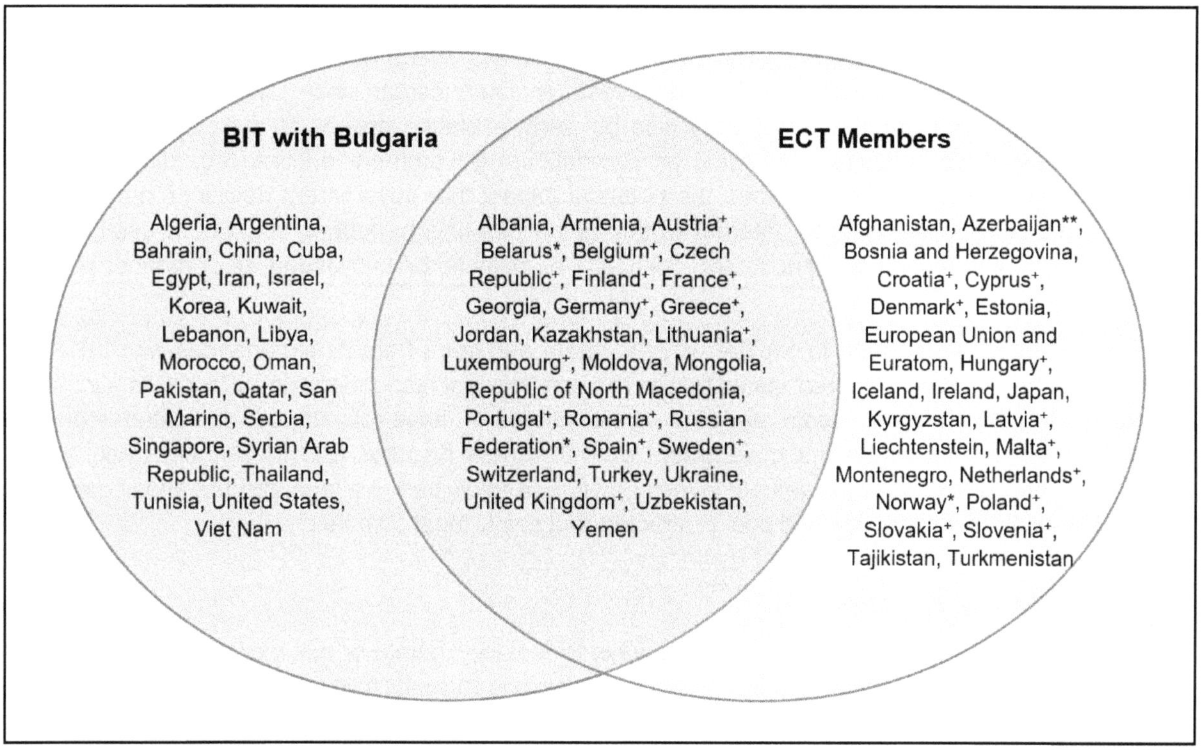

Note: *Belarus, Norway and the Russian Federation have signed but not ratified the ECT; Belarus applies the treaty provisionally. **Bulgaria has signed a BIT with Azerbaijan but it is not in force. + Bulgaria's BITs with EU member states are set to be terminated under the Intra-EU BIT Termination Agreement; 10 of these 19 BIT have already been terminated under the Agreement as of April 2021. The Ministry of Finance also advised during the process of preparing this *Review* that bilateral negotiations are underway to terminate existing Bulgarian BITs with Austria, Finland, Sweden and the United Kingdom, including sunset provisions that would extend treaty effects beyond termination.
Source: OECD investment treaty database.

Developing approaches to prevention of ISDS claims and ISDS case management

Bulgaria may wish to prioritise the development of strategies to prevent and achieve early settlement of investment-related disputes, as well as its approach to case management of ISDS cases. Aside from participating in inter-governmental discussions on these topics, the government may wish to consider taking certain steps at a domestic level.

There is currently no dedicated unit responsible for handling investor grievances before they become ISDS cases under investment treaties. The Litigation Department of the Ministry of Finance (MoF) co-ordinates Bulgaria's legal representation in arbitrations and foreign court proceedings, including any related settlement negotiations, annulment proceedings or enforcement actions. MFA acts as a repository for original versions and certified copies of Bulgaria's concluded treaties.

The government may wish to consider drawing on examples of institutional frameworks in other countries for the prevention of investment disputes and policy-setting activities. At a domestic level, some countries, such as Colombia and Peru, have adopted comprehensive legislative and regulatory frameworks to encourage the early detection and resolution of investment disputes (OECD, 2018b; Joubin-Bret, 2015). Other countries, such as Chile, have opted for an informal prevention system where sectoral agencies directly manage disputes with investors. Some countries including Croatia and Thailand have reported successful outcomes with inter-ministerial committees established to advise line agencies on investor grievances and formulate proposals to update and revise the government's policies regarding investment treaties and domestic legal frameworks for investment protection. As noted above, Brazil does not include ISDS in its investment treaties but instead establishes with each treaty partner a Focal Point or ombudsman within each government to address investor grievances, with a Joint Committee of government representatives to oversee the administration of the agreement. Korea has also had a successful track-record of early dispute resolution with its Foreign Investment Ombudsman since it was established in 1999 (Nicolas, Thomsen and Bang, 2013). It may also be worth exploring options to build awareness within government ministries, agencies and local or sub-national government entities regarding Bulgaria's obligations under investment treaties and the potential impact that government decisions may have on investor rights under these treaties. Internal written guidelines or a handbook could be a useful way to disseminate this information and encourage continuity of institutional knowledge as personnel changes occur over time.

The government may also wish to explore ways to share and learn from its experiences with ISDS and those of other governments. Several states that have been frequent respondents in ISDS cases – including Argentina, Canada, Mexico, Spain and the United States – have developed dedicated teams of government lawyers to advise the government on investment disputes and investment treaty policy. Nurturing an internal expertise to evaluate investor claims candidly before a legal dispute arises can be an important step in preventing time and cost protracted and costly legal disputes.

Procedural considerations: Exit and renegotiation

A growing number of countries are considering ways to replace, update or exit older investment treaties that no longer reflect governments' current priorities. Bulgaria is currently following this course with Türkiye: ongoing negotiations seek to replace an existing BIT concluded in 1994 with a new treaty in line with the government's 2018 model BIT. Negotiations are also underway with Austria, Finland, Sweden and the United Kingdom to terminate existing BITs. Review and renegotiation of investment treaties takes time and significant governmental resources and the option to terminate a treaty is not necessarily available at any moment, as the relevant provisions on temporal validity in the treaty may place limits on exit options (Box 5.3).

Box 5.3. Designs of temporal validity provisions in investment treaties

Unlike most international treaties, which can be denounced at relatively short notice, investment treaties typically contain clauses that extend their temporal validity for significant periods of time. Three designs can be found, often cumulatively in the same agreement. First, most investment treaties set and initial validity period of often 10 years or more, counting from the treaty's entry into force. After that period, many treaties only allow states parties to denounce the treaty at the end of specific intervals of often 10 years or more. Finally, treaty obligations almost universally continue to apply for a sunset period after the termination of the treaty, again for periods of typically 10 years or more. Many treaties thus bind the treaty parties for at least two decades, and in some extreme cases for up to 50 years.

Treaty designs that automatically extend the validity of the treaty for fixed terms are included in around 30% of the global treaty stock, but this design has been used less frequently in recent years. This design tends to prolong the period for which states parties are bound without granting additional benefits in terms of predictability for investors: on the contrary, the oscillating residual treaty validity is hard to predict without detailed study (see illustrative comparison in Figure 5.4).

Figure 5.4. Residual validity of treaties depending on the design of their validity clause

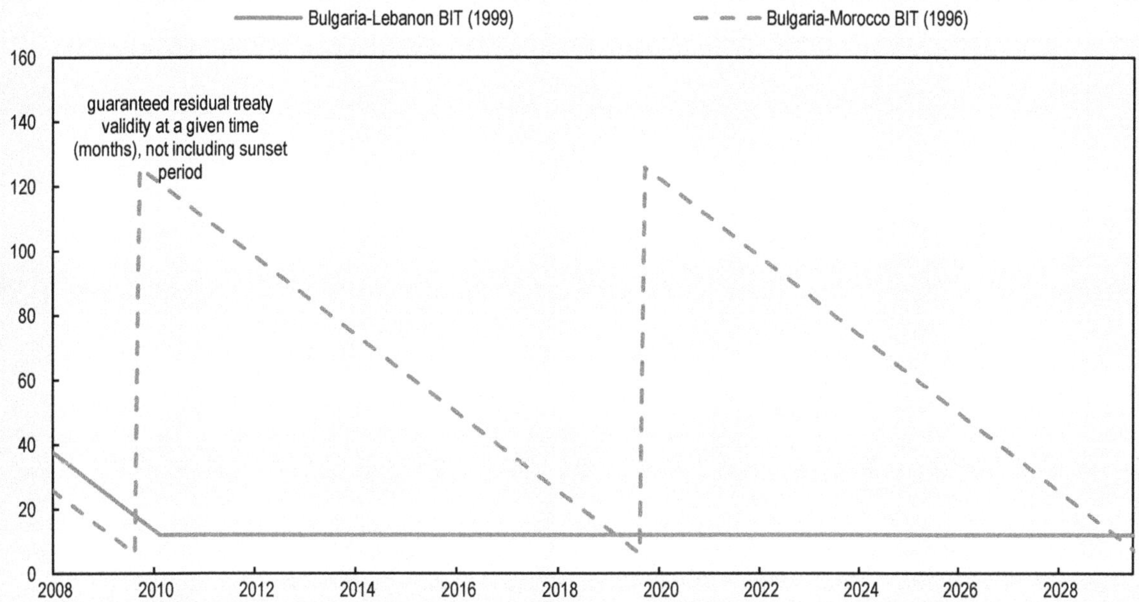

Note: Adapted from OECD work on temporal validity of investment treaties (Pohl, 2013).
Source: OECD calculations based on OECD investment treaty database.

Many Bulgarian investment treaties in force today contain temporal validity provisions that will operate to delay possibilities for unilateral exit from the treaty. Most of Bulgaria's investment treaties contain an initial validity period of 10 or 15 years. Bulgaria's BIT with Kuwait (1997) has a longer initial validity period of 25 years. At least 31 of Bulgaria's BITs in force today provide for an automatic renewal period after the period of initial validity and allow either treaty party to denounce the treaty within six or 12 months (depending on the treaty) of the expiry of the renewed period. Treaties that renew for fixed terms require more monitoring as they limit the possibilities to update or unilaterally end the agreement. If no termination occurs in the defined notice period, the treaty automatically renews for the agreed period, thereby committing Bulgaria to these treaties for a further six or ten years in most cases – and 25 years in the case of the BIT with Kuwait (1997) – before the next opportunity to terminate the treaty will arise.

Even if Bulgaria were to terminate unilaterally some or all of its treaties, most of them would continue to apply for a survival period of at least 10 years or more (often referred to as "sunset" clauses). These provisions are often intended to provide a measure of legal certainty for investors who frequently make long-term capital commitments in the host country. This situation may leave the government potentially exposed to ISDS claims far beyond the termination date. An extreme case is Bulgaria's BIT with Libya (1999), which appears to envisage survival effects for an unlimited duration following termination. Treaty partners may be able to agree mutually to replace or exit an older treaty in such a way that the survival provisions no longer apply.

As a hypothetical example to illustrate the possible effects of these clauses, as of 20 December 21 the earliest occasion that the government could unilaterally withdraw from all of its investment treaties is 2031 (taking into account the automatic renewal periods in some treaties) and the effects of post-termination "sunset" periods could last beyond 2045 even if appropriate actions were started today (Figure 5.5).

Figure 5.5. Projection of the temporal validity of Bulgaria's investment treaties

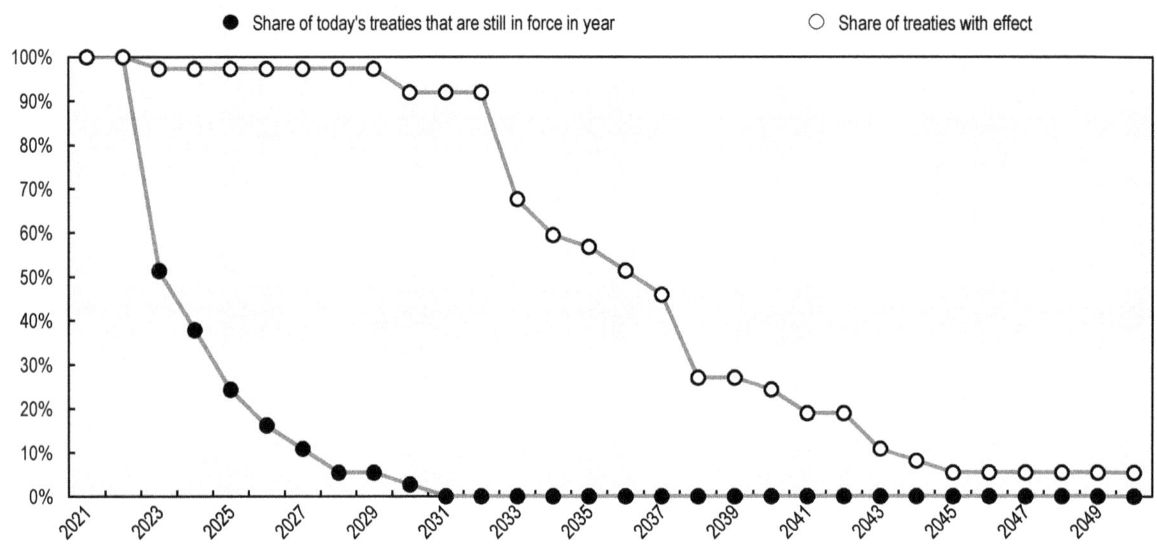

Note: Projections based on a hypothetical scenario of unilateral denunciation of all treaties in the available sample at the earliest possible occasion. Line with black dots shows the share of Bulgaria's existing treaties that would remain in force in a given year. Line with white dots shows the share of those treaties that would remain in effect in a given year based on applicable sunset periods.
Source: Calculations based on OECD investment treaty database.

Unilateral action is not the only option to update or address older investment treaties but the impact of temporal validity provisions may influence how treaty amendments or agreed exits can be negotiated with treaty partners, especially if the renewal period is imminent. Bulgaria may therefore wish to consider whether the current design of its temporal validity provisions can serve its interests in future discussions with treaty partners.

Outlook and policy recommendations

The protection of investment, combined with effective enforcement mechanisms, is an important pillar of a sound investment climate. Bulgaria's domestic legal framework provides protection for investors in line with other EU policy regimes, reflecting the gradual adoption of the EU *acquis* and the country's transition towards a market economy. Bulgaria also benefits from a modern IP legislation that is aligned with the EU norms and standards. Constitutional-level protection to IP rights, in particular to artistic, scientific and technological creativity, as well as inventors' rights, copyrights and related rights, is an important precondition for attracting and retaining investment. Bulgaria is also a party to most international treaties and conventions on intellectual property administrated by the WIPO and its national laws are aligned with EU directives, even going beyond the minimum requirements of the WTO TRIPS.

Contract enforcement is important for investment, since it assures investors that their contractual rights will be respected and upheld, Bulgaria has made sure to create an arbitration and mediation-friendly legal system and is currently making progress in reducing delays related to contract enforcement. Challenges nevertheless remain in the area of contract enforcement, associated to a weak judiciary, delays and additional costs to enforce contracts and obtain reparations, hampering the country's investment climate and economic prospects.

Bulgaria's investment treaty policy also deserves continued attention. Although the EC now plays an important role in setting investment policy for EU member states, the government should be proactive in evaluating whether its existing BITs – many of which were concluded decades ago – align with current priorities. These treaties may play an important role in attracting or retaining FDI in Bulgaria or treaty partner countries for Bulgarian investors abroad but evidence of this impact may be needed to assess whether these and other objectives are being fulfilled. Some aspects of Bulgaria's older BITs discussed in this chapter may render them out of step with EU and/or Bulgarian assessments of the appropriate balance between investor protection and the right to regulate. A more balanced approach in the new model BIT approved by the Cabinet in 2018 represents an important achievement for future treaty negotiations but seeking to update existing treaties is a separate challenge with time, cost and resource allocation constraints. The government is keenly aware of these issues through its participation in reform processes at UNCITRAL and for the ECT as well as EU-led action to terminate intra-EU BITs. Continued engagement in government and other action on investment treaty reforms should be an important part of the government's strategy to address these issues.

Policy recommendations

- Consider recognising foreign-based conciliation commissions and foreign-based mediation procedures as an alternative method of resolution of legal and non-legal disputes, as done with mediation that takes place in Bulgaria. This would avoid the current burdensome requirement for out-of-court settlements to undergo the general procedures for enforcement of contracts.
- Take additional steps to reduce the length of judicial procedures. These measures should include specific rules of procedure to prevent or limit dilatory measures and fixed time limits for the performance of each judiciary step, eliminating the need of interested parties to resort to the superior court to avoid time-delaying tactics.
- Continue to reassess and update the government's priorities with respect to investment treaty policy. An important issue in this regard is an evaluation of the appropriate balance between investor protections and the government's right to regulate, and how to achieve that balance in practice. Clearer specification of key provisions in older BITs would likely help to reflect government intent and ensure policy space for government regulation. It has proven difficult for governments to update older treaties but some multilateral reform initiatives are underway. Depending on whether the parties wish to clarify original intent or revise a provision, it may be possible to clarify language through joint interpretations agreed with treaty partners or treaty amendments. Replacement of older investment treaties by consent may also be an appropriate option in some cases.

- Continue to participate actively in and follow closely government and other action on investment treaty reforms at the OECD, UNCITRAL and for the ECT. Consideration of reforms and policy discussions on frequently invoked provisions in ISDS cases and whether investment treaties are achieving their intended purposes are of particular importance in current investment treaty policy. Emerging issues such as the possible role for trade and investment treaties in fostering responsible business conduct as well as ongoing discussions about treaties and sustainable development also merit close attention and participation.
- Continue to develop ISDS dispute prevention and case management tools. The government advised during the course of this Review that there is currently no dedicated unit responsible for handling investor grievances before they become ISDS cases under investment treaties. The government may wish to consider drawing on examples of institutional frameworks in other countries for the prevention of investment disputes and policy-setting activities. It may also wish to consider ways to promote awareness-raising and inter-ministerial co-operation regarding the government's investment treaty policy and the significance of investment treaty obligations for the day-to-day functions of line agencies.

References

Alfaro, L. (2016), "Gains from Foreign Direct Investment: Macro and Micro Approaches", *World Bank Economic Review*, Vol. 30, https://elibrary.worldbank.org/doi/abs/10.1093/wber/lhw007.

Draguiev, D., A. Georgiev (2015), *The European, Middle Eastern and African Arbitration Review 2016*, Global Arbitration Review, https://globalarbitrationreview.com/insight/the-european-middle-eastern-and-african-arbitration-review-2016/1036942/bulgaria.

Emanuilov, E. (2019), *Arbitration in Bulgaria*, Kambourov & Partners Attorneys at Law, *Lexology*, 18 September 2019, www.lexology.com/library/detail.aspx?g=660a8f97-ebf4-4db1-8e5f-c9ae1b0c7a24.

Energy Charter Secretariat (2020), "Updated statistics on investment arbitration cases under the Energy Charter Treaty", 5 June 2020, www.energycharter.org/media/news/article/updated-statistics-on-investment-arbitration-cases-under-the-energy-charter-treaty/.

Energy Charter Secretariat (2019), "Decision of the Energy Charter Conference on the Policy Options for Modernisation of the ECT", Document No. CCDEC 2019 08 STR, 6 October 2019, www.energycharter.org/fileadmin/DocumentsMedia/CCDECS/2019/CCDEC201908.pdf.

European Commission (2020), "EU text proposal for the modernisation of the Energy Charter Treaty (ECT)", May 2020, https://trade.ec.europa.eu/doclib/docs/2020/may/tradoc_158754.pdf.

European Commission (2018), *Report from the European Commission to the European Parliament and the Council: On Progress in Bulgaria under the Co-operation and Verification Mechanism,* https://ec.europa.eu/info/files/technical-report-bulgaria-2019-swd-2019-392_en.

European Commission (2017), *Report from the European Commission to the European Parliament and the Council: On Progress in Bulgaria under the Co-operation and Verification Mechanism*, https://ec.europa.eu/info/files/progress-report-bulgaria-2017-com-2017-750_en.

Gaukrodger, D. (2020), "Business Responsibilities and Investment Treaties", public consultation paper by the OECD Secretariat, 15 January 2020, www.oecd.org/daf/inv/investment-policy/Consultation-Paper-on-business-responsibilities-and-investment-treaties.pdf.

Gaukrodger, D. (2018), "Appointing Authorities and the Selection of Arbitrators in Investor-State Dispute Settlement: An Overview", March 2018, *OECD Consultation Paper*, www.oecd.org/investment/investment-policy/ISDS-Appointing-Authorities-Arbitration-March-2018.pdf.

Gaukrodger (2017a), "The balance between investor protection and the right to regulate in investment treaties", *OECD Working Papers on International Investment,* No. 2017/02, OECD Publishing, Paris, https://doi.org/10.1787/82786801-en.

Gaukrodger, D. (2017b), "Addressing the balance of interests in investment treaties: The limitation of fair and equitable treatment provisions to the minimum standard of treatment under customary international law", *OECD Working Papers on International Investment*, No. 2017/03, OECD Publishing, Paris, https://doi.org/10.1787/0a62034b-en.

Gaukrodger, D. (2016), "The legal framework applicable to joint interpretive agreements of investment treaties", *OECD Working Papers on International Investment*, No. 2016/01, OECD Publishing, Paris, https://doi.org/10.1787/5jm3xgt6f29w-en.

Gaukrodger, D. (2014a), "Investment Treaties and Shareholder Claims for Reflective Loss: Insights from Advanced Systems of Corporate Law", *OECD Working Papers on International Investment*, No. 2014/02, OECD Publishing, Paris, https://doi.org/10.1787/5jz0xvgngmr3-en.

Gaukrodger, D. (2014b), "Investment Treaties and Shareholder Claims: Analysis of Treaty Practice", *OECD Working Papers on International Investment*, No. 2014/03, OECD Publishing, Paris, https://doi.org/10.1787/5jxvk6shpvs4-en.

Gaukrodger, D. (2013), "Investment treaties as corporate law: Shareholder claims and issues of consistency. A preliminary framework for policy analysis", *OECD Working Papers on International Investment,* No. 2013/3, OECD Publishing, Paris, https://doi.org/10.1787/5jxvk6shpvs4-en.

Gaukrodger, D. and K. Gordon (2012), "Investor-State Dispute Settlement: A Scoping Paper for the Investment Policy Community", *OECD Working Papers on International Investment*, No. 2012/03, OECD Publishing, Paris, https://doi.org/10.1787/5k46b1r85j6f-en.

Gordon, K. and J. Pohl (2015), "Investment Treaties over Time – Treaty Practice and Interpretation in a Changing World", *OECD Working Papers on International Investment*, No. 2015/02, OECD Publishing, Paris, https://doi.org/10.1787/5js7rhd8sq7h-en.

Gordon, K., J. Pohl and M. Bouchard (2014), "Investment Treaty Law, Sustainable Development and Responsible Business Conduct: A Fact Finding Survey", *OECD Working Papers on International Investment*, No. 2014/01, OECD Publishing, Paris, https://doi.org/10.1787/5jz0xvgx1zlt-en.

Joubin-Bret, A. (2015), "Establishing an International Advisory Centre on Investment Disputes? E15Initiative", *Working Paper for the International Centre for Trade and Sustainable Development and the World Economic Forum*, December 2015, https://e15initiative.org/wp-content/uploads/2015/09/E15-Investment-Joubin-Bret-Final.pdf.

Kolev, N. and T. Targot (2019), *The Foreign Investment Regulation Review*, seventh edition, Law Business Research Ltd, https://thelawreviews.co.uk/edition/the-foreign-investment-regulation-review-edition-7/1209420/bulgaria.

Mikov Attorneys (2017), "Litigation in Bulgaria", https://www.mikov-attorneys.com/news/litigation-bulgaria

Miroudot, S. and D. Rigo (2019), "Preferential Trade Agreements and Multinational Production", European University Institute Working Paper, No. RSCAS 2019/14, Robert Schuman Centre for Advanced Studies, Global Governance Programme, http://dx.doi.org/10.2139/ssrn.3332245.

Mistura, F. and C. Roulet, (2019), "The Determinants of Foreign Direct Investment: Do Statutory Restrictions Matter?", OECD Working Papers on International Investment, No. 2019/01, OECD Publishing, Paris, https://doi.org/10.1787/641507ce-en.

Nicolas, F., S. Thomsen and M. Bang (2013), "Lessons from Investment Policy Reform in Korea", *OECD Working Papers on International Investment*, No. 2013/02, OECD Publishing, Paris, https://doi.org/10.1787/5k4376zqcpf1-en.

OECD (2020), "OECD investment policy responses to COVID-19", 17 April 2020,

https://doi.org/10.1787/4be0254d-enhttp://www.oecd.org/coronavirus/policy-responses/oecd-investment-policy-responses-to-covid-19-4be0254d/.

OECD (2016), "The impact of investment treaties on companies, shareholders and creditors", in OECD Business and Finance Outlook 2016, OECD Publishing, Paris, https://dx.doi.org/10.1787/9789264257573-en.

OECD (2015), *Enquiries into Intellectual Property's Economic Impact*, OECD Publishing, www.oecd.org/sti/ieconomy/intellectual-property-economic-impact.htm.

Pohl, J. (2013), "Temporal Validity of International Investment Agreements: A Large Sample Survey of Treaty Provisions", *OECD Working Papers on International Investment*, No. 2013/04, OECD Publishing, Paris, https://doi.org/10.1787/5k3tsjsl5fvh-en.

Pohl, J. (2018) "Societal benefits and costs of International Investment Agreements: A critical review of aspects and available empirical evidence", *OECD Working Papers on International Investment*, No. 2018/01, OECD Publishing, Paris, https://doi.org/10.1787/e5f85c3d-en.

Pohl, J., K. Mashigo and A. Nohen (2012), "Dispute Settlement Provisions in International Investment Agreements: A Large Sample Survey", *OECD Working Papers on International Investment*, No. 2012/02, OECD Publishing, Paris, https://doi.org/10.1787/5k8xb71nf628-en.

UNCITRAL Commission (2019), "Possible reform of investor-State dispute settlement (ISDS): Shareholder claims and reflective loss. Note by the Secretariat", Document No. A/CN.9/WG.III/WP.170, http://undocs.org/en/A/CN.9/WG.III/WP.170.

Urtasun, E. (2020), "Statement on the modernisation of the Energy Charter Treaty", 8 September 2020, www.ernesturtasun.eu/ecologia/statement-the-modernisation-of-the-energy-charter-treaty/.

Annex 5.A. Overview of Bulgaria's investment treaties

Annex Table 5.A.1. Bulgaria's bilateral investment treaties – in force as of July 2021

No	Treaty partner	Date of signature	Date of entry into force
1	Bahrain	26-06-2009	22-12-2011
2	Qatar	08-11-2007 (Bulgaria) 11-11-2007 (Qatar)	20-05-2008
3	San Marino	23-02-2007	26-07-2007
4	Oman	03-02-2007	22-10-2014
5	Korea	12-06-2006	16-11-2006
6	Lithuania	21-11-2005	25-04-2006
7	Singapore	15-09-2003	10-02-2006
8	Thailand	11-09-2003	12-08-2004
9	Jordan	07-08-2002	19-04-2003
10	Yemen	12-04-2002	11-04-2003
11	Pakistan	12-02-2002	26-10-2005
12	Tunisia	24-11-2000	15-10-2003
13	Mongolia	06-06-2000	26-03-2003
14	Syrian Arab Republic	21-05-2000	10-11-2001
15	Libya	19-11-1999	19-01-2004
16	Kazakhstan	15-09-1999	20-08-2001
17	Lebanon	01-06-1999	16-02-2000
18	Czech Republic	17-03-1999	30-09-2000
19	Republic of North Macedonia	22-02-1999	05-06-1999
20	Cuba	16-12-1998	24-05-2000
21	Iran	13-11-1998	24-08-2003
22	Algeria	25-10-1998	06-06-2002
23	Uzbekistan	24-06-1998	31-03-1999
24	Egypt	15-03-1998	08-06-2000
25	Finland	03-10-1997	16-04-1999
26	Kuwait	17-06-1997	16-09-1998
27	Austria	22-01-1997	01-11-1997
28	Viet Nam	19-09-1996	15-05-1998
29	Morocco	22-05-1996	19-02-2000
30	Moldova	17-04-1996	11-06-1997
31	Belarus	21-02-1996	11-11-1997
32	Serbia	13-02-1996	09-01-1997
33	United Kingdom	11-12-1995	24-06-1997
34	Spain	05-09-1995	22-04-1998
35	Armenia	10-04-1995	27-03-1996
36	Georgia	19-01-1995	06-08-1999
37	Ukraine	08-12-1994	10-12-1995
38	Türkiye	06-07-1994	18-09-1997
39	Romania	01-06-1994	23-05-1995
40	Albania	27-04-1994	28-01-1996
41	Sweden	19-04-1994	01-04-1995

No	Treaty partner	Date of signature	Date of entry into force
42	Israel	06-12-1993	17-12-1996
43	Argentina	21-09-1993	11-03-1997
44	Russian Federation	08-06-1993	19-12-2005
45	Portugal	27-05-1993	20-11-2000
46	Greece	12-03-1993	29-04-1995
47	United States	23-09-1992	02-06-1994
48	Switzerland	28-10-1991	26-10-1993
49	China	27-06-1989	21-08-1994 (China) 24-08-1994 (Bulgaria)
50	France	05-04-1989	01-05-1990
51	BLEU (Belgium-Luxembourg Economic Union)	25-10-1988	29-05-1991
52	Germany	12-04-1986	10-03-1988

Note: Listed in descending chronological order based on date of signature. Dates appear in dd-mm-yyyy format. It is difficult to be precise about the exact status of Bulgaria's BITs due to some inconsistencies in publicly available information, especially entry into force dates. Full-text versions of some but not all Bulgarian BITs are available on the Bulgarian State Gazette website: https://dv.parliament.bg/. The Ministry of Foreign Affairs acts as a repository for originals and certified transcripts of Bulgaria's treaties under the Law on International Treaties but the MFA does not maintain an electronic database for these treaties. The Bulgarian Government confirmed during the preparation of this *Review* that the list of BITs in force above is accurate as of September 2020. Some of the information published by Bulgaria on its investment treaties, in particular with respect to dates of signature and entry into force, may nonetheless be inconsistent with information published by Bulgaria's treaty partners. For example, information published on the State Gazette website indicates that the Bulgaria-Qatar BIT was signed on 8 November 2007 while Qatar's legislation portal and its Official Gazette (https://www.almeezan.qa/) indicates 11 November 2007; similarly, the State Gazette indicates that the Bulgaria-China BIT (1989) entered into force on 24 August 1994 while China's Ministry of Commerce (http://tfs.mofcom.gov.cn/) indicates 21 August 1989. Online databases of investment treaties maintained by third parties such as UNCTAD and ICSID indicate a range of other conflicting dates that have not been taken into account for the purposes of this chapter.
Source: OECD investment treaty database; Bulgarian Government.

Annex Table 5.A.2. Bulgaria's bilateral investment treaties – terminated

No	Treaty partner	Date of signature	Date of entry into force	Effective date of termination	Type of termination
1	Indonesia	13-09-2003	25-01-2005	25-01-2015	Unilaterally denounced
2	Latvia	04-12-2003	23-07-2004	28-02-2021	Mutual agreement
3	Netherlands	06-10-1999	01-03-2001	31-03-2021	Mutual agreement
4	India	26-10-1998	23-09-1999	30-03-2017	Unilaterally denounced
5	Slovenia	30-06-1998	26-11-2000	10-03-2021	Mutual agreement
6	Croatia	25-06-1996	20-02-1998	13-12-2020	Mutual agreement
7	Hungary	08-06-1994	07-09-1995	13-12-2020	Mutual agreement
8	Poland	11-04-1994	09-03-1995	04-04-2021	Mutual agreement
9	Slovak Republic	21-07-1994	09-03-1995	13-12-2020	Mutual agreement
10	Denmark	14-04-1993	20-05-1995	13-12-2020	Mutual agreement
11	Italy	05-12-1988	27-12-1990	01-09-2008	Unilaterally denounced
12	Netherlands	08-03-1988	24-05-1990	01-03-2001	Replaced
13	Cyprus	12-11-1987	18-05-1988	13-12-2020	Mutual agreement
14	Finland	16-02-1984	16-07-1985	16-04-1999	Replaced
15	Malta	12-06-1984	07-02-1985	13-12-2020	Mutual agreement

Source: OECD investment treaty database; Bulgarian Government.

Annex Table 5.A.3. Bulgaria's bilateral investment treaties – signed but not in force

No	Treaty partner	Date of signature
1	Azerbaijan	07-10-2004
2	Sudan	03-04-2002
3	Democratic People's Republic of Korea	16-06-1999
4	Nigeria	21-12-1998
5	Ghana	20-10-1989
6	Austria	15-05-1981

Source: OECD investment treaty database; Bulgarian Government.

Annex Table 5.A.4. Bulgaria's trade agreements containing investment protections, investment liberalisation provisions and/or ISDS

No	Treaty	Date of signature for Bulgaria	Date of entry into force	Date of entry into force for Bulgaria
1	EU-Viet Nam Investment Protection Agreement	30-06-2019	-	-
2	EU-Singapore Investment Protection Agreement	19-10-2018	-	-
3	EU-Canada Comprehensive Economic and Trade Agreement	30-10-2016	21-09-2017 (provisional)	21-09-2017 (provisional)
4	Energy Charter Treaty	17-12-1994	16-04-1998	16-04-1998

Source: OECD investment treaty database; Bulgarian Government.

Notes

[1] English version available at: www.minfin.bg/en/1394

[2] Article 14.3 and 14.3 of the Bulgarian Statutory Instruments Act allows, exceptionally for a normative act to be retroactive, however, this retroactive force can never apply to provisions envisaging sanctions, unless they are lighter than the ones revoked.

[3] See Judgment of the Constitutional Court of the Republic of Bulgaria No. 1 of 27 January 2005 on constitutional case no. 8/2004 and Decision No. 13/2018 of 27 July 2018.

[4] The main laws regulating the forcible expropriation of property are the Property Act, the State Property Act (SPA), the Spatial Development Act and the Municipal Property Act. Other laws that may deal with specific expropriations are the Agricultural Land Conservation Act, Property Act and Use of Land Act, Energy Act, Protected Areas Act, Roads Act, Underground Resources Act, Maritime Spaces, Inland Waterways and Ports of the Republic of Bulgaria Act, Safe Use of Nuclear Energy Act and Cultural Heritage Act.

[5] An arbitration is deemed international if one or all of the parties to it are seated (for legal entities) or resident (for individuals) outside of Bulgaria. Respectively, an arbitration is domestic when all parties are seated or resident in Bulgaria.

[6] The arbitration agreement may consist of an arbitration clause or a separate statement (ICAA, Art. 7(3)). This means the Minutes of the arbitration proceedings can also be considered a written arbitration agreement or the written response of the defendant during an arbitration process without questioning the jurisdiction of the arbitration.

[7] Supreme Court of Cassation Decision 71 of 2 September 2011, Commercial Case 1193/2010, Second Commercial Chamber.

[8] Anna Rizova and Oleg Temnikov, "Bulgaria", *The International Arbitration Review,* Edition 11, July 2020.

[9] In particular, if the dispute concerns trade, industrial, invention or fiscal secrets, the public announcement of which would harm defendable interests (Civil Proceedings Code, Article 136).

[10] Agreement for the termination of Bilateral Investment Treaties between the Member States of the European Union, Official Journal of the European Union, 29 May 2020, L169/1-41, https://eur-lex.europa.eu/legal-content/EN/TXT/PDF/?uri=CELEX:22020A0529(01)&from=EN.

[11] Up-to-date information on the entry into force of the Intra-EU BIT Termination Agreement for the Member States and the termination status of related Bulgarian BITs appears at: https://www.consilium.europa.eu/bg/documents-publications/treaties-agreements/agreement/?id=2019049&DocLanguage=en.

[12] Bulgaria signed the two investment protection agreements with Viet Nam and Singapore, which are of a mixed type (i.e. between the EU and its Member States, on the one hand, and Singapore or Vietnam, on the other), in its national capacity and will ratify them at the national level. Related free trade agreements with Viet Nam and Singapore (as well as Japan) are signed and concluded by the EU only in its exclusive capacity; Bulgaria and the other EU Member States are not parties to these related trade agreements.

[13] The ratification procedure for EU-Canada CETA in Bulgaria is now at the stage of first reading. Updates on legislative developments for this ratification process appear at: https://www.parliament.bg/bg/bills/ID/157055/.

[14] Several other EU trade agreements such as the EU-Japan Economic Partnership Agreement (2018) contain investment liberalisation commitments without provisions on substantive investment protections or ISDS. Other EU trade agreements such as the EU-Armenia Comprehensive and Enhanced Partnership Agreement (2017) contain hortatory provisions on the contribution of FDI to sustainable development and envisage future negotiations regarding an investment chapter but do not currently contain provisions on investment protection.

[15] The discussion here refers to known claims only. The number of actual ISDS claims against Bulgaria may be higher on account of confidential pending cases.

[16] *Moti Ramot and Rami Levy v. Republic of Bulgaria* (ICSID Case No. ARB/18/47); *ACF Renewable Energy Limited v. Republic of Bulgaria* (ICSID Case No. ARB/18/1); *ČEZ, a.s. v. Republic of Bulgaria* (ICSID Case No. ARB/16/24); *State General Reserve Fund of the Sultanate of Oman v. Republic of Bulgaria* (ICSID Case No. ARB/15/43); *ENERGO-PRO a.s. v. Republic of Bulgaria* (ICSID Case No. ARB/15/19); *EVN AG v. Republic of Bulgaria* (ICSID Case No. ARB/13/17); *Novera AD, Novera Properties B.V. and Novera Properties N.V. v. Republic of Bulgaria* (ICSID Case No. ARB/12/16); *Accession Eastern Europe Capital AB and Mezzanine Management Sweden AB v. Republic of Bulgaria* (ICSID Case No. ARB/11/3); *Plama Consortium Limited v. Republic of Bulgaria* (ICSID Case No. ARB/03/24).

[17] *ST-AD GmbH v. Republic of Bulgaria*, UNCITRAL, PCA Case No. 2011-06.

[18] *Kornikom EOOD v. Republic of Serbia* (ICSID Case No. ARB/19/12).

[19] Based on publicly available information, at least five Bulgarian BITs contain no reference to fair and equitable treatment – BITs with Cyprus (1987), Malta (1984), Qatar (2007), Sweden (1994), Türkiye (1994). Most Bulgarian treaties refer to "fair and equitable" treatment but some refer to "fair and impartial" treatment (e.g. BITs with Libya (1999), Jordan (2002), Yemen (2002), Mongolia (2000), Pakistan (2002), San Marino (2007) and Tunisia (2000)) and others to "just and equitable" treatment (Bulgaria-France BIT (1989)).

[20] See *Plama Consortium Limited v. Republic of Bulgaria* (ICSID Case No. ARB/03/24) under the ECT; *ST-AD GmbH v. Republic of Bulgaria*, UNCITRAL, PCA Case No. 2011-06. The discussion here refers only to known claims. The number of actual FET claims against Bulgaria may be higher on account of confidential pending cases claims.

[21] See also Argentina-Japan BIT (2018); Australia-Peru FTA (2018); USMCA (2018); Australia-Hong Kong Investment Agreement (2019); Australia-Indonesia CEPA (2019). Recent EU treaties such as the EU-Singapore Investment Protection Agreement and the EU-Viet Nam Investment Protection Agreement also contain clarifications relating to investor expectations. However, they clarify certain exclusions of liability generally rather than referring specifically to the FET provision.

[22] Australia-Singapore FTA (2003), as amended in 2016, Article 6(5); Australia-Peru FTA (2018), Article 8.6(5); Australia-Uruguay BIT (2019), Article 4(5); Australia-Indonesia Comprehensive Economic Partnership Agreement (2019), Article 14.2(3).

[23] For example, Article 2.4 (2) of the EU-Singapore IPA clarifies that: "A Party breaches the obligation of fair and equitable treatment referenced in paragraph 1 if its measure or series of measures constitute: (a) denial of justice in criminal, civil and administrative proceedings; (b) a fundamental breach of due process; (c) manifestly arbitrary conduct; (d) harassment, coercion, abuse of power or similar bad faith conduct."

[24] See Bulgaria's BITs with Iran (1998), Libya (1999), Mongolia (2000), Kazakhstan (1999), Pakistan (2002), Russian Federation (1993) and Yemen (2002).

[25] Multiple references to FET occur in preamble text as well as a substantive provision of the treaty (see, for example, Bulgaria's BITs with Denmark (1993), Finland (1997), Jordan (2002), Pakistan (2002), the Netherlands (1999) and the United-States (1992)) or in several different substantive provisions (see, for example, Bulgaria BITs with Libya (1999), Indonesia (2003), Korea (2006) and Latvia (2003)). Other formulations of FET in Bulgarian treaties may also leave scope for broad interpretations by arbitral tribunals. For example, the Bulgaria-United States BIT (1992) refers to FET as "in no case… less than that required by international law" but does not define FET as MST-FET. Such a formulation creates a "floor" for FET, rather than a "ceiling" that would limit FET to the protections already afforded under international law. There is no guidance in this BIT or any other Bulgarian BIT about the extent to which protections may exceed those under international law.

[26] Gaukrodger, D. (2016) (reviewing the applicable law on joint interpretations of investment treaties without express provisions on the issue); Gordon, K. and Pohl, J. (2015). For a recent example of a joint interpretation, see the Joint Interpretative Declaration between Columbia and India (2018) regarding the Columbia-India BIT (2009).

[27] Notably there are no provisions on MFN treatment in the EU-Singapore Investment Protection Agreement (2018).

[28] Some of the EU's trade and investment agreements contain more detailed sector-specific exclusions. See, for example, the EU-Viet Nam Investment Protection Agreement (2019), which provides that MFN treatment does not apply to government subsidies or investments in some sectors (e.g. audio-visual services, mining, manufacturing and processing of nuclear materials, production of or trade in arms, munitions and war material, national maritime cabotage, domestic and international air transport services, and services supplied and activities performed in the exercise of governmental authority).

[29] See the EU's trade and investment agreements with Canada, Singapore and Viet Nam, as well as the Argentina-Bulgaria BIT (1993) and the EU-Japan Economic Partnership Agreement (2018).

[30] EU-Canada CETA (2016); EU-Vietnam FTA (2018); EU-Japan Economic Partnership Agreement (2018).

[31] EU-Singapore Investment Protection Agreement (2018).

[32] Treaty shopping is a concept used broadly herein to describe the power for a beneficial owner of an investment to choose between investment treaties or between provisions of different investment treaties. See further detail on treaty shopping below.

[33] For a recent discussion of the uncertainty surrounding the interpretation of MFN clauses in ISDS, see Batifort, S. and Benton Heath, J. (2018), "The New Debate on the Interpretation of MFN Clauses in Investment Treaties: Putting the Brakes on Multilateralization", *American Journal of International Law*, Volume 111, Issue 4 (October 2017), pp. 873-913.

[34] See, for example, United States-Mexico-Canada Agreement (2018), Article 14.5(4) ("For greater certainty, whether treatment is accorded in 'like circumstances' under this Article depends on the totality of the circumstances, including whether the relevant treatment distinguishes between investors or investments on the basis of legitimate public welfare objectives"); CPTPP (2018), "Note on Interpretation of 'In Like Circumstances'", www.mfat.govt.nz/assets/Trans-Pacific-Partnership/Other-documents/Interpretation-of-In-Like-Circumstances.pdf

[35] EU-Canada CETA (2016), Annex 8-A; EU-Singapore Investment Protection Agreement (2018), Annex 1; EU-Viet Nam Investment Protection Agreement (2019), Annex 4.

[36] See Bulgaria's BITs with Poland (1994), United Kingdom (1995), Romania (1994), the Netherlands (1988), Kuwait (1997), Indonesia (2003), Italy (1988), Greece (1993), Hungary (1994), Spain (1995), Latvia (2003), Germany (1986), Qatar (2007), France (1989), Egypt (1998), Denmark (1993), Croatia (1996), China (1989), the Slovak Republic (1998), Belgium/Luxembourg (1988), Iran (1998), Libya (1999), Mongolia (2000), Kazakhstan (1999), Pakistan (2002), the Russian Federation (2003), San Marino (2007), Türkiye (1994), Yemen (2002), and Albania (1994).

[37] For example, the Argentina-Bulgaria BIT (1993) provides that: "the denial of an investment authorization shall not itself constitute a dispute between an investor and a Contracting Party."

[38] See Bulgaria's BITs with Egypt (1998), Thailand (2003), Slovenia (1998), the Slovak Republic (1994), Latvia (2003), Lebanon (1990), France (1989), China (1989), Algeria (1998), Jordan (2002), Kazakhstan (1999), Mongolia (2000), Pakistan (2002), Yemen (2002), Argentina (1993) and Albania (1994).

[39] For example, under the Bulgaria-Singapore BIT (2003), investors can choose between ICSID or UNCITRAL arbitration in case of a dispute regarding expropriation, compensation for losses, repatriation, or subrogation, but have no choice other than ICSID arbitration for a dispute that concerns other subject matters.

[40] For example, under the Bulgaria-Oman BIT (2007), covered investors may choose to submit a dispute to international arbitration the UNCITRAL Arbitration Rules, the ICSID Arbitration Rules or an *ad hoc* arbitral tribunal.

[41] See, for example, EU-Singapore Investment Protection Agreement (2018), Article 2.2.

[42] See, for example, EU-Canada CETA (2016), Annex 8-A.

[43] See, for example, EU-Viet Nam Investment Protection Agreement (2019), Article 3.27.

[44] See, for example, EU-Canada CETA (2016), Chapter 22 (Trade and Sustainable Development), Chapter 23 (Trade and Labour) and Chapter 24 (Trade and Environment).

[45] See, for example, Armenia-EU Comprehensive and Enhanced Partnership Agreement (2017), Article 276.

6 Investment promotion and facilitation

This chapter reviews investment promotion and facilitation policy in Bulgaria. It provides an overview of the overall institutional and regulatory framework, relevant strategic documents, available investment incentives and the role of EU funds in mobilising investment. It also analyses the activities of the national investment promotion agency, InvestBulgaria Agency, benchmarking them to the agencies of OECD countries. Finally, it discusses the progress made in facilitating investment and reducing administrative burdens.

Introduction

As highlighted in the *OECD Policy Framework for Investment* (OECD, 2015a), investment promotion and facilitation – if adequately designed and implemented – can be powerful means to attract investment and ensure its contribution to economic development. As such, countries worldwide decide to not only remove restrictions on foreign direct investment and provide high standards of protection to investors, but also to proactively promote and facilitate investment, or certain types of investment, to maximise the benefits to the host economy. Considering that Bulgaria has removed most formal barriers to FDI, and is subject to the EU's regulatory *acquis*, it can benefit from active and well-designed investment promotion and facilitation policies to help attract and retain investment that can assist its transition towards more innovation, diversification and high-quality employment.

Bulgaria has made progress in improving its overall investment climate, as reflected in the existing business surveys and reports by international organisations. For example, the share of firms reporting political instability and corruption as a key barrier to firms diminished by nearly 10 percentage points in the World Bank's *Enterprise Survey* between 2013 and 2019 prior to political crises that Bulgaria faced throughout 2021 and new political crisis in the aftermath of the Government's lost of confidence vote in June 2022 (Figure 6.1). Still, firms identify certain policy areas as continuously important obstacles (Figure 6.2), such as the competition from the informal sector. According to EBRD BEEPS survey, 60% of firms reported they have to compete against unregistered firms. In addition, importance of other factors has increased – notably, the availability of skilled workforce and business licensing and permits. This is consistent with the findings of the survey by the Bulgaria Industrial Association (BIA), which also pointed to a lack of skilled labour force and bureaucracy as major obstacles to firms in 2019.[1]

Figure 6.1. Change in the share of firms identifying a particular area as a major constraint to doing business in Bulgaria, 2013-19

Percentage points

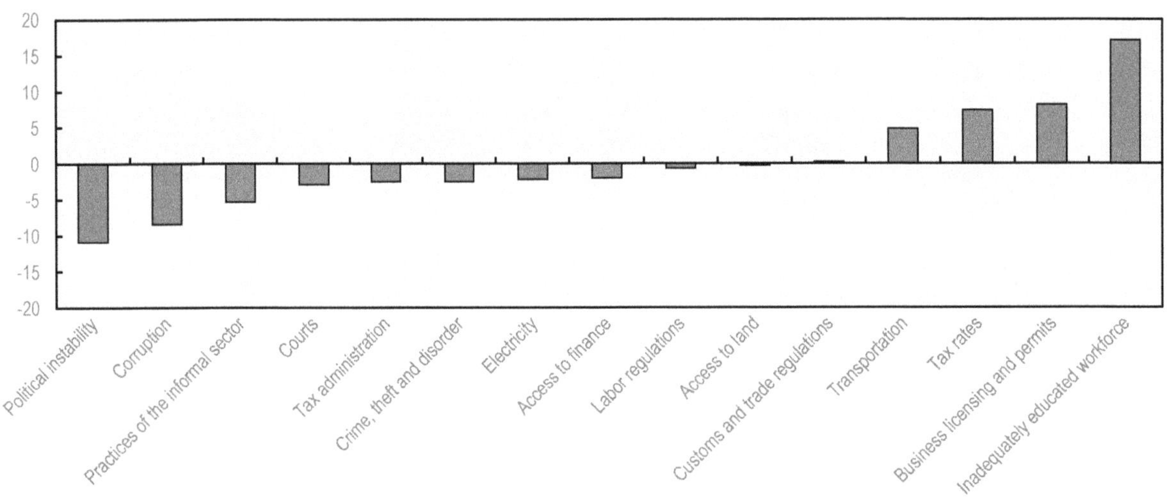

Source: World Bank (2013-19), Enterprise Survey of Bulgaria.

Figure 6.2. Overview of the main obstacles to doing business in Bulgaria and its region

In percentage

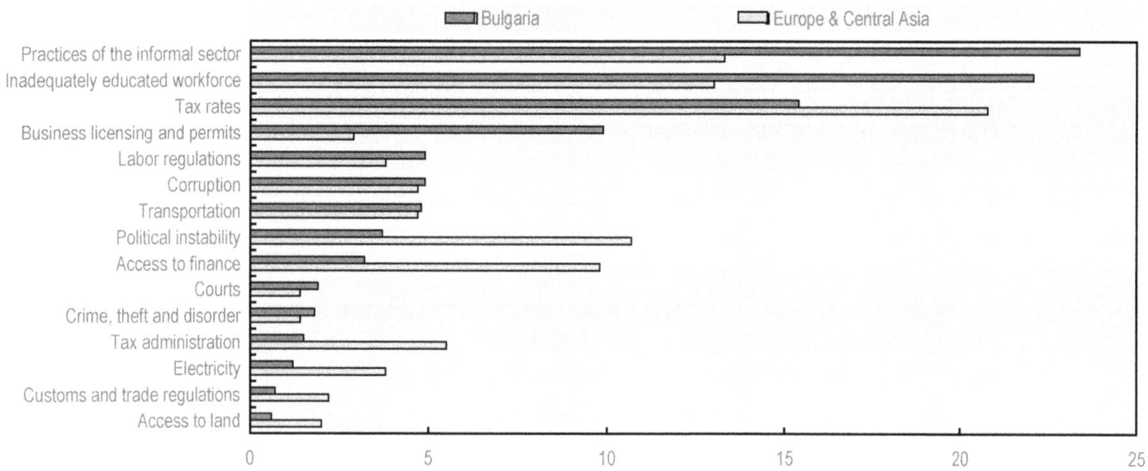

Note: Business owners and top managers in 772 firms were interviewed between January 2019 and March 2020.
Source: World Bank (2019), Enterprise Survey of Bulgaria.

Addressing these various challenges will require a concerted effort on the part of the government, utilising various policy tools at its disposal. This Chapter provides an overview of Bulgaria's recent efforts to improve business climate. It first outlines the legal and institutional framework for investment promotion and facilitation and describes the main policy tools in the area, such as the use of EU funds, investment incentives, industrial zones and SME-specific support programmes. It then reviews the activities of the national investment promotion agency (IPA), InvestBulgaria, benchmarking it relative to OECD IPAs. Finally, yet importantly, it analyses the progress made by Bulgaria in reducing administrative burdens and concludes with key policy recommendations.

National strategy and the institutional set-up

Bulgaria has developed elements of a national strategy for FDI attraction

Over the years, Bulgaria has developed several framework documents that provide the overall vision for the country's medium and long-term socio-economic development and set out key priorities, including in the area of investment policy (Box 6.1). They provide a framework within which the country's investment promotion and facilitation policy intervenes and set the national goals that FDI attraction should support. They also shape the expectations of the private sector on the type of support that investors may expect and delineate the responsibilities of different institutions.

In particular, the Act on Investment Promotion (AIP) is the main legal document outlining the type of support provided by the government to investors. It specifies the conditions, applicable procedures and requirements for obtaining state support and outlines the responsibilities of different government bodies. It is primarily concerned with regulating investment incentives. This is a relatively common approach to investment promotion acts in transition economies that have recently become EU Member States and have undertaken active steps to comply with the EU state-aid rules.[2]

Box 6.1 Strategic objectives of investment promotion and facilitation policy in Bulgaria

Several strategic documents provide an overall vision for the socio-economic development and the role of investment promotion and facilitation policy in Bulgaria:

- The National Development Programme: Bulgaria 2020 has served as an umbrella document for the country's socio-economic policies until 2020. In particular, Priority 5 explicitly targeted investment and innovation policy in Bulgaria, and proposed broad measures to improve domestic productive capacity, such as expanded investment incentives, industrial parks, proactive investment marketing and support for SMEs.
- The National Development Programme BULGARIA 2030 is a strategic document that elaborates the overall vision for Bulgaria's socio-economic development for the next decade in line with the UN Sustainable Development Goals. While it does not explicitly refer to the role of FDI in the national development, it outlines several priority areas that will have incidence on the quality of the overall business climate (e.g. institutional strengthening, developing transport and digital infrastructure and skills upgrading).
- Innovation Strategy for Smart Specialisation 2014-20 outlined objectives for the country's long-term economic development. For example, it identified key sectors with a potential for growth and upgrading of the country's innovation capacity: mechatronics and clean technologies; ICT; biotechnology; nanotechnology; creative industries; pharma; and food industry. It also outlined an institutional framework for co-ordinating the implementation of the plan as well as indicators for monitoring progress. The plan's implementation was supported with EU funds.
- The Act on Investment Promotion (AIP) is the main document setting out the specific objectives of the national investment promotion policy in Bulgaria, delineating responsibilities of different bodies and outlining the criteria for government investment support. The main objectives stipulated in AIP are: 1) raising the competitive capacity of the economy through increase in investment in science, technology, innovation, and high value-added activities; 2) improvement of the investment climate and overcoming the regional socio-economic inequalities; 3) creating new and highly productive jobs. These goals are operationalised through a series of support measures outlined in AIP.
- Several other laws and documents also include relevant elements. For example, the Law on Reduction of Administrative Burden and Administrative Control on Economic Activity (adopted in 2003 with subsequent amendments) outlines measures to reduce administrative obstacles. Several specific programmes have also aimed to support the development of SMEs and entrepreneurship such as the National Strategy for Promotion of SMEs 2014-20 and since then the National Strategy for Promotion of SMEs 2021-27, adopted in 2021.

Source: OECD based on information provided by Bulgarian authorities.

Yet, in order to start addressing the remaining obstacles to doing business in Bulgaria and ensure a co-ordinated whole-of-the-government approach, a more comprehensive approach to business climate reforms may be desirable. The government could hence consider whether it would not be beneficial to formulate a detailed action plan on the implementation of different priority business climate reforms with specific measures to be implemented, responsible authorities identified and timelines set. The plan should be more detailed than the 2015 Action Plan for Improving the Investment Environment, specifying concrete steps to be taken to address bottlenecks while being more comprehensive than the AIP. It could build on the existing analysis and projects, including those realised in the framework of co-operation with the EU, or be part of the next phase of national planning to avoid duplication. By including specific projects aimed at addressing remaining barriers, such an exercise could help operationalise the objective of improving the overall business climate. The plan could be made publically available to allow for tracing of progress achieved. If the government is seeking an inspiration in international good practice, it may be interested in the way that Uruguay – which adhered to the OECD *Declaration on International Investment* in 2021– integrated investment climate reforms in its national planning process.

The newly established Ministry of Innovation and Growth could clearly play a role in the process, being the principal institution responsible for investment policy since early 2022. For the projects involving other ministries or agencies outside of the Innovation and Growth Ministry's responsibilities, support at the highest levels of government and the involvement of the inter-Ministerial co-ordination mechanisms that pre-existed to the creation of the Ministry of Innovation and Growth (see below) would be beneficial to ensure co-operation.

Bulgaria's national strategy for FDI attraction could provide a basis for better cross-governmental co-ordination

In Bulgaria, as in other countries, several different institutions are involved in the elaboration and implementation of the investment promotion and facilitation policy (Box 6.2). Prior to the establishment of a new government in December 2021, and pursuant to the Act on Investment Promotion, the Ministry of Economy was in charge of the development of the national investment promotion policy, aided in implementation by InvestBulgaria Agency (IBA), at the national level, and by regional governors and mayors at the sub-national level.

In addition, several bodies aim to facilitate cross-institutional co-ordination. For example, under the previous administration, the Ministry of Economy had created a high-level permanent Taskforce (composed of Deputy Ministers and Secretary Generals) to co-ordinate support measures for investors. The National Economic Council (NEC), created in 2015[3], has been charged with developing and proposing regulations to encourage investment activity, increase the overall competitiveness, and organise and control the interaction between the executive authorities, other state bodies and business representatives. Meeting regularly, its decisions have been published on the websites of the Ministry of Economy and the Council of Ministers. Finally yet importantly, the National Council for Tripartite Co-operation, which consists of representatives of the Council of Ministers and representative organisations of employees and employers, can also play a relevant role in providing a platform for negotiation of certain reforms (see Chapter 8 on Responsible Business Conduct).[4]

As highlighted in the OECD *Policy Framework for Investment* (OECD, 2015a), the ability to co-ordinate effectively the various activities is critical for successful business climate reforms. As such, the government could consider seeking feedback from relevant stakeholders if they deem the current co-ordination mechanisms to be sufficient. The national planning (described above), with specific deliverables and joint projects identified for different institutions could also facilitate co-ordination. While NEC by its nature could be naturally placed to co-ordinate such horizontal efforts, its technical capacity and the Secretariat may need to be strengthened further to ensure tangible progress in implementing reforms.

Box 6.2. Division of responsibilities for investment promotion in Bulgaria as of December 2021

Responsibilities of different bodies involved in the design and implementation of investment promotion policy in Bulgaria are outlined in the Act on Investment Promotion.

The Minister of Economy:

1. develops a strategy for promoting investment in co-operation with the executive authorities and interested NGOs, which is adopted by the Council of Ministers
2. develops and implements programmes and measures to encourage investment in co-operation with the executive authorities and interested NGOs
3. develops and proposes draft regulatory acts to encourage investment activity in the country
4. represents the country in international organisations in the field of investments
5. makes proposals for inclusion of the necessary funds to encourage investments in the State Budget Law for the respective year under items 7 and 8
6. makes proposals for inclusion in the operational programmes co-financed by the European Union funds of measures to encourage investment
7. issues a certificate for a given investment class and for a priority investment project and submit proposals to the Council of Ministers for the implementation of investment promotion measures under this law
8. submits to the Council of Ministers proposals for the conclusion of memoranda or agreements with investors
9. submits to the Council of Ministers proposals for the designation of industrial zones or technological parks with the necessary technical infrastructure to attract investment for national sites within the meaning of the State Property Act.

The Regional Governor:

1. ensures the implementation of the state policy for promoting investments in the region;
2. develops measures to encourage investment (included in the regional development strategy) and co-ordinates their implementation in line with the strategy for investment promotion
3. co-ordinates the work of the executive bodies and their administrations on the territory of the region under items 1 and 2;
4. exercises control over the legality of the acts and actions of the bodies of local self-government and local administration.

The Mayor of a municipality:

1. ensures the implementation of the policy for encouraging investments on the territory of the municipality in the development and implementation of the municipal development plan and the programme for its implementation;
2. assists in the implementation of the investment promotion measures under this law;
3. issues a certificate for investment projects of municipal importance and apply the promotion measures within its competence.

The InvestBulgaria Agency has two main functions:

1. Supports investors by providing information; acts as a one-stop-shop for contacting different authorities during the investment process; and provides aftercare services;
2. Promotes Bulgaria as an attractive investment location through different marketing activities.

Source: Act on Investment Promotion and Bulgarian authorities (2021).

Main investment attraction tools

Bulgaria's reliance on the provision of investment incentives

Bulgaria has a corporate income tax (CIT) rate of 10%, which is significantly below the OECD average (Figure 6.3). It can make the country an attractive location to certain investors. There are also different kinds of investment incentives available to locally established firms, both foreign and domestic, without differentiation by the origin of capital. As an EU Member State, Bulgaria is also subject to the EU State Aid rules.[5]

Figure 6.3. Statutory corporate income tax rate in Bulgaria and OECD countries

In percentage

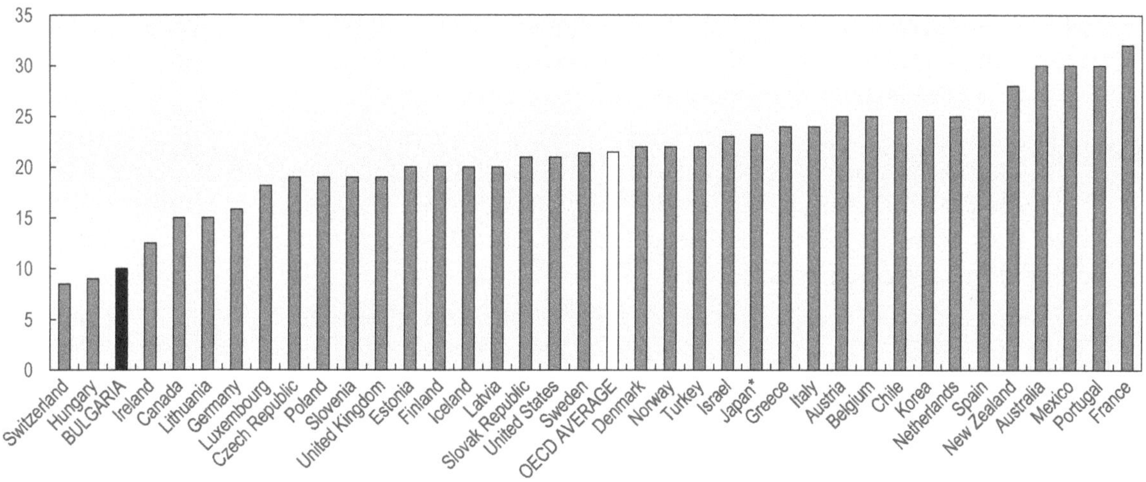

Note:* Data for all countries is available for 2020 and for Japan for 2019.
Source: OECD (2020c), OECD Tax Database, www.oecd.org/tax/tax-policy/tax-database.

The legal framework for regulating investment incentives in Bulgaria is well developed. Fiscal incentives are consolidated in, and regulated by, the respective tax statutes, i.e. Value-Added Tax Act (VAT Act), the Corporate Income Tax Act (CITA), the Social Insurance Code and the Law on Income Tax of Physical Persons. They involve a reduction of and exceptions from CIT payments, accelerated tax depreciation or losses carry-forward; special arrangements for VAT payment; and tax relief concerning pension funds under the Social Insurance Code, among others (see Box 6.3 for an overview). Financial investment incentives are also available to firms in Bulgaria as regulated by the AIP and its implementing regulations.[6]

Overall, there are four types of certified investment projects in Bulgaria – Class A, Class B, Class C and priority investment projects – that can benefit from government support (see Box 6.4). They differ in terms of the eligibility criteria, which relate to the character of the economic activity, size of investment and job creation effect, among others, and the application process. As of November 2021, applications for Class A and B investment project certificates had to be submitted to InvestBulgaria and Class C to the mayor of the municipality where the project would be implemented. Both Class A and Class B certificates were issued by the Minister of Economy; certificates for investment projects with municipal importance (Class C) were issued by the mayor of the municipality. Priority investment project certificates were issued by a Council of Ministers' Decision, which approved either a Memorandum of Understanding or an Agreement between the Government of Bulgaria and the investor.[7]

Box 6.3. Overview of fiscal incentives for investment in Bulgaria

The Corporate Income Tax Act (CITA)

Besides the general corporate income tax of 10%, CITA includes several fiscal incentives:

- Accelerated tax depreciation of machinery, production equipment and apparatuses which are part of the initial investment or have been acquired in connection with an investment made to increase energy efficiency (Art. 55(3) and (6)): The tax incentive consists in accelerated tax depreciation. The annual tax depreciation rate is up to 50% (in the general case the annual tax depreciation rate for these assets is 30%).
- Accelerated tax depreciation (100% per annum) for assets formed as a result of research and development (R&D) activities (Art. 69).
- Tax losses carry forward (Art. 70-74): The right of choice regarding carrying forward of tax loss can be exercised by the persons during the first year in which they have formed positive financial result for taxation purposes before the tax loss is deducted.
- Tax relief for hiring unemployed persons (Art. 177): Employers having employed an unemployed person under certain conditions are entitled to recognising for tax purposes of an amount equal to twice the expenditure on employment remuneration and social security contributions at the expense of the employer (for the first 12 months of employment). There is no restriction regarding eligible economic sectors.
- Exemption of financial instruments admitted to trading on a regulated market (Art. 44 and 196) and of collective investment schemes, admitted to public offering in Bulgaria, national investment funds under the Collective Investment Schemes and Other Undertakings for Collective Investments Act, and the companies with a special investment purpose under the Companies with a Special Investment Purpose Act (Art. 174-175).
- Remission of up to 100% of the corporate income tax for undertakings engaging in manufacturing activities in municipalities with high unemployment (Art. 184-189).

The Value-Added Act (VAT Act)

- Special arrangements for charging value added tax upon importation and reduced 30-day period for refund of the value added tax in the implementation of an investment project (Art 57, Art. 164-167).
- Special arrangements for postponed accounting of VAT upon importation (Article 57(5) and (6) and Art. 167a/b)). This regime has been in force since 1 July 2019.

The Social Insurance Code and the Law on Income Tax of Physical Persons

- Tax reliefs concerning supplementary mandatory pension funds under the Social Insurance Code (Art. 160. (1), Art. 161-162).
- Tax reliefs concerning supplementary voluntary pension funds under the Social Insurance Code (Art. 253-255).

Note: *In the meaning of § 1, item 24 of the Additional Provisions of the Corporate Income Tax Act, "Research activity" shall denote the activity of development, design, creating and testing of new goods, materials, production technology and technology for industrial systems and other objects of industrial property, as well as the improvement of existing products and technology.
Source: Government of Bulgaria, 2021

To be certified as a supported investment project in Bulgaria, investment needs to meet several criteria. First, it must relate to the establishment of a new enterprise, extension of an existing enterprise, diversification of the output into new products, or a material change in the overall production process. For Class A, B and C projects, investment must be implemented in specific economic activities, according to the Statistical Classification of Economic Activities in the European Community (NACE Rev. 2), i.e.: manufacturing (with certain exceptions) or in specific high value-added services sectors (i.e. high technology activities in computer technology, R&D, accounting, tax and audit services, education and health care and storage of goods).[8] The project also needs to satisfy the minimum investment and job creation requirements; and needs to comply with other conditions related to the project's realisation, duration, source of financing, and purchases of inputs, among others.[9] Priority investment projects do not need to belong to a particular sector and are those that are considered essential for the economic development of the country or its regions and are required to have at least EUR 51 million of investment or 200 newly created jobs, unless other conditions apply.[10]

Table 6.1. Eligibility criteria for support under the Act on Investment Promotion

Investment projects with job creation or maintenance		
Region or Sector	Class B	Class A
General case: Manufacturing industry	EUR 1 mln 100 jobs	EUR 2 mln 150 jobs
General case: Services sector	EUR 0.25 mln 100 jobs	EUR 0.5 mln 150 jobs
In municipalities with unemployment rate equal or more than the country average	10 jobs	25 jobs
High-tech activities in the manufacturing industry for the entire country	10 jobs	25 jobs
High-tech activities in the service sector such as: - ICT and computer technologies - R&D - activities of head offices - education - human health care - accounting and auditing - architecture and engineering	25 jobs	50 jobs
Investment projects without job creation or maintenance		
Region or Sector	Class B	Class A
Activities in the manufacturing industry	EUR 2.5 mln	EUR 5 mln
In municipalities with unemployment rate equal or more than the country average	EUR 1 mln	EUR 2 mln
High-tech activities in the manufacturing industry for the entire country	EUR 1 mln	EUR 2mln
Activities in the service sector such as: - warehousing and support activities for transportation - outsourcing of business processes (for administrative and office activities)	EUR 0.75 mln	EUR 1.5 mln
High-tech activities in the service sector such as: - ICT and computer technologies - R&D - activities of head offices - education - human health care - accounting and auditing - architecture and engineering	EUR 0.5 mln	EUR 1 mln

Source: IBA's website, www.investbulgaria.com (accessed: October 2021)

Under the previous administration, the information on certified investment projects in Bulgaria was collected by the Ministry of Economy.[11] According to the data provided by Bulgaria's Ministry of Economy, between 2008 and 2020 a total of 245 certificates were issued under the Investment Promotion Act and the Regulations for its implementation, which resulted in the creation of 38 628 new jobs (Figure 6.4). In addition, according to the data on IBA's website, most of the supported projects were Class A projects and a handful of priority investment projects during that time. Between 2013-20 the Ministry of Economy of Bulgaria allocated BGN 49.4 million (approximately EUR 25.2 million) from its budget to financial incentives dedicated for investment projects certified under the AIP (Figure 6.6).

Box 6.4. Overview of financial incentives for investment in Bulgaria

The Act on Investment Promotion stipulates the type of financial incentives available of firms in Bulgaria as well as outlines the eligibility criteria and explains the application process. These include Class A, B and C and priority certified investment projects explained in turn below.

Class A and Class B Investment Certificates allow for the following incentives:

- Administrative services delivered in one-third of usual time (Class A and B);
- Individual administrative service provided by InvestBulgaria Agency (Class A);
- Acquisition of property rights or establishment of limited rights to real estate state or municipal property without tender or competition after market price determination by two independent assessors (Class A and B);
- Financial support for construction of public infrastructure, i.e. local roads, water supply and sewerage (Class A or for two projects within one industrial zone);
- Financial support for training for attainment of professional qualification for investments in high technology activities or municipalities with high unemployment (Class A and B);
- Financial support for partial reimbursement of the obligatory social insurance contributions made by the investor for the new jobs created with the investment project for a certain period of time (Class A and B).

Class C Investment Certificate allows for the following incentives:

- Administrative services delivered in one-third of usual time provided by the mayor of the municipality in which the investment project is implemented;
- Individual administrative service provided by the mayor of the municipality in which the investment project is implemented;
- Acquisition of property rights or establishment of limited rights to real estate municipal property without tender or competition after market price determination by two independent assessors (the incentive is provided in case that it was not requested by an investor upon the issuing of a certificate for Class A and B or for a priority investment project for the same real estate).

Priority Investment Project Certificate allows for the following additional incentives (in addition to all Class A incentives):

- Acquisition of property rights or establishment of limited rights to real estate could take place at prices lower than the market price (but not below tax assessment) and exemption from state fees for changing the land use;
- Institutional support by an inter-ministerial working group for administrative assistance (convened on an ad hoc basis);
- Public-private partnership with regional authorities and municipalities, with universities and other organisations from the academic community, including for acquisition of real estate (see above) or for technological park development.

Source: Act of Investment Promotion and the Government of Bulgaria (2021).

Figure 6.4. Certified Investment Projects in Bulgaria under AIP, 2008-20

Panel A. Number of projects

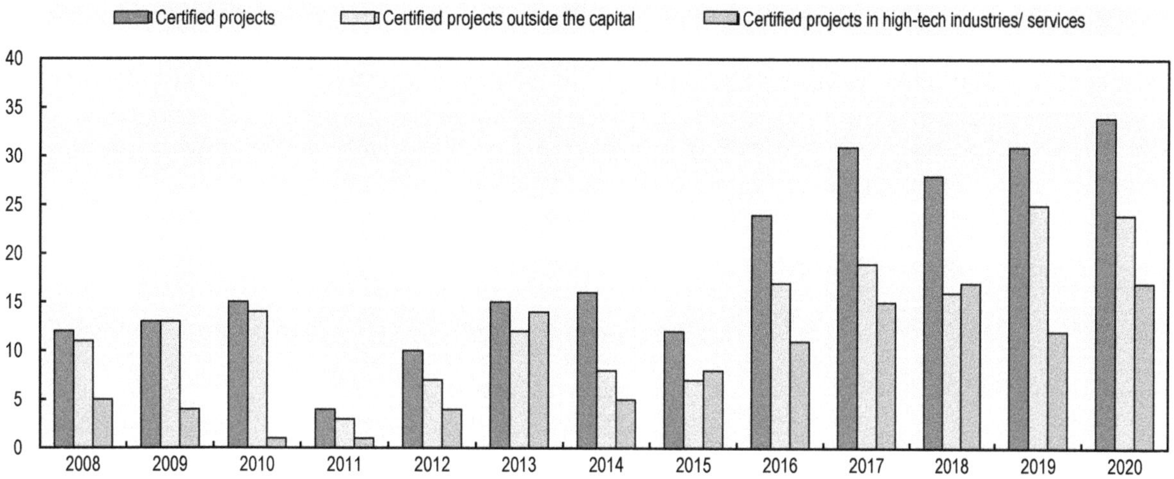

Panel B. Number of new jobs

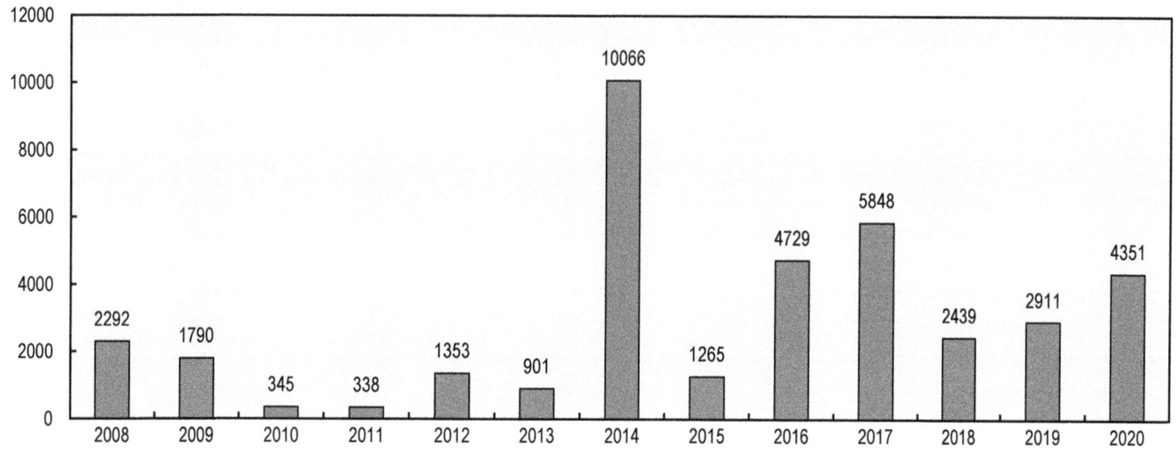

Source: OECD calculations based on data provided by Bulgaria's Ministry of Economy in March 2021.

Figure 6.5. Financial incentives allocated to Certified Investment Projects under AIP

In mln BGN

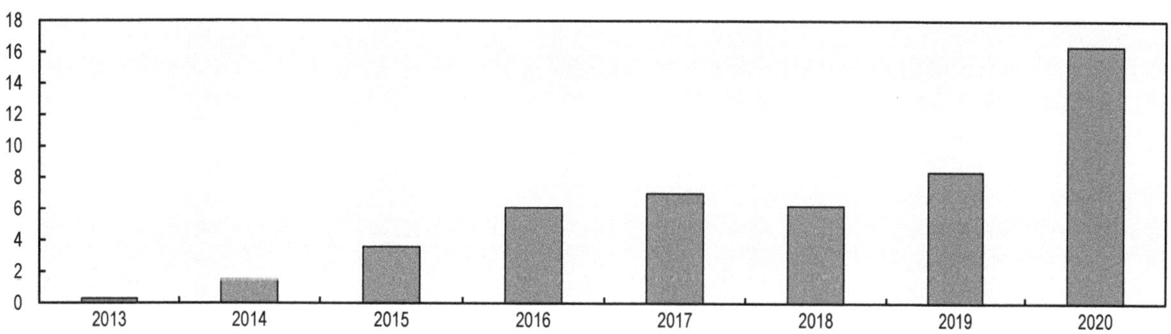

Source: OECD calculations based on data provided by Bulgaria's Ministry of Economy in March 2021.

Industrial zones

Besides investment incentives described above, Bulgaria also offers investors advantages associated with locating in one of its industrial zones. According to IBA's website, there were in 2021 about a dozen of functional industrial zones in Bulgaria and another dozen with the infrastructure ready and available for investment or being under development. Through the catalogue of industrial zones available on IBA's website and the website of the National Company Industrial Zones (NCIZ), detailed information on over 30 such zones is available (Table 6.2). The Bulgarian Chamber of Commerce and Industry also provides information on the different industrial zones and parks available in the country.[12]

Table 6.2. List of selected industrial zones in Bulgaria

No		Region	Available area (in squared metres)	Total area (in squared metres)	Phase	Land ownership
1	Sofia-Bozhurishte Economic Zone*	Sofia	n/a	3 038 527	Functioning	NCIZ
2	Maritsa Industrial Zone	Plovdiv	800 000	3 000 000	Functioning	Private
3	Shumen Industrial Park	Shumen	2 400 000	2 400 000	Developed	Private-Municipal
4	Dolna Mitropoliya Industrial Zone	Pleven	192 136	2 302 494	Functioning	Private
5	Industrial Zone Telish*	Pleven	n/a	2 036 638	Under Development	NCIZ
6	Elin Pelin Industrial Park	Sofia	1 021 000	1 600 000	Functioning	Private-Municipal
7	Sofia Industrial Park	Sofia	1 045 000	1 045 000	Developed	Private
8	Rakovski Industrial Zone	Plovdiv	150 000	1 000 000	Functioning	Private-Municipal
9	Kuklen Industrial and Commercial Zone	Plovdiv	700 000	900 000	Functioning	Private
10	Aytos Industrial and Business Park	Burgas	800 000	800 000	Developed	Private
11	Sofia East Industrial Park	Sofia	700 000	700 000	n/a	n/a
12	Ruse Industrial Park	Ruse	640 000	640 000	n/a	n/a
13	Karlovo Industrial Zone*	Plovdiv	580 000	580 000	Under Development	NCIZ
14	Dobrich Business Zone	Dobrich	424 248	424 248	Developed	Municipal
15	Industrial Zone Varna – West*	Varna	399 000	399 000	Under Development	NCIZ
16	Ruse Free Zone*	Ruse	50 000	370 235	Functioning	NCIZ
17	Vidin Free Zone*	Vidin	0	308 627	Functioning	NCIZ
18	Industrial and Logistics Park Burgas*	Burgas	238 000	238 000	Functioning	Municipal
19	Peristar Razgrad Business Zone	Razgrad	88 585	202 188	Functioning	Municipal
20	Kabile Industrial Park	Yambol	190 000	190 000	Developed	Municipal
21	Dimitrovgrad Industrial Zone	Haskovo	188 704	188 704	n/a	n/a
22	Burgas Free Zone	Burgas	80 000	155 000	Functioning	Private
23	Gorna Malina Industrial Zone	Sofia	153 619	153 619	n/a	n/a
24	Strazhitsa Industrial Zone	Veliko Tarnovo	110 000	110 000	Developed	Municipal
25	Troyan Industrial Zone	Lovech	124 810	124 810	Developed	Municipal
26	First Industrial Zone – Avren	Varna	120 000	120 000	n/a	n/a
27	Industrial Zone Zagore*	Stara Zagora	n/a	115 000	n/a	NCIZ
28	Targovishte Industrial Zone	Targovishte	113 581	113 581	n/a	n/a
	General Toshevo Industrial Zone	Dobrich	112 384	112 384	Developed	Municipal
29	Kaspichan Industrial Zone	Shumen	108 722	108 722	n/a	n/a
	Transit Trade Zone Varna*	Varna	n/a	104 000	Functioning	NCIZ
30	Svilengrad Industrial Zone	Haskovo	n/a	103 653	Functioning	Municipal
31	Industrial Park Kardzhali*	Kardzhali	n/a	94 431	Under Development	NCIZ
32	Montana Technology Park	Montana	84 652	84 652	Developed	Municipal

33	Assenovgrad Industrial Park	Plovdiv	73 362	73 362	Developed	Municipal
34	Svilengrad Economic Zone*	Haskovo	n/a	70 000	Functioning	NCIZ
35	Gabrovo Industrial Zone	Gabrovo	32 000	36 000	n/a	n/a
36	Svishtov Industrial Zone	Veliko Tarnovo	27 930	27 930	n/a	n/a
37	Suvorovo Industrial Zone*	Varna	n/a	24 000	Under Development	NCIZ
38	Delta-S Industrial Park	Sofia	0	15 621	Functioning	Private

Note: *Zones managed by state-owned National Company Industrial Zones (NCIZ).
Source: OECD based on information on the IBA's website (http://www.investbulgaria.com/), the website of the NCIZ (http://www.nciz.bg/en/) and information provided by Bulgaria as part of this *Review*.

There are both private and publically managed industrial zones in Bulgaria. At the time of writing this *Review*, the NCIZ was a company under the guidance of the Bulgarian Ministry of Economy, whose mandate was to design, develop and manage industrial and free zones. In 2021, the company managed 12 industrial zones, seven of which were in operation (Sofia, Burgas, Vidin, Ruse, Svilengrad, Stara Zagora and Varna) and five under development (Kardzhali, Karlovo, Telish, Suvorovo and Varna). According to the information provided by IBA, NCIZ and the National Institute of Statistics of Bulgaria, these zones jointly accounted for a sizable share of the national territory and about 60% of them were located in regions above the national level of poverty.[13]

Importantly, industrial zone users in Bulgaria do not benefit from a reduced profit tax rate. Instead, there are free zones used not only for custom purposes but also aiming at providing investors with high-quality infrastructure. Technological parks also need to satisfy the conditions of an industrial zone and additionally host predominantly scientific research and development activity, education, information technologies or advanced manufacturing, among others.[14] According to AIP, investment projects aiming to create an industrial zone or a technological park are eligible to become certified investment projects. The draft proposal of Industrial Parks Act that aims to regulate the legislative framework for the creation and management of such parks, was adopted by the Bulgarian Parliament in February 2021 and later promulgated in March 2021.[15]

Overall, considering the number of industrial zones in Bulgaria, the pace of creation of new ones and the share of territory that they occupy, they appear to be an instrument that has been encouraged by the government. Yet, creating areas of such type of good quality and that deliver broad-based development impacts for the local economy can be a difficult task. For example, according to a UNCTAD survey (2019), over half of the special economic zones globally are deemed underused. Based on data on the territory available in different zones, the utilisation rate of industrial zones in Bulgaria also appears low.[16]

The government could reflect on the factors needed to increase attractiveness of the existing zones and ensure a good governance framework. While zones in Bulgaria do not offer other benefits than customs duty exceptions and access to infrastructure, thus minimising the amount of tax revenue forgone, the costs associated with creating and maintaining their infrastructure need to be weighed against the benefits of (additional) investment attracted. As a first step, the government could ensure that the information on available facilities and the associated investment and number of jobs is available and monitored in a systematic fashion – for example, via consolidated reports to the responsible ministry, which can be made publically available. In addition, a cost-benefit analysis of zones that benefit from state's involvement and investors' surveys could also be helpful in deciding about the zones current value-added and potential reforms needed.

EU funds' role in mobilising investment

Another aspect influencing Bulgaria's investment attraction policy is the availability of EU funds. Bulgaria is one of the countries that benefits most from the EU support. Under the funding framework for 2014-20, Bulgaria was allocated EUR 9.9 billion via several programmes under the European Structural and

Investment (ESI) funds (Box 6.5). This represented an average of EUR 1 363 per person from the EU budget in 2014-20. This means that an additional source of financing is available for eligible investors operating in Bulgaria. As these funds also support and mobilise additional private financing in certain priority areas, they can increase financial liquidity of firms. In the medium and long run, they can also support building of necessary infrastructure and educating the labour force required by investors to consider Bulgaria an attractive investment destination.

For example, a large share of EU funding goes towards greening of the economy (i.e. increasing resource efficiency, environmental protection and climate change adaptation and risk-prevention) as well as educational and vocational training initiatives, research and innovation and high-quality employment. Programmes related to improving local infrastructure that would increase connectivity, improving competitiveness of SMEs and social inclusion are also important (accounting jointly for nearly 30% of funding). Finally, technical assistance and support to public administration can also support the process of professionalising and improving the capacity of government authorities. The creation of the Technology and Innovation Network (T+IN) or "Sofia Tech Park" – the first science and technology park in Bulgaria – is an example of a project created with EU co-financing, which supports the creation of foundational infrastructure for investment attraction in high-value activities.[17] While recent evaluations show that the park grapples with several governance and management challenges (European Commission, 2018b), its creation marks an important step in the process of strengthening the local technological ecosystem.

Box 6.5. The use of EU funds in Bulgaria

The financial allocation from the EU Cohesion Policy funds* for Bulgaria amounted EUR 9.9 billion in the framework of the Multiannual Financial Framework 2014-20. By the end of 2019, some EUR 7.4 billion (about 85% of the total amount planned) was allocated to projects, while EUR 3.6 billion was reported as spent with implementation levels in line with the EU average.

EU Cohesion policy funding significantly supports structural challenges in Bulgaria. The Cohesion Policy programmes for Bulgaria have allocated EU funding of EUR 1.1 billion for smart growth, EUR 4.1 billion for sustainable growth and sustainable transport and EUR 1.9 billion for inclusive growth. In 2019, following a performance review, EUR 386 million were made available for Bulgaria for these priorities; and EUR 126 million (including national co-financing) need to be reprogrammed by the authorities within the above priority areas.

EU Cohesion policy funding provides investment in research, technological development and innovation, competitiveness of enterprises, sustainable transport, education, employment and social inclusion, among others. According to the Ministry of Finance of Bulgaria, the estimated effect of EU Funds boosted GDP by 7.7% and helped generate approximately 12.5% higher employment by 2020.

Agricultural and fisheries funds and other EU programmes also contribute to addressing the investment needs, such as the European Agricultural Fund for Rural Development and the European Maritime and Fisheries Fund. Bulgaria has also benefitted from other EU programmes such as the Connecting Europe Facility and Horizon 2020.

Note: *European Regional Development Fund, Cohesion Fund, European Social Fund, Youth Employment Initiative, including national co-financing. ‡ Data available on the website of the Ministry of Finance: https://www.minfin.bg/bg/1168 Δ European Regional Development Fund, Cohesion Fund, European Social Fund, European Agricultural Fund for Rural Development Fund and European Maritime and Fisheries Fund.
Source: EU Commission (2020a)

Figure 6.6. Planned European Structural and Investment Funds Allocated to Bulgaria in 2014-20, by area

In percentage

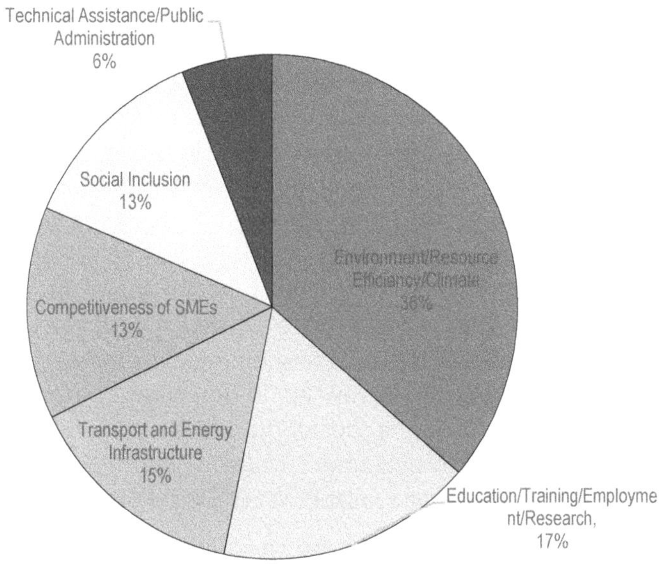

Source: European Commission (2020b).

According to the EU, nearly 5 000 firms have benefitted from support under the ESI funds and nearly twice more are planned to benefit from the support in the future (European Commission, 2020b/d).[18] In addition, EUR 0.14 billion in private match grant aid has already been implemented. In terms of the impact on infrastructure, the EU funds are planned to lead to a reconstruction of 665 km of roads and 166 km or rail as well as the creation of 67 km of new roads. It will also involve a creation of new water supply, waste treatment and flood protection facilities, among others. Finally, it will offer training and improved working prospects to participants. The allocation of EU funds is centralised at the Ministry of Regional Development, and, at the time of writing of this *Review*, there were discussions towards a possible reform.[19] Overall, the allocation of EU funds and additional private financing facilitated through this channel can offer new business opportunities both to domestic and foreign owned firms interested in locating Bulgaria.

Specific programmes to support small and medium-sized enterprises

SMEs play an important role in the Bulgaria economy. They generate two-thirds of total value added and three-quarters of total employment, above the EU average (European Commission, 2019). Meanwhile, their annual productivity, calculated as value added per person employed, is approximately one-fourth of the EU average. Unsurprisingly, as discussed above, a sizeable share of EU structural and investment funds in Bulgaria is allocated to SME development. The SME Initiative is an example of an EU-co-financed programme designed to facilitate SME financing. Moreover, in reaction to COVID-19, additional funds from the “Innovations and Competitiveness” programme were made available to support SMEs (European Commission, 2020c).

The importance of EU funds and policies in shaping the overall framework for supporting SMEs in Bulgaria is evident in the institutional and policy set-up in this area. The main strategic document in this domain until 2021 was the National Strategy for Promotion of SMEs 2014-20, which was based on the Small Business Act for Europe (SBA). In 2021, a new strategy for 2021-27 was adopted with financial support from the European Commission.

At the end of 2021, the main institutions responsible for supporting SMEs, including their internationalisation and access to finance, were: the Bulgarian Small and Medium-sized Enterprises Promotion Agency (BSMEPA); the responsible body for the Operational Programme "Innovation and Competitiveness" under the Ministry of Economy; the responsible body for the SME Initiative Operational Programme; the Bulgarian Development Bank; and the Fund of Funds, managing four operational programmes co-financed by the EU.

According to the European Commission, in 2019 Bulgaria was lagging behind in several areas related to implementing the SBA (European Commission, 2019a). The main challenges for Bulgaria lie in upskilling its workforce, encouraging SME investment in innovation and fostering growth in entrepreneurship as discussed earlier in this *Review.* According to the 2018 survey on SMEs conducted by the European Commission and the ECB, almost 30% of SMEs surveyed identified availability of skilled staff or experienced managers as their biggest challenge (EBRD, 2020). Slow progress in simplifying administrative procedures, discussed in the last section of this chapter, has also been pointed out as affecting SMEs adversely. Meanwhile, Bulgaria has made significant progress in improving the access to finance of SMEs, including through the use of different programmes co-funded by the EU. This is consistent with the results of the World Bank Enterprise Survey (2019) that showed that many firms had access to credit lines in Bulgaria and only 11% of local firms considered access to financing as major concern, which is significantly below the regional and world averages (Figure 6.7). In the recent years, the government offered several additional financial instruments available to SMEs (Box 6.6).

The overall progress in reducing administrative burdens on all firms will be reviewed later. Nevertheless, some initiatives aimed specifically at SMEs are worth highlighting here. For example, the Ministry of Economy and Industry developed a "Business Guide for SMEs", available since 2019, aiming to explain in simple terms the steps that entrepreneurs need to take in commonly encountered situations, ranging from starting a company, hiring staff to resolving insolvency, to comply with 120 most complex and common regulations.[20] The information, organised by themes, was made available online, in both Bulgarian and English. In addition, as part of the overall process of improving the quality of new regulations in the country – discussed in the next chapter – the government has made more systematic use of the "SME Test", i.e. considering *ex ante* the possible impact of proposed regulations on SMEs.

Figure 6.7. Financial constrains faced by firms in Bulgaria and other countries, by firm size

In percentage

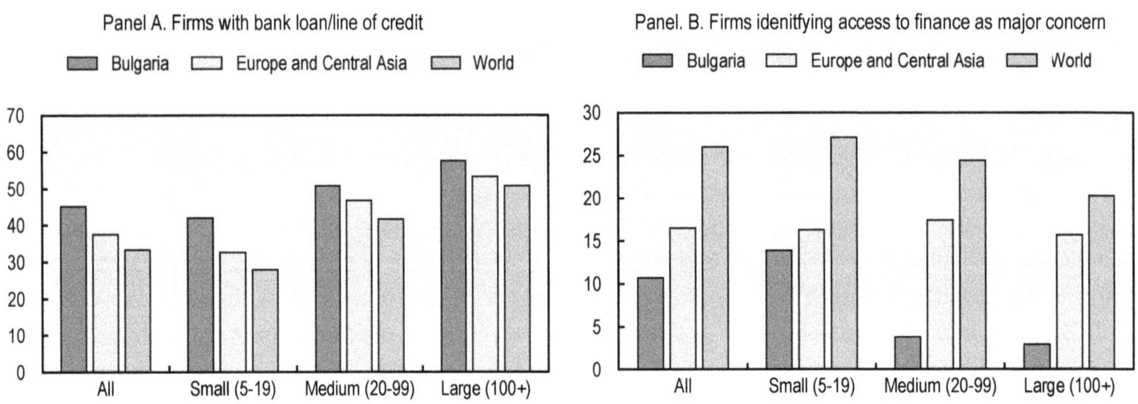

Source: World Bank (2019), Enterprise Survey

Box 6.6. Recent financial instruments to support SMEs' access to finance

Supported by EU funds, the Bulgarian Government announced creation of several financial instruments and other measures to ease SMEs' access to finance in the last few years, e.g.:

- The voucher scheme for the provision of securities-issuing services in the capital markets connecting SMEs with service providers in the field of securities issuance.
- The "Risk-sharing micro-finance facility" funded through the Operational Programme Human Resource Development 2014-20, co-financed by EU finds, that provides micro loans of up to EUR 25 000 to support the establishment and development of start-ups.
- The "BrightCap Ventures capital fund" in which EU co-financed JEREMIE invests EUR 20 million and BrightCap Ventures raise additional private capital. The fund will invest in early stage companies with the potential for significant growth in the global market. The investments will be in the range of EUR 0.5 to EUR 3 million. Part of the fund will be dedicated to supporting newly created companies (accelerator).
- The Venture Capital Fund is making available EUR 24.4 million in public funds for management under another programme, co-financed by EU funds. The Fund provides financial support to start-ups/SMEs during their first five years. The investment in each selected start-up or SME will range from EUR 750 000 to EUR 3.5 million.
- Innovation Accelerator Bulgaria of EUR 15.6 million, co-financed by EU funds, has the mandate to provide access to equity and quasi-equity funding to Bulgarian start-ups. The financing targets entrepreneurs at the earliest stages of business development. Mentoring and strategic support to companies will be provided.
- Finally, the Fund for the support of innovative start-ups will provide financial support (equity and quasi-equity investments) and business support to early stage entrepreneurs.

Source: European Commission (2019).

Overall, further progress in reducing administrative burdens, proposing simplified solutions and e-services can have an important impact on SMEs. Due to important knowledge and skills gaps identified in local SMEs, BSMEPA can play an important role by providing capacity-building support and help local firms reach foreign markets. Its network of regional offices can help it reach firms in different regions.[21] Given the potential learning and upgrading opportunities offered by business linkages between domestic and locally established foreign firms, new programmes and collaboration with the IBA (see next section) could be beneficial in this regard. Moreover, considering the importance of difficulties in hiring skilled labour locally, faced by both foreign enterprises and domestic SMEs, BSMEPA and IBA could consider offering specific services in this area.

Activities of the investment promotion agency

National investment promotion agency can be an important and relevant actor in the institutional landscape for investment promotion and facilitation. The economic literature shows that IPAs help bridge information asymmetries and attract investment into the local economy (Volpe Martincus et al., 2020; Harding and Javorcik, 2011/ 2012/2013; Alfaro and Charlton, 2007). Yet, agencies differ substantially in their characteristics and the type of and quality of services provided to investors, which in turn can affect their effectiveness in FDI attraction (OECD, 2018; Volpe Martincus and Sztajerowska, 2019). In the case of Bulgaria, the InvestBulgaria Agency, serves this function. As the agency participated in the OECD-IDB survey of IPAs (Box 6.7), its characteristics and activities have been compared to agencies in the OECD countries.

Box 6.7. The OECD-IDB survey of IPAs

The OECD and the IDB have partnered to design a comprehensive survey of IPAs. The questionnaire provides detailed data that reflect the recent policy developments and provide rich and comparable information on the work of IPAs in different countries. The survey was shared with IPA representatives from OECD and Latin America and Caribbean countries in the form of an online questionnaire, covering nine areas:

- Basic profile
- Budget
- Personnel
- Offices (home and abroad)
- Activities
- Prioritisation
- Monitoring and evaluation
- Institutional interactions
- IPA perceptions on FDI.

National IPAs from 32 of the 38 OECD countries participated in the OECD- IDB survey. The detailed data gathered through the survey has allowed rich cross-country analysis and served as a basis for a preparation of a mapping report of IPAs in OECD countries (OECD, 2018) as well as benchmarking with other regions, including Latin America and the Caribbean, Middle East and North Africa and South-Eastern Europe.

Invest in Bulgaria: Mandate, governance, and accountability

InvestBulgaria Agency (IBA) is an executive agency public agency, reporting to the government. Its overall objective is to provide free-of-charge information, contacts and project management support services to potential investors (Box 6.8). In 2021, with a total budget of approximately EUR 0.47 million and 27 employees, IBA was one of the smallest agencies across the OECD countries (Figure 6.8).[22] The agency's budget has been increasing progressively in 2014-18 with a small downward adjustment in 2019 (Panel A in Figure 6.8). In 2021, all of the agency's budget came from the state's budget and was allocated by the Ministry of Economy to which it reported. The minister also appointed the Head of IBA. It had annual targets in terms of assisted projects and provided quarterly and annual reports to the Minister of Economy on the completion of its objectives. Unlike most of the OECD IPAs (OECD, 2018), at the time of writing of this *Review*, IBA did not have a Board overseeing its activities. Therefore, based on the different components of the OECD-IDB IPA Institutional Independence Index, IBA showed a relatively low degree of independence (Volpe Martincus and Sztajerowska, 2019).[23] Since early 2022, the new Ministry of Innovation and Growth has been responsible for managing all key state agencies in charge of promoting strategic investments, including IBA.

Box 6.8. Overview of InvestBulgaria

InvestBulgaria Agency (IBA) is a government body providing free-of-charge information, contacts and project management support to potential investors. Its services include:

Pre-investment:

- Provision of macroeconomic data, company and industry profiles
- Legal advice
- Information on FDI incentives and EU funds
- Information on site and facility locations
- Information on industrial and free zones

Investment project support:

- Visa and other administrative support for potential investors
- Identification of potential project location, including identification of facilities for Brownfield projects or office locations for outsourcing and IT projects
- Organisation of bespoke site visits
- Identification of potential suppliers, clients and other business partners
- Legal assistance with setting up a Bulgarian company
- Administrative support with permits and regulations with regards to hiring personnel, purchasing or renting facilities, etc.
- Support with application for government and EU incentives

Post-investment:

- Intermediation with other government and local administration
- Administrative and legal support

Source: IBA (2021)

In 2021, most IBA's staff and budget were devoted to investment facilitation and retention (Panel B in Figure 6.9). This is a common pattern in OECD agencies where investment generation and facilitation account for two-thirds of resources of a typical IPA (OECD, 2018). It also reflects IBA's role in facilitating the process of investors' applications to become a certified investment project, described earlier. The agency also provided support to other potential investors by linking them with local consulting and legal firms, providing information on applicable regulations or facilitating contact with other authorities, for example. In a typical year, IBA assisted about 300 firms, 20 of which were certified investors.[24]

Figure 6.8. Resources of IPAs in Bulgaria and OECD countries

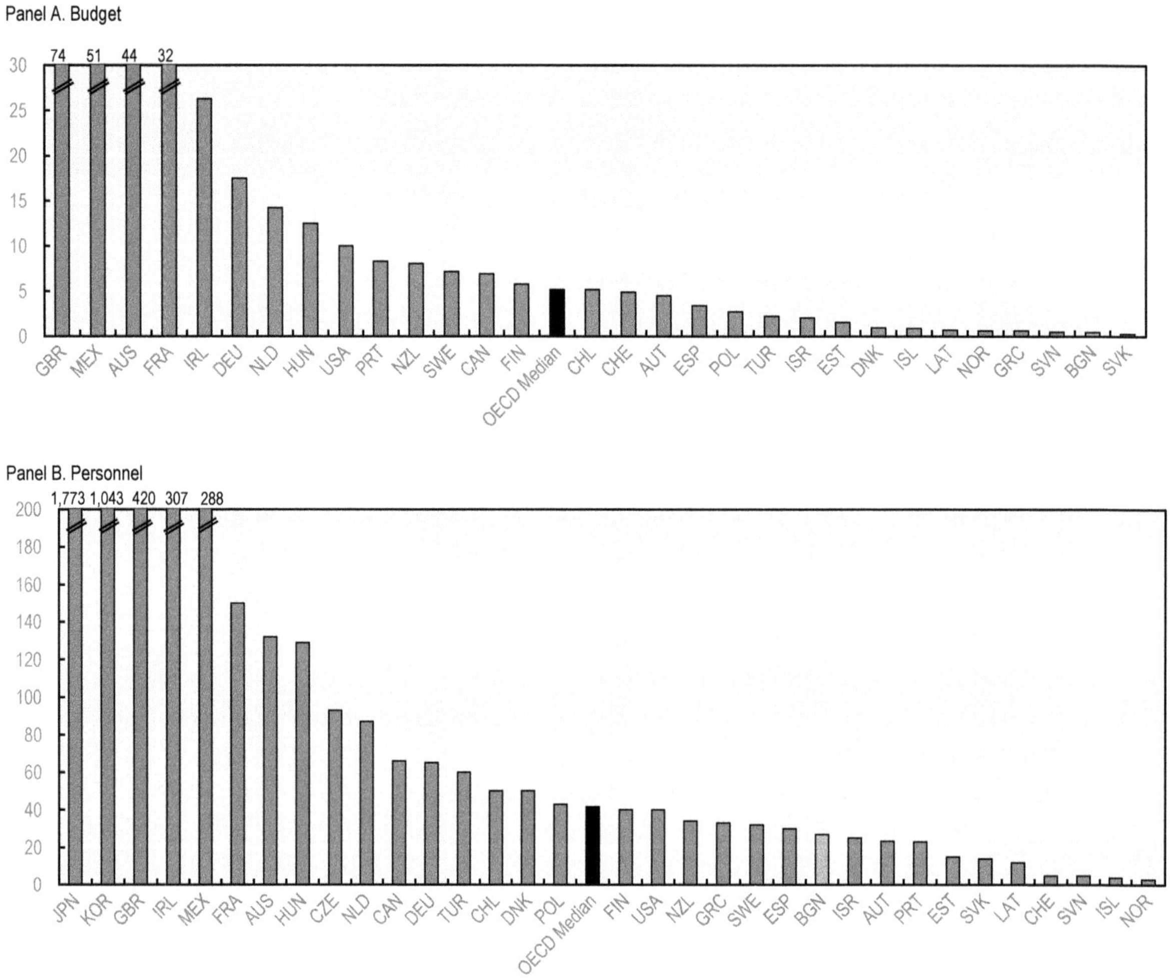

Source: OECD-IDB Survey of Investment Promotion Agencies (2020).

Figure 6.9. Budget and personnel of IBA and other OECD IPAs

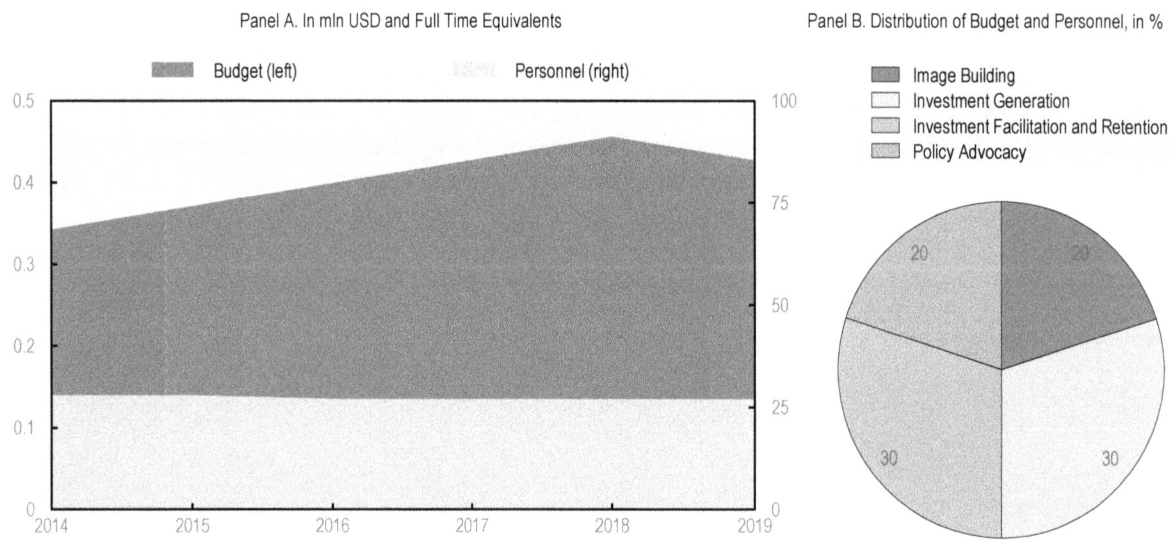

Source: OECD-IDB Survey of Investment Promotion Agencies (2020).

At the time of this *Review*, the agency had several mandates. Besides inward FDI attraction, IBA also assisted domestic investors interested in investment opportunities at home and in foreign markets. As such, it had more official functions than the OECD average (Figure 6.10). Some of them, such as granting of incentives and negotiations of international agreements, were not typically found in OECD IPAs (Figure 6.11). Yet, as explained earlier, IBA's role regarding the former relates mostly to processing of investors' applications, while the ultimate decision regarding state support resided in the Ministry of Economy. While most OECD IPAs perform both investment and export promotion functions, in case of Bulgaria, this task was performed in another agency, BSMEPA, as discussed earlier. BSMEPA also reported to the Ministry of Economy, and, according to IBA, the two organisations co-operated well together.[25] This type of arrangement is also practiced by OECD IPAs, where some agencies merge these two functions and others prefer keeping them apart (OECD, 2018).

Unlike many OECD similar institutions, at the time of writing this *Review*, IBA did not have an explicit regional development mandate. It still rendered some services that support provision of information about investment opportunities across Bulgaria's different regions. For example, it provided a list of all available investment projects and vacant land for investment projects across the country.[26] Yet, in the framework of this *Review*, IBA reported to the OECD Secretariat not to collaborate with regional bodies responsible for investment promotion. It explained that it consulted them or intervened only as necessary, for example to facilitate investor's landing or when a firm encountered a particular problem. As a result, at the time of writing this *Review*, no rules and procedures appeared to be in place to facilitate co-operation between IBA and existing subnational bodies, and the agency did not seem to be fully aware of IPAs operating at the sub-national level. Meanwhile, various major cities have their own municipal-level investment promotion bodies, some of which have well-developed websites and offer investors various services. The lack of explicit co-operation may lead to a duplication or discoordination of efforts, reducing their overall impact.[27]

Figure 6.10. Overall number of official mandates of national IPAs in Bulgaria and OECD

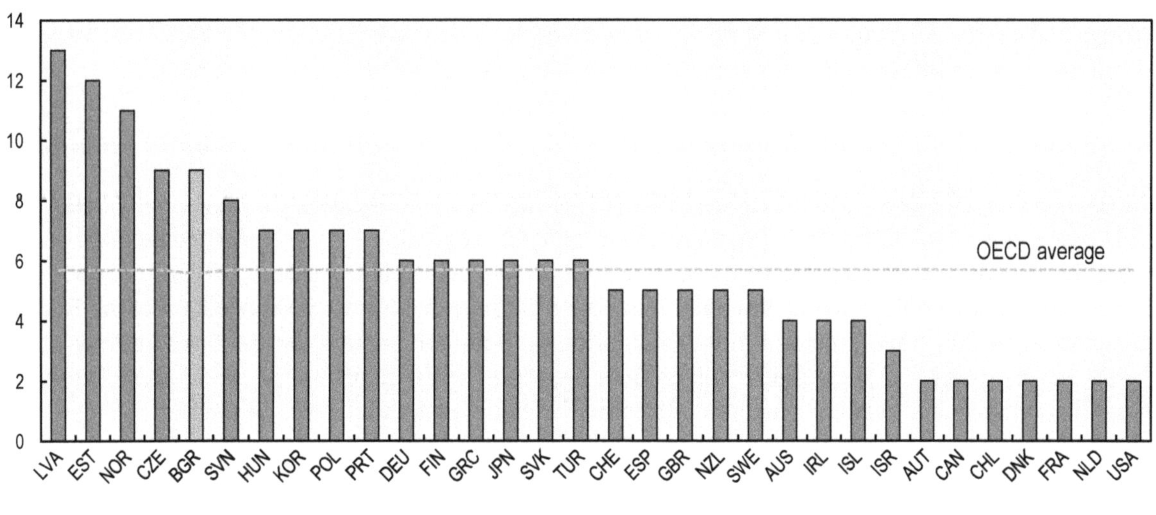

Source: OECD-IDB Survey of Investment Promotion Agencies (2020).

Figure 6.11. Type of official mandates undertaken by OECD IPAs and Bulgaria

In percentage

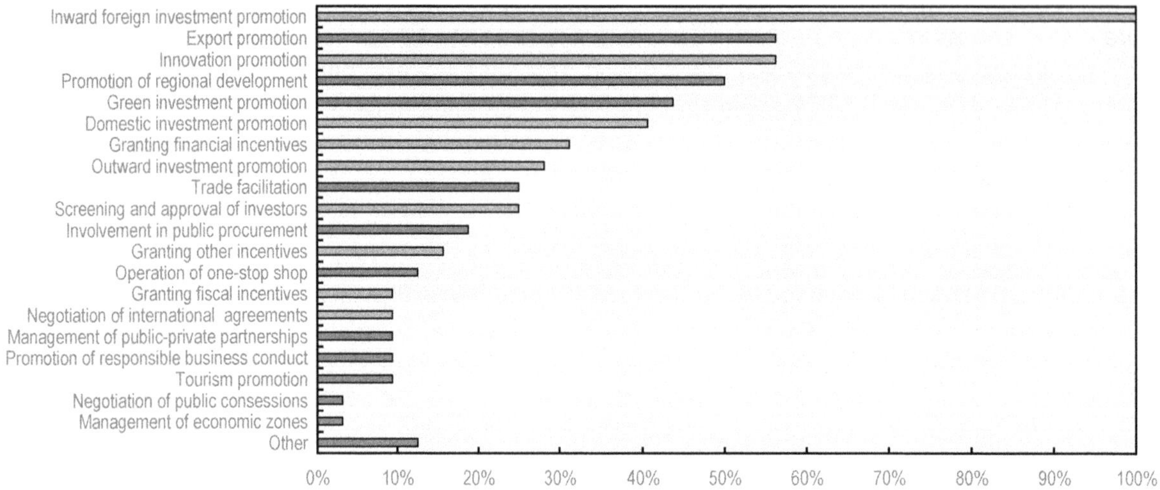

Note: The mandates undertaken by Bulgaria are marked in green. The ultimate decision regarding financial incentives resides in the Ministry of Economy.
Source: OECD-IDB Survey of Investment Promotion Agencies (2020).

Considering that the reduction of social and territorial inequalities is one of the government's priorities, as expressed in the NDP BULGARIA 2030, this area may merit the government's attention. Most OECD IPAs considers regional agencies as strategic partners and report to have frequent contact with them. As such, the ministry in charge of promoting investments could consider if and how to best systematise co-operation between IBA and bodies responsible for investment promotion at the sub-national level. Possible approaches include the use of common guidelines, joint participation in events, access to common information systems, exchanges of staff and incentives for agencies (OECD, 2018).[28] Feedback from regional partners, business and other stakeholders could provide useful inputs in this regard.

The agency's prioritisation strategy is shaped by the provision of investment incentives

In the case of Bulgaria, the process of prioritisation of investors by the IPA appears to be largely determined by EU state aid regulations and the associated national regulations.[29] The AIP, described earlier, establishes IBA as the agency assisting eligible firms in the application process for state support. Yet, some strategic documents, such as the past "Innovation Strategy for Smart Specialization of the Republic of Bulgaria 2014-20", have provided further guidance on potential sectors where Bulgaria may have a competitive advantage. As such, they could provide insight as which activities IBA could usefully target as part of its prioritisation efforts in investment attraction.[30] These sectors broadly correspond to those which were listed on IBA's website at the time of writing this *Review*, and for which the agency provided detailed information and brochures.[31] In order to increase its impact as an IPA, IBA could consider boosting proactive investment generation activities in high-potential sectors.

Proactive prioritisation could also take place by type of investor. The business consultations conducted by IBA when preparing a report on the possible impact of COVID-19 revealed that some firms believed that a successful attraction of one large corporate player could help locate Bulgaria on the radar of foreign investors and facilitate the process of reducing the existing obstacles to doing business. To increase the probability that an investor of such calibre establishes locally, IBA could consider explicitly targeting large or "lead" investors as part of its prioritisation strategy. For example, some OECD IPAs explicitly target companies on "Forbes 2000" list or established brands (OECD, 2018). Considering IBA's small size, it could usefully be supported in this task by the ministry in charge of investment promotion and other government bodies. For example, planned state visits at the highest level could be used to hold relevant meetings with the private sector in a given destination.

Table 6.3. List of priority sectors according to Innovation Strategy and IBA's website

Innovation Strategy (2014-20)	IBA's website (2020)
Mechatronics and clean technologies	Machine Building
ICT	Information Technology
Biotechnology	Business Process Outsourcing
Nanotechnology	Chemistry
Creative industries	Balneology
Pharma	Electrical Engineering and Electronics
Food industry	Healthcare and Medical Tourism
	Food and Agriculture
	Logistics

Source: Government of Bulgaria (2015) and IBA's website, www.investbg.government.bg.

Last but not least, to assist it further in fine-tuning of its prioritisation effort, the agency could improve its monitoring and evaluation system. While the agency did have in 2021 an internal data collection system, it was still rudimentary. Unlike most OECD IPAs, the agency, at the time of writing this *Review*, did not have a Customer Relationship Management (CRM) system. Designing and implementing a CRM could help improve the agency's internal data management, facilitate systematisation of investors' information for proactive targeting and facilitate internal resource management (Sztajerowska, 2019). As development and tailoring of CRM systems takes time and often is a reiterative process, the agency may need to consider future resources required for the upkeep and adjustments of the system and any possible training of staff. The implementation of a high-quality CRM could also help the agency track better the quality and effectiveness of its services. It could also consider undertaking more systematic surveys of firms to gain insights on how to adjust its services and help identify key obstacles to investment attraction and retention.[32] Publishing surveys' results or using them in conversations with the government can be a potent policy advocacy tool (de Crombrugghe, 2019).

Investment facilitation and aftercare is important, especially in the aftermath of the COVID-19 crisis

Studies suggest that the impact of IPAs is strongest when such agencies bridge information asymmetries, for example by providing high-quality and timely information to firms (Volpe Martincus et al. 2020). This is critical for new investors not familiar with the local conditions and those already operating locally that wish to expand their operations encounter difficulties, or face changed business conditions. As such, OECD IPAs give particular attention to investment facilitation and aftercare services (OECD, 2018).

Overall, IBA reported in the framework of this *Review* to provide all standard investment facilitation services associated with project definition and obtaining administrative procedures offered by OECD IPAs (Figure 6.12). In case of certified priority investment projects, IBA can also create *ad hoc* working groups with the relevant government authorities to resolve a particular issue encountered by an investor (upon request). Yet, unlike OECD IPAs, IBA at the time of writing this *Review*, provided a rather limited array of aftercare services to all established investors. For example, it did not provide any matchmaking, linkage, cluster-development, or capacity-building support to local firms. Nor did it offer any personnel recruitment or training support or educational programmes to local staff. Considering the importance of local skill shortages in Bulgaria, as highlighted by business surveys quoted earlier in this chapter and as fully recognised in Bulgaria's most recent development strategies, IBA could consider if it could not usefully support initiative of this type. The experience of the IPA of Costa Rica (CINDE) could provide a useful example in this regard (Box 6.9). Projects designed together with BSMEPA could ensure that such programmes are tailored to SME needs.

Figure 6.12. The share of IPAs conducting different investment facilitation and aftercare services in Bulgaria relative to OECD and LAC

In percentage

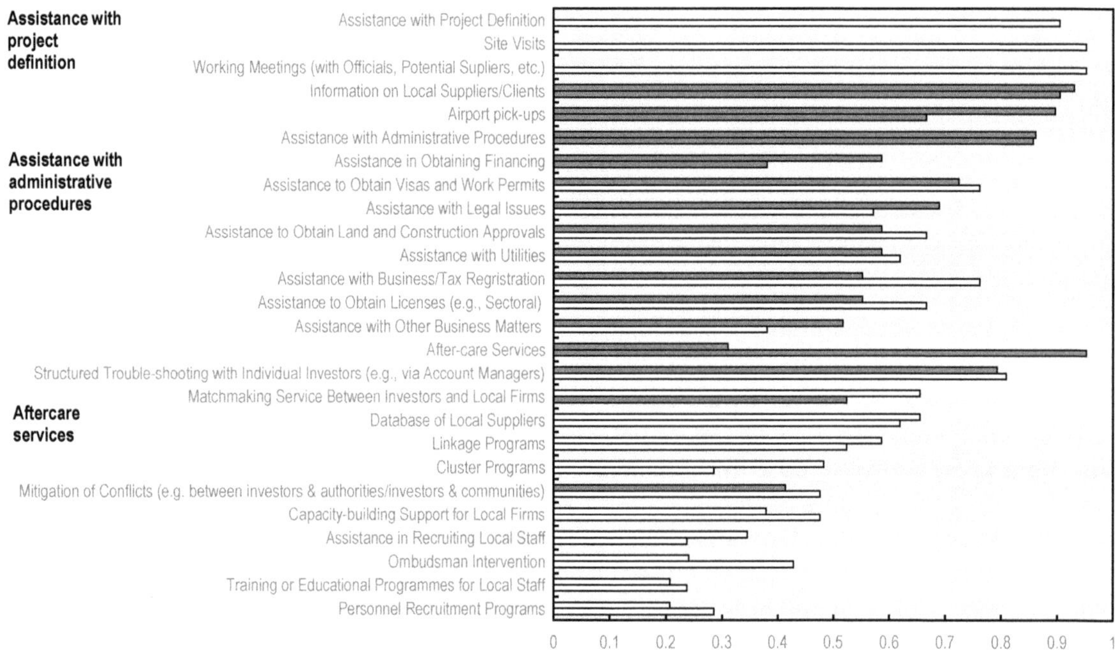

Note: Bars representing activities that IBA did not conduct at the time of survey are highlighted in white.
Source: OECD-IDB Survey of Investment Promotion Agencies (2020).

Box 6.9. IPA's role in supporting better labour market outcomes: The example of Costa Rica

CINDE Invest in Costa Rica is the national investment promotion agency of Costa Rica established in 1982. Its official mandate is the. attraction of foreign direct investment into the local economy. Yet, through its activities, it is also supports broader objectives of sustainable development and improving competitiveness of the local economy. Among others, it aims to strengthen the links between the enterprises it attracts and the local economy, and improve the level of skills and labour market outcomes of the local population through several programmes:

- For example, CINDE helped create an online platform, "The Talent Place" (www.thetalentplace.cr) that provides detailed up-to-date information regarding most in-demand occupations, current vacancies in the companies located Costa Rica, skills required to apply and links to resources to build them and obtain needed certification, including though free-of-charge online courses.
- Aiming at directly linking employers with employees, CINDE also organises, on an annual basis, "CINDE Job Fair" (www.cindejobfair.com), allowing for matching available vacancies in MNEs that were attracted by CINDE with potential jobs seekers. During the 15 years of the fair's operation, 10 000 people assisted the fair and 24% of which have completed the recruitment process.
- Together with the Ministry for Science, Technology and Telecommunications and "Essential Costa Rica", responsible for the country brand, CINDE has also designed a programme for innovation and human capital development (Programa de Innovación y Capital Humano, PINN). The initiative provides Costa Rican nationals with access to scholarships funding educational opportunities in science, technology, engineering and mathematics (STEM). The programme is supported by the Inter-American Development Bank, and CINDE serves as a certification and capacity-building body under one of its pillars.
- In light the COVID-19 crisis, in April 2020, CINDE also created an online platform that offers information on job vacancies available in MNEs located in the country. The goal has also been to facilitate a transfer of employees from sectors most affected by the pandemic (e.g. tourism) to other sectors that have remained relatively intact as well as more generally support worker mobility. As of April 2020, 950 jobs were on offer on the platform.

While being important in normal times, effective investment facilitation has become a critical capacity of an IPA during a crisis such as the COVID-19 pandemic. Unsurprisingly, the majority of OECD IPAs rapidly reoriented their services towards facilitation and policy advocacy support during the COVID-19 outbreak (OECD, 2020a). In 2020, nearly two-thirds of OECD IPAs had a dedicated and regularly updated COVID-19 section in English on their website and many more provided information in other forms. A number of agencies had also readapted their activities to focus on existing clients. For example, they had dedicated most of their staff's time to informing firms about government programmes and support their ongoing investments and operations. In this context, having a list of locally established firms and well-designed CRM have proven useful to identify and prioritise investors quickly. IPAs also activated their existing business networks, particularly in the health sector, to help the government fight the crisis.[33] Both in the immediate aftermath of the crisis and in the medium to long term, many OECD IPAs have also scaled up the use of digital tools for the delivery of services and are rethinking their priority sectors to adapt to the new market reality.[34]

IBA has undertaken many similar steps in face of COVID-19 pandemic. For example, the agency – that also entered a teleworking mode as many other European IPAs – continued operating and servicing clients through digital means during the pandemic. For example, it made use of social media (e.g. YouTube,

Twitter, Instagram) to communicate with clients on the applicable regulations, government support measures and other relevant issues. It also prepared a report on the likely impact of COVID-19 on FDI and projects assisted by IBA and a newsletter.[35] IBA also played an active role in policy advocacy during the pandemic. For example, as a result joint efforts with the Ministry of Economy, a regulation issued by the Ministry of Health allowed certified investors to cross borders without the usually applicable quarantine requirements (Regulation No. RD01 274). Finally yet importantly, in 2020, the agency actively considered potential implications of the crisis for competitive niches available to Bulgaria. In particular, IBA aimed to position Bulgaria as an attractive business location, offering low production costs in close proximity of the EU market, to benefit from potential near- and offshoring opportunities that may arise after the pandemic.[36]

Building on these initiatives, IBA could consider following the examples of OECD IPAs to further adjust its services beyond the COVID-19 crisis. For example, it could follow the example of several OECD IPAs to provide investors with all the relevant information on its website.[37] It could also reflect more systematically how its prioritisation strategy may need to change in light of a projected drop in FDI and its uneven sectoral impact (OECD, 2020b; UNCTAD, 2020).

Investment facilitation and administrative simplification efforts

Bulgaria could reduce administrative burden to further improve business climate

The quality of regulation has a significant influence on the climate for business and investment. Poorly designed or weakly applied regulations can slow business responsiveness, divert resources away from productive investments, hamper entry into markets, reduce job creation and generally discourage entrepreneurship (OECD, 2015a). In this context, the challenge for governments is, on one hand, to balance their need to use administrative procedures as a source of information and a tool for implementing public policies, and on the other, to minimise the interferences implied by these requirements in terms of the resources required to comply with them (OECD, 2009). There are various tools at the disposal of the governments achieve this objective. These include periodic reviews of the stock of regulations, simplifying administrative procedures and introducing e-government services on top of developing better rules on creating new regulations and oversight of regulatory processes, discussed in more detail in the next chapter on public governance.

While the country has made progress in reducing the administrative burden, as captured by the change in its ranking on the World Economic Forum's *Global Competiveness Index* over the past ten years (Figure 6.13), the ease of obtaining licenses and permits, as perceived by businesses, apparently remains a challenge to doing business in Bulgaria. Bulgaria scored 61 out of 190 economies on the World Bank's *Doing Business 2020* and 49 out of 141 economies on the World Economic Forum's *Global Competiveness Index*. While these types of rankings should not be taken at face value, they may point to general tendencies and areas that require government's attention.

For example, the distribution of scores for different aspects covered by the *Doing Business* indicators shows that Bulgaria performs relatively better in trading across borders (21) and protection of minority stakeholders (25), and relatively worse in regards to getting electricity (151), starting a business (113) and paying taxes (97) (Figure 6.14). The average times obtained via interviews of firms through the World Bank's *Enterprise Survey 2019* also point in a similar direction, in particular in regards to the time it takes to obtain a construction permit, electricity connection or an operating license.[38] Surveyed firms also report that over one tenth of senior management's time is, on average, spent dealing with the requirements of government regulation and 10% of firms select business licensing and permits as their biggest obstacle (Figure 6.15), i.e. a share higher than those in other countries. As there are large differences across the regions, in some places these shares are higher.[39]

Figure 6.13. Bulgaria's score on World Economic Forum's Global Competiveness Index, 2007-18

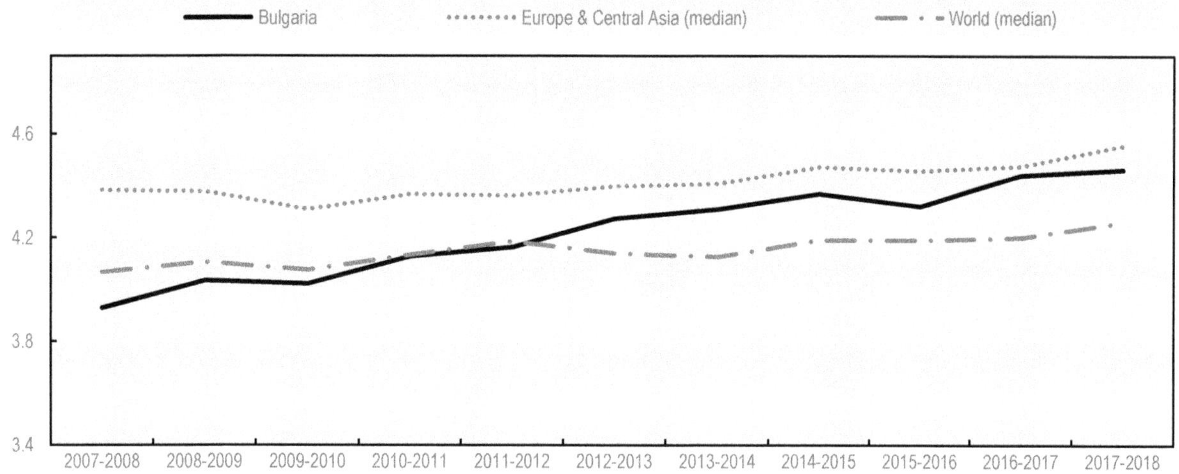

Source: World Economic Forum's Global Competiveness Index (2007-18).

Figure 6.14. Overview of Bulgaria's score on World Bank Doing Business Indicators, 2020

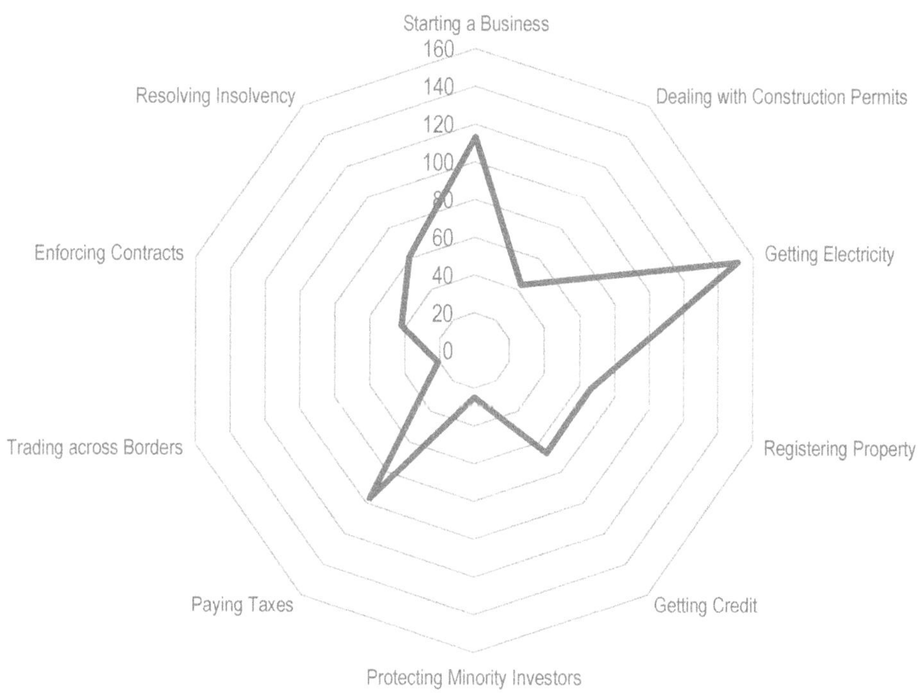

Source: World Bank (2020), Doing Business Indicators.

Figure 6.15. Senior management time spent dealing with the requirements of government regulation and firms choosing business licensing and permits as their biggest obstacle

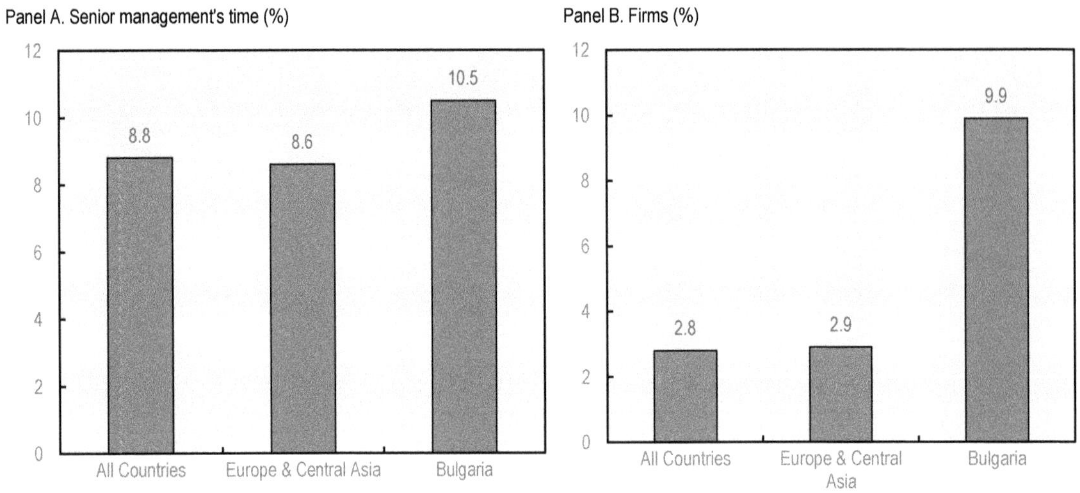

Source: World Bank (2019), Enterprise Survey of Bulgaria.

According to the government, the actual time required to complete administrative procedures and obtain permits is shorter than suggested by *Doing Business*.[40] Yet, its internal analysis identified similar priority areas.[41] As highlighted earlier, while in absolute terms other issues are considered more important barriers to doing business in Bulgaria by firms – notably, the lack of adequately educated workforce and competition from the informal sector; in relative terms, reducing administrative burdens has increased in importance (Figure 6.1). In addition, as the country has transposed significant amount of common EU regulations and will be subject to new ones in the future, this has also increased the importance of effectively reviewing and streamlining the growing stock of regulations. The EC, while recognising progress made by Bulgaria in this area, has repeatedly highlighted the need for further reforms (e.g. European Commission, 2018-20).

Responding to these concerns, the government has implemented three consecutive plans for the reduction of administrative burdens between 2009 and 2018. The first and second plan involved a target to reduce the administrative burdens placed on businesses by 20% each, and the third by 30%. According to the government, the targets have been reached.[42] The Council of Ministers also sought feedback from the private sector on the impact of these changes on business. Yet, the authorities have highlighted that quantifying and reaching targets have been resource-intensive and feedback obtained from firms has suggested that these actions may not have led to improved perception by business (Renda, 2019).

The government has maintained its efforts in this area to achieve tangible progress. For example, in 2017 and 2018, new measures were adopted to ease administrative burdens on SMEs. The Decision 338/2017 of the Council of Ministers ("Reduction of Administrative Burden") withdrew the requirement for presenting notarised documents to the public administration. By Decision of 5 October 2018, the Council of Ministers also approved a new package of 1 528 measures aimed at changing and improving administrative services for citizens and businesses.[43] In addition, as part of the regulatory impact assessment (RIA), introduced in Bulgaria in 2016 – and discussed in more detail in the following chapter – an "SME Test" has been implemented, which aims to explicitly consider the possible impact of regulations on smaller firms, mentioned earlier.

Box 6.10. Overview of selected administrative e-service offered to businesses in Bulgaria

Patents (www.bpo.bg)

- Responsibility: Patent office of Republic of Bulgaria
- Description: The website gives information on multiple services regarding patents (only in Bulgarian). It provides sample templates and information for paid services.

Electronic Signature Certificate for Businesses (www.crc.bg).

- Responsibility: Communications Regulation Commission
- Description: The website gives information on registered providers of certified services in Bulgaria, from whom electronic signature certificate can be requested.

Registration of a new company (www.registryagency.bg).

- Responsibility: Central Government, Ministry of Justice, Registry Agency
- Description: An online commercial register enables the establishment and reorganisation, restructuring and liquidation of a business. Applications in paper form still apply, especially for businesses that do not possess an eSignature certificate. An option to pay electronically is provided. It is necessary to own an electronic signature.

Corporate tax: declaration, notification (www.nap.bg).

- Responsibility: Central Government, Ministry of Finance, National Revenue Agency
- Description: Online information and forms can be downloaded, submitted and signed electronically, allowing for the online submission of corporate taxes.

VAT: declaration, notification (www.nap.bg).

- Responsibility: Central Government, Ministry of Finance, National Revenue Agency
- Description: Online information and forms can be downloaded, submitted and signed electronically, allowing for the online submission of VAT declarations.

Electronic Payments (www.inetdec.nra.bg).

- Responsibility: National Revenue Agency
- Description: The website allows for electronic payments of different type of taxes.

Customs declarations (www.customs.bg/wps/portal).

- Responsibility: Central Government, Ministry of Finance, National Customs Agency
- Description: There are model forms to download, complete and submit.

Public procurement (www.minfin.bg/bg/procurement)

- Responsibility: Central Government, Ministry of Finance, Public Procurement Agency, Small Scale Public Procurement Electronic Market
- Description: Contracting authorities are obliged to publish their tender notices in the Bulgarian State Gazette, and in the web-based Public Procurement Register

The government has made strides in digitising administrative procedures and offering e-government services online, including to businesses (see Box 6.10).[44] For example, the "Strategy for the development of electronic government in Bulgaria 2014-20" aimed to define broad strategic objectives for the delivery of improved e-services; while the roadmap for its implementation listed specific measures for the realisation of strategic orientations. In addition, the State e-Government Agency (SEGA), established in 2016 pursuant to the Electronic Governance Act,[45] has been providing relevant government services via a centralised platform. The number of e-government users has increased since 2018. Yet, many of the e-services provided remain limited to the delivery of information. Further reforms may be considered to facilitate widespread use of e-services and improve the necessary IT infrastructure. One constraint to the e-government expansion has been the challenge to retain IT specialists (European Commission, 2019).

It is worth noting that recognising that complying with administrative requirements may take time. One type of service that allows delivery of different licenses and permits in a streamlined and faster fashion for a large number of firms is an establishment of a one-stop solution (OSS) or a single window for investment. While the specific functionality of OSS will determine which aspect of the investment decision it can simplify, effective instruments of such type provide investors with an ability to issue a whole array of permits beyond the sheer business registration (see e.g. World Bank, 2009). Still, progress in speeding up business registration itself is a welcome step.

Despite recent developments such as the 2019 introduction of a free of charge electronic service under the VAT Act, allowing to submit simultaneously an application for registration with the Commercial Register and a request for VAT registration, it currently takes two times longer to start a business in Bulgaria than in the comparator region and over three times longer than in OECD countries (Table 6.4). While some of the steps in the registration process can already be undertaken online, such as the registration with the Commercial Register at the Registry Agency and registering employment agreements with the National Revenue Agency, potentially in the future all steps could be integrated into one platform.

Going forward, the government could consider if it could not build on international good practices to establish an OSS for investors. An OSS solution for investment can be a physical facility where investors can complete all the required procedures or an online service (Table 6.5). While comparative cross-country data on this issue comes from 2009, already then more than a half of countries worldwide had an OSS solution for investment in place (World Bank, 2009). In addition, such countries tended to have over 30% less procedures and over 50% less time spent dealing with them, according to the World Bank's *Doing Business* than countries without OSS solutions. Regardless of a particular form that such solution could take, the most important component is ensuring that it can successfully integrate the processes of issuing different permits to effectively cut the steps in the process, instead of adding an additional layer. Potentially, a capacity-building project with support of the EU or other international organisation could assist Bulgaria in this task.

Table 6.4. Overview of the number of days, costs and procedures associated for starting a business in Bulgaria

Indicator	Bulgaria	Europe & Central Asia	OECD high income
Procedure (number)	7	5.2	4.9
Time (days)	23	11.9	9.2
Cost (% of income per capita)	1	4	3
Paid-in min. capital (% of income per capita)	0	0.7	7.6

Source: World Bank (2020), Doing Business Indicators.

Table 6.5. Overview of type of one-stop-shop solutions in different countries

Type of OSS	No. of countries	Average No. of procedures	No. of days	WB DB Ranking (out of 183)
A. Commercial Registry with other bodies on the same site	7	7	24	99
B. Commercial Registry which liaises with other bodies	20	6.7	19	61
C. One-Stop Shop (not a Commercial Registry) which liaises with other bodies	13	6.3	27	98
D. Integrated registration function	12	5.8	13	49
E. Online registration facility	15	5.2	14	48

Source: World Bank (2009).

Outlook and policy recommendations

Bulgaria has achieved noticeable progress in improving its investment climate and increasing overall political stability. The proximity of the EU market and availability of EU funds, which have improved financing conditions for firms and can help transform the country's infrastructure and train local workforce, can also be advantageous for investors. The country also has a relatively low rate of corporate taxation and provides a well-developed framework for provision of state support that can be attractive for some projects.

Still, several obstacles hinder the country's investment attraction potential. While Bulgaria has made strides in improving the overall planning and co-ordination of its investment policy, a detailed plan with clearly identified priority reforms and allocated responsibilities of different government bodies and applicable timelines appears to be lacking. The institutions aiming to co-ordinate cross-cutting initiatives and reforms to improve the overall competiveness and business climate are also relatively new and may require further strengthening. In some areas, the rules outlining procedures for co-operation are sometimes lacking, as in the case of IBA's co-operation with subnational bodies. A publically available list of specific initiatives involving different institutions aiming to address key obstacles could help in achieving progress in difficult horizontal reforms – including reduction of administrative burdens – and ensure that the public is aware of the efforts made.

In regards to the investment promotion agency's activities, IBA is primarily responsible for managing applications of investors wishing to be certified as a supported investment project under AIP. It is a relatively small agency with low levels of institutional independence. For example, at the time of this *Review*, it did not have a Board of Directors to oversee its functions, unlike is the case in most OECD IPAs. In the area of investment facilitation, IBA performs most standard services performed by other agencies in OECD countries with a notable exception of aftercare services. For example, it does not offer any linkage or matchmaking programmes between foreign and domestic firms nor personnel recruitment support. Given the skilled labour shortages in the country and potential spillovers from SME-MNE links, IBA could consider designing and implementing initiatives in this area in collaboration with relevant government bodies. Strengthening its prioritisation and monitoring and evaluation capacities could also be beneficial as could greater co-operation with sub-national level bodies.

Besides potentially strengthening aftercare capacities of its IPA, the government could usefully focus on achieving further progress in reducing administrative burdens as foreseen. Considering that the experience with setting and reaching quantitative targets for burden reduction has been mixed, existing diagnostics and feedback from business could be used to identify high-impact reforms. Given the time it takes to establish a business and obtain electrical connection, these could be natural areas of focus. In this context, the government could consider if an OSS solution for investment could be feasible and useful, especially building on the progress made in introducing e-services. Considering the importance of competition from the informal sector, facilitating business registration could potentially contribute to formalisation, in particular if coupled with additional incentives, and be particularly beneficial to SMEs.

Policy recommendations

- *Establish a list of priority investment climate reforms* and specific projects to assist their implementation with clearly identified timelines and responsible institutions. The plan should build on the existing strategic planning documents and diagnostics. It could be made publically available and periodically updated. The NEC and the ministry responsible for investment promotion could play a lead role in this regard, supported by high-level of government.
- *Strengthen regional component in investment promotion* and develop terms of reference for co-operation across agencies at the central and sub-national level. Differentiate investment promotion according to regional comparative advantages. Use the EU Smart Specialisation framework to aid in this exercise. Rules for engagement with sub-national investment promotion bodies appear limited to processing of certified investment projects. For example, InvestBulgaria Agency (IBA) does not have a regional development mandate and lacks terms of reference for engaging with sub-national bodies. The development and implementation of such rules could help ensure complementarity of efforts and attraction of FDI into different regions.
- *Consider strengthening the aftercare services and technical capacity of IBA*. While IBA performs all standard investment facilitation functions in the pre-establishment stage, it does not offer many aftercare services to firms (outside of certified investors). In particular, considering importance of skilled labour shortages in Bulgaria and potential spillover from SME-MNE links, the agency could consider developing such programmes. Specific projects, supported by international donors, could also help strengthen IBA's monitoring and evaluation and prioritisation capacity.
- *Continue reducing administrative burdens.* Administrative burden may be necessary for fair taxation, health, safety, environmental stewardship and other governmental commitments in line with the OECD *Guidelines on Multinational Enterprises* to improve social progress and the overall quality of citizens' life (see Chapter 8). Still, from the perspective of business, administrative burdens can be a cost, delay and source of uncertainty with respect to operations and projects. Given the time it takes to establish a business in Bulgaria, these could be natural areas of focus in the short run. In the medium term, the government could consider whether establishing an one-stop solution for investment would help businesses deal with government regulations. In the long run, progress in improving the quality of regulations (discussed in the next chapter) will also help reduce the stock of burdensome requirements.

References

De Crombrugghe, A. (2019), "Supporting Investment Climate Reforms Through Policy Advocacy", *OECD Investment Policy Insights*, www.oecd.org/investment/investment-policy/Investment-Insights-Supporting-investment-climate-reforms-through-IPA-policy-advocacy.pdf.

EBRD (2019), *Bulgaria Diagnostic*, www.ebrd.com/documents/comms-and-bis/country-diagnostic-paper-bulgaria.pdf?blobnocache=true.

European Commission (2018a), "Reshaping the functional and operational capacity of Sofia Tech Park", Report by an Independent Panel of International Experts, www.ec.europa.eu/knowledge4policy/sites/know4pol/files/report_reshaping_the_functional_and_operational_capacity_of_sofia_tech_park_2018.pdf.

European Commission (2018b), "Country Report Bulgaria: Assessment of progress on structural reforms, prevention and correction of macroeconomic imbalances, and results of in-depth reviews under Regulation No 1176/2011", *Commission Staff Working Document*, SWD(2018)201.

European Commission (2019a), SBA Fact Sheet: Bulgaria, www.ec.europa.eu/docsroom/documents/38662/attachments/4/translations/en/renditions/native.

European Commission (2019b), "Country Report Bulgaria: Assessment of progress on structural reforms, prevention and correction of macroeconomic imbalances, and results of in-depth reviews under Regulation No 1176/2011", *Commission Staff Working Document*, SWD(2019)1001.

European Commission (2019c), *Digital Government Factsheet 2019*, www.joinup.ec.europa.eu/sites/default/files/inline-files/Digital_Government_Factsheets_Bulgaria_2019_1.pdf.

European Commission (2020a), "Country Report Bulgaria: Assessment of progress on structural reforms, prevention and correction of macroeconomic imbalances, and results of in-depth reviews under Regulation (EU) No 1176/2011", *Commission Staff Working Document*, SWD(2020) 501.

European Commission (2020b), "Planned European Structural and Investment Funds (ESIF) 2014-12", www.shorturl.at/lADGJ

European Commission (2020c), "Extra cash for COVID-19 measures in Bulgaria" www.ec.europa.eu/regional_policy/en/newsroom/news/2020/05/22-05-2020-extra-cash-for-COVID-19-measures-in-bulgaria.

European Commission (2020d), "European Structural and Investment Funds: Country Data for Bulgaria", www.shorturl.at/imHOW.

Government of Bulgaria (2015), *Innovation strategy for smart specialisation of the Republic of Bulgaria 2014-20*, www.mi.government.bg/files/useruploads/files/innovations/ris3_26.10.2015_en.pdf.

Harding T. and B. Javorcik (2012), "Investment Promotion and FDI Inflows: Quality Matters," *Economics Series Working Papers 612*, University of Oxford, Department of Economics.

Harding T. and B. Javorcik (2011), "Roll Out the Red Carpet and They Will Come: Investment Promotion and FDI Inflows," *Economic Journal*, Royal Economic Society, Vol. 121(557), pp. 1 445- 1476.

Marshall S. (2019), "Living Wage: Regulatory Solutions to Informal and Precarious Work in Global Supply Chains", *Oxford Labour Law*, Oxford University Press: Oxford, United Kingdom

Novik, A., A. de Crombrugghe (2018), "Towards an International Framework for Investment Facilitation", *OECD Investment Insights*, www.oecd.org/investment/Towards-an-international-framework-for-investment-facilitation.pdf.

OECD (2018), *Mapping of Investment Promotion Agencies in OECD countries*, www.oecd.org/investment/Mapping-of-Investment-Promotion-Agencies-in-OECD-Countries.htm

OECD (2020a), "Investment promotion agencies in the time of COVID-19", *OECD Policy Responses to Coronavirus (COVID-19)*, www.oecd.org/coronavirus/policy-responses/investment-promotion-agencies-in-the-time-of-COVID-19-50f79678.

OECD (2020b), "Foreign direct investment flows in the time of COVID-19", OECD Policy Responses to Coronavirus (COVID-19), OECD Publishing, Paris, https://doi.org/10.1787/a2fa20c4-en.

OECD (2020c), *OECD Tax Database*, www.oecd.org/tax/tax-policy/tax-database.

OECD-IDB (2020), *OECD-IDB Investment Promotion Survey*.

Renda A. (2019), "Feasibility Study: Introducing "One-In-One-Out" in the European Commission", Final Report for the German Ministry for Economic Affairs and Energy Presented by CEPS, www.ceps.eu/wp-content/uploads/2019/12/Feasibility-Study.pdf

Sader F. (2006), "Do One-Stop Shops Work?", Foreign Investment Advisory Service, International Finance Corporation, www.wbginvestmentclimate.org/uploads/Do+One+Stop+Shops+Work.pdf.

Sztajerowska M. (2019), "Monitoring and Evaluation: A Brief Guide for Investment Promotion Agencies",

OECD Investment Policy Insights, www.oecd.org/investment/Monitoring-and-evaluation-a-brief-guide-for-investment-promotion-agencies.pdf.

UNCTAD (2020), "Impact of COVID-19 Pandemic on Global FDI and GVCs", *Investment Trends Monitor*, March 2020, www.unctad.org/en/PublicationsLibrary/diaeiainf2020d3_en.pdf.

Volpe Martincus, C. and M. Sztajerowska (2019), "How to Resolve the Investment Promotion Puzzle – A Mapping of Investment Promotion Agencies in Latin American and the Caribbean and OECD Countries", IDB, Washington, DC, http://dx.doi.org/10.18235/0001767.

Volpe Martincus, C. et al. (2020), "How Effective is Investment Promotion? Firm-Level Evidence", *Integration and Trade Sector, Discussion Paper*, IDB-DP-00741, https://publications.iadb.org/en/how-effective-investment-promotion-firm-level-evidence

World Bank (2009), "How many stops in one stop shop? A review of recent developments in business registration", Investment Climate Advisory Services, World Bank Group, Washington, DC, www.openknowledge.worldbank.org/handle/10986/27886

World Bank (2019), *Enterprise Survey of Bulgaria*, www.enterprisesurveys.org/en/data/exploreeconomies/2019/bulgaria

World Bank (2020), *Doing Business Indicators*.

World Economic Forum (2019) *Global Competiveness Index*, www.weforum.org/reports/global-competitiveness-report-2019

Notes

[1] For more information on the BIA's survey (in Bulgarian), see: www.en.bia-bg.com/news/view/26324.

[2] For example, the OECD *Investment Policy Review of Croatia* (2019) shows that the policy framework there is largely confined to the provision of incentives and allocation of EU funds, governed by the Acts on Investment Promotion and Strategic Investment Projects.

[3] In 2021, it consisted of 11 deputy ministers from different ministries and the chairpersons of the five nationally recognised employers' organizations.

[4] For example, in the past, the Council negotiated and proposed amendments to labour legislation (see Marshall, 2019).

[5] In Bulgaria, the State Aid Act is fully in accordance with EU legislation since 2007. As a consequence of EU State aid modernisation, a new State Aid Act, from October 2017, regulates the terms and procedures related to the allocation, monitoring and evaluation, reporting and penalties related to violations of state aid; All the relevant laws and regulations linked to state aid granting need to be in compliance with the EU state aid rules.

[6] The text of AIP (in English) is available on IBA's website: www.investbg.government.bg/files/useruploads/files/investment_promotion_act_(title_amended,_sg_no._37_2004).pdf as is the text of the implementing regulations: www.investbg.government.bg/files/useruploads/files/regulations_for_application_of_the_investment_promotion_act2020.pdf.

[7] The details are available on the website of the Ministry of Economy of Bulgaria: www.mi.government.bg/en/themes/application-of-the-investment-promotion-act-95-284.html#:~:text=The%20main%20purpose%20of%20the,Rules%20for%20Implementation%20of%20IPA and on the website of IBA: www.investbg.government.bg/en/pages/11-investment-incentives-184.html.

[8] The sectoral classification is available on IBA's website, and at least 80% of the future aggregate income must arise from these activities. All the information pertaining to the eligibility requirements and certification procedures for supported investment project are available (in English) on IBA's website: www.investbg.government.bg/en/pages/getting-certified-under-investment-promotion-act-166.html.

[9] The period of project implementation, i.e. the period between the commencement and completion of the project, must not exceed three years. The investment amount per project must not fall below the minimum amounts specified in the Regulation on the Implementation of AIP. At least 40% of the eligible costs for the investment must be financed by the investor's own or borrowed resources (any resources allocated as state aid or involving an element of state aid, including retained corporation tax, are not considered own or borrowed resources). The jobs created in relation to the investment must be maintained in the relevant region for at least five years in the case of large enterprises and three years in the case of SMEs. The investment must be maintained in the relevant region for at least five years in the case of large enterprises and three years in the case of SMEs, calculated from the date of completion of the investment project. Any long-term tangible and intangible assets acquired shall be new and purchased under market conditions from third parties independent from the investor.

[10] The minimum investment value is EUR 25 million if investment takes place in municipalities with high rates of unemployment or in general manufacturing activities; EUR 15 million if it concerns high technology activities of the manufacturing or service sectors or EUR 7.6 million if it concerns a creation of an industrial zone or a technological park.

[11] Information on the certified projects is available on IBA's website: www.investbg.government.bg/en/pages/certified-investment-projects-in-bulgaria-217.html

[12] The information is available at www.bcci.bg/zones.

[13] Information gathered from the websites of IBA (www.investbg.government.bg/en), the NCZI (www.nciz.bg/en), and the National Institute of Statistics (www.nsi.bg/en)

[14] The definition of an industrial zone as well as a technological park is available in supplementary provisions of AIP. "Industrial zone" shall be a set of one or several adjoining lots with similar characteristics and prevailing assigned use for manufacturing activities, projected by an effective detailed plan, according to the Spatial Development Act. "Technology park" shall be a park which satisfies the requirements for an industrial zone but with a prevailing scientific research and development activity and/or education, and/or information technologies and for innovative activities for technological renovation of manufacturing products and technologies. Complementary investment activities in the manufacturing industry or in another production sector are admissible (Paragraphs 12-13).

[15] See https://dv.parliament.bg/DVWeb/showMaterialDV.jsp?idMat=156334.

[16] Information based on the share of available territory to the total territory of the zones for the functioning industrial zones for which such information is publically available.

[17] The project is co-funded by the European Regional Development Fund through the Operational Programme "Development of the Competitiveness of the Bulgarian Economy". The grant for the project is of the value of about EUR 47.4 million, split in two phases over 2007-14 and 2014-20 period. The owner of the "Science-technology park" project is Sofia Tech Park Joint Stock Company (JSC). The managing authority is the Ministry of Economy – European Funds for Competitiveness Directorate-General. For more information, see EC (2018).

[18] All information in the paragraph is source from European Commission (2020b) and the website with the data on the use of EU funds: www.shorturl.at/imHOW

[19] In 2021, there were ongoing discussions whether to provide a more decisive role to the regions in funds allocation and potentially involving a wider range of stakeholders. The OECD and World Bank were providing support in this process.

[20] The Guide can be found on the website of the Ministry of Economy: www.mi.government.bg/en/pages/msp-info-220.html. The news release also provides further information: www.mi.government.bg/en/news/a-guide-for-smes-has-been-published-on-the-website-of-the-ministry-of-economy-3716.html

[21] BSMEPA has a regional network of representatives distributed in six major cities in Bulgaria: Plovdiv, Stara Zagora, Burgas, Varna, Vratsa and Ruse. Their main goal is to build and maintain an up-to-date register of SMEs and provide capacity-building support.

[22] IBA scores below the OECD average and median and is comparable in size to agencies of other small European economies.

[23] The Index covers the legal status of an IPA, the share of non-public sources in the IPA's budget; the share of non-public members on the IPA's board; the reporting line of the IPA; the approving body of the agency's strategy; the appointing authority of the IPA's head; and the ability to pay wages that are higher than those of the public sector, among others

[24] Information based on data provided by IBA as part of this *Review*.

[25] For example, according to the government, they usually perform joint presentations and share with each other information on relevant forthcoming events.

[26] The former information is available here: www.investbg.government.bg/en/projects.htm; and the latter is available here: www.investbg.government.bg/en/pages/areas-354.html.

[27] As a case in point may serve the differences in articulation of investment prioritisation strategies: sectors targeted by individual subnational IPAs differ from those listed by IBA on its website.

[28] For example, in Sweden, a code of conduct agreement among the national IPA and the 15 regions was established to better communicate on opportunities and encourage exchange of information. The agency also used software that allows sharing information with external partners. Business France has designed a formal information-sharing process to increase the efficiency of the collaboration with France's 13 regions: it created a "marketplace" of investment projects and shares information weekly with its regional partners.

[29] For example, IBA explicitly states that the Investment Promotion Act is in line with the EU Regulation No 651/2014 on categories of aid compatible with the internal market rules.

[30] The strategy was approved the Council of Minister's Decision No 857/03.11.2015.

[31] Project "Promoting the advantages of investing in Bulgaria" BG 161PO003-4.1.01-0001-C0001, of which IBA was beneficiary was implemented with the financial support of the EU through the European Fund for Regional Development and the national budget of Bulgaria.

[32] See Sztajerowska, M. (2019) for more information on monitoring and evaluation by OECD IPAs.

[33] For example, Invest in Canada and Invest in Denmark made their business contacts available to the authorities to support immediate medical and source health care supplies.

[34] For more information on the impact of COVID-19 on OECD IPAs, see OECD (2020a).

[35] The newsletter is available on the agency's website: www.investbg.government.bg/files/useruploads/files/newsletter-march_2020.pdf

[36] Information provided by IBA to the OECD Secretariat as part of this *Review*.

[37] It could consult the website of GTAI of Germany as an example of a well-developed website with all relevant information or the website of Invest in Estonia for the use of artificial-intelligence (AI)-based chat-box. GTAI's COVID-19 website is available here: www.gtai.de/gtai-en/invest/business-location-germany/corona-crisis-and-germany-232102 and the chat-box on the homepage of Invest in Estonia's website: www.investinestonia.com.

[38] For example, firms report to require 46.7 days to obtain a construction permit, 24.8 days for an electrical connection, and 20 days for an operating license. The survey has been conducted on 772 firms were interviewed between January 2019 and April 2020. For more information, see: www.enterprisesurveys.org/content/dam/enterprisesurveys/documents/country/Bulgaria-2019.pdf.

[39] The share of firms reporting licensing and permits as the biggest obstacle in Bulgaria ranges from 0% in Severoiztochen to 15.2% in Severozapaden according to the World Bank's Enterprise Survey (2019).

[40] Information obtained by the OECD Secretariat during the find-finding missions in Bulgaria in 2020.

[41] In 2015, the Ministry of Economy conducted an analysis of the investment bottlenecks related to business regulation and administrative burden for investors in the country. Based on the analysis ten key problematic areas were identified: access to technical infrastructure grids (electricity, gas, water), constructions permits, administrative services, frequently changing legislation, judiciary system independence and corruption, paying taxes, skills mismatch on the labour market, lack (or poor quality) of the transport infrastructure. Special inter-institutional working groups were established and proposed measures to address these barriers.

[42] The first target was achieved in 2012, the second in 2014 and 26% of the 30% target in 2018.

[43] According to the information provided by the government in the course of this *Review*, the changes are based on information from visits of 3 700 points providing services from all central administrations and their territorial units, including all district, municipal and regional administrations.

[44] For more information: www.e-gov.bg/wps/portal/agency-en/strategy-policy

[45] The Electronic Government Act and other strategic documents pertaining to e-government efforts in Bulgaria are available on SEGA's website: www.e-gov.bg/wps/portal/agency-en/strategy-policy/startegical-documents/startegical-documents

7 Public governance

This chapter provides an overview of recent advances and remaining challenges related to public governance in Bulgaria, in particular persisting challenges in the fight against corruption, judiciary and public procurement. It also provides an overview of recent advances and remaining challenges relating to regulatory quality in Bulgaria.

Introduction

Public governance has a significant influence on the climate for business and investment. Poorly designed or loosely applied regulations can slow business responsiveness, divert resources away from productive investments, hamper or delay entry into markets, reduce job creation, and generally discourage entrepreneurship. From an investor's perspective, regulatory policy should provide strong guidance and benchmarks for action by officials and set out what investors can expect from the government regarding regulation. From the citizens' point of view, regulation influences the quality of public services by shaping the behaviour of public and private actors and can influence citizens' involvement in policy making.

The quality of public services also significantly influences the investment climate as well as the citizens' life. In this regard, policies ensuring the transparency, predictability, and effectiveness of the regulatory framework for investment are essential to reduce or eliminate potential or existing obstacles faced by companies when they consider investing in a country.

Integrity is also a crucial determinant of a favourable investment climate. Comparative evidence suggests a link between trust in politicians and public officials, both from the business community and citizens, and the perception of corruption. Integrity tools and mechanisms, aimed at preventing corruption and fostering high standards of behaviour, help diffuse concerns by investors when considering investing in a country. Bribery and corruption also undermines the rule of law and the ethical values upon which democratic societies and their institutions are based.

Ever since the accession of Bulgaria to the EU, the country has made progress in improving the regulatory quality of public governance, control of corruption, and government effectiveness. As discussed in this chapter, Bulgaria has improved its anti-corruption framework. Despite the many encouraging steps undertaken by Bulgaria, the country nevertheless still suffers from a negative image with respect to the regulatory quality of public governance and corruption. Corruption continues to be viewed as being widespread, impacting decisions by entrepreneurs to invest in Bulgaria. Tailor-made specifications for particular companies and the unclear selection or evaluation criteria are also believed to be widespread practices in public procurement. Bulgaria's civil service has also been seen as subject to a high degree of politicisation, a likely consequence of the communist legacy (EC, 2018b). There have also been strong suspicions of favouritism and political connections, especially at the local level, despite some significant steps taken by the government for ensuring the integrity of the country's administrative system. Concerns have also been expressed regarding legal certainty and the quality of public services, which have been seen as affecting the decisions of entrepreneurs to invest in Bulgaria.[1]

Challenges persist in the fight against corruption

Corruption control is a basis for sound governance and an attractive investment climate. Effective rule of law is fundamental to a market economy and an inclusive society as it ensures that everyone is treated equally and consistently under well-defined laws. Despite Bulgaria's progress in addressing corruption over the past 20 years or more, corruption continues to be perceived by investors as an important issue. According to the 2019 EU *Flash Eurobarometer* on businesses attitudes towards corruption in the EU, 85% of respondents operating in Bulgaria described corruption as widespread; 50% of respondents felt that corruption had increased in the previous years and more than 80% considered that bribery was the easiest way to obtain public services.[2] In the Transparency International's *Corruption Perception Index* (CPI) for 2020, Bulgaria ranked 69th – the worst ranking of an EU country along with Romania (69th) and Hungary (69th) among 183 countries surveyed. In the Transparency International's *Corruption Perception Index* for 2021 released in January 2022, Bulgaria ranked 78th among 180 countries surveyed, again the worst ranking of an EU country. Entrepreneurs have regularly considered that corruption was one of the biggest shortcomings when it comes to business conditions in Bulgaria compared to other countries in the region.

The judiciary – in principle the institution of choice for resolving commercial disputes or enforcing contracts- has not been trusted either. Courts have been perceived as corrupt and inefficient. Challenges with respect to Bulgaria's judicial system have been highlighted in numerous reports by international organisations such as the European Commission and the Venice Commission of the Council of Europe. As a consequence, at the time of Bulgaria's accession to the European Union in 2007, the country was placed under the EU's Mechanism for Co-operation and Verification (CVM) to ensure progress in judicial and anti-corruption reforms.

Combatting corruption requires simultaneous actions in many areas, encompassing both preventive and repressive measures. In this regard, Bulgaria, in line with good practices, has been following a holistic approach, engaging in reforms with a view of strengthening repressive measures and enhancing public integrity. Individual reforms have been part of the priorities in a series of long-term anti-corruption strategies.

For example, in the framework of its anti-corruption strategy covering the period 2015-20, Bulgaria carried out reform of its legal and institutional anti-corruption framework, leading to a number of high-level investigations in 2020. The reforms also provided for public access to the property and interests declarations of senior public office holders. They also included the adoption of the Anti-Corruption and Forfeiture of Assets Act (AFAA), which introduced key principles relevant to the fight against corruption such as legality, transparency, independence, impartiality, including provisions on greater responsibility of senior public officials; publicity of the property of the persons holding higher public posts; respect and guarantee of citizens' rights and freedoms. In addition, the AFAA established a single, specialised institutional structure – the Commission for Countering Corruption and Confiscation of Illegally Acquired Property (the Anti-Corruption Commission) – to enforce the law. Since then, the new anti-corruption strategy for the period 2021-27 has been approved, with a new set of priorities, namely strengthening capacity to combat corruption; increasing accountability of local authorities; and creating an environment against corruption capable of timely responses (European Commission, 2021).[3]

Because of these actions, reforms undertaken by Bulgaria in the past few years have been assessed by international organisations as contributing positively to the fight against corruption (European Commission, 2020a; European Commission, 2021). Still, Bulgaria faces continuous challenges, for example with respect to the independence of the judiciary as highlighted by the European Parliament's resolution on the rule of law and fundamental rights adopted in October 2020.[4] A lack of tangible results in the fight against corruption has also been one of the key aspects of fuelling protests in 2020 and in the context of the April and July 2021 parliamentary elections. A solid record of accomplishment of final convictions in high-level corruption cases remains to be established. In addition, although a legal framework is in place with respect to conflict of interest, yet concerns exist as regards lobbying.

Prosecution and sanctioning of corruption

The legal framework to fight corruption is largely in place. Significant progress has been achieved as regards the adoption of criminal legislation reforms and the establishment of law enforcement mechanisms specifically dedicated to the detection, prosecution and sanctioning of corruption (European Commission 2020a). Bulgaria's actions have been guided *inter alia* by its obligations under relevant Council of Europe and EU instruments, the OECD Convention on Bribery of Foreign Public Officials and the UN Convention Against Corruption. Modern criminal legislation has been established, largely meeting international standards. Bulgaria has also paid attention to strengthen procedural means to make Bulgaria's law enforcement agencies more efficient to detect and investigate corruption, although these concern primarily domestic corruption and organised crime with bribery of foreign public officials receiving much lower attention as assessed by the OECD Working Group on Bribery in the framework of Bulgaria's Phase 4 Monitoring Report in October 2021.[5] The institutional setting of the law enforcement system has been a particular focus of reforms as illustrated by the establishment of a unified anti-corruption commission under the 2018 AFAA (Box 7.1).

Box 7.1. The Commission for Countering Corruption and Confiscation of Illegally Acquired Property in Bulgaria

The Commission is an independent and specialised public agency entrusted with the implementation of anti-corruption and seizure policies been established by the Law on Anti-Corruption and Confiscation of Illegal Acquisitions (enacted SG No. 7 of 19 January 2018).

The Commission is the successor to the Commission for Confiscation of Illegally Acquired Property, established by the Law on Confiscation in favour of the State of Illegally Acquired Property (promulgated SG, No 38 of 18.03.2012), and the Commission for Establishment of Property Acquired from Criminal Activities, established by the Law on Seizure in favour of the State of Property Acquired from Criminal Activities (promulgated SG, No 19 of 01.03.2005).

For its activities, the Commission is accountable before the National Assembly of the Republic of Bulgaria. Bulgaria's former Prosecutor General preside the Commission for Illegal Assets Forfeiture (CIAF).

The Commission is empowered to bring forfeiture proceedings for illegally acquired assets when is proved an unlawful acquisition of assets. Such a proceeding can take place if an investigation by the Commission establishes a discrepancy that exceeds BGN 150 000 (approximately EUR 75 000).

The Commission has also to ensure that there is no a conflict of interest among high-ranking officials. Any breaches to the rules on conflict of interest are subject to pecuniary sanctions from the Commission.

Source: The Anti-corruption and Forfeiture of Assets Act; the Commission for combating corruption and confiscation of illegally acquired property website.

Other ways to tackle and deter corruption have involved confiscation of assets, which is being carried out in Bulgaria both permanently and temporarily to recover property derived from corruption. It is widely acknowledged that the confiscation of the proceeds and instrumentalities of a crime constitutes an additional deterrent that may have as great an effect as a fine or prison term; the threat of confiscation is also a preventive measure, as it makes bribes solicitation less attractive to public officials. In this regard, Bulgaria has modern legislation in place, which makes it mandatory to confiscate the proceeds and instrumentalities of crime and largely complies with both the international and European standards concerning the asset recovery process.

Despite these encouraging developments, the lack of results in the fight against corruption has been source of concerns, as illustrated by civil protests in 2020 and Bulgaria's 2021 parliamentary elections, which were all about corruption.[6] While high-level corruption investigations cases increased in 2020, most of them did not have tangible results (European Commission 2020a and 2020b). Concerns have also been expressed with respect to alleged political influence and lack of political independence in the work of the Anti-corruption Commission since its chairperson and members are elected after a simple majority vote in the National Assembly (European Commission, 2020b). For example, in 2020, out of 33 decisions that the Supreme Court of Cassation issued on corruption cases, only two were revived in criminal proceedings (EC, 2021). According to the 2019 Eurobarometer survey on corruption published in June 2020, only 18% of surveyed people trusted the role of the Anti-corruption Commission in addressing cases of corruption – a decrease of 4% compared to previous years. Specific concerns have also been raised regarding the Prosecutor General's power to influence cases and essential immunity from criminal investigation of himself.

As a result, according to the above mentioned Eurobarometer survey on EU citizens' attitudes towards corruption, 80% of the Bulgarians interviewed considered corruption to be widespread in their country and 51% considered that corruption had increased in the previous three years. With respect to Bulgaria's confiscation of assets system, when compared with countries such as Croatia, Moldova and Romania, it has been assessed as less developed than those found in Croatia and Romania (OSCE, 2018).

Judicial reform has advanced but challenges remain

Judicial reform in Bulgaria has advanced. Through the CVM, Bulgaria has undertaken actions to tackle major issues such as concerns about the lack of professionalism and impartiality of the judiciary with the overall objective to enhance the objectivity and transparency of magistrates, including through the election of the new Supreme Judicial Council (SJC), the highest administrative authority in Bulgaria's judiciary (European Commission, 2017, 2018). For example, a reform adopted in 2015 led to a division of the SJC into two categories of professionals – the prosecutorial college (11 members) and the judicial college (14 members) – to prevent prosecutors and investigators from participating in individual decisions for judges.

Other reforms have aimed at strengthening the role of the anti-corruption agency and of specialised prosecutors as well as the Prosecutor General's accountability. In 2020, the Constitutional Court clarified that a Prosecutor General cannot exert his supervisory and methodological guidance role in cases against himself. In early 2021, following recommendations by the Venice Commission, a law on accountability of the Prosecutor General, establishing a special prosecutor to investigate crimes committed by the Prosecutor General or his deputy, was adopted.[7]

As a result of these reforms, the performance of the justice system has been seen as improving. According to the EU Justice Scoreboard for 2018 and 2019, Bulgaria performed rather well with respect to the time needed to resolve civil, commercial and administrative cases, on the number of pending cases, as well as the average length of judicial review cases against decisions of consumer protection. The 2019 EU Justice Scoreboard showed other positive developments such as the fact that Bulgaria had one of the highest numbers of judges per 100 000 inhabitants or that Bulgaria is one of the few EU countries that provide the public with comprehensive online information about the judicial system (European Commission 2019a).

Despite these encouraging policy developments, public perception of judicial independence has improved marginally. In 2018, only 30% of respondents from both public and businesses had a good opinion of the courts and judges in Bulgaria (compared to the EU averages of 56% and 48%, respectively). On the Global Competitiveness Report's scale, which ranges from one (bad) to seven (best), Bulgaria's judicial independence score for 2019 was 3.3. According to the 2019 EU Justice Scoreboard, perceptions among citizens and companies about the independence of the judiciary remained among the weakest in the EU, suggesting recurrent concerns about possible interference in the work of judges or pressure from economic and other interests. In 2021, according to 2021 EU Justice Scoreboard, the level of perceived judicial independence in Bulgaria remained low among the general public, having decreased slightly compared to 2020. Only 31% among the general public considered judicial independence to be 'fairly or very good'. The level of perceived independence among companies remained average, with 43% considering it to be 'fairly or very good' (European Commission, 2021). Investors have been reporting that Bulgaria's justice system not only does not support existing business operations, but also restricts existing opportunities for investment (World Bank, 2019).

Despite the progress made by Bulgaria with reforming the Prosecutor General, the combination of the Prosecutor General's powers and position has been perceived as exerting influence, as the Prosecutor General may annul or amend any decision taken by any prosecutor which has not been reviewed by a judge (European Commission, 2021). As it has been noted by the Venice Commission and the EC, while the establishment of a separate judicial chamber has reduced the influence of the Prosecutor General on the career and discipline of lower court judges, it has increased the General Prosecutor's influence on career and disciplinary questions concerning prosecutors and investigating judges and on the appointment or dismissal of heads of prosecutor's offices (European Commission, 2020b). Similarly, despite progress made with respect to the SJC, its composition and functioning has continued to be subject to concerns by international organisations such as the Council of Europe.[8] To safeguard judicial independence and the rule of law, Bulgaria should implement accountability mechanisms for the Prosecutor General and improve the governance of judges (OECD, 2021). In this respect, the absence of judicial review against a decision of a prosecutor not to open an investigation continued to raise concerns in 2021 (European Commission, 2021).

Another matter of concern has been the low confidence in the ability of the justice system to prosecute and implement convictions of those guilty of corruption: in 2017, only 24% of companies thought that corrupt people or businesses would be caught by prosecutors, much lower than the EU-28 average of 43% (European Commission, 2017). In an October 2019 report, the European Commission noted that more work to detect and convict those engaged in corruption was needed (European Commission, 2019b). Despite significant efforts undertaken by Bulgaria to accelerate courts processes and balance out the uneven workload of judges, notably by amending the civil procedure code to allow cases to be distributed to other courts regardless of jurisdictions, and through amendments to the criminal procedure code, the capacity of the judiciary to deal with corruption and other cases has been an area of concern. As noted earlier in this *Review*, despite legislative efforts, digitalisation of justice is also still lagging behind in practice.

In summary, Bulgaria still faces institutional deficiencies, especially as far as the independence of the judiciary is concerned. There is scope for further strengthening Bulgaria's judiciary to stimulate investor confidence and ultimately growth. This includes strengthening the independence of the prosecution system and more broadly the independence of the judiciary; increasing accountability of the justice system; ensuring more intensive training for judges; and further rebalancing the workload among courts. With respect to the latter, Bulgaria adopted in February 2021 a roadmap with an action plan to implement a new reorganisation of the court system (Box 7.2).

Box 7.2. Action plan for a new model of the judicial structures at district and appellate levels

With a decision of 2 February 2021, the Judges' College of the SJC adopted a Roadmap and an Action Plan for reorganisation of the judicial structures at district and appellate levels, including the opening of territorial divisions at the regional courts.

The new model foresees:

- To unite regional courts to reduce the number of cases to be heard in the regional courts.
- To divide the staff of the regional courts into permanent and non-permanent staff. The permanent staff of judges will work only in the regional court, and the non-permanent will be part of the staff of the higher district court.
- To increase significantly the number of judges in the district and appellate courts. The district courts will hear some of the cases currently triable by the regional courts, while the appellate courts will hear a large part of the appellate proceedings
- To introduce a workload rate for judges in regional, district, and appellate courts to better foresee the needs of judges per region.

Source: Bulgaria, Reform of the Judicial Map, 2021.

Preventing undue relations between business and politics

Fair political parties' funding is crucial not only for preventing the risk of corruption but also for protecting democracy. In 2019, Bulgaria's parliament removed all limits for individual and corporate donations for political parties,[9] a move that has been seen as potentially worsening corruption in Bulgaria. Analysts warned that unlimited donations from companies and private citizens could lead to an unhealthy merging of political and business interests.[10]

Bulgaria does not regulate lobbying activities either. There are no regulations establishing obligations for registration of lobbyists and no transparency standards and disclosure requirements are set in this field. The lack of specific legislation regulating lobbying in Bulgaria has been assessed as potentially increasing the risk of policy capture (European Commission 2020b). Notwithstanding establishing a solid regulation of lobbying is part of Bulgaria's national action plan in response to the EC 2020 Rule of Law Report,[11] concrete steps have not been taken yet (EC, 2021). In this regard, Bulgaria could make use of the *Principles for Transparency and Integrity in Lobbying* adopted by the OECD in 2010, which are international principles providing guidance on how to meet expectations of transparency in the public decision-making process.

Protecting sources of information

Reporting of wrongdoings can play a role in the detection of violations of anti-corruption legislation and public integrity standards (OECD, 2015). A solid legal whistle-blower protection can encourage citizens to disclose cases of corruption and illegal conduct. In Bulgaria, there is no generic, freestanding whistle-blower protection law.

Until now, Bulgaria has been relying on specific provisions built into a number of different statutes: its Administrative Procedure Code (APC), the Labour Law Code, the Law on Civil Servants and the Anti-Corruption and Forfeiture of Assets Act (AFAA). Bulgaria's legal framework for reporting corruption and protecting whistle-blowers remains fragmented and does not provides sufficient guarantees and measures to encourage submission of alerts. For example, the provisions of the APC are applicable to the public administration sector only. According to the AFAA, anyone who has information about corruption or conflict of interests may signal it to the anti-corruption commission and such reporting cannot be anonymous: whistle-blowers are required to disclose their names, address, telephone, fax and electronic address (Article 46 and Article 47, AFAA). Given that anonymous complaints are neither allowed nor protected, the Anti-Corruption Commission cannot thus use the information received from undisclosed sources (European Commission, 2021).

Fear of retaliation has been widely recognised as the main disincentive to report on other's misconduct. According to the 2019 EC *Special Eurobarometer,* 39% of Bulgaria's participants in the survey would not report a case of corruption because of fear of retaliation. Bulgaria's civil society organisations and the public in general have been particularly critical of the current legal framework, which has been seen as insufficient in providing whistle blowers protection (European Commission 2020b).

Continuing efforts to improve the protection regime for whistle-blowers will not only benefit Bulgaria's overall anti-corruption system but also increase pressure on companies to set-up internal compliance programmes, as discussed in Chapter 8. In this respect, it should be noted that, as a result of the 2019 EU Whistleblowing Directive, which entered into force on 16 December 2019, Bulgaria was required to adopt a national whistleblowing legislation no later than December 2021. A Whistleblower Protection draft Act aiming to transpose the European Whistleblower Protection Directive was published on the Council of Ministers' portal for public consultations in April 2022.

Challenges also persist in the area of public procurement

Unfair or opaque procurement processes may send negative signals to businesses and mislead them into considering that corruption is part of the normal course of doing business in a country. In Bulgaria, general government public procurement accounts for approximately 12% of GDP, the same as the OECD average and below the 18-20% average in the European Union percentage (OECD, 2016). Public procurement has been particularly important for the construction sector in the country, with approximately a third of total sector turnover deriving from public procurement in 2013.[12] Given the important share of public procurement in the Bulgarian economy, consolidating the procurement system is important for attracting FDI (OECD, 2017).

Commendable progress has been made in modernizing public procurement in Bulgaria since the launch in 2014 of the National Strategy for the Development of the Public Procurement Sector (2014-20), which aimed at enhancing the efficiency and lawfulness in the public procurement awards, and the adoption, in 2016, of the Public Procurement Act (PPA). The law transposes the EU directives on public procurement into the Bulgarian legislation and is therefore aligned with EU rules in particular with respect to the principles of equal treatment and non-discrimination; free competition; proportionality; and publicity and transparency (PPA, Article 2).

Since 2016, the Public Procurement Agency, which is an independent body established under the Ministry of Finance, has established itself as the leader regarding the implementation of Bulgaria's PPA by ensuring a close inter-agency co-operation for the implementation of common policy in the field of public procurement. In particular, the Agency is responsible for undertaking the following types of external control related to public procurement: control through random selection of public procurement procedures; control on certain negotiated procedures; control on specific modifications to public procurement contracts. Both the National Audit Office in Bulgaria and the Public Internal Financial Control Agency are in charge of the *ex-post* control by ensuring that procurement procedures comply with the provisions of the PPA. According to the PPA, the Commission on Protection of Competition (CPC) is charged with the public procurement appeal procedure while Supreme Administrative Court acts as a second-instance body.

Notwithstanding this new environment, the proportion of businesses that regard corruption in public procurement as very or fairly widespread in Bulgaria's public opinion remains high. According to the 2019 *Business Eurobarometer* survey, 74% of businesses felt that corruption was very common in public procurement. According to another survey, conducted by the German-Bulgarian Industrial-Commercial Chamber in 2019, one of the main challenges for Bulgaria's economy and business environment was the non-transparency of Bulgaria's public procurement.[13] Anecdotal evidence abounds that powerful private operators would exert pressure on the public administration to channel public procurement to major companies linked through circles of influence to them.

Echoing these concerns, the legislation governing public procurement has been amended on several occasions, with each amendments enhancing transparency and control. Reforms initiated to address irregularities and corruption-related issues have nevertheless been perceived by business as jeopardising legal certainty (European Commission, 2020). For example, the PPA was amended 11 times in 2018.[14]

Administrative capacity has been another challenge for the procurement system, causing delays (World Bank 2019), despite support provided by the OECD. For example, the OECD, in 2016, provided Bulgaria with technical assistance on setting training priorities and developing training materials for capacity building programmes in the public procurement sector.[15] Yet, despite continuous training efforts, the professionalization of public purchasers, particularly at the municipal level, has remained challenging (European Commission, 2019b). E-government reforms have reportedly progressed slowly and have not led to a significant improvement in the business environment (European Commission, 2020a), despite actions taken by Bulgaria in this regard. In 2020 mandatory use of the centralised e-Procurement platform (CAIS EPP) was introduced at two stages: as of 1 January 2020 – for central administrative bodies and their territorial structures, the CPB for the needs of central administration, other public bodies established by a law, as well as big municipalities and contracting entities; as of 14 June 2020 – for all other contracting authorities and contracting entities.

There is room for developing expertise of public procurement specialists. The development of a skilled workforce in public procurement meeting high professional standards for integrity and knowledge would improve the public procurement system. Bulgaria should make additional efforts on further enhancing the operational capacity of PPA and countering corruption in public procurement, which could include greater use of e-procurement tools.

Improving the quality of regulations

As noted in the introduction to this chapter, the quality of public regulation is another important component of a sound investment climate. According to the *OECD Policy Framework for Investment*, poorly designed or weakly applied regulations can slow business responsiveness, divert resources away from productive investments, hamper entry into markets, reduce job creation and generally discourage entrepreneurship. To reduce the stock of overtly burdensome, conflicting or poor-quality regulations and to address national and global challenges pertaining to systemic risks (e.g. protection of human health, safety or environment), governments need to articulate better regulations and make continuous progress in regulatory reforms. There are a number of tools at policy makers' disposal to achieve these objectives, including better stakeholder engagement, the use of regulatory impact assessment (RIA) and *ex post* evaluation of regulations, as captured in the *Recommendation of the Council on Regulatory Policy and Governance* (Box 7.3).

Box 7.3. Recommendation of the Council on Regulatory Policy and Governance

The OECD Council adopted the Recommendation of the Council on Regulatory Policy and Governance in 2012. The Recommendation was the first international instrument to address regulatory policy, management and governance as a whole-of-government activity that can and should be addressed by sectoral ministries, regulatory and competition agencies.

The Recommendation sets out the measures that Governments can and should take to support the implementation and advancement of systemic regulatory reform to deliver regulations that meet public policy objectives and will have a positive impact on the economy and society. These measures are integrated in a comprehensive policy cycle in which regulations are designed, assessed and evaluated ex ante and ex post, revised and enforced at all levels of government, supported by appropriate institutions. Many topics such as consultation and citizen engagement, regulatory impact assessment, multi-level coherence, risk and regulation, institutional responsibility for policy coherence and oversight, and the role of regulatory agencies are more developed that in earlier principles.

Together the Recommendation's principles provide countries with the basis for a comprehensive assessment of the performance of policies, tools and institutions that underpin the use of efficient and effective regulation to achieve social, environmental and economic goals. Through its work programme, the Regulatory Policy Committee supports countries in their implementation. In particular, the OECD Regulatory Policy Reviews assess regulatory management capacities in different countries, including policies, tools and institutions for ensuring regulatory quality, using the Recommendation as an assessment framework.

Source: Source: OECD (2012)

Overall, Bulgaria has made strides in improving the quality of its regulations, including as part of the process of adopting the EU *acquis*. As such, it scored best on regulatory quality across the different aspects measured by the World Bank's *World Governance Indicators* in 2018, available for 155 economies globally (Figure 7.1).[16] In addition, it is one of the countries that improved most its capacity in this area between 2000 and 2018, scoring much above the OECD average in this regard (Figure 7.2). While to some extent this captures the low starting point in Bulgaria, it is also indicative of an impressive catching up process, accomplished over the years.

Figure 7.1. Bulgaria's rank on World Governance Indicators, 2018

Note: The percentile rank is calculated based on a given country's score and that of 154 other ranked countries.
Source: World Bank's World Governance Indicators (2018).

Figure 7.2. Change in the quality of regulations in Bulgaria, 2000-18

In percentage

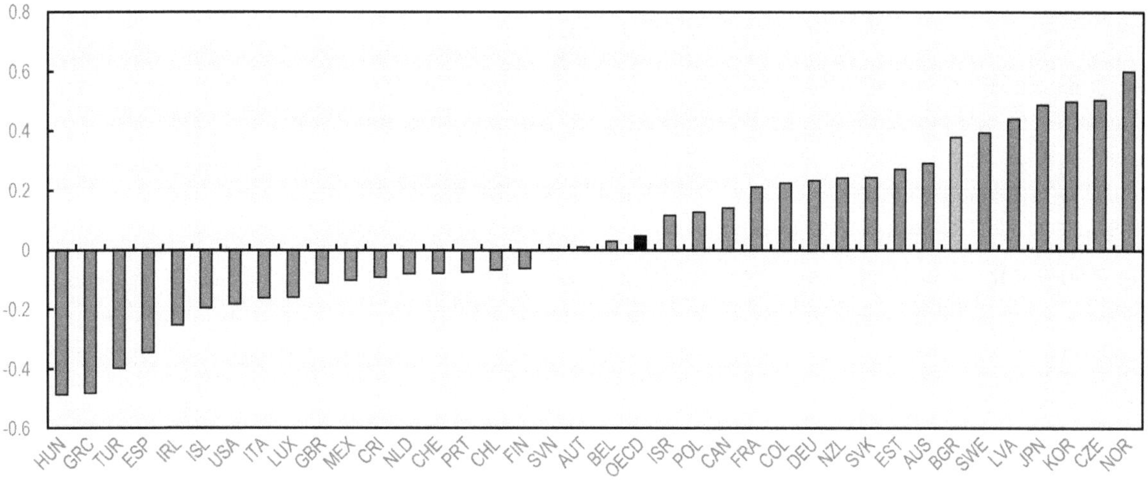

Note: The graph shows a change in the country's score on regulatory quality between 2000 and 2018.
Source: World Bank's World Governance Indicators (2018).

Most recently, Bulgaria has also made legislative changes aiming at improving specific aspects of regulatory quality, as highlighted in the OECD report on quality of regulatory practices across the EU Member States (OECD, 2019) and in the OECD *Regulatory Policy Scan of Bulgaria* (OECD, 2022). In particular, Bulgaria has significantly reformed its regulatory management system as a result of the entry into force of the Law on Normative Acts in 2016. The law extended minimum consultation periods with stakeholders to 30 calendar days,[17] and resulted in the establishment of a central consultation portal, which is now better integrated with Bulgarian impact assessments for regulatory proposals (OECD, 2019). Before being adopted, a draft regulation needs to be made available both at the main internet page of the initiating institution and via the central consultation portal (www.strategy.bg) where stakeholders can also provide their comments.[18] The portal also provides direct feedback to participants that explains how their submission has helped shape final regulatory proposals. As a result of these changes, in 2018, Bulgaria scored above average on stakeholder engagement in developing regulations on OECD Indicators of Regulatory Policy and Governance (iREG) (Figure 7.3). Still, relative to the EU average, it needs to strengthen the oversight function and transparency of the stakeholder engagement process. To this end, "Standards for Holding Public Consultations" were adopted by the Council for Administrative Reform in 2019.

The law also introduced a new RIA system, whereby regulatory proposals are now subject to either a partial or full assessment requirement. Bulgaria established an oversight body for RIA quality control at the end of 2016 (see Box 7.3 for an overview of the institutional set-up for regulatory oversight in Bulgaria). The methodological framework applicable to the executive branch was developed: a Guidance for *Ex Ante* Impact Assessment and a Guidance for *Ex Post* Impact Assessment were adopted by the Council of Ministers in 2019 and 2020, respectively. Annual Reports on the RIA are adopted by the Council for Administrative Reform, identifying the progress, but also the weaknesses and challenges. Still, mainly due to the need to further systematise the use of RIA at parliamentary level as well as increase its transparency, Bulgaria is scoring slightly below the OECD average in this area.[19] As part of its RIA, Bulgaria has also started introducing an SME Test to assess the effects of proposed regulations on SMEs, and developed a business guide for SMEs (see Chapter 6). In addition, it is worth noting that the same RIA and consultation requirements apply to the transposition of EU regulations in Bulgaria as domestic regulations although

Bulgaria does not routinely undertake consultations or impact assessment at the development or negotiation stage but only once the regulations is being transposed into domestic law (Table 7.1).

Box 7.4. Institutional setup for regulatory oversight

The Council of Ministers is responsible for promoting overall regulatory policy in Bulgaria, including in relation to stakeholder engagement, RIA, and ex post evaluation. An oversight body in the Administrative Modernisation Directorate of the Council of Ministers in Bulgaria is responsible for quality control of regulatory management tools. No evaluations have yet been conducted in Bulgaria to assess the efficiency and effectiveness of any of its regulatory management tools.

The Council for Administrative Reform, established under Decree 192 of 5 August 2009, acts as an advisory body to the Council of Ministers for the co-ordination of regulatory burden reduction on both business and citizens.

Source: OECD (2019).

Figure 7.3. Indicators of Regulatory Policy and Governance (iREG): Bulgaria, 2018

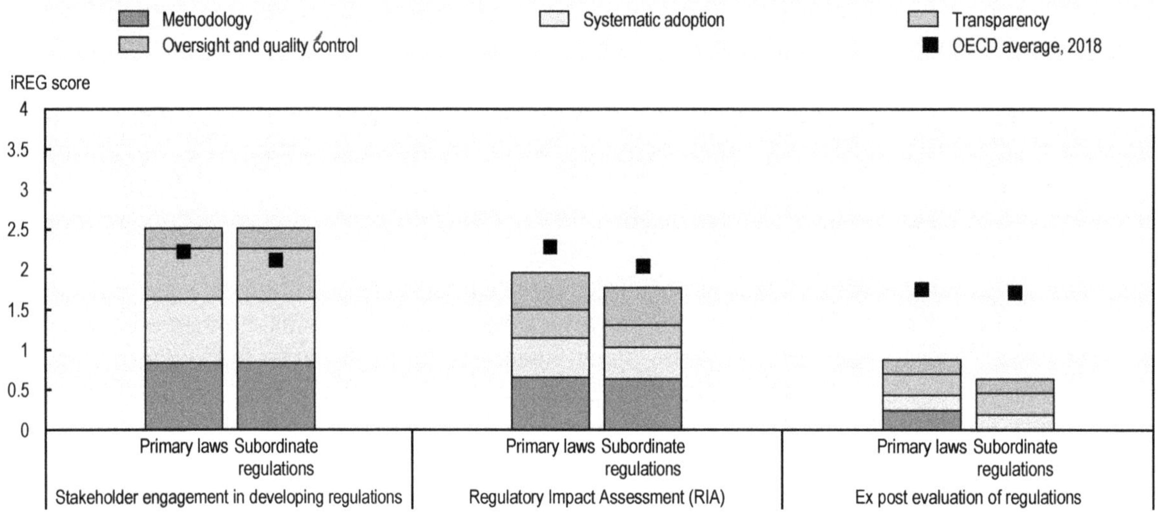

Note: The more regulatory practices as advocated in the OECD Recommendation on Regulatory Policy and Governance a country has implemented, the higher its iREG score. The indicators on stakeholder engagement and RIA for primary laws only cover those initiated by the executive (42% of all primary laws in Bulgaria).
Source: Indicators of Regulatory Policy and Governance Survey and its extension to all EU Member states; see OECD (2019).

Finally, yet importantly, since the entry into force of the law, all new laws, codes and sub-statutory acts of the Council of Ministers are subject to *ex post* evaluation within five years of their entry into force. Still, even though *ex post* evaluations are conducted in Bulgaria, they are limited in number and in scope, primarily focusing on administrative burdens for business. Assessing a wider range of impacts would help to ensure that regulations remain appropriate over time. This is an area where Bulgaria lags most behind both the EU and OECD averages according to iREG indicators and could make further progress. The expiry in 2021 of the five-year period for holding *ex post* evaluations and the adoption of a comprehensive methodological document (Guidance for Ex Post Impact Assessment) is expected to provide a favourable base for improvement. As discussed in Chapter 6, advances in reviewing, streamlining and improving the stock of existing regulations can help reduce administrative burdens with positive effects on business climate. Yet, the experience thus far has been mixed, including in regards to meeting specific quantitative reduction target, and remains an ongoing challenge.

Table 7.1. Requirements to use regulatory management tools for EU-made laws: Bulgaria

Stakeholder engagement		Regulatory impact assessment	
Development stage			
The government facilitates the engagement of domestic stakeholders in the European Commission's consultation process	No		
Negotiation stage			
Stakeholder engagement is required to define the negotiating position for EU directives/regulations	No	RIA is required to define the negotiating position for EU directives/regulations	Yes
Consultation is required to be open to the general public	NA		
Transposition stage			
Stakeholder engagement is required when transposing EU directives	Yes	RIA is required when transposing EU directives	Yes
The same requirements and processes apply as for domestically made laws	Yes	The same requirements and processes for RIA apply as for domestically made laws	Yes
Consultation is required to be open to the general public	Yes	RIA includes a specific assessment of provisions added at the national level beyond those in the EU directives	No
		RIA distinguishes between impacts stemming from EU requirements and additional national implementation measures	NA

Source: Indicators of Regulatory Policy and Governance Survey and its extension to all EU Member states, http://oe.cd/ireg, see OECD (2019).

Despite these improvements, at times significant changes to applicable rules and regulations may nevertheless take place in the parliament without an obligation of prior consultation or impact assessment. For example, the National Centre for Parliamentary Research (NAPR) has shown in a recent analysis, covering the period April 2017-December 2019, that 37% of the adopted normative acts amend other legal acts (NAPR, 2019). Such amendments are currently not subject to the requirement of conducting public consultation nor a RIA. In addition, public consultation and RIA are required only for the first reading of the proposed regulation in the National Assembly. Changes can potentially be introduced by legislators and voted on without the necessity to consult stakeholders (although amendments that contradict the principles or the scope of the proposed regulation should *a priori* not be discussed).[20]

As signalled in recent reports of the European Commission, Bulgaria continues introducing legislative amendments through amendments to other acts via transitional provisions and adopting important amendments between the first and second reading in the National Assembly without public consultation which affects not only the quality of regulation but also the rule of law (EC 2020 and 2021 Rule of Law report). To help ensure alignment with the available international best practices and further improve the quality of its regulations, Bulgaria should also implement any recommendations identified as part of the OECD *Regulatory Policy Scan of Bulgaria* (OECD, 2022).

Outlook and policy recommendations

An assessment of Bulgaria's public governance leads to a number of general conclusions. Bulgaria has made perceptible progress by strengthening its anti-corruption institutional framework: over the past decade, Bulgaria has consolidated its legal and institutional framework concerning judicial reform and the fight against corruption. In spite of these reforms, businesses' trust in the government's ability to combat against corruption remains low. Bulgaria continues to face challenges, for example with respect to the independence of the judiciary and the lack of results in the fight against corruption – which led to protests in 2020 and a surge of votes for anti-corruption parties at the time of the parliamentary elections in 2021. A solid record of accomplishment of final convictions in high-level corruption cases remains to be established.

In addition, although Bulgaria has taken steps to improve its legal framework with respect to conflict of interest (a verification system for asset declaration and conflict of interest is in place), there is limited evidence as to the effectiveness of these measures as highlighted in the July 2021 European Commission Rule of Law Report (European Commission 2021). Concerns also exist as regards lobbying. Bulgaria should make concrete efforts to improve the political funding system, notably by imposing limitations on donations and subjecting political parties to the disclosure of financial resources and auditing.

Public procurement in the country has been modernised with the gradual introduction of the eProcurement platform and regular amendments to the legislation governing public procurement, with each version enhancing transparency and control but this has also affected legal certainty, an issue that the country should address. Given that the public procurement system in Bulgaria suffers from low trust by businesses and citizens alike, the country could make use of the OECD *Principles for Integrity in Public Procurement* while undertaking additional reforms.

Bulgaria has also made strides in improving the overall quality of its regulatory system. For example, recent legislative changes improved the legal framework for publishing draft laws, conducting public consultations, and preparing regulatory impact evaluations and improved the regulatory oversight. Still, in the area of conducting *ex post* evaluations of regulations, Bulgaria can achieve further progress to reach the levels found in other OECD countries. In particular, reducing administrative burdens and mixed feedback in reaching quantitative reduction targets point that this area is an ongoing challenge and will require further effort to review and, wherever possible, streamline most burdensome regulations.

Policy recommendations

- *Build on the progress made in improving the overall quality of regulations* by systematising and improving the oversight and transparency of regulatory processes. In particular, ensure that the requirements of prior publication, public consultations and ex ante regulatory impact assessment of draft regulations are respected in practice at the parliamentary level. Also, *advance on conducting* ex post evaluations to reduce administrative burdens and implement any specific recommendations identified as part of the 2022 OECD Regulatory Policy Scan of Bulgaria.
- *Continue ongoing reforms to combat corruption*, notably by perfecting Bulgaria's public integrity framework. Significant challenges remain concerning the effectiveness of measures related to the integrity of public administration, lobbying and whistleblowing protection. With respect to the latter, *develop an adequate framework for the protection of whistle-blowers* in compliance with the 2019 EU Whistleblowing Directive, which requires EU Member States to adopt a national whistleblowing legislation no later than December 2021 and launch a campaign to enhance officials and the public's acceptance of whistleblowing.
- *Continue judicial reforms* to strengthen judicial independence and increase public confidence; implement an effective and transparency accountability mechanism for the Prosecutor General in line with international standards.

References

Centre for study of democracy (2016), *Управление на обществените общества България:*

корупционни рискои и криминална прокуратура [Public procurement governance in Bulgaria-corruption risk and criminal prosecution], Sofia, https://csd.bg/bg/publications/publication/governance-of-the-bulgarian-public-procurement-sector-corruption-risks-and-criminal-prosecution/

European Commission (2021), 2021 *Rule of Law Report: Country chapter on the rule of law situation in Bulgaria*, SWD (2021) 703 final, Brussels 20 July 2021, https://ec.europa.eu/info/sites/default/files/2021_rolr_country_chapter_bulgaria_en.pdf

European Commission (2020a), *Country report Bulgaria 2020*,

https://eur-lex.europa.eu/legal-content/EN/TXT/?qid=1584543810241&uri=CELEX%3A52020SC0501

European Commission (2020b), 2020 *Rule of Law Report Country chapter on the rule of law situation in Bulgaria*, https://ec.europa.eu/info/sites/info/files/bg_rol_country_chapter.pdf.

European Commission (2019a), *The 2019 Justice Scoreboard,* https://ec.europa.eu/info/sites/info/files/justice_scoreboard_2 019_en.pdf

European Commission (2019b), *Report from the European Commission to the European Parliament and the Council: On Progress in Bulgaria under the Co-operation and Verification Mechanism*, https://ec.europa.eu/info/sites/info/files/progress-report-bulgaria-2019-com-2019-498_en.pdf.

European Commission (2018a), *Report from the European Commission to the European Parliament and the Council: On Progress in Bulgaria under the Co-operation and Verification Mechanism*,

https://ec.europa.eu/info/sites/info/files/progress-report-bulgaria-com-2018-850_en.pdf.

European Commission (2018b), *Public administration characteristics and performance in EU28: Bulgaria*, http://ec.europa.eu/social/BlobServlet?docId=19942&langId=en.

European Commission (2017a), Report from the European Commission to the European Parliament and the Council: On Progress in Bulgaria under the Co-operation and Verification Mechanism, https://ec.europa.eu/info/sites/info/files/comm-2017-750_en_0.pdf.

European Commission (2017b), *Businesses' attitudes towards corruption in the EU*, Flash Eurobarometer 457, December 2017

NAPR (2019), Study of the legislative activity of the 44 National Assembly, www.strategy.bg/Publications/View.aspx?lang=bg-BG&categoryId=&Id=301&y=&m=&d=&fbclid=IwAR1P1CLY2H02ODkYQBM23622hA9qkXmSCDXDkEvLaiHqLLcVQgv3h233CIQ

OECD (2022), *Regulatory Policy Scan of Bulgaria*, OECD Publishing, Paris, www.bia-bg.com/uploads/files/analysis/OECD-Regulatory-Scan-of-Bulgaria.pdf

OECD (2021), *OECD Economic Surveys: Bulgaria*, OECD Publishing, Paris, https://doi.org/10.1787/19990626

OECD (2020) *OECD Indicators of Regulatory Policy and Governance* (iREG), www.oecd.org/gov/regulatory-policy/indicators-regulatory-policy-and-governance.htm.

OECD (2019), *Better Regulation Practices across the European Union*, OECD Publishing, Paris, www.doi.org/10.1787/9789264311732-en.

OECD (2018), *Anti-Corruption and Integrity Guidelines for State-Owned Enterprises*, OECD Publishing, www.oecd.org/fr/gouvernementdentreprise/anti-corruption-integrity-guidelines-for-soes.htm

OECD (2017), *General guide on the public procurement legislative environment in Bulgaria*,

OECD Publishing, www.oecd.org/governance/procurement/toolbox/search/guide-public-procurement-legislation-bulgaria.pdf.

OECD (2016), *Public Procurement Training for Bulgaria: Needs and Priorities*, OECD Publishing, www.oecd.org/governance/procurement/toolbox/search/public-procurement-training-bulgaria_EN.pdf.

OECD (2015), *Policy Framework for Investment- 2015 Edition*, OECD Publishing, Paris, https://doi.org/10.1787/9789264208667-en.

OECD (2013), *Transparency and Integrity in Lobbying: 10 Principles for Transparency and Integrity in Lobbying*, www.oecd.org/corruption/ethics/Lobbying-Brochure.pdf.

OECD (2012), *Recommendation of the Council on Regulatory Policy and Governance,* OECD Publishing, Paris, https://oe.cd/374.

OSCE (2019), *Opinion on the Act on Amendment of the Act on the 2019 State Budget of the Republic of Bulgaria,* 3 December 2019, www.osce.org/odihr/441685

OSCE (2018), *Asset Recovery: A Comparative Analysis of Legislation and Practice – Bulgaria, Croatia, Moldova and Romania*, www.rai-see.org//wp-content/uploads/2018June 20180611-AssetRecovery_OSCE_final.pdf

State Agency for National Security (2020), National Risk Assessment of Money Laundering and Terrorist Financing, published on 9 January 2020, www.dans.bg/en/msip-091209-menu-en/results-from-national-risk-assessment.

Transparency International (2004), Tools to Support Transparency in Local Governance, https://images.transparencycdn.org/images/2004_TI_UNHabitat_LocalGovernanceToolkit_EN.pdf.

World Bank (2019a), *Understanding Barriers to doing Business – Survey Results of how Justice System impacts the Business Climate in SEE*,
http://documents.worldbank.org/curated/en/168701564080491520/Understanding-Barriers-to-Doing-Business-Survey-Results-of-How-the-Justice-System-Impacts-the-Business-Climate-in-South-East-Europe.

World Bank (2019b), Оценка на системата за обществени поръчки в Република България [Evaluation of the public procurement system in the Republic of Bulgaria], www2.aop.bg/wp-content/uploads/2019/05/Bulgaria-RAS-Procurement-Report-Component-3-BG.pdf.

Notes

[1] See "Foreign Investment has collapsed say Bulgarian industrialists", *BalkanInsight*, 28 August 2018.

[2] See Special Eurobarometer 502, *Corruption*, December 2019, https://ec.europa.eu/commfrontoffice/publicopinion/index.cfm/Survey/getSurveyDetail/instruments/SPECIAL/yearFrom/1974/yearTo/2020/surveyKy/2247.

[3] In the framework of this new stratwegy, new priorities have been established as regards high-risk sectors, including strengthening capacity to combat corruption; increasing accountability of local authorities; and strengthening the ability of insitutions to provide timely responses to alledged cases of corruption.

[4] European Parliament resolution on the rule of law and fundamental rights in Bulgaria, 2 October 2020, https://www.europarl.europa.eu/doceo/document/B-9-2020-0309_EN.html.

[5] www.oecd.org/daf/anti-bribery/bulgaria-oecdanti-briberyconvention.htm

[6] See https://euobserver.com/opinion/149503.

[7] See Law supplementing the Code of Criminal Procedure, https://parliament.bg/bg/laws/ID/163448.

[8] GRECO Fourth evaluation round – Second compliance report, recommendation V, paras. 13-15; CCJE Bureau, 2019 edition of the Report on judicial independence and impartiality in the Council of Europe member States.

[9] See https://www.lex.bg/laws/ldoc/2135501352.

[10] See "Bulgaria slashes state subsidy, allows unlimited donations for political parties", *Euractiv*, 5 September 2019, www.euractiv.com/section/elections/news/bulgaria-slashes-state-subsidy-allows-unlimited-donations-for-political-parties/

[11] In November 2020, Bulgaria adopted a "Plan for the implementation of measures in response to the recommendations and the identified challenges in the European Commission's Rule of Law Report" (Action Plan), covering issues related justice system, anti-corruption framework, media pluralism, and media freedom, other institutional issues related to checks and balances.

[12] Based on data in the Public Procurement Register, the total value of awarded public procurement contracts for works as a result of public procurement procedure is, as follows:

2017 – 2, 591, 723 563 BGN (VAT excluded).

2018 – 2, 937, 885 708 BGN (VAT excluded).

2019 – 8, 831, 743 878 BGN (VAT excluded).

2020 – 2, 650, 237 291 BGN (VAT excluded)

[13] See https://bulgarien.ahk.de/bg/infothek/umfragen.

[14] Council of Ministers Administration (2019), Impact Assessment Annual Report 2018.

[15] Under the project "Support for the Design and Implementation of the Bulgarian Public Procurement Training and Development Programme in the Frame of ESIF Ex-ante Conditionality Action Plan".

[16] See Kaufmann, Kraay and Mastruzzi (2010) for the methodology.

[17] In exceptional cases, the project developer may set another time limit, but not less than 14 days.

[18] There are no restrictions for participating in the public consultation (a registration in the portal is required).

[19] It is worth noting that the OECD indicators on stakeholder engagement and RIA for primary laws cover processes carried out by the executive, which initiates approximately 42% of primary laws in Bulgaria. While there are requirements to conduct RIA to inform the development of primary laws initiated by parliament, they are relatively less stringent than those for laws made by the executive.

[20] According to Art 43(3) of the Rules of Procedure for the Organisation and Activity of the National Assembly "On the proposals submitted by Members of Parliament for a second vote, the chairman of the leading commission may request an opinion from non-governmental organizations." According to Art 84(2) of the Rules of Procedure for the Organisation and Activity of the National Assembly: "During the second voting shall be discussed only proposals of Members of Parliament, received by the order of art. 83, as well as proposals of the committee responsible, included in its report. Editorial corrections are also allowed. Proposals that contradict the principles and scope of the bill passed at the first vote are not discussed and voted on".

8 Promoting and enabling responsible business conduct

Responsible Business Conduct (RBC) is an important part of the investment climate and is increasingly integrated within policies aimed at integrating quality investment and enhancing sustainable investment. This chapter provides an overview of the RBC landscape in Bulgaria and Bulgaria's plans for its National Contact Point for the OECD *Guidelines for Multinational Enterprises*.

Introduction

Governments that adhere to the OECD *Declaration on International Investment* aim to encourage the positive contributions that businesses can make on economic and social progress. They commit to promote Responsible Business Conduct (RBC) principles and standards, as set out by the OECD *Guidelines for Multinational Enterprises* (the *Guidelines*). The *Guidelines* are the most comprehensive set of government-backed recommendations on RBC currently in existence (See Box 8.1). Observance of the *Guidelines* is supported by their unique implementation mechanism – the National Contact Points (NCPs).

RBC is a key element of a healthy business environment – one that attracts quality investment, minimises risks for businesses, ensures stakeholder rights are respected and ultimately leads to broader value creation. RBC principles and standards set out an expectation that businesses should avoid and address adverse impacts of business activities, while contributing to sustainable development in countries where they operate. RBC emphasises the integration and consideration of environmental and social issues into core business operations. A key element of RBC is risk-based due diligence – a process through which businesses identify, prevent and mitigate actual and potential adverse impacts, and account for how these impacts are addressed. RBC expectations extend to business activities throughout the entire supply chain and linked to business operations, products or services by a business relationship.

Many businesses, governments and stakeholders are familiar with the term corporate social responsibility (CSR), which has historically been used to describe business interactions with society. Over the last years, CSR has increasingly been used alongside RBC and Business and Human Rights (BHR), with some using the terms interchangeably (e.g. the European Union). All these concepts reflect the expectation that businesses should consider the impact of their operations and supply chains on people, the planet and society as part of their core business operations and not as an add-on. A key characteristic of CSR, RBC and BHR is that they refer to corporate conduct beyond simply complying with domestic law and call on business to contribute positively to sustainable development while managing risks and any harm that may result from their activities and from that of suppliers and partners. These concepts are not and should not be understood to be equivalent to philanthropy.

While it is the role of businesses to behave responsibly, governments have a primary duty to protect the public interest and an important role in promoting and enabling RBC. The RBC chapter in the OECD *Policy Framework for Investment* is a useful reference for designing and implementing a strong RBC policy framework. This entails establishing and enforcing an adequate legal framework that protects the public interest and underpins RBC, while monitoring business performance and compliance with the law. Setting and communicating clear expectations on RBC and providing guidance on what those expectations mean is important, while encouraging and engaging industry and stakeholders in collective initiatives and providing recognition and incentives to businesses that exemplify good practice is encouraged. It also entails ensuring that RBC principles and standards are observed in the context of the government's role as an economic actor.

Bulgaria adhered to the *Declaration on International Investment and Multinational Enterprises* in June 2022. This chapter examines Bulgaria's convergence with OECD standards on RBC as enshrined in the Declaration and other instruments which form part of adherence, as well as Bulgaria's steps to establish a fully functioning NCP.

Box 8.1. Understanding the OECD Guidelines for Multinational Enterprises

Addressed by Adherents to the OECD *Declaration on International Investment and Multinational Enterprises* to businesses operating in or from their jurisdictions, the *Guidelines* set out principles and standards in all major areas related to RBC, including information disclosure, human rights, employment and industrial relations, environment, bribery and corruption, consumer interests, science and technology, competition, and taxation.

Their purpose is to ensure that business operations are in harmony with government policies, to strengthen the basis of mutual confidence between businesses and the societies in which they operate, to improve foreign investment climate, and to enhance the contribution of the private sector to sustainable development. The *Guidelines*, together with the UN Guiding Principles and the fundamental ILO Conventions, are one of the major international instruments on RBC.

The *Guidelines* do not aim to introduce differences of treatment between multinational and domestic enterprises – they reflect good practice for all. Adherents wish to encourage the widest possible observance of the *Guidelines* to the fullest extent possible, including among small- and medium-sized enterprises even while acknowledging that these businesses may not have the same capacities as larger enterprises.

The *Guidelines* are supported by a unique implementation mechanism of National Contact Points (NCPs), agencies established by adhering government to promote and implement the Guidelines. The NCPs assist enterprises and their stakeholders to take appropriate measures to further the implementation of the *Guidelines*. They also provide a mediation and conciliation platform for resolving practical issues that may arise.

To support implementation of the *Guidelines*, the OECD has developed due diligence guidance, which provide practical recommendations to businesses on how to identify and respond to risks of adverse impacts associated with particular products, regions, sectors or industries. OECD RBC Due Diligence instruments are: the *Due Diligence Guidance for Responsible Supply Chains of Minerals from Conflict-Affected and High-Risk Areas*, the *OECD-FAO Guidance on Responsible Agricultural Supply Chains*, the *Due Diligence Guidance for Meaningful Stakeholder Engagement in the Extractive Sector*, the OECD *Due Diligence Guidance for Responsible Supply Chains in the Garment and Footwear Sector* and the OECD *Due Diligence Guidance for Responsible Business Conduct*. For more information, see https://mneguidelines.oecd.org/duediligence/

Pursuing efforts to align with international standards and expectations on RBC can advance Bulgaria's national development objectives

The notion that businesses should contribute to society is not new in Bulgaria. Early forms of economic entities with a defined social mission date back from the second half of the 19th century (European Commission, 2019). RBC in its modern sense was introduced along with Bulgaria's transition to an open, market-based economy in the 1990s. International actors including international organisations, international financial institutions, business associations and multinational companies have played an important role in raising awareness of the concept, and disseminating standards, tools and business practice. Large multinational companies have also contributed to the dissemination of knowledge and practices through links with suppliers and investees (Stefanova, 2015).

Bulgaria's transition to an open economy was concomitant with global trends placing increased emphasis on RBC, reflected by a proliferation of high-level statements, policies and regulations (See Box 8.4). The

EU, for example, has over the years asserted its commitment to promote and enable RBC, and translated this commitment in a mix of voluntary and mandatory measures (European Commission, 2021). In the years 2000, Bulgaria's EU accession process created an impetus to promote RBC and align with EU standards and priorities on the matter (Stefanova, 2015; Lyubenova, 2014). Pursuing efforts to align with international expectations and standards on RBC remains highly relevant to achieve Bulgaria's national development objectives, and increasingly necessary for any country willing to attract investment and participate in global value chains.

Box 8.2. Rising international demands on RBC

The 2030 Agenda for Sustainable Development and the 17 Sustainable Development Goals (SDGs) adopted in 2015 call for robust involvement of the private sector in global development efforts. UN member states have also committed to foster a well-functioning business sector and protect labour rights and environmental and health standards in accordance with relevant international standard. Several high-level commitments to promote RBC in line with internationally recognised standards at G20 and G7 forums have also made it clear that RBC issues were a priority in the international agenda.

RBC expectations are also reflected in domestic legislations. Several countries have passed legislations aimed at strengthening due diligence requirements to address supply chain and sustainability risks. Importantly, in April 2020 the European Commission announced its commitment to introducing rules for mandatory corporate environmental and human rights due diligence, which will ultimately be applicable to all EU member states. The UK Modern Slavery Act, adopted in 2016, requires that commercial organisations prepare an annual statement and report on their due diligence processes to manage the risks of slavery and human trafficking within their operations and supply chains. Australia passed a similar act on 29 November 2018, which includes expectations for the government itself to report on its own activities. In France, since 2017, the French Due Diligence law requires certain companies to develop and implement due diligence plans to identify and address risks related to human rights, fundamental freedoms, health and safety, and the environment. In the United States, the US Trade Facilitation and Trade Enforcement Act of 2015 repealed the exceptions to the prohibition on imports of goods mined, produced or manufactured in any foreign country by forced or indentured child labour, including child labour.

RBC is also increasingly referenced in various economic instruments, such as trade or co-operation agreements. For example, the EU commonly includes RBC in its Trade and Sustainable Development chapters. The OECD Recommendation of the Council on Common Approaches for Officially Supported Export Credits and Environmental and Social Due Diligence encourages members, via their Export Credit Agencies (ECAs), to promote the *Guidelines*, consider the outcomes of NCP cases when undertaking project reviews, as well as to give consideration to policy coherence with the *Guidelines*.

Promoting RBC aligns with Bulgaria's national priorities

In the last two decades, the government has made important commitments toward RBC. As discussed earlier in the context of this *Review*, Bulgaria adopted in 2020 the National Development Programme BULGARIA 2030, which lays out Bulgaria's vision and general goals for the country's development policies and achievement of the global Sustainable Development Goals (SDGs). The plan gives a strong role to the private sector across its goals and priorities, and includes specific objectives to encourage companies to develop and implement CSR programmes, as a way to promote the inclusion of vulnerable groups (Government of Bulgaria, 2020a). RBC is also as a cross-cutting topic relevant to various national priorities laid out in Bulgaria 2030, including for example the transition to a circular and low-carbon economy, clean air and biodiversity, sustainable agriculture, or education and skills (See Box 8.3).

The role of the private sector to achieve sustainable development is also reflected in Bulgaria's Voluntary National Review (VNR) of the implementation of the SDGs completed in 2020. The VNR recognises that the private sector has the resources to make many of the SDGs come true, and argues that private sector's commitment to the SDGs is mainly related to the adoption of the concept of corporate social responsibility (CSR) (Government of Bulgaria, 2020c).

Box 8.3. Observing the Science and Technology recommendations of the Guidelines to boost innovation and skills

Chapter 3 of this review already noted that boosting innovative capacities and addressing shortages of skills in areas including ICT, engineering, finance and mathematics is a strategic priority for Bulgaria. Bulgaria's national plan Bulgaria 2030 includes several goals and priorities to boost innovation, education and scientific infrastructure. The government has also adopted several national strategies and measures to foster innovation and enhance competitiveness, including important efforts to improve the vocational education and training (VET) system. The highly centralised VET and limited financial resources however have constrained the potential of these reforms. R&D spending remains relatively low compared to other EU countries, and more could be done to ensure equity within VET provision, and include vulnerable groups (OECD, 2019b). Engaging businesses in national efforts to enhance innovation and competitiveness is key to address the skills mismatch and promote innovative capabilities. Promoting RBC can go a long way in fostering a dialogue between businesses and the government, and encouraging business practices that contribute to the dissemination of scientific and technical knowledge.

The chapter on Science and Technology of the *Guidelines* specifically aims to promote the diffusion by multinational enterprises of the fruits of research and development activities among the countries where they operate, contributing thereby to the innovative capacities of host countries. Specific recommendations addressed to companies include, where feasible, adopting practices that permit the transfer and rapid diffusion of technologies and expertise, with due regard to the protection of intellectual property rights. The *Guidelines* also recommend that companies perform science and technology development work in host countries to address local market needs, as well as employ host country personnel in an S&T capacity and encourage their training, taking into account commercial needs. Where relevant to commercial objectives, companies are encouraged to develop ties with local universities, public research institutions, and participate in co-operative research projects with local industry or industry associations.

Source: OECD Guidelines for Multinational Enterprises (2011), https://mneguidelines.oecd.org/mneguidelines/

In 2019, Bulgaria adopted a new National Strategy for Corporate Social Responsibility (hereafter: the CSR Strategy) for the period 2019-23. It follows a previous iteration, which covered the period 2009-13 (Stefanova, 2015). The development of the new strategy was led by the Corporate Social Responsibility Advisory Council to the MLSP, an entity established in 2017 which is also in charge of monitoring its implementation. The CSR strategy affirms the government's commitment to improve the quality of life of the population through transparent, socially responsible business practices, and explicitly references key international RBC standards, including the OECD *Guidelines*, UN Guiding Principles, the ILO MNE Declaration, the UN Global Compact, and the ISO 26 000 on Social Responsibility (MSLP, 2019a).

The strategy includes a situation analysis, which lays out key challenges that CSR policy in Bulgaria should focus on, including insufficient awareness of the concept, weak stakeholder engagement, different levels of implementation between small and large businesses, and insufficient integration of principles into company's policies (MSLP, 2019a). Implementation of the strategy is supported by an action plan covering the periods 2019, 2020-21, and 2022-23,[1] which define specific activities and performance indicators for the implementation of the CSR Strategy, including the organisation of events, and development of tools and knowledge products (MLSP, 2019b).

The EU accession process has supported alignment with global standards in policy areas covered by the Guidelines (e.g, disclosure, consumer interests, competition, taxation)

The EU accession process initiated with Bulgaria's application for EU membership prompted a set of reforms to align with the EU *acquis communautaires,* which is the body of common rights and obligations that are binding on all EU member countries. During the process of Bulgaria's accession negotiations, the *acquis* were divided into 31 chapters, many of which are relevant to the policy areas covered by the OECD *Guidelines* (e.g. company law, competition policy, social policy and employment, science and research, environment, consumer health and protection, etc.). Reforms and initiatives undertaken in the context of this process contributed to strengthen the regulatory framework underpinning RBC in all these areas. Since Bulgaria's accession to the EU in 2007, Bulgaria has an obligation as a member state to transpose EU Directives into national laws.

For example, in 2015, Bulgaria transposed in national law the landmark EU Accounting Directive, amended by the EU Non-Financial Reporting Directive, which requires certain large undertakings and groups to disclose, amongst other things, non-financial and diversity information in order to better understand the development, performance, position and impact of the entity's activity. Such requirement can contribute to align business practices with the disclosure expectations laid out in the OECD *Guidelines*, making relevant information available to the public and improving understanding of companies operations. Ensuring compliance with the requirements established in the EU Directive is therefore of importance to enable and promote RBC. In July 2020, the EU sent a letter of formal notice to inform Bulgaria of an infringement procedure for failing to correctly transpose the Directive into Bulgarian law. In particular, the assessment concluded that the law did not explicitly require companies to disclose information required by the Directive, such as information concerning human rights, corruption and bribery matters, and risk management and due diligence processes (European Commission, 2020d; EU Business, 2020). In response, and with a view to achieve full compliance with the Directive, amendments were made to the Bulgarian Accountancy Act. Bulgarian authorities have indicated in the framework of this *Review* that they provided additional information to the European Commission on the steps taken to fully transpose the Directive into national law.

Amendments to Bulgaria's legal framework to align with EU standards were also made in other policy areas covered by the *Guidelines*. For example, as discussed in Chapter 3 of this *Review*, in the field of competition, the 2008 Protection of Competition Act is the direct application of the articles 101 and 101 of the Treaty on the functioning of the European Union. The Protection of Competition Act notably aims to provide protection against agreements, decisions and concerted practices, abuse of monopolistic and dominant positions on the market. As part of EU membership requirements, Bulgaria has aligned its legal and institutional framework with EU standards.

Concerning consumer interests, the Consumer Protection Act, in force since 2005, was amended in 2020 to further align with the European Directives on Consumer Law and Consumer Protections (ICLG, 2020). The Consumer Policy Unit within the Ministry of Economy responsible for the formulation of consumer policy, for the protection of economic interests, consumer safety and for taking initiatives in favour of consumers. It is also responsible for drafting consumer protection legislation and for the alignment with the EU legislation in the field of consumer protection. As noted in Chapter 3 of this *Review,* despite significant progress in that field, further steps could be taken to ensure consistency and implementation of the Bulgarian competition framework.

Bulgaria's National Reform Programme 2020, prepared as part of the European Union monitoring and informed by findings from the European Commission, includes objectives to implement measures to curb tax fraud, to prevent tax evasion and non-payment, to limit the prerequisites for manifestation of the shadow economy, and to optimise the control activity of the revenue administrations (Government of Bulgaria, 2020). This aligns with the OECD *Guidelines*, which call on enterprises to comply with both the letter and spirit of the tax laws and regulations of the countries in which they operate. In June 2021 however, the European Commission sent a letter of formal notice to Bulgaria drawing its attention to the tax treatment of undertaxed subsidiaries. At that time, the Commission considered that the current legislation transposing the Council Directive (EU) 2016/1164 of 12 July 2016, laying down rules against tax avoidance practices that directly affect the functioning of the internal market, included an undue exemption for subsidiaries that constitute an infringement to the Directive (European Commission, 2021). In July 2021, Bulgaria made commitments to amend the national legislation and remedy the situation through a formal position of the Republic of Bulgaria to the European Commission, approved at the meeting of the Council of European Affairs on 19 July 2021.

Initiatives by various actors have contributed to raise awareness of RBC in Bulgaria, although understanding of the concept varies

Various actors have been involved in the promotion of RBC in Bulgaria. International organisations, for example, have contributed to raise awareness of RBC in the country. From 2007 to 2009, the United Nations Development Programme (UNDP) implemented a regional CSR project to promote CSR standards in the region (Blancpain et al., 2011). Between 2007 and 2010, the United Nations Industrial Development Organization (UNIDO) also carried out awareness raising and training activities under the project "Sustainable development of enterprises in Bulgaria" (BILSP, 2021).

International business networks have also played an important role in the diffusion of RBC in Bulgaria. In 1998, the International Business Leaders Forum supported the establishment of the Bulgarian Business Leaders Forum (BBLF), a group of Bulgarian companies united by RBC values and commitments (Stefanova, 2015; BBLF, 2021). Since its creation, the BBLF has initiated various projects including the development of a code of Business Ethics, the launch of annual Responsible Business Awards, as well as CSR research studies and charity events (BBLF, 2021). The creation of the local chapter of the UN Global Compact in 2003 was an important milestone for the promotion of RBC in the country. According to UNGC's official website, the Bulgarian network counts 40 members from various industries and sizes to date (UNGC, 2021).

Bulgarian business associations have spearheaded various initiatives, including the creation, adaptation and dissemination of RBC standards and tools. Between 2014 and 2016, the Bulgarian Chamber of Commerce and Industry (BCCI) participated at a regional EU-funded project to promote RBC and multi-stakeholder dialogue (CSR for All, 2021). The "CSR for All project" enabled the development and translation in Bulgarian language of a Handbook of Good Practices for Corporate Social Responsibility. The Association of Bulgarian Industrial Capital, together with the Association of Bulgarian Investor Relation Directors supported the dissemination of the Handbook, which had been taken on by over 100 Bulgarian companies by 2014 (Lyubenova, 2014; BBLF 2021). Other business groups have also developed standards and tools for the benefits of their members. For example, the Bulgarian Chamber of Mining and Geology established its own Sustainable Development Standard in 2012; since 2005, the Union of Brewers in Bulgaria have a Code of Commercial Communication and Ethical Standards and Human Resources (MLSP, 2019).

The adoption of a National Corporate Governance Code, applicable (on a voluntary basis) to companies listed in the Bulgarian Stock Exchange (BSE), in 2012, was an important milestone in the promotion of good corporate practice in Bulgaria. The Code, which amended an earlier version from 2007, was developed and approved by the National Corporate Governance Committee, a legal non-profit entity and consisting of representatives from various stakeholder groups (NCGC, 2012). In 2019, 53 publicly listed companies declared compliance with the Code (MLSP, 2019). In November 2020, BSE became a partner exchange in the Sustainable Stock Exchange initiative, with the goal to promote responsible investment in sustainable development and advance corporate performance on environmental, social and governance issues in Bulgaria (BSE, 2020).

Several organisations have also been established with a specific goal to promote RBC. The Balkan Institute of Labour and Social Policy (BILSP) for example was established in 2001 as a non-profit organisation and works with a range of national and international actors to foster social innovation, including through projects and conferences to promote CSR (BILSP, 2021). The Bulgarian Association of CSR Professionals was created in 2018, with the goal to create and promote professional standards and a positive attitude towards the profession of specialists in corporate sustainability and social responsibility. The Association included about 40 CSR specialists in 2019 (MLSP, 2019). In 2020, the Association of CSR Professionals adopted Rules for ethical conduct of CSR specialists. Awareness of RBC varies among businesses.

Civil society organisations and trade unions have been active supporters of RBC promotion and dissemination in Bulgaria. In 2013, the Economic and Social Council (ESC) of Bulgaria – an independent consultative body established to express the will and interests of civil society – adopted a Resolution expressing support for any policy and / or action of the State bringing Bulgaria closer to OECD standards, including adherence to the OECD *Declaration* and the OECD *Guidelines*, and the establishment of an NCP (ESC, 2013). The role and importance of civil society organisations and trade unions in promoting RBC and participating in the due diligence process is discussed later in this chapter.

The government has collaborated with various stakeholders on a number of initiatives. For example, on 30 September 2020, the MoE participated in a national conference on Corporate Social Responsibility, co-organised by the magazine "Enterprise" and the multimedia analytical and educational programme of the "Kauzi" Foundation "CSR AdviceBox". The conference on "Corporate Social Responsibility: Sustainable Development for the Bulgarian Business" was held under the patronage of the Ministry of Labour and Social Policy. The government has indicated in the context of this *Review* that six information seminars led by the MLSP had been organised in 2019, as part of the plans laid out by the CSR Strategy.

Efforts by various stakeholders are paying off and contributing to gradually raise awareness of RBC and align understanding of RBC with internationally recognised RBC standards. A recent survey carried out among Bulgaria's largest employers found that 76% of respondents considered the engagement of their company on CSR as high or very high – a 9-percentage point increase since the previous survey of this kind carried out in 2018. The main reported obstacles for further uptake were a lack of human resources and knowledge, lack of capacity, and lack of finance (Stefanova, 2018-20). The outlook for overcoming these challenges is positive: according to a 2015 CSR Managers regional survey by Deloitte, 60% of Bulgarian managers consulted believe that CSR will flourish and there will be a continued growth in the number of socially responsible businesses. Another 30% believe that CSR will become more mature whereby it will include social and environmental issues in the business model (Deloitte, 2015).

Despite encouraging trends, awareness of RBC in Bulgaria, although increasing, is not yet widespread. Understanding of the concept varies across businesses. Several studies have noted that RBC in Bulgaria is traditionally understood and practiced in the form of corporate philanthropy, and that integration of RBC principles and standards into core activities, while increasing, is not the norm (Stefanova et al., 2015; Lyubenova, 2019). For example, supply chain due diligence –-a key element of RBC – is rarely mentioned in the public discourse, business initiatives and literature on CSR or RBC. Furthermore, RBC standards tend to be more prevalent within large companies that are subsidiaries of multinational enterprises. Thus the importance for Bulgaria to play an active role in promoting the *Guidelines* and related due diligence guidance.

Promoting and facilitating RBC risk-based due diligence

The *Guidelines* call on business to carry out risk-based due diligence, for example by incorporating it into their enterprise risk management systems, to identify, prevent and mitigate actual and potential adverse impacts, and account for how these impacts are addressed. The OECD has developed a set of guidance to provide practical support to enterprises on the implementation of the *Guidelines*, providing plain language explanations of its due diligence recommendations and associated provisions. Adherents to the *Declaration* commit to adhere to all of the related OECD legal instruments aimed at supporting the implementation of the *Guidelines*, including the *Due Diligence Guidance for Responsible Supply Chains of Minerals from Conflict-Affected and High-Risk Area*s, the *OECD-FAO Guidance on Responsible Agricultural Supply Chains*, the *Due Diligence Guidance for Meaningful Stakeholder Engagement in the Extractive Sector*, the OECD *Due Diligence Guidance for Responsible Supply Chains in the Garment and Footwear Sector* and the OECD *Due Diligence Guidance for Responsible Business Conduct* (See Box 8.4).

Box 8.4. OECD Due Diligence Guidance for Responsible Business Conduct

One of the key expectations reflected in the *Guidelines* is that companies should contribute positively to environmental, economic, and social progress worldwide, with a view to achieving sustainable development ("do good"). Another key expectation is that companies should avoid causing or contributing to adverse impacts and seek to prevent or mitigate adverse impacts related to their activities or business relationships (including throughout supply chains) "(do no harm") through conducting risk based due diligence.

Due diligence is the process enterprises should carry out to identify, prevent, mitigate and account for how they address adverse risks and impacts in their own operations, their supply chain and other business relationships, as recommended in the *Guidelines*. Effective due diligence should be supported by efforts to embed RBC into policies and management systems, and aims to enable enterprises to remediate adverse impacts that they cause or to which they contribute.

Due diligence addresses actual adverse impacts or potential adverse impacts (risks) related to the following topics covered in the *Guidelines*: human rights, including workers and industrial relations; environment (including biodiversity issues); bribery and corruption; disclosure; and consumer interests (RBC issues).

For many enterprises, the term "risk" means primarily risks to the enterprise – financial risk, market risk, operational risk, reputational risk, etc. Enterprises are concerned with their position in the market vis-à-vis their competitors, their image and long-term existence, so when they look at risks, it is typically risks to themselves. The *Guidelines* and the OECD due diligence process, however, insist on the impacts on people, the environment and society that enterprises cause, contribute to, or to which they are directly linked. In other words, it is an outward-facing approach to risk.

By actively promoting these instruments, governments can help businesses operationalise RBC principles and standards. In addition to disseminating and building capacity on due diligence standards, governments can also facilitate supply chain due diligence, notably by removing legal and regulatory obstacles to RBC. This not only requires creating an environment that encourages responsible behaviour and enables dialogues between relevant stakeholders, but also a policy environment that is clear and predictable and allows for mechanisms to ensure accountability when RBC expectations are not met. This section highlights areas where the government could focus its policy efforts to build the capacity of businesses in carrying out due diligence, and facilitate supply chain due diligence.

Facilitating and removing obstacles to RBC risk-based due diligence to advance fundamental rights

Bulgaria is party to all but two of the nine core UN human rights treaties, and all eight fundamental ILO conventions (ILO, 2021). The State is also party to Council of Europe's European Convention on Human Rights and the European Social Charter. As noted earlier in this *Review,* as part of the EU Accession process, Bulgaria had to meet a number of pre-conditions, which include having the institutions to preserve democratic governance and human rights (EUR-Lex, 2021). Months of uninterrupted protests in 2020 however have put a spotlight on particular issues that affect the rule of law, including corruption, undue relations between business and politics, as well as the independence of the judiciary. As noted in Chapter 7 of this *Review*, the EU Parliament adopted in October 2020 a resolution on the rule of law and fundamental rights in Bulgaria (European Parliament, 2020), which expressed regrets for a significant deterioration in respect for the principles of rule of law, democracy and fundamental rights, including the independence of the judiciary, separation of powers, the fight against corruption, and freedom of the media. The resolution furthermore expressed its solidarity with the people of Bulgaria in their legitimate demands and aspirations for justice, transparency, accountability and democracy (European Parliament, 2020). Addressing these issues is of particular importance to ensure that businesses can effectively carry out human rights due diligence.

Facilitating stakeholder engagement

A key component of what constitutes an enabling environment for RBC is one where meaningful stakeholder engagement and dialogue is a way of doing business. The *Guidelines* explicitly recommend that enterprises engage with relevant stakeholders in order to provide meaningful opportunities for their views to be taken into account in relation to planning and decision making for projects or other activities that may significantly affect local communities. Enterprises are also encouraged to co-operate with governments in developing and implementing policies and laws, and to consider the views of other stakeholders in society. Additionally, the OECD *Policy Framework for Investment* emphasises that greater participation of stakeholders in policy design and implementation leads to better-targeted and more effective policies. Creating an environment where stakeholders are empowered to express their views and actively participate in policy design as well as consultations organised by businesses, the government or a group of stakeholders, is therefore essential for RBC.

Foreign investors, especially those for which implementing RBC standards is a legal obligation, may also have concerns about their ability to conduct risk-based due diligence when stakeholders cannot actively engage in the due diligence process. The OECD *Due Diligence Guidance for Responsible Business Conduct* lays out clear expectations that due diligence should be informed by meaningful engagement with stakeholders such as workers, workers' representatives, trade unions (including global unions), community members, civil society organisations, investors and professional industry and trade associations. Meaningful stakeholder engagement is characterised by two-way communication, through which enterprise and stakeholders freely express opinions, share perspectives and listen to alternative viewpoints to reach a mutual understanding. The government can play an important role in supporting this process by ensuring that the legal and judicial framework empowers stakeholders to express their views and engage with businesses.

Bulgaria enjoys a vibrant civil society, which can be leveraged to promote a broad consensus on RBC and support in key policy processes and business practices related to RBC. In recent years however, various actors have raised concerns over the environment enabling civil society organisations to raise human rights, environmental or social concerns (Freedom House, 2020; Za Zemiata, 2020). In 2019, legal proceeding initiated by the VMRO party – a partner in Bulgaria's coalition government at the time – for the de-registration of the Bulgarian Helsinki Committee (BHC), one of the main human rights organisations in the country, was widely condemned by the international community (CoE, 2019; Amnesty International,

2019). In 2020, the UN Special Rapporteur on the rights to freedom of peaceful assembly and of association expressed concerns that a draft law submitted in July 2020 by a group of members of the Bulgarian Parliament aimed at amending the Law on Non-Profit Legal Persons/Entities could, if adopted, hamper the work of independent non-profit organisations, including those that promote and protect human rights, (OHCHR, 2020c). These concerns were echoed by the European Parliament resolution on the rule of law and fundamental rights in Bulgaria (European Parliament, 2020; OHCHR, 2020d). The 2021 EU Rule of Law report indicates that following the publication of the previous similar report (the 2020 report), the draft legislation was not further pursued. The 2021 report notes that civic space remains narrow and that, in some occasion, members of the civil society appear to be under pressure (European Commission, 2021d).

Bulgarian law provides for the right of workers to form and join independent labour unions, bargain collectively, and conduct legal strikes. Anti-union discrimination is also prohibited. Workers alleging discrimination based on union affiliation can file complaints with the Commission for Protection Against Discrimination (United States, 2019). Observers however have noted limitations to the right to association and collective bargaining. The ITUC has been rating Bulgaria at rank 3, on a scale from 1 to 5+ (1 being the best possible rating), and domestic trade unions have reported cases of employer obstruction (ITUC, CITUB, 2019). Collective bargaining in Bulgaria is predominant in larger companies, while no union structure is in place in most small companies, meaning that there can be no company agreement. Moreover, most small companies are not members of an employers' association, which means that industry level agreements do not apply (Fair Wear, 2019).

The media environment is also of importance to enable RBC. Information relayed by the media is often a key source of information to identify RBC risks and make them known to the public. In Bulgaria, freedom of the media is protected by the Constitution, and by the Radio and Television Act. In the past decade, and particularly in recent years, concerns have been raised about the independence of the media and working conditions for journalists (European Parliament, 2020; CoE, 2020; OHCHR, 2020a; Freedom House, 2020). Bulgaria ranked 111 out of 180 countries in the 2020 World Press Freedom Index, which is the lowest performance within the European Union. This is a significant deterioration from 2008, where Bulgaria ranked at 59 (RSF, 2020). In 2020, a new legislation was adopted to strengthen the independence of the media regulator (CEM), and an increase in the resources of the regulator was foreseen in the 2021 State Budget to enhance its effectiveness. While this is a welcome development, in March and April 2021, the government decreased the budget of the regulator. The 2021 EU Rule of Law of report noted in this context persisting challenges, including the lack of transparency of media ownership, as well as the working environment and safety of journalists (European Commission, 2021d).

Continuing efforts to ensure access to effective remedy, including through state-based non-judicial grievance mechanisms

Access to remedy is an essential part of the state duty to protect against adverse impacts by private actors such as businesses. States are expected to take appropriate steps to ensure, through judicial, administrative, legislative, and other appropriate means, that when such abuses occur within their territory or jurisdiction, those affected have access to effective remedy. At the same time, the independence of the judiciary is a crucial foundation of law enforcement that affects investment as highlighted in this IPR, as business enterprises and the public need a reliable and impartial mechanism for resolving disputes, whether labour, commercial, environmental or otherwise, as well as for combatting corruption.

As highlighted in Chapter 7 of this *Review*, despite noticeable progress in judicial reforms, challenges remain to ensure the full independence and accountability of the judiciary, free from executive and other interferences, and with respect to the transparency and professionalism surrounding judicial selection and proceedings. As a result, effective access to remedy for corporate harms is still a work in progress, although positive developments can be noted in the area of state-based non-judicial grievance mechanisms. In 2019, the Bulgarian National Human Rights Institution (NHRI) or Ombudsman was re-accredited with "A status", meaning that the institution is now considered fully compliant with the international benchmarks for NHRIs (the so-called "Paris Principles"). The Ombudsman has the mandate to receive and review complaints concerning the violation of rights and freedoms by the state and municipal bodies and their administrations, as well as by public services providers, thus providing an avenue to resolve RBC issues falling within that scope (Ombudsman, 2021).

Individuals may also pursue discrimination cases through the Commission for Protection against Discrimination (CPD). The CPD was created as a specialised government agency under the Law on Protection against Discrimination with a mandate to prevent and protect against discrimination, specifically in relation to persons with disabilities and hate speech. The CPD hears individual complaints and can impose fines and administrative measures in case of violations (Government of Bulgaria, 2019). According to the CPD, the majority of discrimination complaints received in 2019 related to employment, predominantly concerning persons with disabilities (United States, 2019). The Bulgarian state 2021-23 budget forecast foresees an increase in financial and human resources of both the NHRI and the CDP, including a 10% increase of the personel funds for both institutions (European Commission, 2021d).

In 2019, as part of Bulgaria's request to adhere to the *Declaration on International Investment*, Bulgaria made steps to establish a National Contact Point within the Bulgarian Government. The creation of this entity would offer another important avenue for remedies for victims of business-related abuse (see section below on Bulgaria's plan for the establishment of an NCP).

The *Guidelines* state that when causing or contributing to adverse impacts, companies are expected to provide for or co-operate with legitimate remediation mechanisms through which affected stakeholders can raise complaints and seek to have them addressed. Today, little evidence is found of businesses providing or co-operating in such mechanisms. The government, together with business associations, should consider taking actions to raise awareness about the importance of establishing effective company-based grievance mechanisms to address concerns by potentially affected stakeholders and adverse impacts at an early stage.

Combatting bribery, bribe solicitation and extortion

Tackling corruption is another important component of building this enabling environment. The *Guidelines* emphasise that bribery and corruption discourage investment and distort international competitive conditions. In particular, the diversion of funds through corrupt practices undermines attempts by citizens to achieve higher levels of economic, social and environmental welfare, and it impedes efforts to reduce poverty. Both businesses and governments have a role to play in addressing corruption. For example, the *Guidelines* specify that enterprises should not, directly or indirectly, offer, promise, give, or demand a bribe or other undue advantage to obtain or retain business or other improper advantage, and should also resist solicitation of bribes and extortion. Governments also have a responsibility to ensure that a legal and regulatory framework is in place and enforced to deter corruption. They can also lead by example by observing the highest integrity standards in their own actions as economic actors.

As discussed in Chapter 7 of this *Review*, corruption continues to be a challenge in Bulgaria. The country has carried out important reforms to address the issue. The National Development Programme BULGARIA 2030, a strategic framework document that determines the vision and the overall goals of development policies in all sectors of state governance, recognises that strengthening the independence of the judiciary and reducing the risk of corruption would improve the business environment and the international competitiveness of Bulgaria's economy. The programme includes priority actions dedicated to the fight against corruption, including ensuring transparency of legislative processes, strengthening the independence of the judiciary and ensuring a balanced workload of courts (Government of Bulgaria, 2020). As noted in Chapter 7, Bulgaria has adopted long-term anti-corruption strategies. The lack of significant results from Bulgaria's efforts to address corruption nevertheless fuelled civil unrest in Bulgaria in 2020 and led to political instability during most of the year 2021.

Civil unrest in Bulgaria in 2020 and 2021 resulted primarily from allegations of corruption in the public sector. Promoting a culture of business integrity and responsibility can play an important role in reducing corruption. Efforts so far in that regard have been timid. During the first quarter of 2022, Bulgaria was in the process of transposing the EU Directive 2019/1937 – the so-called "EU Whistleblowing Directive". As Bulgaria goes through this process, promoting RBC and the *Guideline*s can help align business practices with international best practice, thereby facilitating implementation of the legislation once in force. The *Guidelines* include a recommendation for enterprises to introduce safeguards in their own policies to protect bona fide whistle-blowing activities, including protection of employees who, in the absence of timely remedial action or in the face of reasonable risk of negative employment action, report practices that contravene the law to the competent public authorities.

Strengthening environmental safeguards for a sustainable use of resources

Bulgaria has traditionally had a well-established and robust environmental protection framework. Environmental protection is enshrined in the Bulgarian Constitution, which stipulates that the country shall ensure the protection and reproduction of the environment, the maintenance and diversity of wildlife, and the rational utilisation of the minerals and the resources of the country. Bulgaria is a party to the vast majority of global and regional multilateral environmental agreements (MEAs), including the UN Convention on Biological Diversity, the UN Framework Convention on Climate Change, and the Paris Agreement. The National Development Programme BULGARIA 2030 includes a development axis focused on the sustainable management of resources, to satisfy the needs of the economy and society while maintaining environmental sustainability. Globally, Bulgaria ranks 41 out of 180 countries rated by the Environment Performance Index in 2020 (Yale, 2020).

The main law governing environmental management in Bulgaria is the Environment Protection Act (EPA) of 2004. Key secondary legislation specifying the EPA include the 2003 Ordinance on the conditions and procedure for carrying out environmental impact assessment (EIA), and the 2004 Ordinance on the conditions and the procedure for carrying out environmental assessment of plans and programmes (SEA Ordinance). Since the EU accession, Bulgaria has strengthened various aspects of its environmental legislation. In 2008, the Liability for Prevention and Remedying of Environmental Damage Act was adopted. The law transposed the 2004 Directive 2004/35/EO on environmental liability with regard to the prevention and remedying of environmental damage. The EPA has also been amended and a number of ordinances were issued to transpose other EU Directives. According to the UN and the European Commission, Bulgaria has nevertheless been slow in implementing the EU environmental legislation (UNECE, 2017, European Commission 2019b).

There is growing attention by stakeholders to environmental protection and to the environmental performance of business enterprises. The important rise in complaints related to environmental protection filed with the Ombudsman of the Republic of Bulgaria, the independent national human rights institution, illustrates such trend and offers an in indication of the type of business-related environmental challenges facing the country (see Box 8.5).

Box 8.5. Complaints received by the Ombudsman of the Republic of Bulgaria on environmental issues

In 2019, the Ombudsman received 412 complaints from citizens and associations in relation to the right to a healthy environment. This is a significant increase from the 213 complaints received in 2017.

Issues raised in complaints included: failure to take into account the threats to health caused by industrial pollution of the air, water and soil; allowing for industrial burning and other activities with waste without a permit or under unclear rules; insufficient measures to prevent environmental and health risk through the procedures of environmental impact assessment of investment proposals; providing exploitation rights for natural resources and subsoil, in disregard of the rules for sustainable development and land use; failure to observe the citizens' procedural rights to information, participation in the decision making process on matters of the environment and challenging them, harmful impact on the environment with cross-border consequences; adverse impacts of harmful emissions from industrial sources and, more specifically, the burning and processing of waste, generation of electricity from biomass, and the extraction and initial processing of building materials.

Source: Ombudsman of Bulgaria (2019).

Among other issues, ensuring air quality and a reduction in the levels of some pollutants is an important challenge for Bulgaria. While domestic fuels-based heating and road transport are large sources of particulate matters in Bulgaria, various industry sectors also contribute to air emissions (UNECE, 2017). The energy sector, dominated by coal-fired power plants, was found generally responsible for the greatest share of emissions to air for most pollutants compared to all other industrial sectors (Ricardo, 2018). The European Environment Agency has found concentrations of pollutants, especially particulate matter (PM10) and PM 2.5, to be above the annual limit value at times (EEA, 2020). In 2020, the European Commission referred Bulgaria to the European Court of Justice for failing to fully comply with a 2017 court judgement finding that Bulgaria had breached its obligations under the EU's ambient air quality legislation – in particular, the limit values for PM10, and adoption of appropriate measures to keep the period of exceedance as short as possible (European Commission, 2020). In July 2019, the European Commission had issued another referral to the European Court of Justice for Bulgaria's failure to respect limit values of SO2, noting persisting non-compliance in the South-East area of the country, where the largest thermal power plants in Bulgaria are located (European Commission, 2019c).

Air pollution is a major cause of premature death and disease. In 2015, the European Environment Agency estimated that about 14 200 premature deaths were attributable to fine particulate matter concentrations, 350 to ozone concentrations and 640 to nitrogen dioxide concentrations (European Commission, 2019b). In relative terms, when considering years of life lost per 100 000 inhabitants, the largest impacts were observed in Bulgaria and other central and eastern European countries, where the highest concentrations of PM2.5 were observed (European Environment Agency, 2018). The issue of air pollution attracted significant attention in 2020, as the health risks of air pollution compounded with that of the COVID-19 pandemic (Euractiv, 2020).

The government recognises the significance of the problem and has taken steps to address it. Improving air quality is one of the key priorities of NDP BULGARIA 2030, which acknowledges that excess levels of particulate matter (PM10) are a major problem at national level in terms of ambient air quality. In 2019 the government adopted the National Ambient Air Quality Improvement Programme 2018-24 to address and reduce fine dust pollution, in particular at municipal level (Government of Bulgaria, 2020). Another strategic document is the National air pollution control programme (2020-30) in order to limit annual anthropogenic emissions of SO_2, NOx, NMVOC, $PM_{2,5}$ and NH_3 into the air, which implements the Directive (EC)

2016/2284 on the reduction of national emissions of certain atmospheric pollutants, amending Directive 2003/35/EC and repealing Directive 2001/81/EC. At local level, municipal governments with poor air quality have also adopted their own air quality plans, such as in the town of Galobovo, which sits in the vicinity of large coal plants and has experienced exceeding levels of pollutants (Municipality of Galobovo, 2019-23). In addition, the government's seventh National Communication on climate change lists a number of measures aimed at reducing greenhouse gas emissions, including improvement of production efficiency in existing coal-fired power plants, and fuel substitution from coal to natural gas (Government of Bulgaria, 2018).

Besides air quality, another area requiring continuing efforts is waste management. The legal framework is broadly in place, with the Waste Management Act transposing the EU Waste Framework Directive and introducing the hierarchy of waste management and the 'polluter pays' principle. However, progress in ensuring compliance with wastewater collection and treatment obligations has been slow (European Commission, 2019a). Among issues raised is the overreliance on landfilling as a method of waste disposal, the low recycling rate compared to EU average and targets, (European Commission, 2019a and 2020). Efforts have been made over the years to reduce the share of landfilled waste, and a national strategy on circular economy is being developed (Ministry of Environment and Water). While the waste management issue is to a large extent related to domestic and municipal waste management, industries also play a role in waste creation, management and prevention. With regards to coal waste management, a recent study on one large plant in the country has shown frequent releases of contaminated waste waters to the local environment from sites where ashes generated by the plant are stored (Greenpeace, 2021). Another issue has been the burning of waste by coal power plants, which has prompted local opposition (Euractiv, 2020; Greenpeace, 2021).[2] Only one coal power plant has permit to burn waste in Bulgaria. However, civil society organisations have raised concerns related to the illegal burning of waste, alongside coal, without the required permit, in violation of EU regulations. In 2020, environmental lawyers from ClientEarth and Za Zemiata Access to Justice brought a complaint to the European Commission to investigate and put an end to alleged illegal waste incineration in Bulgaria (Spasik, 2020; Euractiv, 2020).Finally, an important element of environmental prot ection is the ability of stakeholders to access environmental information, participate in public debates and access remedy for environmental matters. Civil society organisations have raised concerns in this regard, notably in relation to a 2017 Supreme Administrative Court decision to deny legal standing to citizens and environmental organisations to challenge air quality plans. In May 2020, as part of its infringement procedures, the European Commission sent a letter of formal notice urging Bulgaria to remove barriers to access to justice in relation to air quality plans (European Commission, 2020). Concerns related to public participation and access to justice (in connection among others with air quality plans) in environmental matters as well as protection of the members of the public against penalisation, persecution and harassment, were also raised by NGOs in a submitted October 2018 communication to the Aarhus Convention Compliance Committee (ACCC/C/2018/161), alleging violations of the Convention (of which Bulgaria is a party) (UNECE, 2018-20).

Promoting RBC standards in the energy sector in particular could support government's efforts to improve ambient air quality and environmental risk management more broadly. The environment chapter of the *Guidelines* calls on enterprises to take due account of the need to protect the environment, public health and safety, and generally to conduct their activities in a manner contributing to the wider goal of sustainable development. This entails sound environmental management that aims to controlling both direct and indirect environmental impacts; establishing and maintaining appropriate environmental management systems; improving environmental performance; being transparent about the environmental impacts and risks, including also reporting and communicating with outside stakeholders; being proactive in avoiding environmental damage; working to improve the level of environmental performance in all parts of their operations, even where this may not be formally required; and training and education of their employees with regard to environmental matters.

The *Guidelines* include specific recommendations on providing adequate, measurable and verifiable (where applicable) and timely information on the potential environment, health and safety impacts of the activities of the enterprise available to the public. The *Guidelines* also encourage companies to engage in adequate and timely communication and consultation with the communities directly affected by the environmental, health and safety policies of the enterprise and by their implementation. Bulgaria's government could further encourage businesses in that direction, and leverage the potential of the vibrant civil society engaged in environmental protection to hold businesses accountable. In addition, Bulgaria should ensure that the legal and institutional framework in place allows stakeholders to access environmental information, raise issues and access effective remedy.

Addressing RBC risks in strategic sectors by building capacity on due diligence

While awareness of RBC has been on the rise in Bulgaria, there is scope to improve businesses' understanding of due diligence as a key process through which RBC principles can be operationalise, and to build the capacity of businesses in carrying out due diligence. The OECD has developed a range of due diligence instruments to provide practical guidance to businesses on how to implement the *Guidelines*, including in key sectors particularly relevant to Bulgaria. This section provides examples of how due diligence instruments can be applied to address risks prevalent in selected Bulgarian sectors.

Promoting decent work in the garment industry

Bulgaria has a large garment and textile industry. The total number of employees under labour contract in the textile, apparel, leather and otherwise-related products within the manufacturing sector was close to 118 000 persons in 2017 (Fair Wear, 2019). Some NGOs estimate the total number might be around 130 000, accounting for those with semi-formal contractual conditions. In 2018, the export turnover of Bulgarian companies from the sector reached EUR3.86 billion euro. Almost 95% of the export production of the Bulgarian industry goes to EU member states (Fair Wear Foundation, 2019). The dominant type of production consists in sub-contracting of work done with materials provided by clients. The latter are predominantly foreign-owned, attracted by low cost sources of labour and energy, as well as a skilled workforce guaranteeing quality (Iankova, 2021).

Across sectors, Bulgaria has been facing issues with low wages, associated with some of the highest levels of poverty and income inequality in the EU (European Commission, 2020c). The issue is particularly salient in the garment industry, where workers receive amongst the lowest wages in the country, hovering around the national minimum wage. In 2019, Bulgaria had the lowest gross minimum wage (EUR 286) across the 22 out of 28 EU members that have national legal minimum wage[3] (Eurostat, 2019). A 2019 study by Fair Wear found that the most common non-compliance issue with the Code of Labour Practices (CoLP) to date falls under 'payment of a living wage', usually found during social audits (Fair Wear, 2019). As a result, workers often face difficult living conditions and live under or close to the poverty line. The Clean Clothes Campaign estimated that in 2018, the average net salary in the garment sector, without overtime, was slightly below the statutory minimal net wage, and below the EU poverty threshold (Clean Clothes Campaign, 2018).

The absence of collective bargaining agreements (CBA) in the garment and textile industry makes it difficult to negotiate better wages and conditions. According to trade unions and NGOs, there has been no CBA in the garment industry since 2008, and none for the textile industry since 2012. Trade union and employer organisation density are low, partly because there are many small enterprises in the sector that remain difficult to unionise. A 2021 mapping of social dialogue in Bulgaria carried out by the Cornell University School of Industrial and Labor Relations and the Strategic Partnership for Garment Supply Chain Transformation noted serious problems for garment industry workers trying to exercise their right to Freedom of Association, including attempts by employers to eradicate trade union organisations, as well as an unwillingness to sign collective bargaining agreements (CBAs) at both the industry and company levels (Iankova, 2021). There has however been some CBAs signed at company level. However, even when they are signed, CBAs are not always fully complied with. Furthermore, overall, 90% of the company-level collective agreements negotiate wages that are at the level of the mandatory minimum wage for the country (Iankova, 2021).

The OECD *Due Diligence Guidance in the Garment and Footwear Sector* provides practical recommendations to help businesses identify and address risks that are prevalent in the industry. For example, the *Guidance* includes dedicated modules on the questions of working time, trade union and collective bargaining, and wage. Widely disseminating and promoting the *Guidance* could contribute to ensure compliance with national law in the sector, but also to ensure that wages and working conditions satisfy the basic needs of workers and their families. The government could also consider promoting social dialogue, and taking advantage of collective initiatives present in the country to facilitate international partnerships and encourage responsible purchasing practices across the garment value chain, including among foreign buyers.

Protecting workers health and local communities in the mining sector

Contrary to the situation in the garment and textile industry, low wages are less of an issue in the mining sector, where workers enjoy higher wages up to EUR 800-1 000. Nonetheless, there is some evidence that sub-contracting is used to pay lower wages to many workers (Free Information Surveys, 2019). Other challenges in the mining sector relate to occupational health and safety and well as environmental and social impacts on communities.

There have been reports that conditions in sectors such as mining, but also construction, chemicals, and transportation pose risks for workers (CITUB, 2019). The mining industry, which remains the main source of energy production in the country, has been under scrutiny for years for unsafe working conditions and pollution affecting both workers and communities (Euractiv, 2020). The issue is one of implementation rather than policy, as the legislative framework to ensure occupational safety and health is in place, including ordinances on particular sectors such as construction, and on the order, manner and frequency of risk assessment, among others. The "General Labour Inspectorate" is mandated to carry out inspections to monitor employers' compliance with laws protecting the rights of workers, including the Law on Healthy and Safe Working Conditions. The government has also made efforts to enforce regulations requiring companies to conduct occupational health and safety risk assessments and to adopt measures to eliminate or reduce any identified risks (United States, 2019).

The expansion of coalmines in certain areas have also led to alleged adverse impacts and created tensions with local communities. One case involving the main mining state-owned enterprise was taken to the EBRD complaint mechanism (See Box 8.6).

The OECD Due Diligence Guidance for Responsible Supply Chains of Minerals from Conflict-Affected and High-Risk Areas and the OECD Due Diligence Guidance for Meaningful Stakeholder Engagement in the Extractive Sector can provide useful frameworks to address some of the issues that Bulgaria still faces in the coal mining industry. The latter lays out concretely why engaging with stakeholders makes good business sense and how to go about it.

Box 8.6. The Maritsa East Mines case with the EBRD

Maritsa East Mines EAD, also called Mini Maritsa East, in Stara Zagora province, operates the largest lignite coalmines in Bulgaria. The mines provide coal to the four thermal power plants in the nearby Maritsa East complex and account for about 96% of Bulgarian coal production. Maritsa East Mines is a subsidiary of Bulgaria Energy Holding (BEH), a fully state-owned holding company with a portfolio revolving around electricity generation, supply and transmission, and coal supply mining.

The mines' operations and expansion since 2005 have reportedly resulted in a range of impacts on the surrounding communities in Beli Bryag and Troyanovo, which are set to be expropriated and destroyed by 2023 and 2030, respectively. The inevitability of the mine expansion prevented any development in the two villages since the start of the expropriation process from 2010 on.

Residents raised concerns with the company over the expropriation process on numerous occasions. In late 2017, residents of Beli Bryag turned to the Project Complaint Mechanism of the European Bank for Reconstruction and Development (EBRD). The complaint is connected with the EBRD's Bulgaria Energy Holdings Bond Issue and the Kozloduy International Decommissioning Support Fund relating to Maritsa East Mines.

In the complaint to the EBRD, residents raised concerns that the resettlement action plan proposed by Maritsa East Mines was made without their participation and consent, and that it did not include a fair compensation methodology for housing and agricultural land, with prices offered below market prices. Residents, many of whom were retirees, noted that as a result of such low compensation for housing, and the loss of agricultural and grazing land, they were likely to find themselves in poverty. In addition, due to the mine's proximity (500-600m) to the village, mining operations, including explosions, caused losses and destruction and damage to properties, and the noise level was impacting their health.

The EBRD conducted a problem-solving exercise from late 2017 to July 2020. This process is said to have facilitated communication and resulted in the signing of over 25 voluntary bilateral agreements, as well as, according to the Ministry of Energy, in the safeguarding of the cemetery outside the territory of the mine (although the EBRD final report notes that the relocation of the cemetery may take place in 2021). The EBRD problem-solving exercise did not however result in a final settlement agreement between the complainants and the company within the deadline set in the Resettlement Action Plan (RAP). The EBRD mechanism noted that it had been agreed, as part of the mediation process, that an addendum to the RAP would be drafted in consultation with the community, yet no addendum was shared. The EBRD noted the lack of agreement on the estimation of compensation costs, and the differing interpretations between parties of applicable legal provisions, the company claiming it could not cover non-monetary damages based on Bulgarian law.

Tensions between the remaining residents and the company rose subsequently. In June 2020, while the EBRD mediation was in its final stage, Maritsa East Mines allegedly submitted what appears to be an eviction notice to residents, flagging that it will rely on the police to conduct the eviction. The residents complained to the Ministry of Energy (which manages ownership of Maritsa East Mines) about the inappropriate nature of this letter. As of mid-2020, around 80% of properties in Beli Bryag had been expropriated, and it is unclear whether expropriation for the remaining properties has started.

Sources: Ministry of Energy; Bulgaria Energy Holdings (https://bgenh.com/en); EBRD, 2017 and 2020; Bankwatch (https://bankwatch.org)

Fostering policy coherence on RBC

Policy coherence is crucial to ensure sound policy design and implementation. This is recognised in the *Policy Framework for Investment*, which encourages governments to co-operate internally as well as externally with foreign governments and stakeholders to ensure coherence and support of policies relevant to RBC. Such co-operation should involve all relevant stakeholders, including among government agencies, companies, worker associations, professional associations, employer associations, civil society, and local communities.

As noted earlier in this chapter, Bulgaria has made important strides in mainstreaming RBC in national policies and strategies. Bulgaria has also adopted an overarching framework defining Bulgaria's priorities for the country on RBC. As Bulgaria plans to develop a National Action Plan on RBC, ensuring consistency and complementarity with existing plans will be essential to build on progress made and ensure clarity on messages and expectations communicated around RBC.

Ensuring co-ordination between various ministries and government agencies relevant to RBC will also be key to support implementation of these commitments. In particular, attention should be paid to ensuring co-ordination between the MLSP, in charge of the implementation of the CSR strategy, and the MoE, where under current plans the National Contact Point for RBC, in charge of promoting RBC and furthering the effectiveness of the *Guidelines*, will be hosted (see below plans for the establishment of the NCP). In a similar manner, clear delineations of roles and areas of collaboration between the multi-stakeholder working group established within the National Economic Council, the Economic and Social Council, and the Advisory Body on CSR located at the MLSP, would be important to maximise the potential of the different institutions to represent and liaise with stakeholders.

Policy coherence also means leading by example on RBC in the activities of the state as an economic actor. In that regard, important efforts have been made to enhance the corporate governance of state-owned enterprise. Besides the current reforms, the Accountancy Act, which regulates enterprises' accounting practices, includes requirements on transparency and disclosure of non-financial information, such as on environmental, social and employee matters, human rights, and anti-corruption. These requirements also apply to "public interest enterprises", which include several SOEs identified by name or business activity in the Act (Government of Bulgaria, 2015; OECD 2019).

As noted in Chapter 3, SOEs dominate strategic sectors, some of which such as energy, mining and transport are associated with high environmental and social risks. Coupled with the fact that some SOEs are large employers, this creates an opportunity for the government to promote good practices on responsible business, which could make a significant positive mark on these sectors and send a strong signal to other business enterprises. The *Guidelines* apply to all entities within the enterprise sector whether private, state or mixed. The *Guidelines on Corporate Governance of State-Owned Enterprises* (SOE *Guidelines*) also recommends that SOEs "observe high standards of responsible business conduct" and state that "expectations established by the government in this regard should be publicly disclosed and mechanisms for their implementation be clearly established". The SOE *Guidelines*' Annotations further encourage measures to report on foreseeable risks, including in the areas of human rights, labour, the environment, and risks related to corruption and taxation.

Public procurement can also be used strategically to promote and incentivise RBC. As noted in Chapter 7 of this *Review*, general government public procurement in Bulgaria accounts for approximately 12% of GDP, presenting a considerable opportunity for the government to leverage its purchasing power. Efforts have been made to integrate RBC criteria into public procurement. The Public Procurement Act, adopted in 2016, transposes EU directives on public procurement, according to which tenders should be awarded based on the Most Economically Advantageous Tender ("MEAT") criteria, which gives more prominence to non-financial considerations. In practice, however, the World Bank has observed that according to the PPA, in 2017 65% of procedures subject to ex-ante checks used the lowest price as evaluation criteria –

compared to 55% EU average. Against this backdrop, business and public stakeholders surveyed for the World Bank 2019 report concurred that the lowest price criteria was the least favoured option, and privileged a combination of price, quality, favouring SMEs, and environmental criteria, and were also open to including social aspects. The World Bank noted other avenues for the inclusion of environmental and social considerations in public procurement: for instance, through the application of exclusion grounds in the PP Act (disrespect of environmental or labour laws, criminal convictions such as bribery and child labour), or in the supervision and inspection phase, through the conduct of inspections on environmental and labour standards (World Bank, 2019).

The government has reported that in June 2019, the PPA completed the implementation of its project 'Methodological Support for the Development of Green Public Procurement in Bulgaria', funded under the Swiss-Bulgarian Co-operation Programme and aimed at raising the awareness on benefits of green public procurement, promoting the award of green public contracts and creating conditions for a coherent and targeted policy in this area. After a study on the potential of the national green public procurement market and identification of 12 product groups suited to the award of green procurement in the long term, a practical handbook has been developed containing the selected product groups, appropriate green criteria for each of them, practical advice on how to apply those criteria in the awarding process, as well as other useful information.

Current efforts to integrate RBC considerations into the public procurement process are positive steps that should be pursued in addition to addressing the issues raised in Chapter 7 related to the transparency and integrity of public procurement processes.

Bulgaria's NCP

According to the *Decision of the OECD Council on the Guidelines*, all Adherents to the OECD *Declaration on International Investment* are required to set up an NCP. NCPs have a mandate to further the effectiveness of the *Guidelines* by undertaking promotional activities, handling inquiries, and contributing to the resolution of issues that arise if the *Guidelines* are not observed by businesses in specific instances. NCPs provide one of the few government-based, non-judicial grievance mechanisms with such an effective and broad application.

Adherents are required to make human and financial resources available to their NCPs so they can effectively fulfil their responsibilities, taking into account internal budget priorities and practices. In accordance with the Procedural Guidance of the Decision of the Council on the *Guidelines*, NCPs are expected to operate in accordance with the "core criteria" of visibility, accessibility, transparency and accountability.

In early 2020, the Bulgarian authorities hosted a technical workshop in Sofia with the OECD Secretariat on the obligations of adherence in relation to RBC. The workshop provided information on the *Guidelines* and due diligence guidance, and included a dedicated session on the role and functions of NCPs, and process for establishing an NCP. Representatives from various ministries were present, along with representatives from trade unions, business associations and stakeholders. In July 2020, the government, together with the NCPs from France and the United Kingdom and the OECD Secretariat, held a second workshop with Bulgarian policy makers and stakeholders to discuss NCP structure and functioning, and learn from peers. Due to COVID-19 related measures in place at the time, the workshop was held in virtual format. The Bulgarian authorities have also engaged with OECD institutional stakeholders (BIAC, TUAC, and OECD Watch) to request advice on the draft plans for the NCP.

Based on this experience and engagement, Bulgarian authorities undertook the following actions and designed the following plan for Bulgaria's NCP prior to adherence to the Investment Declaration.

Institutional arrangements

NCP Structure

On 17 September 2021 the Council of Ministers of Bulgaria adopted Decision № 682 for the establishment and organisation of the activities of the National Contact Point for the implementation of the OECD Guidelines for Multinational Enterprises in Bulgaria. The Decision includes details on the composition and functions of the NCP. Bulgaria envisions an NCP consisting of an NCP Head, a Secretariat, a multi-stakeholder Working Group and an Oversight Body.

In July 2021 the Minister of Economy appointed the Executive Director of the Bulgarian Small and Medium Enterprises Promotion Agency (BSMEPA) to serve as the Head of the NCP. He will perform his duties in addition to his responsibilities with BSMEPA. The Head of the Bulgarian NCP will be in charge of facilitating co-ordination between Bulgarian institutions, businesses, workers and stakeholders, and the OECD Secretariat. He will also lead and co-ordinate the work of the NCP, including undertaking promotional activities, handling inquiries and contributing to the resolution of specific instances. He will be the main contact point for the reception of specific instances.

The Secretariat will count two full-time members within the structure of each respective administration – one at the MoE and one at the BSMEPA. The government is also looking into the possibility of expanding the Secretariat after the adoption of the Decision, through the gradual involvement of additional staff members from other Ministries (tentatively, the Ministry of Environmental and Water and / or the Ministry of Labour and Social Policy). The Secretariat will have operational functions, providing administrative and technical service to support the NCP's activities, and ensuring co-ordination with the Working Group and oversight body. The Secretariat will also ensure institutional and organisational memory by keeping a record of activities and relevant information. The Head of the NCP and one staff member of the Secretariat will have their offices at the premises of BSMEPA. The other Secretariat staff member will sit in the office of the Ministry of Economy.

The Bulgarian authorities planned to give the role of oversight body to the National Economic Council (NEC), created in 2015 to advise the Council of Ministers on the definition and implementation of Bulgaria's economic policy. As discussed earlier in this *Review*, the NEC is chaired by the Minister of Economy, and composed of Deputy Ministers from various ministries, as well as Chairpersons of the five Bulgarian Employers Organisations.[4] According to the Bulgarian Government, this will allow benefitting from an established and well-functioning entity, with a mandate and structure that are suited for NCP oversight functions, and help avoid duplication and overlap of entities.[5] The NEC, which meets on a regular basis (at least once a month), will be holding additional meetings on an ad hoc-basis as required by specific instances or other circumstances related to the Bulgarian NCP. The NEC will serve its oversight functions by reviewing the annual or ad-hoc activity reports of the Bulgarian NCP to ensure consistency in practice and provide general recommendations for better implementation of the NCP's mandate. The oversight body will also aid the NCP in promoting the *Guidelines* by regularly disseminating the relevant information regarding specific instances, policy changes or future developments in the strategic framework for RBC through its stakeholder network since it includes representatives of the public authorities and business organisation. The oversight function of the NEC entails a formal reporting process: the Head of the NCP will submit annual as well as mid-term reports on the implementation of the NCP's activities in Bulgaria to the Minister of Economy for approval, then the Head of the NCP in his/her capacity as chairperson of the WG shall submit these reports to the NEC for review of the NCP's activities and provision of general recommendations for better efficiency of the Bulgarian NCP.

As a follow-up to the adoption of the Decision No. 682 for the establishment and organisation of the activities of the National Contact Point for the implementation of the OECD *Guidelines for Multinational Enterprises* in Bulgaria, a multi-stakeholder Working Group will be established by Order of the Minister of Economy. At the time of writing of this *Review*, the multi-stakeholder Working Group was on its way to be established before the end of 2021. The Working Group will be established as a subsidiary body to the NEC (which, as indicated above, also has the function of oversight dody to the NCP), with an independent decision-making mandate. The Working Group will be chaired by the Head of the NCP and composed of approximately 15 members, representing four stakeholder groups:

Government institutions will include the Ministry of Economy, the Ministry of Labour and Social Policy, the Ministry of Environment and Water, and the National Revenue Agency of the Republic of Bulgaria (on behalf of the Ministry of Finance).

Business organisations will include the Bulgarian Chamber of Commerce and Industry, Bulgarian Industrial Association – Union of the Bulgarian Business; the Confederation of Employers and Industrialists in Bulgaria, Bulgarian Industrial Capital Association, and the Union for Private Economic Enterprise.

Trade Unions will include the two largest union confederations in Bulgaria, i.e. the Confederation of Labour "Podkrepa" and the Confederation of Independent Trade Unions of Bulgaria.

Civil society organisations will include the Centre for the Study of Democracy, the Bulgarian Association of CSR Professionals, and the UN Global Compact Network Bulgaria.

After being formally appointed to be part of the NCP Working Group (WG) through a letter from the Ministry of Economy, each institution will elect their representative to participate in the Working Group. Furthermore, external experts from other government institutions, business organisations, trade unions, non-governmental organisations and/or the academic sector, will be involved on an ad-hoc basis in the activity of the Working Group. For that purpose, each stakeholder group, after internal deliberation within the group, will have the possibility to put forward an official request to involve an external expert on an ad-hoc basis. As explained by Bulgaria, the authorities have designed an open construct for the WG by providing stakeholders with the option if necessary to call for the involvement of external experts from other institutions, business organisations, trade unions, NGOs and academia. All stakeholders in the WG will be provided with equal voting rights. According to Bulgaria, the addition of ad-hoc experts will not in any way affect the total amount of votes that each stakeholder group is allocated – six votes.

The Working Group will be the only body of the Bulgarian NCP with decision-making power, notably when it comes to specific instances (see below). The Rules of Procedure developed by the WG will clarify the full decision-making procedure – simple majority during the initial assessment of cases of alleged incompliance with the OECD Guidelines, internal and external communication processes, transparency and promotional activities, etc. or qualified majority voting (QMV) during further deliberations when handling specific instances. Bulgaria views the majority voting system as more operational since, according to Bulgaria, it provides more flexibility to the WG when making decisions as opposed to consensus which would slow down the reaching of a mutually acceptable decision. The Working Group will make decisions on topics including future measures for the promotion of the OECD *Guidelines* and the role of Bulgarian NCP in this process; adoption of National Strategy/National Action Plan for the implementation and promotion of the MNE Guidelines; adoption of the Annual Activity Reports of the NCP; and specific instances. One of the WG's prerogatives will be to develop and apply the Internal Rules of Procedure regarding the organisation and operation of the NCP mechanism and the co-ordination of the NCP with the WG itself and the Oversight Body. The Working Group will also be in charge of developing rules of the procedures for the Bulgarian NCP. During the first formal meeting of the WG, it will be tasked with drafting the Rules of Procedure in which the WG will envisage specific provisions/mechanisms for ensuring its impartiality from the Oversight Body and equity when executing its decision-making functions. After the drafting and consultation processes have been finalised, the Working Group will send the rules of procedures for approval and official adoption by an Order of the Minister of Economy.

Every year, the NCP will submit an annual report on its activities to the Minister of Economy. After approval, the report shall be submitted to the NEC by the Chairperson of the Working Group, and then to the OECD Secretariat. Furthermore, the Minister of Economy in his capacity as Chair of the NEC shall report to the

Council of the Ministers on the decisions of the NEC including any deliberations on the activities of the Bulgarian NCP. Annual reports will be made available online in the NCP section of the MoE and BSMEPA websites.

Stakeholders have been consulted throughout the process of defining the NCP structure and institutional modalities. In addition to the two workshops co-hosted with the OECD Secretariat, Bulgarian authorities held bilateral meetings and carried out e-consultations on their draft plans for the NCP from 16 to 27 July 2020. A total of 20 people were consulted, including representatives from five ministries, one government agency, five business associations, three research centres, one academic, two trade unions, and three associations focused on CSR and corporate governance research and promotion. After incorporation of the feedback and finalisation of the NCP structure, a public consultation was organised on 26 July 2021. An open invitation was sent by the Ministry of Economy to civil society, business representatives, trade unions, academia, OECD institutional stakeholders and interested parties. The consultation took place at the premises of the Ministry of Economy in a hybrid format – physically and virtually for anyone who could not participate in person.In the framework of this *Review*, the Bulgarian Government has expressed its commitment to review the NCP structure and planned activities one year into the establishment of the NCP, through both internal and public consultations aiming at gather feedback and general recommendations. As a result of this built-in review mechanism of the Bulgarian NCP, a Summary Report will be elaborated with recommendations and specific actions to be taken for the improvement of the NCP's structure and efficiency in the future.

Stakeholder engagement

On 30 September 2020, the MoE participated in a national conference on Corporate Social Responsibility, co-organised by the magazine "Enterprise" and the multimedia analytical and educational programme of the "Kauzi" Foundation "CSR AdviceBox". The conference, entitled *"Corporate Social Responsibility: Sustainable Development for the Bulgarian Business"*, was held under the patronage of the Ministry of Labor and Social Policy. At this occasion, a representative from the MoE presented the role of the NCP and called on various stakeholders to work together to support this mechanism.

The Bulgarian authorities have created a dedicated webpage providing information and updates about the Bulgarian NCP on the MoE website. The webpage includes details about the NCP's role and function, structure, and activities. The email address of the NCP is publicly available on the NCP webpage. The government plans to use this webpage to publish documentation included OECD instruments on RBC. At the time of writing, Bulgarian authorities have translated the *Guidelines* and made them available in both English and Bulgarian languages. The website will also provide links to OECD instruments and relevant webpages. Once they have been developed, the rules of procedures will be made publicly available. As mentioned previously, annual reports on the activity of the NCP will also be posted online. Additionally, key RBC documents and information on the Bulgarian NCP's structure and activities will also be published on the BSMEPA webpage.

After the formal establishment of the NCP, stakeholders will primarily be involved in the NCP's activities through the multi-stakeholder Working Group, which has been formed to represent diverse views and act as a platform for dialogue and consultations on matters related to the NCP functioning. It is also foreseen that stakeholders will be consulted throughout the process of developping rules of procedures, including through an open consultation to be organised prior to their adoption. In addition, it is envisaged that the NCP will hold regular meetings with stakeholders, as well as an Annual Information Event to present the activities and results of the NCP.

Resources

The MoE has committed to fund the NCP's establishment and activities, the financial resources for which will be allocated from the budget of the MoE depending on the NCP's needs. The staffing resources will be allocated on behalf of the MoE and the BSMEPA as follows: 1) For the Head of the NCP/the Executive Director of the BSMEPA, which according to the Decision of the Council of Ministers is tasked with the execution of this function on a full-time basis effective immediately with no additional payment; 2) For the two experts of the NCP's Secretariat – two currently employed experts from both institutions will be appointed on a full-time basis to execute the sole functions of a Secretariat to the NCP. At the time of this *Review*, according to Bulgaria, dedicated resources were specifically envisaged in the MoE's budget for 2022 amounting to BGN 35 000 (approximately EUR 18 000) to cover the activities of the Bulgarian NCP for the implementation of the *MNE Guidelines* and establishing a network of stakeholders (including for the purpose of participation in NCP meetings and forums at OECD level; of maintaining an up-to-date website of the NCP; of adopting a National Action Plan (NAP) to promote the Guidelines; of holding regular consultations/meetings with the stakeholders such as seminars, roundtables and workshops; of translating and making publicly available key RBC documents in Bulgarian and English, etc.).

Since the activities of the NCP will be covered by the MoE's budget, each year the NCP will elaborate a draft budget according to its needs to be approved for the following year. This will allow Bulgaria to have the NCP budget (as part of the MoE's budget) approved one year in advance.

Handling of specific instances

The Head of the NCP will be the main contact point for the submission of specific instances. Upon reception, specific instances will be transmitted to the Working Group, which will handle cases and make decisions related to the resolution of specific instances. In order to ensure impartiality, each of the four stakeholder groups represented in the Working Group will be given an equal number of votes (six votes each), when making decisions on specific instances, regardless of the number of representatives participating in each group. The Head of the NCP will also have one vote.

As previously mentioned, external experts may be involved on an *ad hoc* basis to provide additional expertise and support the work of the Working Group. When this is the case, *ad hoc* experts will have access to all relevant documents keeping in mind that they will be bound to respect the confidentiality of the stakeholders and the matters under review. External experts' role will depend on the needs of each stakeholder group that they are a part of; it will mostly be to consult the given stakeholder group, to give them an opportunity to express their views on a given matter openly and to advise according to their competences so that the specific stakeholder group can form its general opinion/position. The involvement of external experts will not affect voting rights, which will remain evenly distributed between the four stakeholder groups (with one additional vote for the Head of the NCP). It is also envisioned that external professionals with mediation expertise be involved to handle specific instances. These professional mediators will support the Working Group when handling specific instances and share knowledge and expertise on the mediation process.

Promotional activities and next steps

The Bulgarian Government has elaborated a draft plan for various activities for the first two years of functioning of the NCP (See Table 8.1). Planned activities include the creation of an NCP section in MoE website (available in both Bulgarian and English) as well as on the BSMEPA webpage, translation of the *Guidelines*, the elaboration of a digital booklet on the implementation of the *Guidelines*, and the development by the WG of a National Action Plan (NAP) on RBC to promote the *Guidelines*. Bulgaria recognises that the development NAP will be important as it will serve as an effective way to unify concrete efforts at national level to promote the *Guidelines* by active engagement with different stakeholders and co-ordination of measures to reinforce policy actions for coherence of the RBC-related policy instruments including coherence between the NAP for the implementation and promotion of the *MNE Guidelines* and the National CSR Strategy (2019-23). The NAP on RBC will be subject to an open public consultation prior to its adoption by a Decision of the Council of Ministers in the first few months of 2022. Each year will be marked by the publication of an annual report followed by an Annual Information event for the presentation of the NCP's activities.

In the first two years of activity, the NCP will aim to raise awareness of the *Guidelines* and learn from experiences in other countries, for example by contacting diplomatic missions to identify effective ways to promote the Guidelines, and by researching and publishing case studies on the implementation of *Guidelines* in other countries. These case studies could be presented at different events where information about the NCP would be shared.

Table 8.1. Timeline for the establishment of the Bulgarian NCP

Timeline	Milestones / Actions
July 2021	Appointment of the Head of the NCP in Bulgaria
Q3 2021	The Council of Ministers of Bulgaria adopted Decision № 682 for the establishment and organisation of the activities of the National Contact Point for the implementation of the OECD Guidelines for Multinational Enterprises in Bulgaria on 17 September 2021
Q4 2021	Establishment of the Working Group through an Order of the Minister of Economy
Q4 2021	First meeting of the newly established NCP
Q4 2021	Participation at the OECD NCP meeting in Paris (or virtually)
Q4 2021	Start of the development of rules of procedures by the Working Group
Q4 2021	Start of the development of a NAP on RBC by the Working Group, including stakeholder consultations
Q4 2021	Public awareness raising event with stakeholders and policy makers to promote and disseminate information about the Bulgarian NCP
Q4 2021	Publication of the first report on the activities of the NCP
Q4 2021	Public consultation on the final draft of the rules of procedure
Q4 2021	Adoption of the rules of procedures by MoE
Q1 2022	Adoption of the Bulgarian NAP on RBC
Q1-Q2 2022	Participation at the meeting of the OECD NCP network in Paris
Q2 2022	Public awareness raising event with stakeholders and policy makers to promote and disseminate information about the Bulgarian NCP
Q3 2022	Start the reception of specific instances
Q4 2022	Publication of the results of the mediation process on the NCP webpage
Q4 2022	Open consultation to review the structure and planned activities of the Bulgarian NCP Publication of a summary report including lessons learned and next steps as an outcome of the consultation

Outlook and policy recommendations

Bulgaria has taken steps to promote RBC, including through the adoption of a National CSR Strategy and the mainstreaming of RBC principles and several policies and sectoral strategies. Various actors, notably business associations have been active in RBC promotion. These efforts have resulted in a growing awareness of RBC in the country. Understanding and implementation of RBC however varies significantly across businesses. Moreover, the concept of due diligence – a key process for the implementation of RBC principles – is not yet at the forefront of the public discourse and national efforts on RBC. Promoting a common understanding of RBC based on internationally recognised RBC standards, can help promote sound business practices, while supporting the government national priorities for Bulgaria's sustainable development.

Furthermore, deepening efforts to promote RBC due diligence could go a long way in addressing some of the main environmental and social risks that are associated with certain industries, for example the garment, mining and energy production sectors. The government could consider leveraging and actively disseminating international standards and tools to help businesses better manage such risks, improve industrial relations and maximise the contribution of the sectors to economic, but also environmental and social outcomes.

Beyond promoting standards, the government can play a role by facilitating the due diligence process, and creating an enabling environment for RBC. Ensuring that stakeholders, workers and journalists can play their role in consultative and accountability processes is key to ensure that businesses can meet international RBC standards. More broadly, a sound regulatory and judicial system, as well as predictable and transparent processes are important elements to underpin RBC. The government has made efforts in that regard, and is encouraged to deepen reforms to support further uptake and implementation of RBC.

Policy recommendations

- *Establish an effectively functioning NCP to further the effectiveness of the OECD Guidelines.* All Adherents to the OECD *Declaration* have an obligation to establish an NCP, in accordance with the Decision of the Council on the OECD *Guidelines for Multinational Enterprises.* Bulgaria should ensure that structure of the NCP retains the trust of stakeholders and guarantees its impartiality. In this context, further clarify the relations between the NCP's Chair, Secretariat and Working Group as well as its relation with the National Economic Council with respect to NCP's impartiality as highlighted in the OECD *Procedural Guidelines.*
- *Promote policy coherence and ensure co-ordination on RBC-related policies within the government.* In particular, the government should ensure that the mandates of different bodies, including those created through the process of establishing the NCP, are clearly delineated and co-ordinate adequately. As Bulgaria plans to develop a NAP on RBC, ensuring consistency and complementary with the existing CSR Strategy will be of particular importance. The government should also make sure that the development of the NAP follows international best practice notably with regards to the consultation processes and involvement of stakeholders.
- *Set clear expectations as to what RBC entails, including in relation to due diligence.* The governments could leverage the presence of large business associations active in RBC promotion to translate and disseminate the OECD *Guidelines* as well as all OECD due diligence guidance, to establish a common understanding across businesses of what RBC means and what government expectations are in that respect.
- *Actively promote the OECD Guidelines and the NCP among businesses operating in Bulgaria and Bulgarian companies operating abroad, as well as workers and stakeholders.* This entails organising awareness raising events, capacity building activities and consultations on RBC with all stakeholders to identify priorities and needs. Ensuring that RBC principles and standards, as well as the NCP mechanism, are known among all relevant stakeholders is an important aspect of ensuring that the NCP can effectively fulfil its mandate.
- *Promote the use of the OECD sectoral due diligence guidance*, in particular the *OECD Due Diligence Guidance in the Garment and Footwear Sector, OECD Minerals Guidance and OECD Guidance in Extractive Industries*, through active support to these enterprises in implementing the recommendations of the due diligence instruments. Countries that adhere to the OECD Declaration

commit to also adhere to all of the related OECD legal instruments aimed at supporting the implementation of the OECD *Guidelines,* including the OECD *due diligence guidance*. Promoting and supporting implementation of these instruments will contribute to facilitate businesses in meeting RBC expectations in Bulgaria.

- *Facilitate meaningful stakeholder engagement in the design and implementation of RBC policies and processes.* This includes ensuring that all stakeholders are empowered to express their views and take part in the public debate and encouraging companies to consider the views of stakeholders and affected communities. The *OECD Due Diligence Guidance for Meaningful Stakeholder Engagement in the Extractive Sector* can provide a useful framework that can be particularly relevant for the coal industry.
- *Ensure full compliance with EU legislations related to RBC, including the EU Non-Financial Reporting Directive*, and support businesses in observing RBC-related laws and expectations. The government could consider leveraging the NCP to identify challenges faced by businesses and provide relevant tools and guidance to facilitate businesses in meeting RBC expectations.
- *Seize the momentum created by SOE reforms to promote and implement RBC standards within SOEs.* As an economic actor in its own right and owner of enterprises, the government could take steps to establish clear expectations and requirements for SOEs with regards to RBC performance and due diligence, and reporting on RBC-related risks. The government could rely on OECD due diligence guidance to practically operationalise RBC in Bulgarian SOEs.

References

Amnesty International (2019), Amnesty Condemns Call to Ban Bulgarian Helsinki Committee, https://balkaninsight.com/2019/10/02/amnesty-condemns-call-to-ban-bulgarian-helsinki-committee/

Amundi (2020), *The day after. COVID-19 and the ESG transformation of the asset management industry,* #3 update, November 2020.

Balkan Institute for Labour and Social Policy (2021), *Corporate and Social Responsibility,* https://bilsp.org/csr/

Bulgarian Industrial Association (2020), *Responsible Businesses During the crisis,* https://en.bia-bg.com/standpoint/view/26728/

Bulgarian Business Leaders Forum – BBLF (2021), *CSR in Bulgaria,* www.bblf.bg/en/content/59/csr-in-bulgaria

Bulgarian Stock Exchange – BSE (2020), www.bse-sofia.bg/en/sustainability

Blanpain, R, W. Bromwich, O. Rymkevich,, I, Senatori, (eds) (2011); *Rethinking corporate governance: From shareholder value to stakeholder value*; Bulletin of Comparative Labour Relations Series, Kluwer Law International, Alphen aan den Rijn.

Clean Clothes Campaign (2019), *Bulgaria country profile 2019*, https://cleanclothes.org/file-repository/2019_ccc-countryprofile-bulgaria_eng.pdf/view

Client Earth, Greenpeace and Za Zemiata (2021), *Additional information on Bulgaria's systemic and persistent violation of the limit values for SO2 and case C-730/19 CJEU* (Commission v. Bulgaria), 19 January, www.clientearth.org/latest/documents/additional-information-on-bulgaria-s-systemic-and-persistent-violation-of-the-limit-values-for-so2/

Client Earth (2021) *ClientEarth partners sue as toxic EU coal plant scores permission to pollute 'indefinitely'*; www.clientearth.org/latest/latest-updates/news/clientearth-partners-sue-as-toxic-eu-coal-plant-scores-permission-to-pollute-indefinitely

Confederation of Independent Trade Unions of Bulgaria- CITUB (2019), *Annual report on trade unions: 2019*

Council of Europe (2019) *Concern over legal proceedings for de-registration of the Bulgarian Helsinki Committee.*

CSR for All (2021). *Project overviez;* www.csrforall.eu/en/project_overview.php

Deloitte (2015). *CSR Managers Survey 2015 in Central Europe. How CSR has influenced Central European societies and economies. Lessons learnt and future trends.* https:/www2.deloitte.com/content/dam/Deloitte/lt/Documents/strategy/LT_CSR_Managers_Report.pdf

Euractiv (2020a). *Air pollution: Covid-hit Bulgaria faces compound risk.* https://www.euractiv.com/section/health-consumers/news/air-pollution-covid-hit-bulgaria-faces-compound-risk/

Euractiv (2020b). *Challenging Bulgarian coal plants' new waste burning obsession.* https://www.euractiv.com/section/air-pollution/opinion/challenging-bulgarian-coal-plants-new-waste-burning-obsession

European Environmental Agency – EEA (2020). *Bulgaria – Air pollution country fact sheet.*

European Commission (2020). *Air quality: Commission decides to refer BULGARIA to the Court of Justice over its failure to comply with previous judgement.* https://ec.europa.eu/commission/presscorner/detail/en/IP_20_2150

European Commission (2020b), Commission Staff Working Document, Assessment of the final national energy and climate plan of Bulgaria, SWD(2020) 901 final, 14 October, https://ec.europa.eu/energy/sites/default/files/documents/staff_working_document_assessment_necp_bulgaria.pdf

European Commission (2019). *Social enterprises and their ecosystems in Europe. Updated country report: Bulgaria.* Author: Maria Jeliazkova. Luxembourg: Publications Office of the European Union. Available at https://europa.eu/!Qq64ny

European Commission (2019b), Commission Staff Working Document, The EU Environmental Implementation Review 2019: Country Report Bulgaria, SWD(2019) 113 final, 4 April, https://ec.europa.eu/environment/eir/pdf/report_bg_en.pdf

European Commission (2019c), *Air quality: Commission refers Bulgaria and Spain to the Court for failing to protect citizens from poor air quality.* https://ec.europa.eu/commission/presscorner/detail/EN/IP_19_4256

European Parliament (2020). *European Parliament resolution of 8 October 2020 on the rule of law and fundamental rights in Bulgaria (2020/2793(RSP)).* https://www.europarl.europa.eu/doceo/document/TA-9-2020-0264_EN.html

Eurostat (2019). *Disparities in minimum wage across the EU.* https://ec.europa.eu/eurostat/web/products-eurostat-news/-/DDN-20190131-2#:~:text=In%20January%202019%2C%20Bulgaria%20had,percentageE2%82%AC286)%20across%20the%20EU.

Economic and Social Council – ESC (2015). *Opinion on Corporate Social Responsibility – achievements and challenges.* https://www.eesc.europa.eu/ceslink/sites/default/files/document-file-uploads/-opinion-_corporate_social_responsibility_signed_en-2015.pdf

Freedom House (2020), Freedom in the World: Bulgaria, https://freedomhouse.org/country/bulgaria/freedom-world/2020

Fair Wear Foundation (2019). *Bulgaria country study 2019.* https://api.fairwear.org/wp-content/uploads/2020/05/Bulgaria-Country-Study-2019-DEF.pdf

GAN Integrity (2021). *The EU Whistleblowing Directive: Finding the Right Solution.* https://www.ganintegrity.com/blog/eu-whistleblower-directive/

Government of Bulgaria (2018), Seventh National Communication on climate change: United Nations Framework Convention on Climate Change, https://unfccc.int/files/national_reports/annex_i_natcom/submitted_natcom/application/pdf/0917254_bulgaria-nc7-br3-1-vii_nc_bulgaria_2018.pdf

Government of Bulgaria (2020a). *National Development Programme BULGARIA 2030.* https://www.minfin.bg/en/1394

Government of Bulgaria (2020b). *National Reform Programme* https://www.minfin.bg/en/867

Government of Bulgaria (2019a), Eighth periodic report submitted by Bulgaria to the UN Committee on Discrimination against Women (CEDAW), CEDAW/C/BGR/8, https://documents-dds-ny.un.org/doc/UNDOC/GEN/N19/332/18/PDF/N1933218.pdf?OpenElement

Government of Bulgaria (2019b), Public Procurement Agency, Annual Report on Public Procurement Agency Activity in 2019, https://www2.aop.bg/en/ppa/annual-reports/

Government of Bulgaria (2015a), Accountancy Act, Decree No 237

Government of Bulgaria (2015b), Protection of Competition Act.

Heal (2018). *Health professionals on derogations for coal power plants: no exemptions for pollution.* https://www.env-health.org/wp-content/uploads/2018/12/Letter_BG_derogations.pdf

ILO (2021) *Safety and Health at Work.* https://ilostat.ilo.org/topics/safety-and-health-at-work/

International Comparative Legal Guide – ICLG (2020), *Bulgaria: Consumer Protection Laws and Regulations*, Global Legal Group, https://iclg.com/practice-areas/consumer-protection-laws-and-regulations/bulgaria

ITUC (2019). ITUC Global Rights Index 2019 report. https://www.ituc-csi.org/IMG/pdf/2019-06-ituc-global-rights-index-2019-report-en-2.pdf

KRIB (2021). Institutional website, accessed 26 01 2021. http://krib.bg/en/

Lyubenova, M.E. (2014). *Corporate Social Responsibility in Bulgaria: Advantages and challenges*. in The Małopolska School of Economics in Tarnów Research Papers Collection, vol. 25, iss. 2, December 2014. Academy of Economics D.A Tsenov. Bulgaria.

Matev, D; Gospodinova, Z.; Peev, G.; Yordanov, K. (2009). *The Corporate Social Responsibility in Bulgaria.* Management Prospective edition. In Management & Avenir. Retrieved from https://www.cairn.info/revue-management-et-avenir-2009-3-page-47.htm

Ministry of Labour and Social Policy – MLSP (2019a). *Corporate Social Responsibility Strategy 2019-23.* https://www.mlsp.government.bg/uploads/1/2019-pr-36-strategy-en.doc

Ministry of Labour and Social Policy – MLSP (2019b). *Plan for the implementation of the Corporate Social Responsibility Strategy for the period 2020-21.*

OECD (2019), *OECD Review of the Corporate Governance of State-Owned Enterprises: Bulgaria*

OHCHR (2021). Status of ratifications. https://tbinternet.ohchr.org/_layouts/15/TreatyBodyExternal/Treaty.aspx?CountryID=26&Lang=EN

OHCHR (2020a), Universal Periodic Review: Bulgaria, Compilation of UN documents, A/HRC/WG.6/36/BGR/2, https://documents-dds-ny.un.org/doc/UNDOC/GEN/G20/052/95/PDF/G2005295.pdf?OpenElement

OHCHR (2020b), Special Rapporteur on violence against women, Report on visit to Bulgaria, A/HRC/44/52/Add.1, https://documents-dds-ny.un.org/doc/UNDOC/GEN/G20/114/17/PDF/G2011417.pdf?OpenElement

OHCHR (2020c), UN Special Rapporteur on freedom of peaceful assembly and of association; Special Rapporteur on human rights defenders; and Independent Expert on sexual orientation and gender identity, *Communication to Bulgaria*, OL BGR 3/2020, https://spcommreports.ohchr.org/Tmsearch/TMDocuments

OHCHR (2018). *Contribution by the Government of Bulgaria to the UN Special Rapporteur on Human Rights and the Environment – call for inputs on air pollution and human rights.*

https://www.ohchr.org/Documents/Issues/Environment/SREnvironment/Pollution/Bulgaria.pdf

OHCHR (2016), UN Special Rapporteur on Human Rights Defenders, *Communication to Government of*, AL BGR 2/2016, https://spcommreports.ohchr.org/Tmsearch/TMDocuments

Ombudsman of Bulgaria (2019), Annual report 2019, https://www.ombudsman.bg/pictures/SUMMARY_%202020%20_ENG(1).pdf

OECD (2019), *Vocational Education and Training in Bulgaria*, OECD Publishing, Paris, https://doi.org/10.1787/25bad018-en.

Ombudsman (2021). *What issues can the Ombudsman help me with?* https://www.ombudsman.bg/

RSF (2020). Bulgaria. https://rsf.org/en/bulgaria

Ricardo Energy and Environment (2018), Industrial emissions policy country profile – Bulgaria : Report for European Commission, 070201/2016/741491/SFRA/ENV.C.4

Spasic, V (2020). *Environmental organisations ask EU to stop waste burning in coal power plants in Bulgaria*. Balkan Green Energy News. https://balkangreenenergynews.com/environmental-organisations-ask-eu-to-stop-waste-burning-in-coal-power-plants-in-bulgaria/

Stefanova, M.D (2018). *State of CSR in Bulgaria. Annual Review 2018.* CSR Advice Box. Junction Bulgaria.

Stefanova, M.D, Simeonov, S. (2015). *CSR in Bulgaria: the Current State of the Field.* in Idowu S.O., Schmidpeter R. & Fifka M.S. (eds.): Corporate Social Responsibility in Europe. United in Sustainable Diversity. Springer International Publishing Switzerland, pp. 313-332

Transparency International (2020). *Whistleblowers' protection in Bulgaria.* https://transparency.bg/en/what-we-do/whistleblowers-protection-in-bulgaria/

UN Global Compact (2021). *Our participants. Bulgaria.* UN Global Compact website, accessed 25.01.2021. https://www.unglobalcompact.org/what-is-gc/participants/search?page=2&search%5Bcountries%5D%5B%5D=17

United States (2019), *Human Rights Report: Bulgaria*, Washington, D.C.: U.S. Dept. of State, https://www.state.gov/wp-content/uploads/2020/02/BULGARIA-2019-HUMAN-RIGHTS-REPORT.pdf

World Bank (2005). *Opportunities and Options for Governments to Promote Corporate Social Responsibility in Europe and Central Asia*. Evidence from Bulgaria, Croatia, and Romania. Working Paper. Retrieved from http://www-wds.worldbank.org/external/default/WDSContentServer/WDSP/IB/2006/04/18/000012009_20060418133128/Rendered/PDF/358740rev0CSR0in0Europe01PUBLIC1.pdf

UNECE (2017). *3rd Environmental Performance Review of Bulgaria*. https://unece.org/environment-policy/publications/3rd-environmental-performance-review-bulgaria

World Bank Group (2019), *Assessment of the Public Procurement System in Republic of Bulgaria*, February, https://openknowledge.worldbank.org/bitstream/handle/10986/34184/Assessment-of-the-Public-Procurement-System-in-Republic-of-Bulgaria.pdf?sequence=4&isAllowed=y

Yale (2020). Environmental Performance Index 2020. https://epi.yale.edu/

Za Zemiata (2018), *Communication to the Aarhus Convention Compliance Committee regarding the Republic of Bulgaria's failures to comply with the Aarhus Convention, ACCC/C/2018/161; and (2020), Additional information from the communicant, both available at:* https://unece.org/acccc2018161-bulgaria.

Notes

[1] At the time of writing, the preparation of the CSR Action Plan for the period 2022-23 was ongoing.

[2] In 2020, NGOs filed a complaint with the European Commission against Bulgaria, alleging that several power plants were burning non-hazardous waste alongside coal, in violation of EU regulations, and with potential air pollution risks (Euractiv, 2020). NGOs have also expressed concerns with regards to the adequacy of the permits granted, as earlier permits for 'exploratory purposes' were not made public and, at least in one case, allowed for the burning of waste beyond EU limits.

[3] Denmark, Italy, Cyprus, Austria, Finland and Sweden do not have any minimum wage.

[4] The Ministries that are part of the NEC are: Ministry of Economy, Ministry of Labour and Social Policy, Ministry of Finance, Ministry of Regional Development and Public Works, Ministry of Foreign Affairs, Ministry of Education and Science, Ministry of Energy, Ministry of Tourism, Ministry of Environment and Water, Ministry of Transport, Information Technology and Communications, Ministry of Agriculture, Food and Forestry. The five business associations represented are: the Bulgarian Chamber of Commerce and Industry, the Bulgarian Industrial Association – Union of the Bulgarian Business, the Confederation of Employers and Industrialists in Bulgaria, the Bulgarian Association of Industrial Capital in Bulgaria Association and the Union for private economic enterprise.

[5] The specific functions of the NEC under Decree No75/2015 are to: i) analyse and propose measures to support innovative and investment activities in order to increase the competitiveness of the economy; ii) draw up recommendations and consult the government on the problems of the general economic development of the country; iii) to develop and propose economic and legal regulators to promote the investment activity in the country; and iv) organise, analyse and control the interaction between the executive authorities, other public authorities and the business representatives.

Annex A. Bulgaria's list of exceptions to National Treatment in accordance with the third revised decision of the Council on National Treatment

A. Exceptions at national level

I. Investment by established foreign-controlled enterprises

Land for real estate and business purposes: Companies established outside the EU/EEA can only acquire land (for real estate and business purposes) by virtue of an international treaty or by inheritance.

Authority: Constitution of the Republic of Bulgaria, articles 21 and 22.

Agricultural land: Acquisition of agricultural land by foreign-owned companies requires a mandatory 5-year establishment in Bulgaria. In addition, it is restricted to joint-stock companies with no bearer shares whose shareholders are:

- Nationals from EU/EEA countries; or
- Foreign legal entities established in the EU/EEA; or
- Natural and legal persons from third countries with whom Bulgaria has concluded an international treaty containing provisions on the acquisition of agricultural land; provided they are not, either directly or indirectly, legal entities registered in jurisdictions with preferential tax regimes.

Authority: Agricultural Land Ownership and Use Act, Articles 3 and 3c.

Forestry: Non-EU/EEA foreign legal persons may acquire wooded areas pursuant to the provisions of an international treaty or by way of legal inheritance. In the absence of such treaty, foreigners that have acquired right to ownership of wooded areas by way of legal inheritance must, within three years from discovery of such inheritance, transfer ownership thereof to Bulgarian or EU/EEA persons or companies.

Authority: Constitution of the Republic of Bulgaria, Article 22; Forestry Act, articles 23.5 and 24.

Air transport: Licenses for the provision of air transport can only be granted to companies that are owned at least 51% and controlled, directly and indirectly by EU/EEA Member States or EU/EEA nationals.

Authority: Civil Aviation Act, Article 64; Regulation (EC) No 1008/2008 of the European Parliament and of the Council.

Maritime and inland waterways transport: Transportation within the territory of Bulgaria (cabotage) can only be provided by vessels using the Bulgarian flag or that of an EU country. Third-countries may only provide these services by entering into an international treaty with Bulgaria or via a decision of the Council of Ministers.

Authority: Shipping Merchant Code, Article 6.

Rail transport: Non-EU railway operators may only carry out passenger and/or freight transportation by rail, and access the relevant infrastructure of Bulgaria only if so provided in an international agreement ratified by Bulgaria.

Authority: Railway Transport Act, Article 43, paragraph 2.

Legal services: Companies providing legal consultancy services (law firms) and partnerships can only be created by groups of lawyers authorised to practice in Bulgaria, the EU/EEA or Switzerland. In addition, law firms must be locally incorporated and registered in the Bar Council.

Authority: Bar Act, articles 57 and 61.

Mining: Foreign companies registered in preferential tax treatment jurisdictions and those related, directly or indirectly, to such companies are not allowed to participate in open procedures for mining permits or concessions, and to operate an existing permit or concession. This restriction extends to the registration of geological or commercial discoveries of a deposit, as a result of exploration.

Authority: Law on the Economic and Financial Relations with Companies Registered in Preferential Tax Treatment Jurisdictions, with the Persons Controlled by Them and with Their Beneficial Owners, Article 3, Point 7.

II. Official aids and subsidies

None.

III. Tax obligations

None.

IV. Access to local finance

None.

V. Government purchasing

None.

B. Exceptions by territorial subdivisions

None.

Annex B. Measures Reported for Transparency under the National Treatment Instrument

A. Measures Reported for Transparency at the Level of National Government

I. Measures based on public order and essential security considerations

a) Investment by established foreign-controlled enterprises

The following activities are reserved to Bulgarian companies and companies incorporated in the EU/EEA and Switzerland:

- Fire safety of facilities and/or maintenance and servicing of devices, systems and installations related to fire safety, such as firefighting, firefighting maintenance.
- Activities in connection with the manufacturing, trading, acquisition, safe-keeping, carrying and use, transportation, import, export and transit, repair, discarding, destruction and utilisation of explosives, weapons, ammunition and pyrotechnical products.
- Activities related to the export, import, transfer, transport, passage, carriage and transit of defence-related products and dual-use items import, brokering services with defence-related products and dual-use items and the control over such activities.
- Private security activities.

Authority: Ministry of Interior Act, Article 129; Weapons, Ammunition, Explosives and Pyrotechnical Products Act; Defence-Related Products and Dual – Use Items and Technologies Export Control Act of 2011 Law on Private Security Activities.

II. Other measures reported for transparency

a) Investment by established foreign-controlled enterprises

None.

b) Corporate organisation

Air transport: Airlines and companies for the management and operation of civilian airports in Bulgaria must be controlled, directly or indirectly by EU/EEA Member States or EU/EEA nationals; this is, more than half of the members of the managing body of the company or those otherwise exercising decisive influence on the process of making decisions relevant to the operation of the company.

Authority: Civil Aviation Act, Article 48c.

Maritime and inland waterways transport: companies must employ ship crew consisting of qualified seafarers, of which Bulgarian citizens must account for minimum 25% of the management and operational functions and 25% of the support level functions. In addition, the master and the chief engineer of a vessel must be Bulgarian citizens or citizens of the EU/EEA or Switzerland.

Authority: Shipping Merchant Code, Article 88.

Private security services: persons working as security guards or security guard manager must be citizens of Bulgaria, EU/EEA or Switzerland.

Authority: Law on Private Security Activities, Article 50.

Banking and private pension: At least one of the two required managers of a bank and of a private pension company providing services in Bulgaria must be fluent in Bulgarian language.

Authorities: Law on Credit Institutions, Article 10(1); Social Insurance Code, Article 121f.

c) Government purchasing

None.

d) Official aids and subsidies

None.

B. Measures reported for transparency at the level of territorial subdivisions

None.

C. Activities covered by public, private, mixed monopolies or concessions

At the level of national government

I. Public monopolies

- Bulgargaz EAD
- Bulgartransgaz EAD
- Electricity System Operator EAD
- National Railway Infrastructure Company (NRIC)
- Independent Bulgarian Energy Exchange EAD
- National Electricity Company EAD
- State Enterprise radioactive waste (SERAW)
- National Health Insurance Fund.

II. Private or mixed (public/private) monopolies

None.

III. Concessions

- Mining
- Wood-processing
- Transport
- Mineral water extraction
- Port Administration

- Airport administration
- Exploitation of protected areas.

At the level of territorial subdivisions

None.

www.ingramcontent.com/pod-product-compliance
Ingram Content Group UK Ltd.
Pitfield, Milton Keynes, MK11 3LW, UK
UKHW051500290926
15471UKWH00008B/1329